COMPUTER GRAPHICS
FOR
DESIGNERS
& ARTISTS

SECOND EDITION

Isaac Victor Kerlow
& Judson Rosebush

 VAN NOSTRAND REINHOLD
New York

Library of Congress Catalog Card Number 93-8490
ISBN 0-442-01430-9

I(T)P   Van Nostrand Reinhold is an International Thomson Publishing company. ITP logo is a trademark under license.

Printed in Hong Kong.

Van Nostrand Reinhold
115 Fifth Avenue
New York, NY 10003

International Thomson Publishing
Berkshire House, 168-173
High Holborn, London WC1V 7AA
England

Thomas Nelson Australia
102 Dodds Street
South Melbourne 3205
Victoria, Australia

Nelson Canada
1120 Birchmount Road
Scarborough, Ontario
M1K 5G4, Canada

International Thomson Publishing GmbH
Königswinterer Str. 518
5300 Bonn 3
Germany

International Thomson Publishing Asia
38 Kim Tian Rd., #0105
Kim Tian Plaza
Singapore 0316

International Thomson Publishing Japan
Kyowa Building, 3F
2-2-1 Hirakawacho
Chiyada-Ku, Tokyo 102
Japan

16 15 14 13 12 11 10 9 8 7 6 5 4 3 2 1

Library of Congress Cataloging-in-Publication Data

Kerlow, Isaac, 1958–
    Computer graphics for designers and artists / Isaac Victor Kerlow,
Judson Rosebush. —2nd ed.
        p.   cm.
    Rev. ed. of: Computer graphics for designers & artists. c1986.
    Includes bibliographical references and index.
    ISBN 0-442-01430-9
    1. Computer graphics. I. Rosebush, Judson. II. Kerlow, Isaac Victor, 1958–
Computer graphics for designers and artists.
III. Title.
T385.K47   1993   93-8490
006.6'0247—dc20   CIP

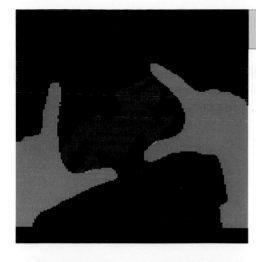

ACKNOWLEDGMENTS

Books evolve through the efforts of many people. As active participants in the field of computer graphics and animation, hundreds of interactions over the years with friends, co-workers, clients, students, teachers, and the press have helped shape our attitudes and concepts.

The actual production of this book began with the help of Dorothy Spencer, then our editor at Van Nostrand Reinhold, and with suggestions from David Sachs and Donna Rossler, all of whom have moved on in their careers. This second edition was instigated by Lilly Kaufman and shepherded through the aisles at VNR by our always able editor, Amanda Miller, and Ron McClendon, our production editor.

Line illustrations for the first edition were done by Patrice Bolté, Shane Kelly, Peter Morrison, and Mark Sudell. These have been augmented by illustrations by Nora Barker, Luis A. Camargo, Suk-Il Hong, and Dick Rauh. Credits for the photographs and images are provided throughout the book and adjacent to the art.

The clerical and research staff on the first edition included Gail Goldstein, Elaine Goodman, and Ted Panken. In the second edition this has been augmented with work by Dena Slothower and Gwen Sylvan, and enriched by collaborations with Laurin Herr and Natile van Osdale of Pacific Interface. Our parents and our families, especially Linda Marchand and Christine Shostack, have also provided us with support, peace, and oftentimes careful discussion about how to present ideas.

Finally, we want to thank you, our readers, who made the first edition of this book a success by buying and using it, recommending it to colleagues, distributing it to your clients and potential clients so they might better understand this new world, and sharing it with your students. There are a few of you who have actually written out suggestions, both in reviews and in correspondence to us, and we especially appreciate your thoughts.

INTRODUCTION

The decreasing price of computers, the proliferation of efficient programs, and the design of better systems have facilitated the incorporation of computer technology into design and fine arts; computer-based visual creation is a phenomenon that is currently changing the way we produce images. Graphic designers and artists, students and professionals, must therefore recognize the new possibilities that computers offer for more diverse, more efficiently executed, and more elaborate designs. This text describes, in nontechnical terms, the functions and limitations of computers in the creation of images and objects.

The merging of print, film, and broadcasting, the birth of communication channels, such as videotex and video games, and sophisticated systems with methods for generating and assembling images on a computer have revolutionized our visual environment. Systems alone, however, cannot produce effective designs at the touch of a button. Computer technology can only routinize some production and design tasks; the basic design challenges—style, functionality, and quality—must be effected by skilled professionals. Customers place new demands on designers as a result of more sophisticated graphics techniques, while designers are rewarded with new creative possibilities, new challenges, and an expanding market. Innovative artists can produce graphics that are as precise as vision, yet can simulate fantastical images, limited only by the imagination.

This text is intended as a reference tool designed to address questions that arise in the course of a career in graphics, not as a guide for programming computer graphics. This is reflected in the organization of the book, which is divided into three sections, made up of eleven chapters. The first section contains background material and basic terminology, which are essential for mastering the more complex graphic procedures included in the second section. The third section describes specific applications. Definitions throughout the book appear in boldface italic and are included in the index. Figures are sequentially numbered within each chapter. A bibliography is included, with select bibliographic references scattered throughout the text.

I-0. Mondo Condo by Ned Greene. Courtesy of New York Institute of Technology, Computer Graphics Lab.

PREFACE

COMPUTERIZED GRAPHICS
COMPUTERIZED APPLLICATIONS
WHERE WE ARE GOING

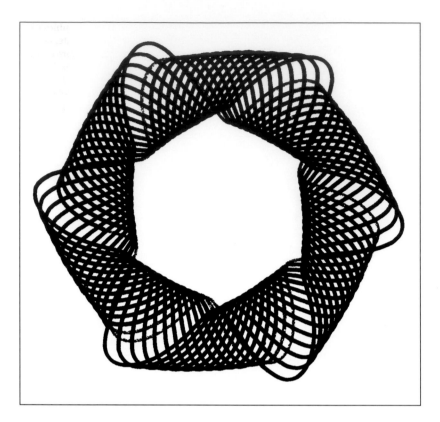

0-1. Mechanical drawing machines existed long before the computer. This picture is made using a harmonic synthesizer, a machine that rotates circles inside circles, and is called a harmonogram. (Courtesy of Judson Rosebush.)

COMPUTERIZED GRAPHICS

The use of images to communicate across space and time lies deep in our history and is a process we as people have been practicing for about 1,000 generations. The introduction of simple machines to aid the imaging process is a more recent development, and began in earnest with your ancestors about 200 generations ago. By the last century—the era of your great-great-grandparents—mechanical drawing was a high art, and steam or mechanically powered drawing machines were developed to address many specialized applications (fig. 0-1).

The fusion of logical processes and drawing also emerged during the nineteenth century, and by the middle part of this century the programmable computer was fused with the cathode ray tube display and the pen and ink plotter so that pictures could be defined and manipulated in a computer and then displayed on a screen or hard copy device. **Computer graphics** is the art and science of incorporating a computer in the process of image creation and display. Today computerization has penetrated all the design and image-making industries. There are many reasons why, in just a few decades, artists, designers, publishing companies, architects, engineers, sculptors, videographers, and animators have elected to adopt this new way of working. But in almost all cases it is because the incorporation of the computer into the imaging process provides both practical benefits as well as expanded creativity.

COMPUTERIZED APPLICATIONS

It is unlikely that there will ever be a time when everything is computerized, and indeed we believe and hope that some people always work with classical means: pencil and paper, charcoal, pen and ink, paint, clay, chisels, and so on. Notwithstanding, the urge to incorporate creative and design tasks into the digital world is compelling. There are many reasons for this:

The most basic technical reason is that digital systems allow images to be reproduced with no loss of quality. Loss of fidelity is a chronic problem in all classical analog media, be it a phonograph record wearing out from needle contact, or the degradation of making a copy of a copy of a copy. In a digital system every copy is identical to the original—there is no difference. This is "the offer no producer can refuse," because the issue of quality reproduction is solved.

Computer design systems can simulate a raft of classical methods, like painting and drawing to create two-dimensional graphic artwork (fig. 0-2). Computer graphics is also employed to design and build three-dimensional objects and is important in industrial design: anything from designing a tube of toothpaste, a car, or a building (fig. 0-3). In almost all of these cases the computer aids the creative process by providing design-specific tools that can be used interactively on the screen. Many people enjoy this process of working with a computer to make things. The experience can be "exciting, not boring, I can fix my mistakes as I go along; I'm in control, and I can do it myself," to quote a person who just "discovered" computers. The computer is an engaging environment.

But there is more still: the designer and artist is seldom a solitary figure. He or she needs to be connected with other similarly interested individuals, with an audience perhaps, and often with a community of people who are working on a common project. This might be a magazine, a TV show, a building, but it is a social product of many people: writers, graphic artists, page or frame design specialists, editors. So it makes sense for the work product of the designer or artist to merge into this digital information/production matrix (fig. 0-4).

But this digital world is not limited to sideways colleagues, it applies to the downstream production process as well. Carefully crafted digital data bases of automobiles are used to draw blueprints, but they are also used to control the ordering of parts, as well as the actions of robots and machines that actually build the car. In other words, once digital, the information stays digital and may be used to actually manufacture the product. The situation is no different for two-dimensional crafts; for example, in embroidery manufacturing an image from a program is analyzed to construct a stitching pathway that in turn controls the actual stitching machine (fig. 0-5). The critical idea here is that computerization consolidates the entire design and production.

Finally, a caveat for the intellectual. Computer graphics provides us with a tool of thought, a way to think about what pictures are, how we represent them, and how they are made. In other words, in order to make pictures using a computer,

0-2. Computer graphics can completely simulate, and in many ways improve, the two-dimensional design process. (*Design Circus*, design by John Weber and Rudy VanderLans.)

0-3. Three-dimensional computer graphics let us build virtual worlds, like the inside of a building, complete with realistic objects, color, and lighting. (Still image from an architectural visualization walk-through produced by Marc Pasini of SPRII using SOFTIMAGE for "Les jeux de la francophonie," France.)

0-4. Multimedia combines computer graphics with sound, television and interactivity. Much of the art we make today is the product of teamwork. (Courtesy of Clement Mok, Doris Mitsch, and Peter Vargas.)

0-5. Computer graphics allows the design and visualization of two- and three-dimensional objects to be fused with the production process. (Courtesy Chenille Products Inc.)

you must employ a language, a set of statements that describe the task. The "statements" may be textual, graphical, or even gestures made with the hands. Before computer graphics we often talked about pictures in vague, imprecise terms. Computer graphics has changed that, and required that we invent a formal language of graphics. To a very large extent, this book is a primer on computer graphics language—the concepts and variables involved in creating pictures.

WHERE WE ARE GOING

We have long passed the point of introduction of digital graphics and animation into the design industries and fine arts. But the conversion from traditional, manual methods is by no means complete. There are jobs for people willing to learn the craft. Even at state-of-the-art facilities it appears there will be continuing innovation for an indefinite future. The quest for the believable image has passed Comet cans (fig. 10-19) in search of more complicated images, like walking human figures (fig. 0-6). In due time we will probably be able to simulate much of how Mother Nature looks and behaves.

Reality is not just about realistic graphic images, it is also about realistic behavior. In the future, computer graphics will be increasingly involved with other media, not just text (its traditional partner), but

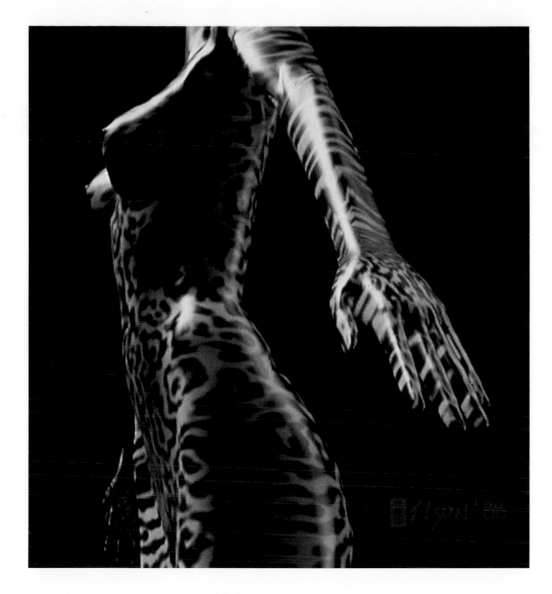

0-6. One of the most difficult challenges in computer graphics is the simulation of the human figure in motion. The solutions demand realistic representation as well as realistic behavior. (Scene from *The Little Death* © 1989 Matt Elson.)

also sound, video, and touch. The driving force behind this is the computer because it can digitally represent any and all media. Everything is going digital and the implications are profound. What were previously different media, like books and movies, that were produced in very different ways (printing versus film production) may now all be produced on a single machine (a computer), and recorded on a single medium (for example, a CD-ROM, a floppy disk). Media is no longer something physical, but is represented on a computer virtually, as graphics (fig. 0-7).

More and more we are rushing toward building not just virtual media on the desktop, but virtual worlds into which we can actually enter and participate (fig. 0-8). These virtual realities are perceived wearing head-mounted displays, with stereoscopic vision and position tracking so that the virtual world is created in real time and interactive with current events. There is a tendency to add interface instrumentation to other parts of the body as well, including data gloves that

0-7. The digital computer and graphical user interface permit us to represent and manipulate media virtually on the desktop. This is a sound waveform. (Screen shot of Farallon *SoundEdit*.)

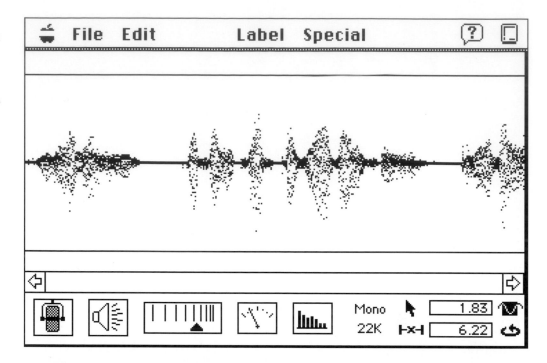

0-8. Virtual reality takes us inside the virtual word— instead of viewing the virtual world through a screen we actually enter into it and look around. (*CyberSex* scene from "The Lawnmower Man," © 1992 Allied Vision Lane Pringle Productions. All rights reserved. Computer animation by Angel Studios, Carlsbad, CA.)

track the position of the hand and the fingers, or even full body suits that track the entire figure. Inside the virtual environment you see three-dimensional objects that you can move around, hear sounds properly located in space; if you are wearing a glove you can see your own virtual hand, and of course you may encounter virtual representations of both real or synthesized people.

In the near future, the virtual world and

0-9. Multisensory feedback—vision, sound, smell, and especially physical force—and combining to form a virtual world that is increasingly similar to the familiar real world. (*Virtuality System* courtesy of Horizon Entertainment, Inc., St. Louis.)

in particular the interaction paradigm will be augmented with a dynamic new medium: force. Force feedback will enable the virtual world to not only look real and behave real, but to *feel* real as well (fig. 0-9). You will be able to touch a wall, feel a paintbrush on a rough surface, or lift a weight.

In this book we begin our journey with an introduction to the basic concepts of computer graphics, followed by a discussion of hardware, software, peripherals, and the interface. In the first edition of this book these opening chapters were a stumbling block for teachers and students alike: teachers assumed that their students already knew this material, and students often found the material completely new. Classes will have to work together on this. Some instructors begin

the book with the second section, which talks about color, and two- and three-dimensional concepts, but sooner or later one must master the basic concepts if one is to communicate in the profession. The third part of the book deals with applications: the chapters on two-dimensional and three-dimensional craft focus on issues like digital typography, prepress, and industrial design. And there are new chapters devoted to interactive multimedia and animation. We understand many of you will read the book in no particular order and hope that it will be a source you can turn to for many years to answer questions, or to simply be inspired by the many wonderful images artists and designers have contributed to share with you.

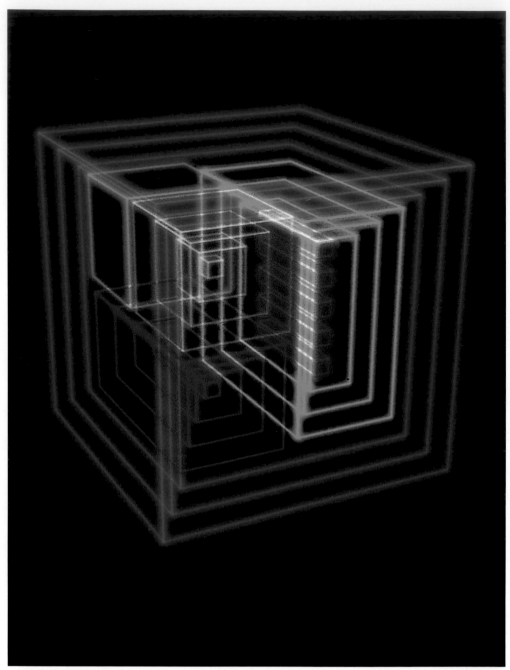

1-0. Hierarchically orga-
nized data structures.
(Courtesy of Digital
Effects Inc.)

1

BASIC CONCEPTS OF COMPUTER GRAPHICS

BITS, BYTES, AND WORDS
NUMBERS AND CODES
DATA AND PROGRAMS
DATA STRUCTURES
DIMENSIONALITY AND COORDINATE SYSTEMS
CONTINUOUS AND DISCRETE GRAPHICS
CONVERSIONS, HYBRID FORMS, AND ZELS
ANALOG AND DIGITAL
ALIASING

☞ **RELATED READING**

Bradbeer, Robin, Peter DeBono, and Peter Laurie. *The Beginner's Guide to Computers.* Reading, MA: Addison-Wesley, 1982.

Davis, William S. *Computing Fundamentals, Concepts.* 2d ed. Reading, MA: Addison-Wesley, 1989.

Greenberg, Donald, Aaron Marcus, Allan H. Schmidt, and Vernon Gorter. *The Computer Image: Applications of Computer Graphics.* Reading, MA: Addison-Wesley, 1982.

Jankel, Annabel, and Rocky Morton. *Creative Computer Graphics.* Cambridge, England: Cambridge University Press, 1984.

Laurie, Peter. *The Joy of Computers.* Boston: Little, Brown, 1983.

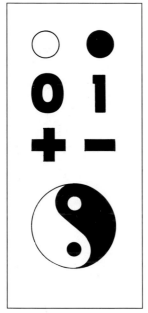

1-1. Bits can represent one of two states: void, ether; +, –; 0, 1; yin, yang.

☐
A BIT

▭▭▭▭▭▭▭▭
A BYTE

▭▭▭▭▭▭▭▭▭▭▭▭▭▭▭▭
A 16-BIT WORD

▭▭▭▭▭▭▭▭▭▭▭▭▭▭▭▭▭▭▭▭▭▭▭▭▭▭▭▭▭▭▭▭
A 32-BIT WORD

1-2. A bit, a byte, a two-byte word, and a four-byte word.

The principles of computing explained at the beginning of this chapter are general—not limited to computer graphics—but understanding and mastering them are essential for attaining computer graphics literacy. These basic principles are therefore followed by more specialized graphics information (fig. 1-0).

The introductory concepts needed for the development of computer graphics applications include numbers and codes; data structures; dimensionality, particularly that of two- and three-dimensional spaces; and the representation of multidimensional objects. Continuous and discrete methodologies are introduced, along with the basic building blocks of graphics—points, lines, planes, pixels, volumes, and voxels. The chapter concludes with a discussion of analog and digital techniques, including an explanation of the mechanics of digitizing, analog and digital conversions, and aliasing. A thorough mastery of the terms and definitions found in this chapter will facilitate understanding of the rest of this book.

BITS, BYTES, AND WORDS

A **bit** is the quantum, indivisible, unit of information, the result of a choice between two alternatives in logic or numbers. The two states of the bit correspond to the differentiation of the ether from the void, yin from yang, male from female, zero from one, and positive from negative electrical charges (fig. 1-1). Bits in a computer are used to control information as well as to represent information.

Memory in a computer is made possible by organizing bits into fixed-length strings or modular units. One of the two modular units used is the **byte,** a string of eight bits that can represent a number from 0 to 255, or a code (for example, a letter, numeral, or punctuation mark). The other modular unit is the **word,** which has a length defined by the hardware of the machine; typically it is a byte or some even multiple of bytes. Thus a word in a sixteen-bit machine contains two bytes, and a double word (or a single thirty-two-bit word) contains four bytes (fig. 1-2).

A **kilobyte** (Kbyte) is 1,024 bytes. Calling the number 1,024 a kilobyte is a bastardization of the metric term for one thousand, and has a different meaning. A **megabyte** is 1,024 kilobytes, or about one million. A **gigabyte** is 1,024 megabytes, about one billion, and a **terabyte** is 1,024 gigabytes, or about one trillion.

☛ **RELATED READING**

Brand, Stewart. *The Media Lab, Inventing the Future at MIT.* New York: Viking, 1987.

Dictionary of Computing. 3d. ed. New York: Oxford University Press, 1990.

Friedhoff, Richard Mark, and William Benzon. *Visualization, The Second Computer Revolution.* New York: Harry N. Abrams, 1989.

Rivlin, Robert. *The Algorithmic Image, Graphic Visions of the Computer Age.* Redmond, WA: Microsoft Press, 1986.

Understanding Computers. The Editors of Time-Life Books. 22 volumes. Alexandria, VA: Time-Life Books, 1988.

NUMBERS AND CODES

Words and bytes of information can store numbers and codes.

Numbers are used to count. **Integer numbers,** 36, for example, are whole and cannot be fragmented into smaller units. **Floating point numbers,** 98.64, for example, denote continuously varying quantities and have a decimal point. So, 98.64 implies a value between 98.635 and 98.645.

Codes represent objects or concepts and have no numerical value. A code may stand for the suits of playing cards (fig. 1-3), for letters and numbers (fig. 1-4), or many other things.

Inside a computer, numbers are represented with bits and are called **binary numbers,** because only two digits (0 and 1) are used. Like decimal numbers, binary numbers can represent integers as well as floating point numbers (fig. 1-5). Integer binary numbers are counted just like decimal numbers and employ a system of positional notation with zeros. Like decimal numbers, binary numbers can be added, subtracted, multiplied, and divided. Positive and negative signs may be indicated by the left-most bit.

But note that binary numbers must not be mistaken for binary codes! The number 1 can be added, but the alphanumeric code for 1 is merely a symbol. For example, the ASCII code number 5 is expressed as 00110101, the number 5 is 101.

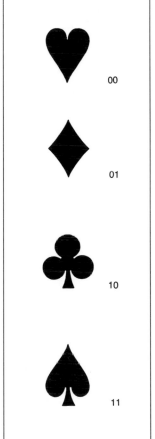

0	0011	0000
1	0011	0001
2	0011	0010
3	0011	0011
4	0011	0100
5	0011	0101
6	0011	0110
R	0101	0010
S	0101	0011
T	0101	0100
U	0101	0100
V	0101	0110
W	0101	0111
X	0101	1000

1-3. Code table for suits of cards. The two-digit binary number represents the graphical symbol inside the machine.

1.4. Fragment of the ASCII code table. The eight bits allow 256 different characters to be defined.

☛ **RELATED READING**

Foley, James, Andries Van Dam, Steve Feiner, and John Hughes. *Computer Graphics, Principles and Practice.* 2d ed. Reading, MA: Addison-Wesley, 1990.

Newman, William M., and Robert F. Sproull. *Principles of Computer Graphics.* 2d ed. New York: McGraw-Hill, 1979.

Rogers, David F., and J. Alan Adams. *Mathematical Elements for Computer Graphics.* New York: McGraw-Hill, 1976.

Decimal	Binary
0	000
1	001
2	010
3	011
4	100
5	**101**
6	110
7	111

$$1 \times 2^2 \quad 0 \times 2^1 \quad 1 \times 2^0$$

$$4 \ + \ 0 \ + \ 1 \ = \ 5$$

1-5. Binary and decimal numbers can be converted back and forth using computer procedures.

DATA AND PROGRAMS

Bits, or binary media, are the common elements for representing data as well as logic instructions. **Data** is the information provided for a problem; for example, in 4 + 5, the *4* and the *5* are data. In general, data refers to organized information and not to process. Numbers, letters and symbols, colors, pictures, buildings, and animation can all be stored in a computer system and are represented by numbers and codes. Data can denote material things, like a package, as well as abstract nonmaterial things, like pork belly futures.

Computers not only manage information but store, organize, and manage processes as well. Processes are executed with a **program,** a well-defined series of steps that yield a singular result. A program may be a simple function like plus (+) or minus (–) or a complicated one like "expand the contrast ratio in the photograph of the fireman."

Numerous processes in computer graphics can be expressed as programs (fig. 1-6). Two-dimensional graphic processes include freehand drawing, color mixing, making a negative, contrast expansion, and block pixing. Three-dimensional processes include perspective drawing, determining visible surfaces, texturing, and shading. Processes also exist for analyzing three-dimensional designs, controlling milling machines that fabricate parts, assembling parts, controlling factories, and auditing operations. Some processes even analyze other processes and seek to optimize the performance of a system—metaprocesses, so to speak.

When using a computer both data and programs are represented notationally. In an addition problem

$$4 + 5$$

the computer stores both the data (4, 5) and the process (+) internally as bits. The numbers are represented as binary numbers—100, 101—and the function + is represented as an instruction or operation code. Here is a simple table:

$$00 +$$

$$01 -$$

$$10 \times$$

$$11 \div$$

The entire addition problem reads 10000101. Binary codes are also used for logical functions (not, and, or), test conditions (greater than, less than, equal to), branches, and instructions that receive and transmit data to peripherals and memory.

DATA STRUCTURES

Data is organized as a sequence of bits, bytes, or words that are in turn organized into increasingly complex forms such as matrices, records, and hierarchies.

Words in a computer are organized in memory as a numbered list starting with the word zero and continuing through the word for the highest number in the machine (fig. 1-7). The **address,** or index, of the word is its position in this numbered sequence, where it can be found if one wants to retrieve data from or add data to that specific location. Note that the content of a word is different from its address.

Users of computers, both graphic artists and programmers, seldom reference a word by its specific address, though this is possible. A word is typically referenced by a ***variable name,*** an English language mnemonic that the computer converts to the internal storage address. Thus, words referenced by names are called variables, because the contents of the word can vary, that is, the string of bits that make up the word can be modified by an artist or a programmer.

The computer has two primary instructions for dealing with variables in memory. The first is an operation called ***read,*** which locates the contents of a variable; its complementary operation is called ***write,*** which stores a value at the variable location. These commands extract information from and store information into a computer memory (fig. 1-8).

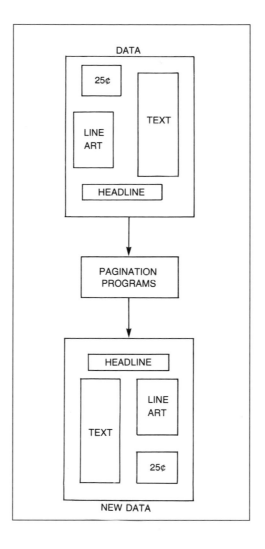

1-6. The process of designing a page is contained in a program.

Decimal			Binary	
Address	**Value**		**Address**	**Value**
0	36		000	00100100
1	38		001	00100110
2	24		010	00011000
3	47		011	00101111
4	50		100	00110010
5	12		101	00001100
6	45		110	00101101
7	20		111	00010100

1-7. Memory organization, where each location has an address and a value.

```
Instruction              Variable Name
and Result               and Contents

WRITE A 30           A    30

WRITE B 21           B    21

WRITE C 10           C    10


WRITE 15 INTO A      A    15

READ A               B    21

15                   C    10


WRITE (A+B) INTO C   A    15

READ C               B    21

36                   C    36
```

1-8. Variable names permit us to read, modify, and write the contents of the computer's memory using Englishlike words.

Columns

	1	2	3	4	5	6	7
1	2	76	32	12	64	38	31
2	92	20	39	13	28	3	89
Rows **3**	37	56	42	51	2	49	78
4	71	43	15	58	7	80	11
5	16	43	72	35	95	27	44

MATRIX D

1-9. The shape of this matrix of numbers is 5 × 7, or the number of rows by the number of columns. The matrix can have a single variable name, and each individual element is addressed by row and column: READ D[3,4] reads the contents of the address where the third column intersects the fourth row (15).

Variables in a computer are not necessarily single numbers and can be constructed with two- and three-dimensional addressing schemes. Often data is stored in a *matrix*—a well-organized collection of numbers (fig. 1-9). Each individual value in the matrix has a row and column address. The number of rows and columns when expressed as a relation (for instance, 5 × 7) is known as the *shape* of the matrix.

In addition to being stored as matrices, data may be stored as *records*, where each record is a row in a table that may contain several different data items or attributes (fig. 1-10). Data may also be organized as *trees*, which allow records, matrices, and single words to be hierarchically structured (fig. 1-11). *Relational* data structures permit information to be organized in a network fashion, so it can be accessed in a variety of ways (fig. 1-12).

Matrices, records, and networks are different ways to build *data bases.* These organized collections of information are compiled so that individual pieces of information can be retrieved by searching and sorting its attributes.

Images and objects as well as nongraphic data, such as accounting information, schedules, and descriptive textual information, are all stored in data bases. They can relate graphic data, like the representation of a bolt, to nongraphic data, such as its part number.

DIMENSIONALITY AND COORDINATE SYSTEMS

A close relationship exists between the ability to structure data and to create graphics. By definition graphics is a two-dimensional activity, though it involves other dimensions as well. For example, letters are an ingenious way of representing a one-dimensional sequence of phonetic symbols as unique two-dimensional patterns. Pictures also use perspective projections to represent volumes with three dimensions, and sequences of pictures often involve time, the fourth dimension.

Country	Capital	Population	Latitude	Longitude	Area (km²)	Map
Thailand	Bangkok	34,152,100	13.45 N	100.31 E	514,000	
France	Paris	51,000,000	48.52 N	2.20 E	543,998	
Mexico	Mexico City	55,000,000	19.24 N	99.09 W	1,972,544	
Hungary	Budapest	10,428,000	47.30 N	19.05 E	93,032	
Indonesia	Djakarta	119,252,000	6.05 S	106.48 E	2,000,000	

1-10. This example depicts a data set of geographic information, including a table of countries and their capitals (alphanumeric data), population (numerical data), and a contour plot of the country (pictorial data). It might also contain abstract dimensions and relationships like the per capita annual earnings. It is often used to search for attributes—for example, how many of the countries have capitals in the northern hemisphere with a population greater than one million?

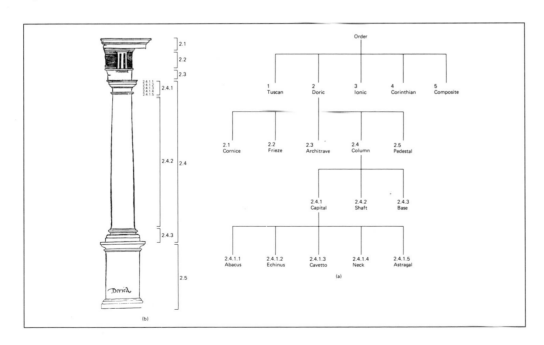

1-11. Tree-structured data base showing hierarchy of the Doric column. (Reprinted, by permission, from Mitchell, *Computer Aided Architectural Design*, 140.)

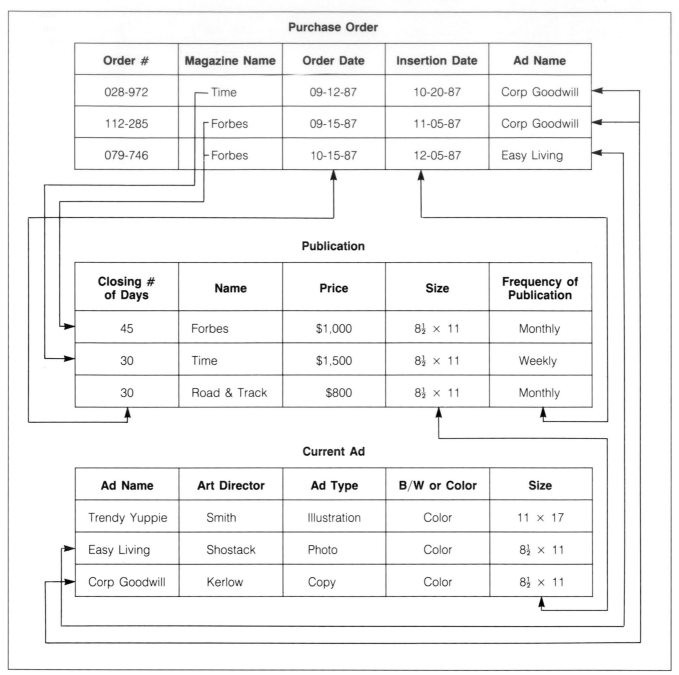

Purchase Order

Order #	Magazine Name	Order Date	Insertion Date	Ad Name
028-972	Time	09-12-87	10-20-87	Corp Goodwill
112-285	Forbes	09-15-87	11-05-87	Corp Goodwill
079-746	Forbes	10-15-87	12-05-87	Easy Living

Publication

Closing # of Days	Name	Price	Size	Frequency of Publication
45	Forbes	$1,000	$8\frac{1}{2} \times 11$	Monthly
30	Time	$1,500	$8\frac{1}{2} \times 11$	Weekly
30	Road & Track	$800	$8\frac{1}{2} \times 11$	Monthly

Current Ad

Ad Name	Art Director	Ad Type	B/W or Color	Size
Trendy Yuppie	Smith	Illustration	Color	11×17
Easy Living	Shostack	Photo	Color	$8\frac{1}{2} \times 11$
Corp Goodwill	Kerlow	Copy	Color	$8\frac{1}{2} \times 11$

1-12. This relational data base integrates several records associated with placing an advertisement in a magazine and might be used by a purchaser in an ad agency. The ad order specifies the work requested; the publication record contains data about the individual publications; and the ad description covers the ad itself.

Spatial dimensions progress from the primitive **point,** a dimensionless entity. A point extended in one direction becomes a one-dimensional **line,** also called a *vector* or *axis.* A line extended along a second axis forms a **plane,** a two-dimensional surface upon which graphics may be composed. A plane extended along an axis perpendicular to the plane forms a **volume,** which has three dimensions. A volume extended along an axis perpendicular to the volume forms **space-time,** which has four dimensions (fig. 1-13), and which describes the progression of a volume through time.

The computer fuses these different dimensional representations into a common digital form. Text (a one-dimensional sequence of phonetic symbols), pictures (two-dimensional graphics as well as projections of three-dimensional objects), books (a serial array of two-dimensional areas), volumetric representations (three-dimensional objects), and animation (a four-dimensional representation of three-dimensional objects across time) all inhabit a common environment.

Cartesian coordinates represent the two-dimensional plane (such as the surface of a piece of paper) with two perpendicular axes that meet at a right angle and have quantitative scales. The **origin** is the point at which the axes cross and has the value of zero (fig. 1-14). The horizontal axis is the **X axis** and the vertical axis is the **Y axis.** A location on a two-dimensional area is defined by two numbers: the X and Y coordinates. The scales are typically linear so that the distances between numbers are constant; scales can also be logarithmic, where distances between numbers are not constant. The axes may extend in both directions with positive and negative numbers, or they may count with positive numbers only, in which case there are four different origin possibilities (fig. 1-15).

A **three-dimensional Cartesian coordinate system** is represented by three mutually perpendicular axes intersecting at an origin. The axis into the third dimension is labeled the **Z axis.** Because paper only has two dimensions it is not possible to actually draw the Z axis on the plane, so it

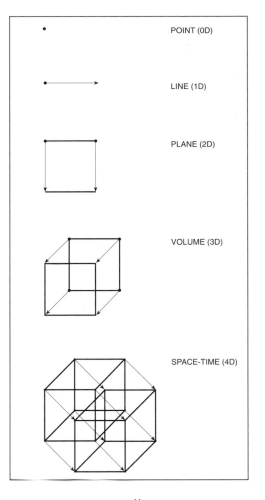

POINT (0D)

LINE (1D)

PLANE (2D)

VOLUME (3D)

SPACE-TIME (4D)

1-13. The progression of dimensions. A point extended becomes a line, a plane, a volume, and space-time.

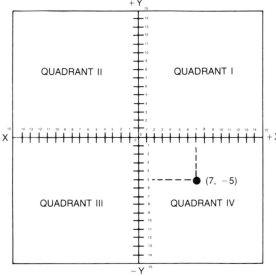

+Y

QUADRANT II   QUADRANT I

−X   +X

(7, −5)

QUADRANT III   QUADRANT IV

−Y

1-14. Two-dimensional Cartesian coordinate system. The X and Y axes are at right angles to each other and intersect at the origin, twice bisecting the plane into four quadrants. Scales may extend in both the positive and negative directions.

1-15. There are four different ways to orient the axes of a two-dimensional Cartesian coordinate system. If only one quadrant is used, the origin may be located in any of the four corners. The direction of the positive axes is different in each.

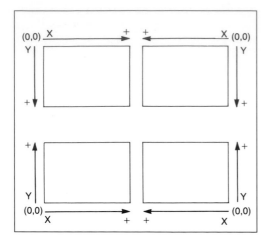

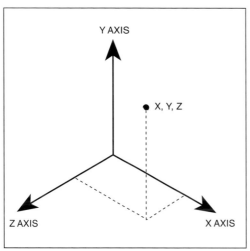

1-16. A three-dimensional Cartesian coordinate system, with X, Y, and Z axes that lie at right angles to each other and intersect at the origin. The axes may have positive and negative values and divide the volume up into eight sectors of space. A location can be defined by three numbers, X, Y, and Z. The X value is the distance of the point from the ZY plane. The Y value is the distance of the point from the XZ plane. The Z value is the distance from the point to the XY plane.

is drawn at an oblique angle as if it were projected onto the plane (fig. 1-16). The axes have scales, and a location in three-dimensional space is defined by the XYZ triplet of coordinates. In the figure the positive X axis points right, the Y axis up, and the Z axis toward the viewer. Eight different axes orientations may be configured (fig. 1-17).

Another way to specify locations is to use angles instead of orthogonal distances. **Polar coordinates** define two-dimensional locations in terms of an angle and a radius (fig. 1-18). The center origin is also called a **pole,** and a single **polar axis** defines the rotational origin.

In three-dimensions one may also express a location using angles instead of Cartesian coordinates, either in terms of two magnitudes and one angle, or in terms of two angles and one magnitude, a technique called **altazimuthal coordinates** (fig. 1-19). These systems are often preferred when one wants to describe a location from the standpoint of an observer. In altazimuthal coordinates the **horizon** forms a 360° circle around the observer. The **azimuth** is the angle around the circle of the horizon. The polar axis of the azimuth scale (0°) points north and the scale increments clockwise (in a NE-SW direction). When the angle of the azimuth is thought

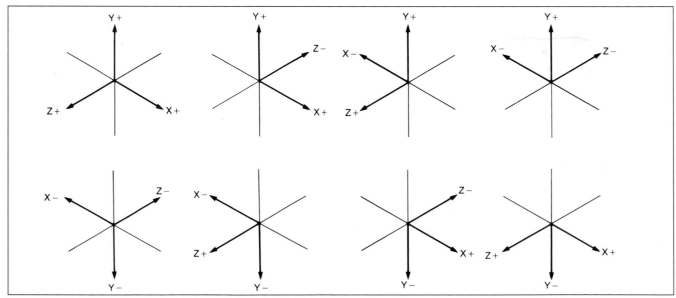

1-17. There are eight different ways to orient the axes of a three-dimensional Cartesian coordinate system. It is imperative to know which orientation is being used in order to navigate successfully.

of as a direction of travel it is called a *bearing*. The **altitude** or *elevation* is the angle from the reference plane of the horizon up to an object. Finally, the **distance** to the object is the straight-line distance from the observer to the object.

Another useful three-dimensional coordinate system relates position to the three axes of rotation: yaw, pitch, and roll (fig. 1-20). Yaw, pitch, and roll are usually conceptualized as relative to an object or an observer, for example, the motions of an airplane from the point of view of the pilot. **Yaw** is rotation around the vertical axis and is equivalent to panning left and right (Y-axis rotation); **pitch** is rotation around the horizontal axis and is equivalent to tilting up and down (X-axis rotation); and **roll** is rotation around the direction of travel (Z-axis rotation). In a real airplane, yaw, pitch, and roll are controlled by a joystick and a pair of foot pedals.

Methodologies do exist to convert three dimensions to two dimensions—**perspective**—and to convert two dimensions to three dimensions—**reconstruction.** The perspective calculation takes points in three-dimensional space and collapses them as points on a two-dimensional plane; in humans, perspective is a calculation made by the lens of the eye. Reconstruction works by comparing points in two or more pictures so that a point in three-dimensional space can be determined; in humans, reconstruction is a calculation made by the brain. Computer techniques for both processes are discussed in chapters 6 and 7.

CONTINUOUS AND DISCRETE GRAPHICS

We have already noted that numbers can be expressed either as integers or floating point numbers. Computer graphics employs either integer or floating point numbers depending on whether the data being measured is discrete or continuous. *Discrete* data occurs in distinct units. Individuals, playing cards, and letters of the alphabet must all be represented by dis-

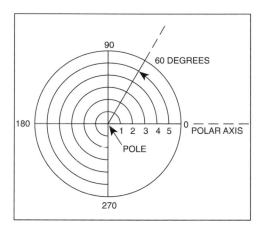

1-18. Polar coordinates consist of two values, an angle and a radius. The angle is measured from the polar axis in either a clockwise or counterclockwise direction. Here the polar axis points right (east) and angles increment counterclockwise. The location of the point has an angle of 60° and a radius of five units.

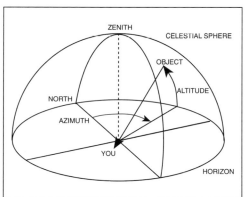

1-19. Altazimuthal coordinates consist of three values: the azimuth angle around the horizon, the altitude angle above the horizon, and the distance to the object. The zenith is a point directly overhead. The measurement of the azimuth is accomplished with the aid of a compass; the altitude with a sextant.

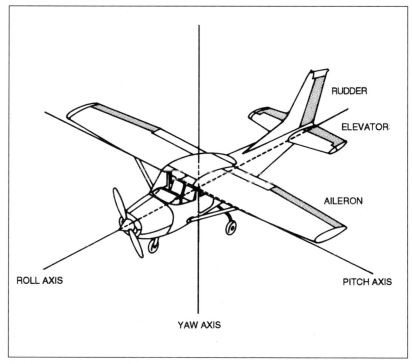

1-20. Yaw, pitch, and roll describe the three axes of rotation local to an object, such as a camera or airplane.

crete data, as they cannot be divided and still retain their identity. Likewise, the pages of this book come in integer whole numbers and are not counted in fractional units.

Data is **continuous** if the axis or dimension that is measured has no apparent indivisible unit from which it is composed. Examples abound in our space-time-matter environment, such as weight, length, and temperature as well as an intelligence quotient or a readability index; no matter how precise the scale of measurement, a finer resolution always exists.

The continuous/discrete dichotomy applies to graphics as well as to Cartesian spaces. Both incorporate an origin, axes, and equal-interval scales. If the Cartesian space is floating point and continuous, then a location is expressed as a decimal number and called a **point,** which is an XY number pair. If the Cartesian space is discrete, a location is expressed using a pair of integers and is called a **pixel** (fig. 1-21). Pixels cannot be fractional.

The distinction between point (line) and pixel representations is analogous to the distinction between line copy and halftones in traditional graphics. Logos, diagrams, and type—objects with sharp edges and no continuous tone—are best represented as line copy, while photographs, paintings, and shaded color areas (benday) are best represented using continuous tone methods. Of course, it is possible to represent logos, type, and rules using halftone methods and to represent photographs using line copy techniques, but this crossover seldom improves visibility and is not recommended except to achieve a particular artistic effect.

Many aspects of computer graphics can be either discretely or continuously represented—time and color for example. Pixels and points are everyday tools that illustrate the fundamental differences between the two.

Pixels: Two-dimensional Discrete Images

A **pixel** is the basic quantum unit of an image (fig. 1-22). Pixels are discrete, modular units often organized in a rectangular matrix akin to a piece of graph paper. Each pixel corresponds to one square on the graph paper and is addressed with an integer X and Y value. The value of each pixel represents the intensity value for that area of the image. The entire matrix of pixels is called a **bitmap.** Pixel matrices have a long tradition in the graphic arts, including needlepoint, the halftone, and weaving.

A simple bitmap or **bitplane** is only one bit deep and stores either a zero or a one in each pixel location and can represent black or white. Characters and symbols are often represented as pixel patterns in the shape of the letter.

The **spatial resolution** of a bitmap is the number of pixels used to represent the image from top to bottom and from right to left. Typical resolutions range from 5×7 dot

1-21. Continuous and discrete Cartesian areas. Points are best thought of as locations on a plane that are recorded at a precision useful to the task at hand. Points specify a location, but do not have an area. They are often used to define objects—entities that have an identity distinct from the area, or environment, in which they exist. Pixels, because they are discrete whole numbers, represent a minute area of a two-dimensional image, similar to each square on a piece of graph paper. A pixel representation is a description of a two-dimensional image, and each pixel is individually accessible. It is the collection or matrix of pixels that compose an image.

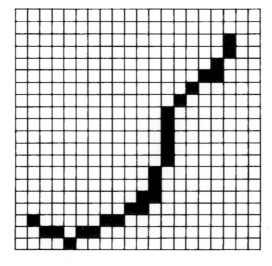

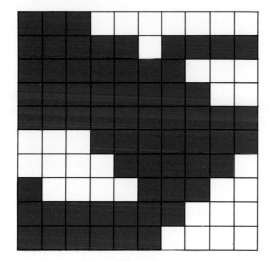

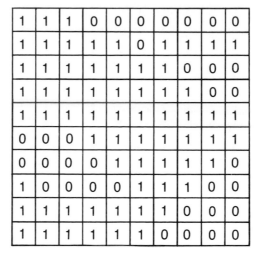

1-22. An enlarged section of a digitized image shows the grid of pixels with its corresponding numerical values. An individual pixel is the quantum unit of an image.

matrices for characters to bitmaps of 1,000 pixels square and larger for images. The *aspect ratio* of a bitmap image is equal to the number of horizontal pixels divided by the number of vertical pixels (fig. 1-23).

The *intensity resolution* or *dynamic range* is a function of how many bits are used to store each pixel. Computers process images the same way they process all information, as numbers; thus the value of each pixel is represented by a number within a range or scale. Should there be two bitplanes where each pixel has two bits, four numerical possibilities exist. If there are three bitplanes, then there are eight possibilities (fig. 1-24). If there are eight bitplanes of memory, then each pixel is one byte and could have a value 0, 1, 2, 3, up to 255. The luminance value or intensity of a pixel is often stored in one byte of computer memory using binary integer numbers. A value of zero might specify black and a value of 255 white, with values between representing shades of gray (fig. 1-25).

Pixels do not have to be arranged in rectilinear grids; they are sometimes organized into triangular grids (fig. 1-26), whereby each pixel touches three adjacent pixels rather than four. Pixels may also be rectangular instead of square, and in these situations the aspect ratio of the image is not equal to the aspect ratio of the bitmap (fig. 1-27).

Pixels and bitmaps may be represented by a stadium full of people with placards or with computer hardware. Computers store

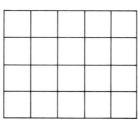

5 / 4   1.25 : 1 ASPECT RATIO

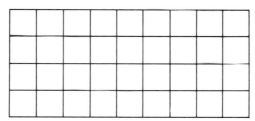

9 / 4   2.25 : 1 ASPECT RATIO

1-23. Aspect ratios are the width divided by the height of an image.

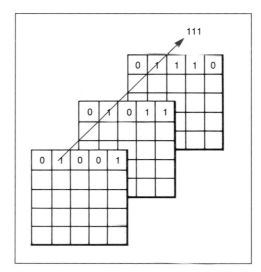

1-24. A pixel in a three-level bitmap can have any of eight intensity or color values. The value of the pixel is determined by reading in sequence the value from each one of the three levels. Eight values can be represented with a three-bit-long number: 000, 001, 010, 011, 100, 101, 110, and 111.

1-25. Pixels can specify intensity values in the image. The numbers (right) express a decimal pixel value, which is the number formed by the binary values from eight bitplanes. The decimal values are expressed as gray levels in the final image (left).

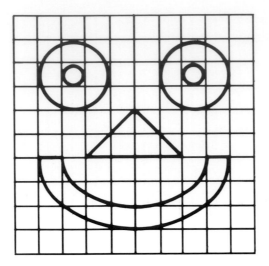

60	95	60			60	95	60
95	20	95			95	20	95
60	95	60			60	95	60
			50	50			
		50	100	100	50		
95	5					5	95
45	85	20			20	85	40
	20	85	100	100	85	20	

1-26. Triangular pixel grids.

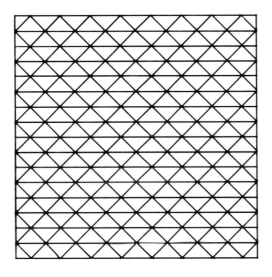

1-27. Rectangular pixels. Each pixel has an aspect ratio of 1.5:1, and the aspect ratio of the image is 2:1.

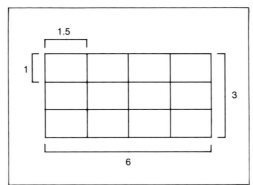

bitmaps in memory, where they can be simultaneously addressed by the central processing unit (CPU) and by a video processor, which displays the image on a raster television monitor.

Points, Lines, Planes: Two-dimensional Continuous Graphics

As indicated before, the differences between points and pixels stem from their continuous and discrete origins. Whereas a pixel represents an area, a point represents a location in a Cartesian environment. Points may be used to compose more complex objects.

On a plane, a point has two addresses, and two points define a straight line, also called a *vector.* The orientation of the line on the plane is called its *slope.* A more complex line can be described with several points (fig. 1-28). The term *vector graphics* has come generically to mean computer graphics defined by lines. A *polygon* is a closed shape formed by lines. The shapes may be simple—a square or circle—or they may be more complicated—the letter **S** or the contour of Australia (fig. 1-29). The simplest polygon is made of three points—a triangle—but the number of sides a polygon can have is unlimited. The corner points of a polygon are called *vertices,* and the sides, *edges.*

Voxels: Three-dimensional Discrete Volumes

Three-dimensional graphics can employ both continuous and discrete methods. A point in three dimensions is still called a *point;* the discrete quantity of three-dimensional volume is the *voxel,* a microscopic cube, a quantum unit of volume (fig. 1-30) in a three-dimensional lattice of space. Voxels

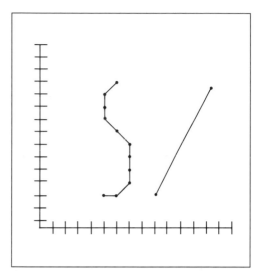

1-28. A vector is defined by two points. Many short vectors are needed to make smooth curves. The individual points, or vertices, that make up an object are often listed in se-quence, with the assumption that a connecting line will be drawn between them. The list for the line is: 9, 3; 13, 12 and for the curve: 5, 3; 6, 3; 7, 4; 7, 5; 7, 6; 7, 7; 6, 8; 5, 9; 5, 10; 5, 11; 6, 12.

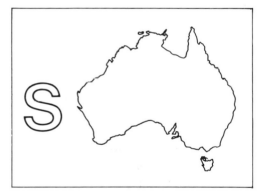

1-29. Polygons are closed shapes defined by lines.

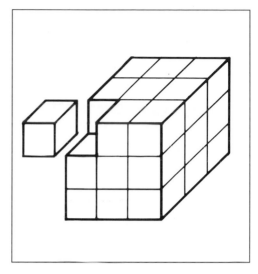

1-30. Voxels are discrete quantum units of volume.

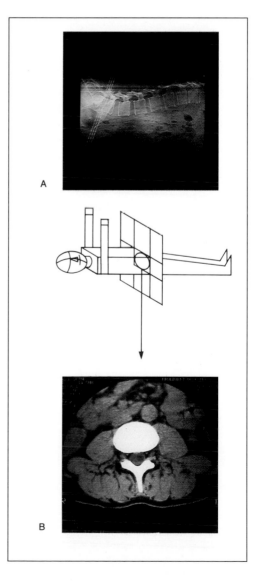

1-31. A cross section of a human body recorded by a CAT scanner (A). A three-dimensional density of this section of the volume is represented by assigning different intensity values to the different tissue densities (B). (Courtesy of General Electric Company.)

do not represent a square area or a grid of reflected light values; rather, they represent volume. A matrix of voxels is three dimensional and represents the densities of matter that occupy the space.

Voxels are digitized using density scanners, such as a Computer-Aided Tomography (CAT) scan. The scan is made as a series of discrete sections or contours, and although individual CAT scan sections might look like images, their source is not reflected light values but tissue densities (fig. 1-31).

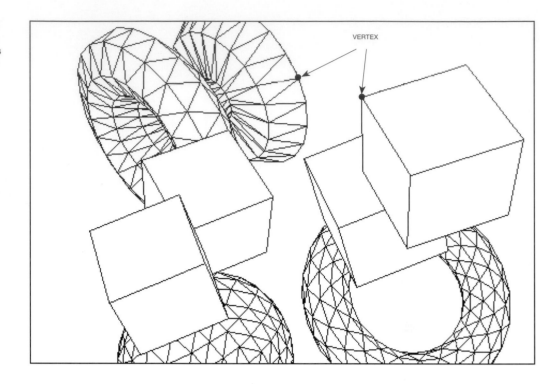

VERTEX

Polyhedra: Three-dimensional Continuous Solids

Points can be three dimensional, and lines, planes, and polygons can exist in three-dimensional spatial environments, such as the volumetric world around us. Three-dimensional environments can also contain *polyhedra*—volumetric solid objects such as a cube, sphere, or ship (fig. 1-32); each face is a *facet*.

A point, line, or polygon in three-

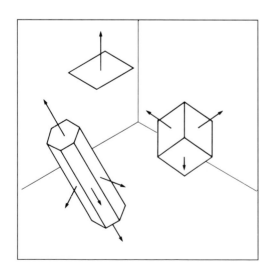

dimensional space has three spatial coordinates. All the points in a polygon lie flat on a two-dimensional plane, but they reside in a three-dimensional space. The orientation of a surface is described by a *normal,* which is the direction it is facing. A normal is specified by three numbers that indicate a line drawn perpendicular from the face of a surface (fig. 1-33). A normal is not a coordinate or position but a direction, an orientation.

Three-dimensional solid objects are defined several ways in a computer. Polyhedra may be constructed as surfaces, where a polygon, or a network of polygons, describes the surface. The simplest polyhedron, composed of four points, is the tetrahedron. Solid objects may be regular shapes in which the surfaces are bounded planes, such as a cube bounded by squares, or they may be objects whose surfaces are curvilinear, such as a sphere constructed as a mesh of polygons (fig. 1-34). Solid objects may also be mathematically defined, so that the surface of a sphere is a mathematical equation and not a series of facets. Obviously voxels can be converted to polyhedra too. We will use

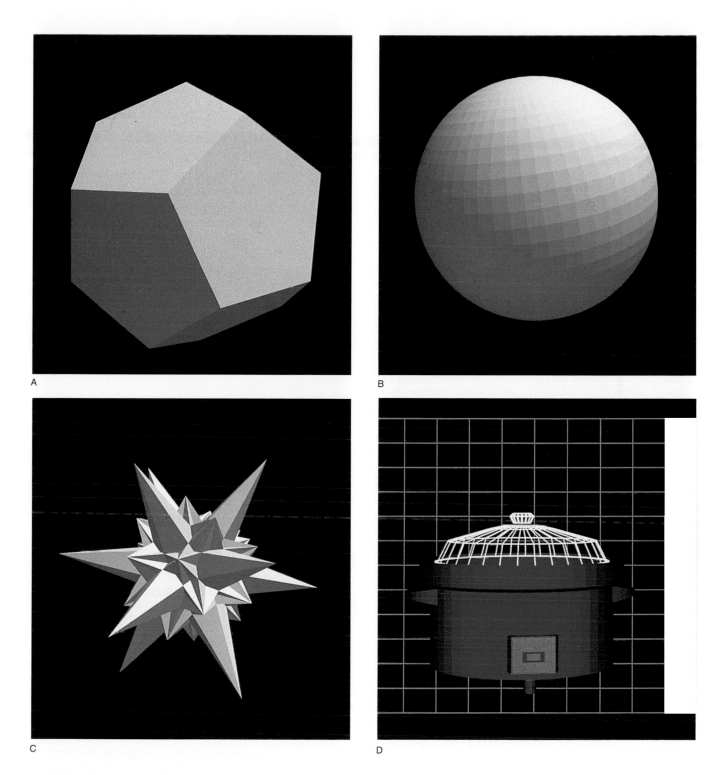

A

B

C

D

1-34. Volumes can be uniform, like the dodecahedron (A) or the second stellation of the icosahedron (C), mathematical like a sphere (B), or irregular like the crockpot (D). (Courtesy of Digital Effects Inc.)

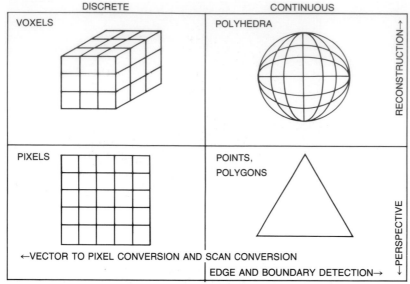

1-35. **Cross reference table of two-dimensional/three-dimensional and discrete/ continuous.** *Rasterization* **is a technique that converts lines to pixels. Techniques that convert contours of pixels into lines are called** *edge detectors.* **Procedures that convert polygon representations into pixel area representations are called** *scan conversions.* **And techniques that identify areas of pixels that have a uniform value and convert them to polygons are called** *boundary detectors.*

1-36. Zels are discrete numbers in a two-dimensional bitmap that store three-dimensional or depth information. In this case the depth values, or Z elements, express the distance between an object and the image plane. Two depth values are shown.

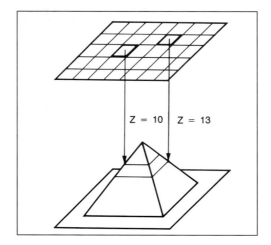

1-37. An analog signal represents continuous information.

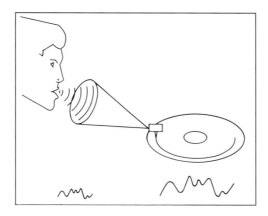

the term *solid models* to refer to three-dimensional solid objects in general, regardless of how they are constructed.

CONVERSIONS, HYBRID FORMS, AND ZELS

A graphic cross-reference table (fig. 1-35) summarizes the two-dimensional/three-dimensional and discrete/continuous distinctions discussed in this section. In practice the distinctions are not always clear-cut; hybrid forms such as the *zel*, which will be discussed shortly, can also be used. Conversions between the different representations are also frequently performed, although the results are often unsatisfactory. For example, a point can be approximated by a pixel, and a pixel by a point. A line can be approximated by a collection of pixels, and a collection of pixels can be converted into a line. Polygons can be approximated by areas of pixels, and areas of pixels can be converted to polygon outlines. These conversions are detailed in chapter 6.

Typical of the hybrid possibilities are **zels**, a method of storing three-dimensional information in two-dimensional bitplanes by using bitplanes to store a matrix of depth values—Z distances from the image plane to a three-dimensional surface or object located in the space behind it (fig. 1-36). Zels are similar to pixels in that they are discrete representations, but are different in that pixels represent luminance at each point in the image, whereas zels represent depth.

ANALOG AND DIGITAL

Analog and digital aspects of computer technology are the keys to understanding operations related to the creation of images. Computers use numbers to represent our world, which is made up of objects that can be counted with whole numbers as well as those that continuously vary and do not exist in discrete quantities, such as the height or weight of a person.

Analog media propagate messages as continuous signals; for example, in voice communications the medium of air pressure is continuously modulated by the muscles of the throat; and in photography, the intensity of light determines the outcome of chemical reactions. Analog media record the varying analog signals in nature by mechanically or electrically converting it to a different physical representation. A phonograph recording is a good example, because it essentially freezes the signal into matter (fig. 1-37).

A *digital medium* represents the continuously varying signal as a sequence of numbers. Such numbers can be whole or fractional and represent the changes in the amplitude or intensity of the signal.

Measurement (Digitizing): Sampling and Quantization

In order to convert a continuous analog variable into a number, it is necessary to sample and quantify. Both of these concepts are concerned with resolution—the number of samples made and the number of steps for each sample.

A *sample* is a measurement made at a particular instant in space and time, according to a specified procedure. In graphics each pixel represents one sample of the image area. The pixel matrix divides the image area into a uniform two-dimensional grid. The number of pixels across a line or down a column corresponds to the number of samples and represents the spatial resolution to which the picture has been sampled. The more lines or columns, the more pixels, the bigger the sample, and the finer the spatial resolution.

The second step in digitizing is *quantization,* which gives each sample a numerical value (fig. 1-38). This requires that the continuously varying quantity be measured with a defined precision or scale. In other words, a continuous variable is represented using a number with a certain precision, or number of decimal places. All real number measurements are approximations

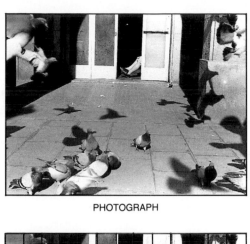

PHOTOGRAPH

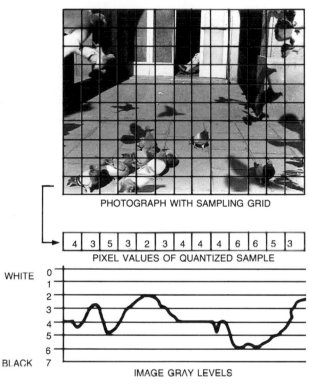

PHOTOGRAPH WITH SAMPLING GRID

| 4 | 3 | 5 | 3 | 2 | 3 | 4 | 4 | 4 | 6 | 6 | 5 | 3 |

PIXEL VALUES OF QUANTIZED SAMPLE

IMAGE GRAY LEVELS

1-38. The photograph depicts continuously varying light intensities with two spatial axes, X and Y. A grid of a specific resolution, here 10×13 squares, is overlaid and indicates where samples of the intensities will be taken. The number of squares in X and Y is the spatial resolution of the sample in X and Y. Each square is then quantized by determining the numerical magnitude of each sample on a brightness scale. In the drawing, the intensities of only the last row are represented as an intensity curve, with brighter luminance at the top. The numerical measurements, or digits, are listed at the bottom. In a computer system these numbers would be stored in bitplane memory as pixels.

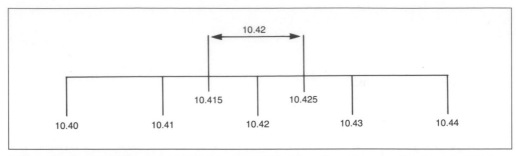

1-39. A quantized sample, even when it is represented with real numbers, implies an approximate value that lies within a range of values. In the illustration the value of 10.42 implies a continuous variable 10.415 < 10.425. Because the resolution of the quantization is fixed, it is also possible to think of the real number 10.42 as 1042 hundredths, a whole number, but remember that measurement involves an approximation, whereas counting with whole numbers does not.

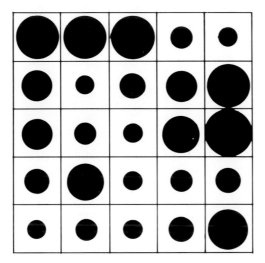

6	6	6	2	1
4	1	3	4	6
4	2	1	5	7
3	5	1	2	3
1	2	1	3	5

1-40. To quantify or digitize a halftone, the diameter of each dot could be measured with a ruler. This measurement could then be written down at the corresponding location on a piece of graph paper.

since it is not possible to measure exactly, only to measure to some resolution (fig. 1-39). The resolution of the quantization is the precision of the measurement along the axis of the variable itself. For example, a yardstick might resolve ⅛ inch; the resolution of a good foot ruler might be 1/64 inch. Quantization requires that you approach the continuous variable (what it is you are going to measure with yardstick in hand) with the understanding that although the resolution of the continuous variable is infinite, you are going to measure at some accuracy, say eight units to one inch. The resolution of the quantization should not be confused with the spatial resolution, which is the number of samples along the size or area of the medium. The accuracy of measuring tools have practical limits, and, of course, integers and real numbers are subject to reading and recording errors made both by humans and machines.

Analog and Digital Conversions

Analog signals, like the grooves in a phonograph, consist of a continuous modulating signal; digital signals consist of discrete samples quantized into numbers. Most graphics media involve a combination of both techniques. Motion picture film, for example, records time discretely in a sequence of frames, but each image is a continuous photograph. Data that is discrete is not necessarily digital. The suits of playing cards are discrete, but not digital, unless they are represented with numerical codes. A halftone, seen on the front page of virtually any newspaper, represents an image as an orderly (discrete) sample of pixel dots, but the diameters and areas of the dots vary continuously and are analog (fig. 1-40).

An **analog to digital conversion** (commonly called an "A to D") involves transforming what is usually a real-world quantity into a numerical (digital) representation. It is a process that involves measurement (sampling and quantization) at a specific resolution.

For example, if you point a light meter at a subject, look at the dial, and write down an exposure, you have digitized the light reading. You have converted an analog continuous quantity existing in nature into a numerical representation. The light is continuous, and the movement of the needle on the dial is continuous, but the scale is read at some precision and recorded as a number.

Machines can do this quickly and are able to measure each pixel in an image. In a **video digitizer,** a television camera pointed at a subject outputs an analog waveform; the amplitude of the wave indicates the relative brightness of the picture at that particular area. The video digitizer samples this waveform hundreds of times for each scan line and converts the analog voltage into a binary number, which is stored in the CPU.

The resolution of the digitizer is expressed as the **color resolution,** which is the number of possible colors (or brightness levels), and as the **spatial resolution,** which is the number of samples across each line in X and the number of scan lines in Y.

A **digital to analog conversion** (a "D to A") changes digital representations to continuous waveforms. High resolution is important if digital data are to appear continuous. For example, a pentagon with five straight sides can approximate a circle, but an octagon is a better approximation, and a centagon (100 sides) is better still (fig. 1-41).

ALIASING

A common problem encountered in measurement is *aliasing,* the loss of information resulting from insufficient or poorly integrated samples. In graphics aliasing occurs in both spatial and temporal dimensions. *Temporal aliasing* is concerned with the integration of the exposure over time; *spatial aliasing* is concerned with the integration of exposure over area.

The mechanics of the motion picture camera illustrate temporal aliasing. When shooting a frame of film the sample does not represent an instantaneous event in time, but rather an interval the length of which is determined by the shutter speed (the time that the shutter is open). In motion pictures, because the film needs some time to advance, the exposure time must be less than the frame rate; this will cause some action to be *blanked* or to go unrecorded (fig. 1-42). Short exposure times leave most of the sample interval blanked and thus are highly aliased, producing sharp images with little blur of motion. Longer exposure times record more motion; the resulting individual frames are blurred, but they appear smoother and more realistic when viewed in motion.

The amount of aliasing in a sample is inversely proportional to how integrated it

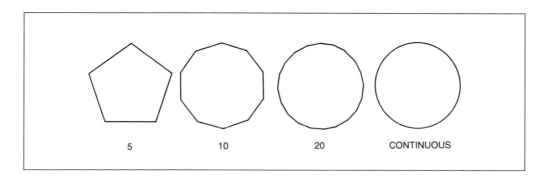

1-41. The better the resolution of the discrete approximation, the more continuous the circle appears.

5   10   20   CONTINUOUS

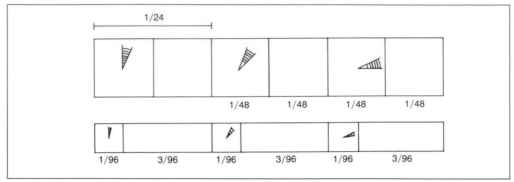

1-42. A camera is recording twenty-four frames (samples) per second. If the shutter is open for one-half of the cycle, the film records the continuously moving clock as a ¼₈-of-a-second-long time-elapsed exposure blur. It then records nothing for the next ¼₈ of a second, which results in temporal aliasing. If the sample is even shorter, say ⅟₉₆ of a second, the picture is less blurred, but only represents about ¼ of the event—¾ of the event would never have been recorded.

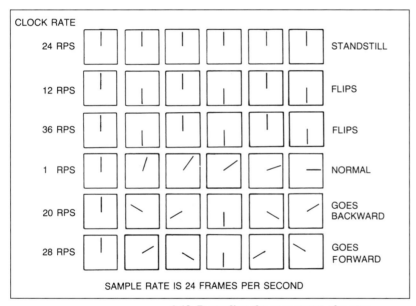

1-43. Recording the movement of wagon wheels with short exposures produces temporal aliasing. The wheels might be rotating at a speed that positions them on a sequence of frames where their rotational continuity differs from their actual continuity, causing them to appear to be standing still, chattering, or going backward. As the wheels change speed, the illusion changes.

is; if the exposure is completely integrated it has minimal aliasing. By and large aliasing is undesirable, because, like objects under a strobe light, the visual image produced may be incorrect, as when the spokes of wagon wheels appear to be going backward in movies (fig. 1-43).

When each pixel is sampled so that the measurement does not incorporate information about its total area, spatial aliasing results. This is particularly prevalent in sampling techniques that only measure the intensity of a point in the center of the pixel (fig. 1-44). A *moiré pattern,* an irregular, wavy finish on a fabric, results from interference between patterns at two different spatial frequencies. This will result when a tweed clothing pattern is printed, because there is interference between the halftone screen and the pattern.

Aliasing affects computer-generated pictures as well, particularly those created on low-resolution displays and in animation. The most common spatial-aliasing effects encountered in computer-generated images are the *jaggies*—jagged lines that represent diagonals or curves. These are reduced (but not eliminated) by increasing spatial resolution. Proper solutions require computing and displaying the integrated value of each pixel area (fig. 1-45).

Understanding aliasing is a way to better understand, control, and direct graphic arts media, whether these are computerized and digital, or traditional.

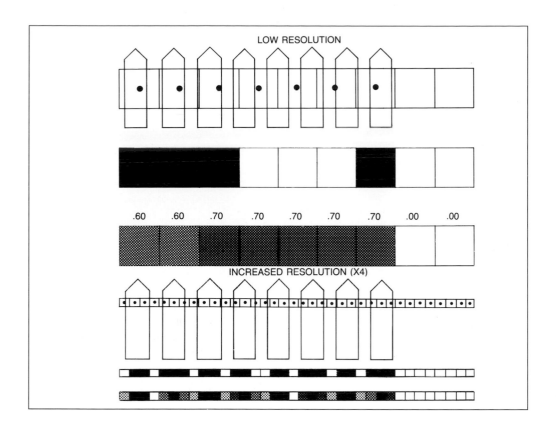

1-44. If, when digitizing a black picket fence on a white background, the image of each black picket is slightly smaller than the width of a pixel, then point sampling would produce a spatially aliased picture in which most pixels would be black, a few would be white, and the continuity of the fence would be lost. Increasing the sample resolution improves, but does not solve the problem. A proper solution requires that the exposure of the entire area of each pixel must be integrated and digitized, not point sampled as in figure 1-38. Digitization produces a gray blur that represents the average contents of each pixel in the image. The blur does not have the precision of the original, because the sample resolution is too coarse to capture every detail, but the sample is anatomically complete.

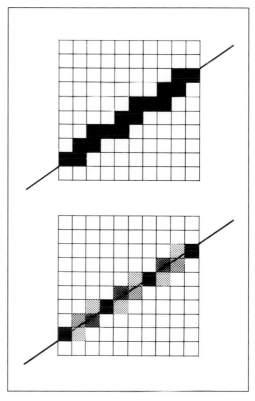

1-45. A common technique for improving the definition of a line uses gray levels in proportion to the area of the grid occupied by the sampled line.

**2-0. This proceduralist
image, entitled *The Gold
Triptych—Artifacts from
an Alien Religious Site*, is
the product of software—a
sequence of instructions
that tell the computer how
to make the image. (Cour-
tesy of Peter Schröder,
Thinking Machines Corpo-
ration.)**

HARDWARE AND SOFTWARE

HARDWARE: THE BASIC ELEMENTS
SOFTWARE
LANGUAGES
DISTRIBUTED PROCESSING AND
COMPUTER NETWORKS

☞ **RELATED READING**

Apple Computer, Inc. *Understanding Computer Networks*. Reading, MA: Addison-Wesley, 1989.

Adobe Systems. *PostScript Language, Tutorial and Cookbook*. 2d ed. Reading, MA: Addison-Wesley, 1990.

Mitchell, William J., Robin S. Liggett, and Thomas Kvan. *The Art of Computer Graphics Programming, A Structured Introduction for Architects and Designers*. New York: Van Nostrand Reinhold, 1987.

Prusinkiewicz, Przemyslaw, and Aristid Lindenmayer. *The Algorithmic Beauty of Plants*. New York: Springer-Verlag, 1990.

Upstill, Steve. *The RenderMan Companion, A Programmer's Guide to Realistic Computer Graphics*. Reading, MA: Addison-Wesley, 1990.

Hardware in computer systems is the physical configuration of a machine, its steel and silicon. *Software* is a series of commands written in an unambiguous language, for example, a program. The hardware executes the program; the program governs the performance of hardware. Notations as diverse as music, arithmetic, word processing, typesetting, graphics, and robot control are processed by the computer. A computer is therefore similar to any device that is used to compose and execute a sequence of events.

Hardware in a computer system is changed by disassembling and reassembling the machine. Software is changed by rewriting the program, which causes the computer to perform a different task. Software is an erector set for logic and is much easier to change than the physical configuration of the computer. A player piano can execute many programs written in a single kind of notation, but it cannot perform other tasks, because its mechanism is fixed. A computer, limited only by its software and its user's invention, can perform innumerable tasks. Computerized media, which combine data and reprogrammability, like clay, can be added to, subtracted from, and reshaped indefinitely. Computers are tools, never substitutes for the imagination.

HARDWARE: THE BASIC ELEMENTS

All computers, regardless of their size or purpose, share a similar basic structure and perform similar functions. The term *hardware* refers to all the physical components in general, including the hardwired circuits inside the machine.

A computer has five basic components: the bus, clock, central processing unit (CPU), memory, and ports (fig. 2-1).

The Bus

A *bus* is a collection of wires that electronically connects all the parts of a computer and has as many wires as the

2-1. A block diagram of a computer system.

machine word size has bits. If a bus is thirty-two bits wide, then thirty-two parallel wires connect the processor, memory, and peripherals; a single thirty-two-bit word may be simultaneously transferred across the bus.

The bus transfers data of all types. For example, when a CPU is programmed to retrieve information from memory, it sends an address via the bus to memory. The memory then returns, through the bus, the data contained in the specified address. Instructions travel on the bus from memory to execution registers, data moves on the bus to and from ports.

The Clock and Cycle Time

In a computer, time is treated discretely and is defined by a **clock**—a device that produces electrical pulses, zeros and ones, at a regular rate. The clock drives the CPU, so at each clock pulse an event occurs: transferring bus data, loading a register, decoding an instruction. The time it takes to execute an instruction is called the **instruction cycle time.** Often the speed of the clock may be faster than the instruction cycle time. Clock speed is a measure of computer performance and is often expressed in a frequency—clock speeds upward of 25 megahertz are common in personal computers. The instruction cycle time is often expressed as the number of instructions that a computer can execute per second, either as **mips,** million of instructions per second, or **gips,** gillions of instructions per second. A related performance variable is the number of floating point operations per second, expressed as **mflops** or **gflops.**

The Central Processing Unit (CPU)

The **central processing unit (CPU)** is the switching and operations center of the computer. By executing the instructions that constitute programs, the CPU controls the entire system, including the handling and processing of data. In desktop and workstation computers, the CPU is usually contained on a single microprocessor chip (fig. 2-2), which is mounted on a mother board

2-2. Microphotograph of a 68000 CPU. The electrical circuitry includes registers, counters, and arithmetic/logic unit circuits that interpret the software and perform an operation. The CPU links software to hardware. (Courtesy of Signetics Corp.)

that contains the bus, memory, and ports. A **microcomputer** consists of a mother board, main memory, a disk drive, and a power supply all mounted in a case, along with a keyboard and/or a mouse, and a screen.

The CPU operates by fetching an instruction word from memory and loading it into an **instruction register.** This register has an address and can store one word. Its contents flow into the **arithmetic and logic unit (ALU),** the logical circuits of the machine, which decode the instruction and perform a computation, such as adding two words. **Status registers** display test results and error conditions, such as dividing by zero. The **program counter** indicates where the next program instruction is stored.

Factors that affect the performance of a CPU include the above-mentioned instruction cycle time (mips, mflops), the width of the registers and bus (bits), the number of registers, the amount of addressable memory, and the richness of the instruction set. A computer with wider registers can operate on larger numbers and address more memory. A CPU with a wider bus can move more data faster. Some machine instructions can cause hardware to perform floating point arithmetic in the ALU, causing execution to be faster than on machines that simulate floating point arithmetic in software. Specialized graphics applications, such as trigonometric functions, complex arithmetic, analytical geometry, and image processing may also be supported as part of the hardware. These variables make it difficult to compare the performance of CPUs. For example the Motorola 68000 microprocessor has thirty-two-bit registers but a sixteen-bit bus: two fetches are required to load each register. The chip runs significantly faster than a competitor chip, the Intel 8086, with sixteen-bit registers and a sixteen-bit bus. It would seem that the 68000 is superior. Neither chip handles floating point, but a coprocessor, the 8087, complements the 8086 in this regard, and when using floating point, the 8086/8087 is faster. Thus, the performance of the chip is determined by the instructions that make up a program.

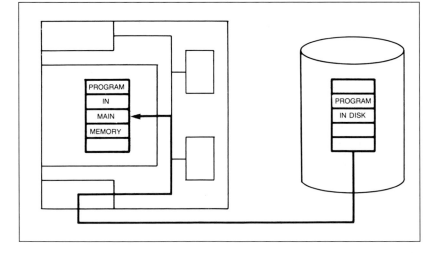

2-3. The CPU loads main memory by transferring a copy of a program on a peripheral disk into main memory.

PROGRAM IN MAIN MEMORY

PROGRAM IN DISK

Memory

Memory is the section of the computer where information is stored. All information is represented with binary digits, including instructions, programs, text, images, and numerical data.

Information encoded in a binary form is stored as a sequence of words, each with an address. Through the bus the CPU can fetch, or read, the contents of a word at a certain address and direct or write it to another location. The CPU can also move data between memory and its own registers, as well as between memory and *ports* (input and output channels).

Main memory is a high-speed memory that is addressed directly by the CPU and may be read and written in any order. In the first computers, main memory was made out of magnetic rings or cores. The term *core memory* now refers to this active working space, though today core is actually made up of semiconductor chips.

Main memory serves as an "erasable blackboard," a working memory space that is loaded with a program and the data that is to be manipulated. The program is loaded by copying a program from a peripheral memory across the bus into main memory. The computer then executes the instructions that constitute the program (fig. 2-3). Memory that can be read and written in any order is called *random access memory (RAM)*. In fact, the semiconductor chips used for this memory are commonly called *RAM*. *Sequential memory* must be read in a particular order.

Main memory is not always writable. Memory that is fixed and can only be read is called *read only memory (ROM)*. ROM is typically part of the address space of the CPU, but its contents are fixed. ROM is often used to store the information required for the computer to work properly—instructions for loading a program and performing self-test diagnostics and the dot matrix patterns of the character generators are typical examples.

Any program or data can be "etched" or "burned" into ROM. This is done by some manufacturers to distribute software, including languages like BASIC and video game programs. ROM ensures that a user cannot erase or modify certain critical programs and is thus a protection against

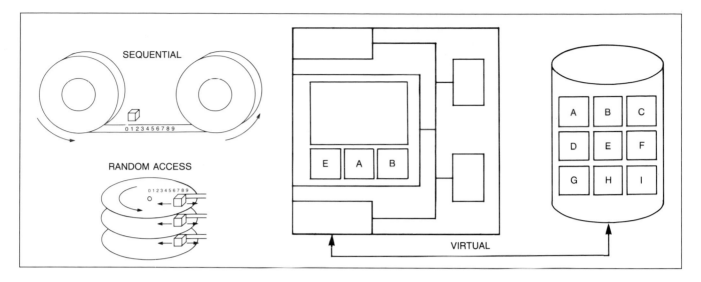

human programming errors and hardware failure.

Like RAM, ROM is made up of semiconductor chips on the CPU board or on a memory board and is connected to the bus. ROM is sometimes created and distributed in switchable plug-in cartridges. Since different ROM can be plugged into the hardware, yet its contents are software, it has aspects of both hardware and software and is therefore sometimes called **firmware.**

Peripheral memory is memory that is not addressed directly by the computer and is connected to the bus by a port. The computer accesses it by dispatching a device name or number and a file name onto the bus. Another processor, located within the peripheral memory, resolves the storage address within the memory system and then returns the requested data to the CPU bus. The advantages of peripheral memory are that large amounts of information (more than the address space of the machine) can be stored cheaply, and that the memory is nonvolatile, that is, it does not vanish when power is turned off.

Peripheral memories may be classified according to the type of medium employed, whether they are sequential or random access, and whether they are read only or rewritable. Originally, peripheral memory used punched paper tape or cards, but today peripheral memory is usually stored on magnetic tape or random access disks (hard drives or floppies). Emerging technologies employ optical recording techniques, sometimes combined with magnetic techniques in what is called magneto-optical recording. Because of the extra address calculations as well as the mechanics, information on disks takes longer to access than information stored in the main memory. And information on tape takes even longer to access (fig. 2-4), because it must be read or written in sequence.

Most peripheral memories can be read or written, although a disc may be "write protected," and only be read. Optical technologies use a laser to read bits. Some, like the **CD-ROM** and the **videodisc,** are read-only technologies. Their strength is that they are inexpensive to manufacture and have very large storage capacity (fig. 2-5). A **WORM,** or Write Once Read Many times disc, can only be written once, although it can be played many times. It is valuable in situations where a permanent trail is desired.

Virtual memory is like main memory in that it is addressed directly by the CPU as if it were RAM, whereas in fact it is memory stored on a peripheral like a disk drive. The illusion is accomplished by the system, which swaps programs and data back and forth between the peripheral memory and main memory as needed (fig. 2-4). This allows a program to operate as if there is

2-4. Sequential, random, and virtual memories. A tape must be read and written sequentially, but a disk can be randomly accessed. Virtual memory operates as if it were part of main memory, but is actually stored on a peripheral device and organized in pages (here, A through I). Pages used by the program are moved into main memory when needed (here, E, A, B).

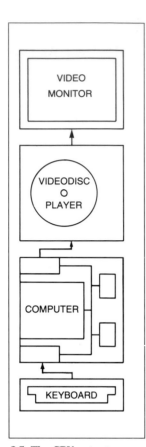

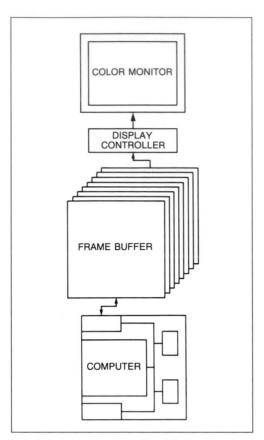

more main memory than actually exists on a machine.

In addition to regular disk and tape peripherals, specialized memories are used to store images. A **frame buffer,** more popularly known as a **video card,** is specialized memory for storing bitmaps and displaying them on a screen. A frame buffer is organized like a pixel matrix and is dual ported; an individual pixel can be read or written by the computer through one port, while a display controller continually reads the contents of the frame buffer through a second port and converts the pixels into a video signal. This can be viewed on a color video monitor (fig. 2-6).

Frame buffer memory is composed of one or more bitplanes with the binary value of each pixel stored in the successive layers. Thus as more bitplanes are added to the frame buffer, more intensity levels can be displayed. The number of intensity levels is equal to two raised to the power of the number of bitplanes.

A *display list memory* is another specialized memory designed for storing lists of numbers, typically points and polygons. Display list memories also provide ways to organize tree-structured hierarchies of objects, define colors and surface properties, and specify compound actions, for example a walking robot.

2-5. The CPU outputs addresses to the videodisc, often in the form of frame or page numbers. The disk then returns either programs, text, or images to the CPU, or outputs text or images to a video monitor. The disk controller may contain a microprocessor that interprets the commands from the master computer and uses them to control the machine.

2-6. A frame buffer with eight bitplanes can display 2^8 or 256 intensity levels. The numerical values written by the computer into the frame control the intensity of the video signal.

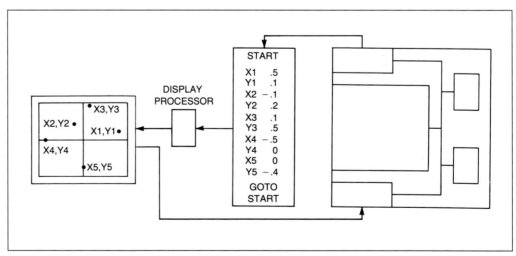

2-7. Display list memories consist of an input port, the memory itself, and an output port, which is connected to a display processor. The user directs the CPU to move points using an input peripheral. When the CPU changes a value in display list memory—for example, makes the value of −.4 equal to −.8—the object on the screen changes.

Like frame buffers, display list memories are dual ported: one port allows the memory to be read or written by the CPU; the second port allows the memory to be read by a display controller, which continually reads the contents of the memory and displays the output onto a monitor as lines or solid objects (fig. 2-7).

Display list memories and frame buffer memories complement each other—frame buffer memory is image oriented and stores pixels, whereas display list memory is object oriented and stores points. Both memories allow a graphic artist to manipulate the objects on the screen while looking at them in real time. The CPU captures the artist's commands as input, and then writes or modifies the contents of the memory accordingly. As these contents are changed the corresponding image on the screen changes. This is discussed in more detail in chapter 3.

Ports and Peripherals

The CPU is a switching device that retrieves and stores information from and into the ALC, the memory, and the peripherals. Peripherals include not only memory but also input and output devices such as keyboards, alphanumeric displays, and graphics devices. (Peripherals

are explored in detail in chapter 3.)

A computer connects to a peripheral via a *port,* typically a hardware board of interface circuitry that is attached both to the bus and the peripheral. All input and output of the computer is performed through the ports, also called channels because of their communicative nature. Ports can connect standard hardware to different computers and can also connect several computers.

Ports may be serial or parallel. A *serial port* receives a word from the bus, stores it, and then transmits a sequence of bits, one after another, to the peripheral on a single wire. A *parallel port* simultaneously passes the word to the peripheral on many wires—as many wires as there are bits in the word (fig. 2-8). Although ports run at different speeds, parallel ports run faster.

Ports, like memory locations, have addresses. A CPU passes information to a port first by transmitting the port address on the bus and then by transmitting the data itself. Whereas a memory cell simply holds data, the port hardware reformats the data into signals that the peripheral, such as a printer or terminal, can act on. Ports can be read as well as written and, like memory locations, can have variable names, also called *unit names.*

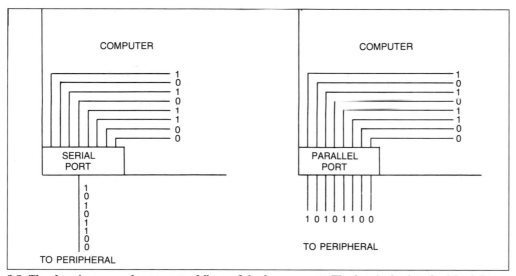

2-8. The drawing, an enlargement of figure 2-1, shows a port. The bus is depicted with eight parallel lines. The serial port converts a simultaneous transmission to a sequential transmission on one wire; the parallel port maintains the simultaneous aspect of the transmission, but requires eight wires.

`/square`	A procedure for drawing a square with four lines is going to be defined. The square will not be drawn until later in the program, when the `square` procedure is called.
`{ 0 0 moveto`	The left curly bracket indicates that this is the beginning of the procedure. The two numbers (0 for the x position, and 0 for the y position) indicate the starting point for drawing, the origin in this case. 0 and 0 are the arguments, and `moveto` is the operator.
`0 50 rlineto`	A line is drawn from the starting point to the arguments preceeding the `rlineto` operator.
`50 0 rlineto`	A second line is drawn from the last point defined in the previous command line to the arguments preceeding this `rlineto` operator.
`0 -50 rlineto`	A third line is drawn from the last point defined in the previous command line to the arguments preceeding this `rlineto` operator.
`closepath`	The `closepath` command will draw a line from the last point defined in the previous opearion to the starting drawing point, therefore closing the path.
`} def`	The right curly bracket indicates the end of the arguments in this procedure. The command `def` indicates that the procedure has been defined. From now on, every time a square is required the `square` procedure can be invoked. This procedure is made of several simpler instructions (i.e. `moveto`, `rlineto`, and `closepath`).
`.5 setgray`	A new color value is chosen with the `setgray` operator. In this case .5 equals a 50% grey tint.
`100 100 translate`	The origin, or starting drawing point, is translated to a new location before the square is actually drawn.
`square fill`	The `square` procedure is called, and it is shaded with the `fill` function.
`200 200 translate`	A new starting drawing point is chosen for future drawings (the origin is translated again before another square is drawn).
`2 setlinewidth`	A new line weight is set for future drawings using the `setlinewidth` operator, in this case 2 equals a 2-point line weight.
`square stroke`	The `square` procedure is called again, and it is drawn in the new location as an outline with the `stroke` function.

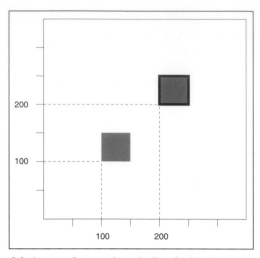

2-9. A procedure, written in PostScript, is created to define a square, and then that procedure is invoked twice to draw two squares. (Note that the grid in the figure has not been generated by the program.)

include computer programs and system documentation, the paper-and-pencil method of long division, and media products like books and movies.

Machine executable software dates as far back as the early 1800s, when the Jacquard loom was developed using punched cards to guide the thread when weaving complex patterns. The term itself is quite modern; software now contains the coded instructions that were previously built into hard-wired circuits. In a computer only the most basic functions are part of its hardware, which is capable of executing a primitive yet complete logic set. The software is a coded sequence of instructions that specify what logical operations the computer hardware should perform. Logic is thus not limited by mechanics.

Programs

A ***program*** is an organized sequence of instructions that defines a function not existing on the computer itself. For example, a computer with an addition but with no multiplication instruction can be programmed to multiply simply by using successive additions.

A program organizes the flow of control information in a series of notational commands. It is a means by which a process is

SOFTWARE

Software comprises the formal procedures used to accomplish a task as well as the data these procedures evaluate. Examples of software in the broad sense defined; programs follow a script that has alternate routes and conclusions. A properly composed program can be referred to by a single name or a symbol and can have its own **arguments,** variables that it evaluates to determine a result. Some programs, like the arithmetic functions +, −, ×, and ÷, are usually implemented as primitive machine language instructions and are executed in hardware. More complicated programs or functions, like the sum of a group of numbers, are constructed using primitive functions (fig. 2-9). These higher-level programs, like primitive functions, may also have arguments and can, in turn, be used by even higher-level procedures.

$$N \leftarrow 5\ 6\ 7\ 8$$

$$SUM\ N$$

$$26$$

In fact, the program will calculate the sum of any list of numbers, for example:

$$A \leftarrow 1\ 2\ 3\ 4\ 5$$

$$SUM\ A$$

$$15$$

The sum divided by the **shape,** or the quantity of numbers, is the average. This can be composed into a single new function called *Average:* (SUM N) ÷ (SHAPE N). If we wanted an average of N, we could just type: AVERAGE N. The computer would respond as if the entire text had been entered and print 6.5, the answer.

A program is said to **call,** or use, a more primitive procedure, and a program that is called is said to be **invoked.** Invoked programs are sometimes referred to as *subprograms,* or *subroutines,* and many different programs might call the same subprogram (fig. 2-10)—subroutines can call other routines, and so on. Programs and subroutines are also referred to as *functions* or *procedures.*

A **language** is a set of procedures with a consistent syntax and is used to communi-

2-10. Procedures are the building blocks of software. Procedures call procedures and are in turn called by other procedures.

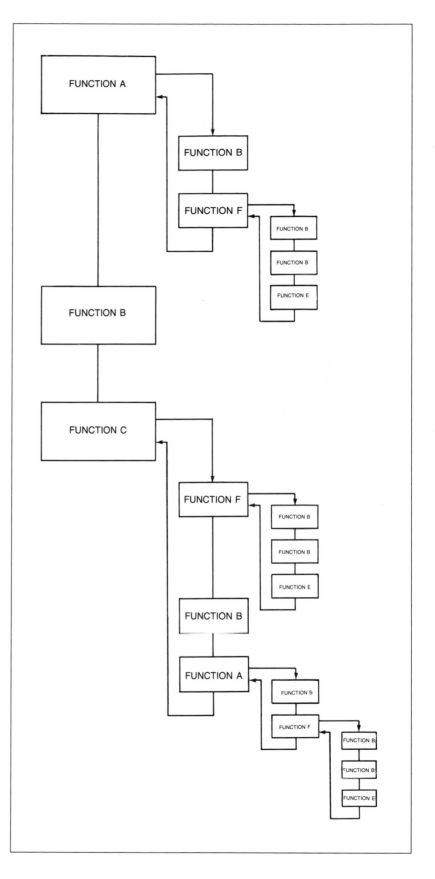

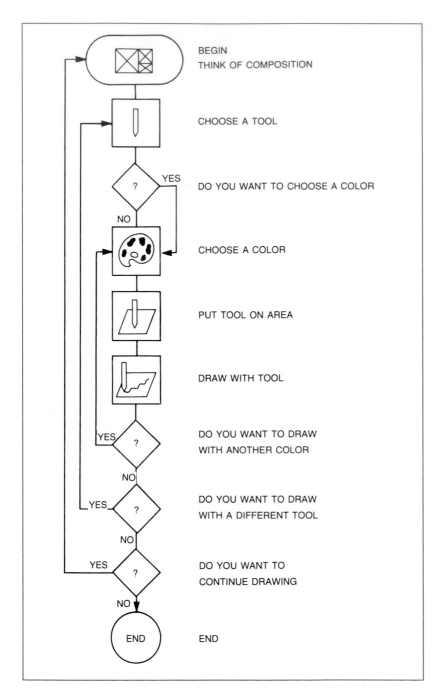

BEGIN
THINK OF COMPOSITION

CHOOSE A TOOL

DO YOU WANT TO CHOOSE A COLOR — YES

NO

CHOOSE A COLOR

PUT TOOL ON AREA

DRAW WITH TOOL

DO YOU WANT TO DRAW
WITH ANOTHER COLOR — YES

NO

DO YOU WANT TO DRAW
WITH A DIFFERENT TOOL — YES

NO

DO YOU WANT TO
CONTINUE DRAWING — YES

NO

END

2-11. Algorithm for drawing a scene.

define a process and generate a specific result in a finite number of steps. A program is the implementation of an algorithm in a computer language. Executing a program involves reading arguments, following a series of steps, determining a result, and terminating (fig. 2-11).

Not all sequences of instructions on a computer form an algorithm. A process that repeatedly adds one then subtracts one to a variable is not an algorithm, because it will go on computing until it is externally terminated. A programmer would say the program has gotten "hung up" and that it had to be "aborted."

Another such sequence is a program that writes its results back into the same memory locations that stores its instructions, thus destroying itself and its ability to conclude the task in the process. The programmer would say that the program "crashed," probably because it executed its results as if they were instructions.

Most of the paper-and-pencil methods we employ for solving problems arithmetically are algorithms. Long division, for example, is an orderly procedure composed of even more fundamental arithmetic functions, particularly multiple subtractions and a test to determine the end. The procedure by which long division is executed on a computer is similar to the pen-and-paper method (fig. 2-12).

Algorithms are solution strategies that are independent of particular processes. Many different algorithms can often be implemented to solve the same problem. Mathematicians have long sought new algorithmic formations to reduce the number of operations required to solve a problem. For example, our function SUM works by adding together a series of numbers. To add together the first one hundred numbers, 1 + 2 + 3 and so on to 100, would require one hundred separate additions. At the end of the eighteenth century, a German schoolboy, Carl Friedrich Gauss, was given this task as a homework assignment. He observed that to solve the problem it was only necessary to multiply the number of numbers

cate directions to a computer as well as to represent numbers. Languages are to programs what musical notation is to musical compositions. Programming languages, as in the above SUM and AVERAGE functions, use elements of human, mathematics, and design languages.

An *algorithm* is the essence of a program, the step-by-step instructions that

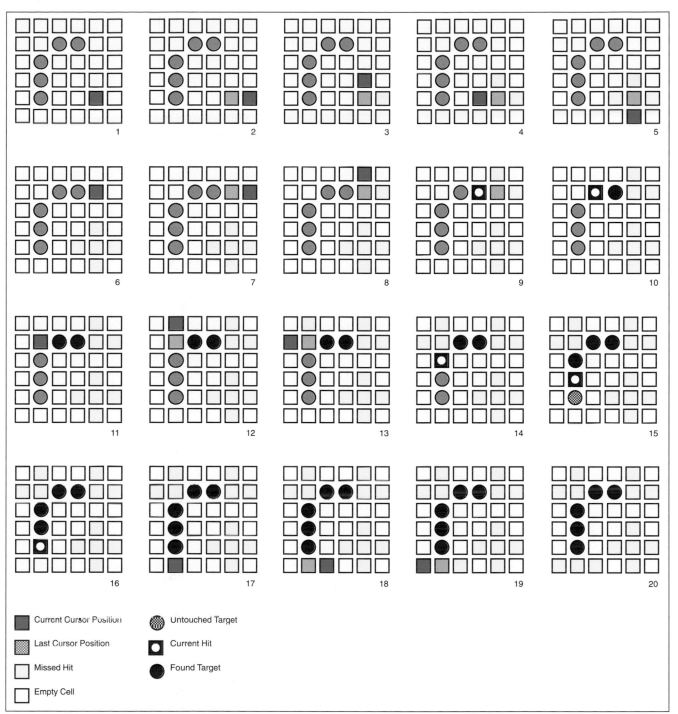

Current Cursor Position   Untouched Target

Last Cursor Position   Current Hit

Missed Hit

Found Target

Empty Cell

2-12. This sequence of drawings illustrates an algorithm that finds contiguous red pixels in a bitmap. In the illustration the bitmap is six pixels square; the empty squares represent empty pixels, the green square represents the current cursor position, and the pink circles represent "undiscovered" red pixels. The program begins searching at a random location within the bitmap and it keeps track of hits and misses (see the key). The procedure first searches the current cursor position to see if it is a hit (1). If not, it moves one pixel to the right and checks again (2), then one pixel up (3), left (4), and down (5). If no hits occur, then the cursor moves three pixels up (6), and the algorithm is repeated (7, 8). This time, upon moving left, a hit is detected and marked (9). The search algorithm now advances the cursor in the direction in which the pixel was found, left in this case (10) where it scores another hit, and left still again (11), where it finds nothing, and reverts to searching up (12), left (13), and down (14), where it again scores and is set marching in a new direction, hitting twice more (15, 16), before it detects an empty pixel (17). It makes a final search right (18) and left (19) and then stops (20), because there are no more contiguous red pixels to be found. (Courtesy of Isaac V. Kerlow.)

2-13. The operating system supports applications programs and provides a way for them to communicate with files, data bases, and systems utilities.

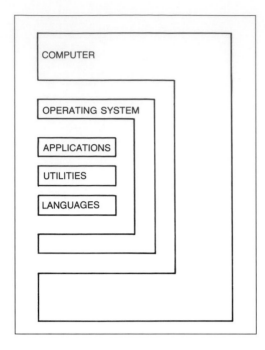

by a number one greater (101) and divide by two.

$$N \leftarrow 100$$
$$N \times (N + 1) \div 2$$
$$5050$$

Gauss reduced an algorithm requiring one hundred steps to an algorithm that required three steps—one addition, one multiplication, and one division. The algorithm remains the same when adding the first one million numbers.

Gauss did this not by employing more hardware but by using the hardware in an economical way. Intuition led him to manipulate algebraic symbols, which represented the primitive arithmetic processes. The proof of the new algorithm was not only in testing it against the known method and getting identical results, but in the ability to symbolically translate the initial algorithm into an improved one using a series of successive substitutions, or a proof.

The **operating system** (OS) is a special program designed to schedule and manage other programs and to manage the flow of operations in the computer. You might think of the operating system as an algorithm for running a machine; it is the framework for the creative tool. OS lets you run different languages, such as BASIC or Pascal, as well as utilities, application programs and file managers, and data-base systems.

Utilities programs perform a restricted set of operations. These are often basic system-oriented tasks required by the operating system and by users, including file managers, librarians, sort and merge procedures, backups, archives, maintenance and diagnostic routines. Communications, not only between the user and the machine, but between peripherals and the machine, are also handled by utility programs (fig. 2-13), as are tasks like job scheduling, loading programs from the disk into core memory, monitoring the flow of program execution, spooling output until it can be printed, error tracking, and logging usage information.

Application programs usually focus on specialized areas of use, including word

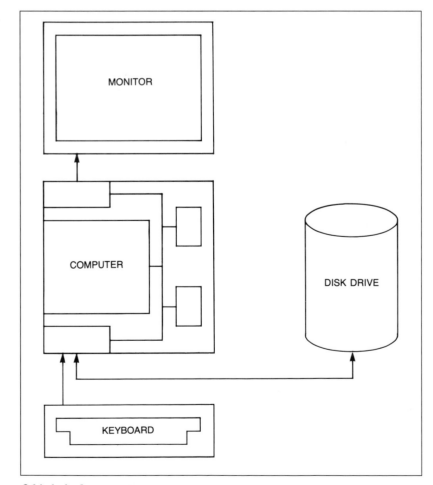

2-14. A single-user system.

processors, paint systems, electronic mail, and spread sheets.

Operating systems are accessible to either one or many users. In a ***single user system*** only one person can use the system, and has access to all the system files (fig. 2-14). A ***multiuser system*** is structured to support several users or tasks simultaneously, each with his or her own application program and files. An OS utility manages core memory and assures that application programs do not interfere with each other. Another OS procedure determines how the resources are shared among the users, another lets users control who can access their files.

Single or multiuser systems can function in interactive or batch mode. ***Interactive*** systems allow an artist to create and modify images in real time. If, however, the image is a complex one, the computer may not be able to calculate interactively the image display.

An OS, just like a language, often has an ***interactive command interpreter,*** which responds to a user's input, either typed on a keyboard or selected from a menu. A command interpreter, discussed in detail in chapter 4, employs a languagelike syntax similar to a programming language.

In multiuser systems, interactivity is supported by a process called ***time-sharing,*** which allows several users access to the CPU resources (fig. 2-15). It is assumed that the time-sharing users do not require the full service of the CPU, so each gets to use it a fraction of the time, which should be sufficient for the CPU to evaluate the user's input and produce results without delay.

Batch processes are collections of transactions processed as single units, and need not communicate with the user during execution (fig. 2-16). Batch computations are not constrained to situations where processing must be done in real time; therefore more complex imagery can be calculated. These processes work by aggregating related operations and then executing them as a unit. For example, in motion picture production

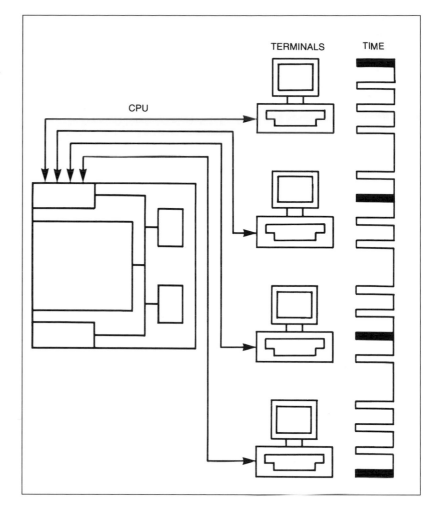

an entire roll of film is shot, then developed and edited, and finally screened. The production process would be very different if each frame had to be individually shot, developed, edited, and screened.

Batch and interactive technologies parallel compositional and improvisational techniques. Composing is command oriented and literal. Improvisation is interactive and nonliteral (fig. 2-17).

2-15. A multiuser time-sharing system divides memory and time among different users, so each has access to the processor for a fraction of the time. Here, four users each get about one quarter of the memory and are able to use the CPU one quarter of the time.

LANGUAGES

A computer programming language is a standardized notation that defines operations between arguments. Different languages have different syntaxes, or grammar rules, for the composition of statements

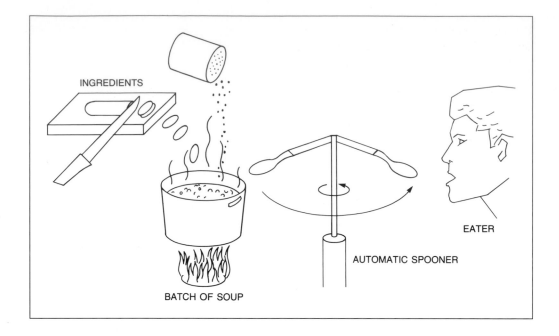

INGREDIENTS

EATER

AUTOMATIC SPOONER

BATCH OF SOUP

as well as for performing different operations. Languages include machine languages, assemblers, high-level languages, and special-purpose graphics languages.

The syntax of a language may be rich or sparse. A typesetting language, for example, operates on textual data, letters and words, and may have commands for font, height, line width, leading, and weight. This set of commands is finite and includes processes that have already been defined in the language program. Sometimes a language provides more than one way of doing something; sometimes a task is inaccessible. For example, if a particular typesetting language lacks an upside-down command, you cannot set type upside down. The feature can be added to the language (by a systems programmer), augmenting the fundamental program and creating the extra command in the typesetting language.

A language is ideally more than a collection of related functions and should include syntax for variable names, assignments, arithmetic, if-then scenarios, and iterative operations.

Machine Language

The interface between software and hardware is the binary machine instruction word that, when loaded into an instruction regis-

ter, is decoded in a precise and exact way.

An ***instruction word*** contains an opcode and an operand. The ***opcode*** specifies functionality, such as +, −, ×, or ÷, and is represented by a binary code. The ***operand*** is the data, the numbers or characters that will make up the arguments of the function.

A group of instruction words, or an instruction set, make up the ***machine language*** and define the functionality of the basic machine. Each computer has its own instruction set that is decoded by the computer circuitry. A machine language for one brand of computer usually cannot run on another.

Assembly Language

Machine language is the only language that the central processor can act on. When computers were first invented all programs had to be written in machine language. ***Assembly language*** was then invented to make programming easier by using mnemonic instructions that translate to opcodes; decimal numbers and alphanumeric variable names are converted to binary digits and assembled into binary addresses (fig. 2-18).

The assembly language is converted into machine language by a program called the *assembler* (fig. 2-19). As you can see, assemblers optimize the programming resources tremendously with virtually no resources wasted. Nonetheless, programming in assembly language remains a tedious, time-consuming process. For that reason even more English-like languages have been developed. Although these languages do not execute as quickly, they are easier and faster to write.

Compilers and Interpreters

Languages, like assembly languages, have to be converted into machine language to run. Programs that convert commands into machine code can be either compilers or interpreters. A *compiler* is a program that translates an entire source program, written in a high-level programming language, into machine code and then saves it as a binary file, which can then be loaded and executed. In this sense the assembler just described is a compiler. A statement in assembly language typically represents a single primitive machine instruction; a statement in a high-level language typically represents several machine instructions. The process of compiling, loading, and executing is one method of processing information in batches. Here the first step is to convert all the high-level statements into machine instructions, then to load the instructions, and then run them. The strategy is basically the same as the assembler depicted in figure 2-19.

An *interpreter,* on the other hand, reads each command, determines its intent, and then calls a preexisting machine language subroutine to execute that action. Inter-

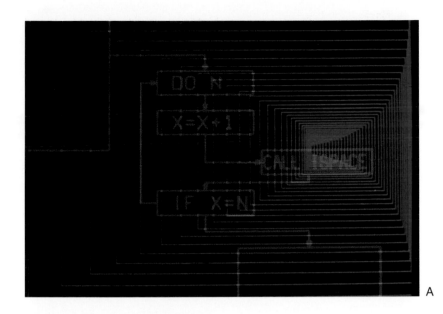

A

B

2-17. Image A was generated with a program—a compositional technique. Image B was produced with an interactive paint system—an improvisational technique. (Image A provided by Judson Rosebush. Image B courtesy of New England Technology Group. Image by Tom Christopher.)

Symbolic HLL	Assembly Language	Machine Language
NOT 1	NOT 1	1000 000000000001
3 + 4	PLUS 3,4	0000 000011000100

2-18. Table shows corresponding instructions for NOT and PLUS written in a symbolic high-level language, an assembly language, and machine code. All contain an opcode and an operand(s). An assembler program converts the assembly language to machine language. An instruction can be *monadic,* having one operand, or *dyadic,* a function with two operands. An example of monadic function is "NOT 1": *NOT* is the opcode, *1* is the operand, and *0* is the result. An instruction with two operands is *PLUS,* where + is the opcode, *3* and *4* are the operands, and *7* is the result.

preters run interactively, often in time-sharing environments. The interpreter itself is a program, as is the information it reads and processes. The interactive mode gives the user access to the program while it is running, so it can respond in real time to the user's commands (fig. 2-20).

Compilers and interpreters each have their purposes and advantages. The interpreter is immediate, but compiled programs run faster, because the high-level language is translated to machine code only once. In an interpreter the program is translated every time it is run.

High-level Programming Languages

The first high-level languages (HLL) were invented in the 1950s. FORTRAN and COBOL, two early entries, eliminated any references to the CPU's registers, incorporated a simple way of passing data to and from subprograms, and permitted data to be represented as arrays of two or more dimensions or as sequential character records. FORTRAN was first used in science, COBOL in business.

Thousands of programming languages are available today; some even have dialects. Programming languages are both general purpose, like FORTRAN, and special purpose, like Synthavision, a language to simplify the creation and manipulation of three-dimensional graphic animation.

High-level languages are *portable,* that is, compilers and interpreters for common high-level languages can be written to trans-

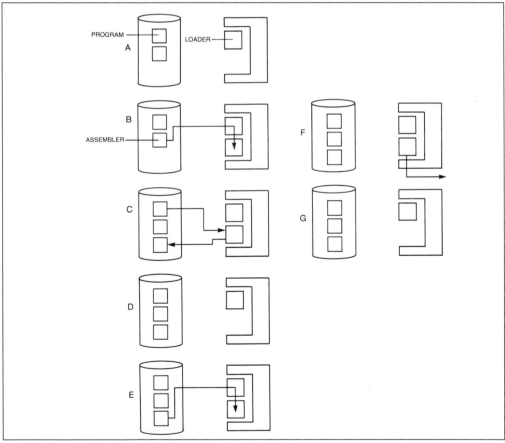

2-19. Assembly language instructions are first composed as a file of text (A). A program called the *assembler* is loaded into main memory (B). The assembler reads the alphanumeric files of assembly language statements, then translates them into a file of binary machine language instructions that are saved on peripheral memory (C). The function of the assembler program is finished and is erased from main memory (D). A program called the *loader* now retrieves the newly created binary machine language file into main memory (E) and the computer executes it (F). The system is then ready to execute the next task (G).

late the language into the machine language of many different CPUs, from microprocessors to mainframes (fig. 2-21).

High-level languages are written in lower-level languages, often assemblers, and very-high-level languages (VHLL), such as a paint system, are written in high-level languages. Indeed, an artist or designer working on a system might be three or more levels above the machine language. It is helpful to know the level of language you are communicating at. This is less important, however, than knowing how to communicate using that particular notational language.

The most relevant high-level languages have been designed for a variety of applications, including graphics, but no one language has been adopted as the standard for the computer industry. Indeed, general-purpose languages are very useful in writing special-purpose tools. Special-purpose graphic languages also exist and are discussed later in the chapter (fig. 2-22).

FORTRAN (Formula Translation) was developed in the late 1950s by an IBM research team headed by John Backus. It became the first portable language and is still widely used for scientific and mathematical applications.

ALGOL (Algorithmic Language) was developed by European and American scientists led by Alan J. Perlis and Nicholas Wirth between 1958 and 1960. ALGOL was the first language to recognize the use of a formal notation for syntax and was used by academics to publish algorithms. Its concepts and structural design have influenced other languages.

COBOL (Common Business Oriented Language) was created by a team headed by Joseph Wegstein and A. Eugene Smith. Its syntax is geared toward simple English commands that post entries to journals and perform bookkeeping arithmetic.

LISP (List Processor) was designed by John McCarthy while working at MIT in 1958 to 1960. LISP allows a programmer to construct logical assertions, or rules, and then invokes an action that must follow the rules. It is widely used for artificial intelligence applications, also known as expert systems.

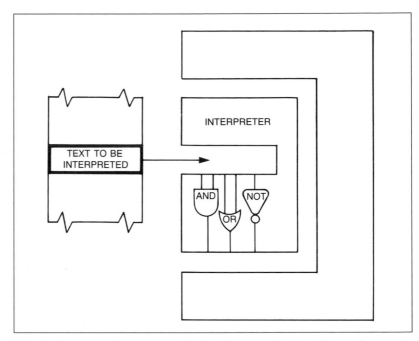

2-20. An interpreter is a program that has been previously written and converted into an executable file of binary machine language instructions. Once this program is loaded into main memory, it operates by evaluating an input file one statement at a time, and then executing an interpreter code, calculating the result. The input file is either interactively typed on the keyboard or read from a disk.

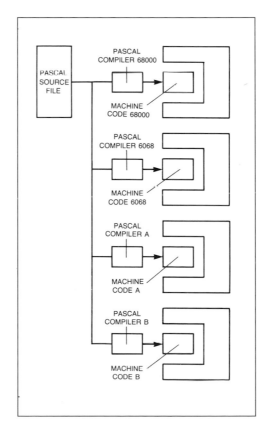

2-21. Programs written in high-level programming languages are *portable*, because they can be compiled, or translated, into the machine code of different CPUs. In this example a single Pascal file is processed by different compilers that generate their own machine language instructions.

BASIC

```
10 HGR:HCOLOR=3
20 X=50; Y=70
30 HPLOT X,Y TO X+20,Y
   TO X+20,Y+20
   TO X,Y+20
   TO X,Y
60 END
```

FORTRAN

```
SUBROUTINE RECT (CENTX, CENTY,
   WIDTH, HEIGHT, XA, YA, N)
DIMENSION XA(4), YA(4)
XA (1) = CENTX - (WIDTH/2)
YA (1) = CENTY - (HEIGHT/2)
XA (2) = XA (1)
YA (2) = CENTY + (HEIGHT/2)
XA (3) = CENTX - (WIDTH/2)
YA (3) = YA(2)
XA (4) = XA(1)
YA (4) = YA(3)
N=4
RETURN
END
```

PostScript

```
1 setlineweight
50 50 moveto
100 50 rlineto
100 100 rlineto
50 100 rlineto
closepath
stroke
showpage
```

Logo

```
TO BOX

REPEAT 4 (FD 50 RT 90)

END
```

Pascal

```
PROGRAM SQUARE;
      USES TURTLEGRAPHICS;
      VAR SIDE: INTEGER;
   BEGIN
      INITTURTLE;
      PENCOLOR (BLUE)
      FOR SIDE:= 1 TO 4 DO
         BEGIN
             MOVE (50)
             TURN (90)
         END
   END
```

C

```
#include "c:\targa\tg.h"

main()
{
   TGinit();
   TGclear_screen(BLACK)
    TGfilled_rect(10,10,20,20,RED)
   TGend();
}
```

2-22. **Making a rectangle in six different programming languages.**

BASIC (Beginners All Purpose Symbolic Instruction Code) was developed in 1967 by John Kemeny and Thomas E. Kurtz of Dartmouth College and was the first interpreted language. BASIC uses simple commands and was designed to broaden access to the computing process by making program-writing easier. Initially, BASIC was implemented on interactive, time-sharing systems, and it was the first language to port to microcomputers. Recent variations, like Visual Basic, make it easy to construct graphical user interfaces.

PASCAL (named for the French mathematician Blaise Pascal) was developed by a team headed by Nicholas Wirth and introduced in 1971. It is a language that encourages the production of well-structured programs using nested functionalities (IF-THEN-ELSE). PASCAL's clarity makes it popular in academia, and it is also used as an alternative to C in the real world.

C was developed in the 1970s by Dennis Ritchie and Brian Kernighan at Bell Laboratories. C expands the features of FORTRAN and allows a pointer and a variable with mixed datatypes to be defined. The multi-user operating system **Unix** is written in C, a combination that has enabled Unix to be portable and run on different processors.

Logo was developed during the 1970s by a group headed by Seymour Papert at MIT seeking to make computer programming accessible to children. It is an interactive (interpreted) language, and incorporates the idea of issuing commands to a handler. A child can draw by commanding a goal-oriented "turtle."

HyperTalk was developed by Bill Atkinson and is a message-passing language. It contains a rich collection of functions, called handlers, which pass messages when screen actions, such as clicking a button with a mouse, occur. A message hierarchy enables messages to be processed locally or upstream, at a more centralized headquarters.

More and more languages like HyperTalk, Visual Basic, and even C are being programmed not only by textual commands, but by **graphical programming interfaces.** These graphical interfaces are not necessarily languages for programming graphics, but rather present a graphical metaphor of the programming process to programmers.

Graphics Languages

Graphics languages are specialized computer languages that include vocabulary (textual syntax or menu commands) with graphic primitives. These primitives include instructions for creating shapes (TRIANGLE, CIRCLE), positioning directions (MOVE TO, ROTATE, SIZE), and page controls. High-level graphics languages exist to manipulate pixels and images, as well as to make charts and graphics, paintings and drawings, and even realistic three-dimensional environments. Graphics languages are often specialized, but a common theme is that single high-level commands in the graphics language invoke complicated graphical procedures (fig. 2-23).

Many graphics languages employ textual commands, for example, **PostScript,** a specialized language for two-dimensional page description, **RenderMan,** a language for rendering three-dimensional objects, or **Phigs,** a language for interactive three-dimensional object manipulation. But many graphics languages are operated graphically, with the media represented virtually, and actions that mimic the user's methods of working are controlled by the cursor. Examples of these graphical paradigm languages include *Freehand,* a program for two-dimensional drawing, and *Photoshop,* a program for two-dimensional image manipulation. Oftentimes it is desirable to use a language in interactive graphical mode or to construct a textual representation that can run in batch mode.

Graphics software should be portable, or adaptable to different computers. It should also be *device independent,* or able to interface with various graphic peripherals. Thus a graphics subroutine library provides a standardized, portable interface between applications programs and graphics peripherals by isolating device dependent routines, which are commands unique to a specific model of a peripheral, from the body of the subroutine library, which contains only device independent subroutines. Because the device

2-23. High-level graphics languages, like low-level languages, are composed of operations and operands, and calculate results. The difference is that individual commands can be very effective and specific. For instance, in a graphics system, a command or process, "NEGA-TIVE," coupled with an argument or data, a "PIC-TURENAME," performs photographlike picture processing, in this case making a negative of the image.

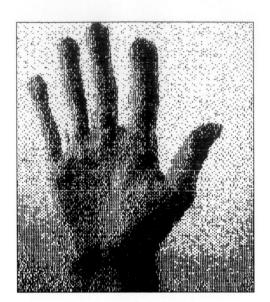

LOAD PICTURE

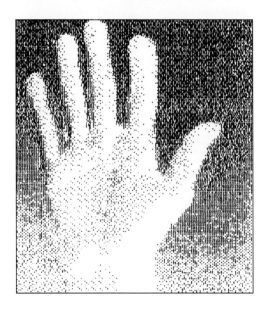

NEGATIVE PICTURE

the full repertoire of the high-level language. Examples of subroutine libraries include the ACM Core System for vector graphics and the Graphics Kernel System (GKS) for raster graphics. These packages define basic drawing interfaces such as a routine to draw a line between two points (fig. 2-25). Subroutine packages support basic two- and three-dimensional geometric operations, perspective, and the drawing of text, lines, and areas of color.

A *graphics preprocessor* is an extension of the compiler and permits the syntax of an existing language to be augmented by new (graphics) commands. It works by recognizing and incorporating extensions to the language. The preprocessor program is executed prior to the interpreter or compiler, and its output, which combines native language commands with expanded commands, is passed to the high-level language compiler and compiled normally (fig. 2-26). The advantage of this technique is that it uses a graphics language that fully incorporates an existing high-level language as well as new commands.

A *complete programming language* with syntax to express logic, store and manipulate variables, and create graphics is yet another approach to developing, manipulating, and displaying visual images. Complete programming languages are often interpreters and can be controlled by graphic menus (fig. 2-27) as well as by text (fig. 2-28). Complete programming languages exist for creating two-dimensional as well as three-dimensional graphics, but unless they are extremely comprehensive they will have limited command and logical structures compared to high-level languages.

DISTRIBUTED PROCESSING AND COMPUTER NETWORKS

The role of the computer in society began with a monolithic central computer surrounded by a plotter, disk drives, memory, and terminals and managed by a set of professionals, who focused on cramming

dependent routines constitute a small portion of the system, they are written anew for each physical display (fig. 2-24). Another feature is *device intelligence,* where software detects the capabilities of hardware, performing only necessary calculations and letting the hardware do more of the work.

Three techniques have emerged for the creation, manipulation, and display of visual images: subroutine libraries, preprocessors, and complete languages. *Subroutine libraries* are collections of functions that can be used with and called by a preexisting high-level language, thereby retaining

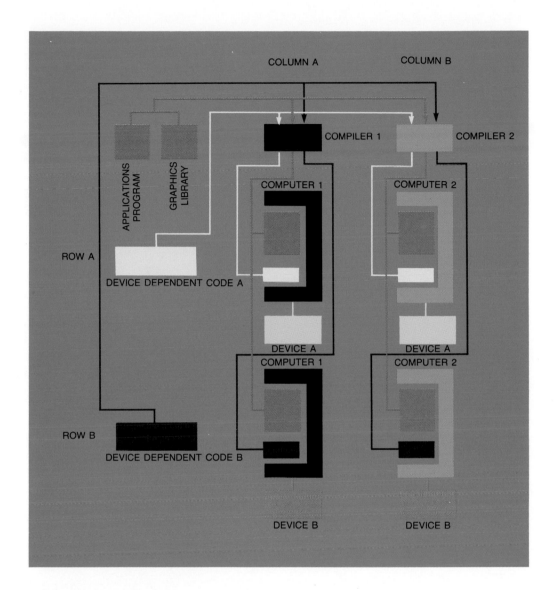

COLUMN A   COLUMN B

COMPILER 1   COMPILER 2

APPLICATIONS PROGRAM   GRAPHICS LIBRARY

COMPUTER 1   COMPUTER 2

ROW A

DEVICE DEPENDENT CODE A

DEVICE A   DEVICE A

COMPUTER 1   COMPUTER 2

ROW B

DEVICE DEPENDENT CODE B

DEVICE B   DEVICE B

2-24. Four permutations of device-independent and device-dependent graphics software are illustrated in this drawing: two pairs of computers, each with its own compiler (columns A and B), and two pairs of graphic peripherals (rows A and B). Each peripheral is driven by each type of computer. One common applications program and the device-independent routines contained in the graphics subroutine library (top left) are shared by all systems. The device-dependent code is shared only by peripherals of the same type and is compiled with different compilers.

work through a finite resource.

With the advent of the microprocessor and the personal computer it became possible for laboratories, offices, and individuals to acquire their own machines. These personal computers are not as comprehensive as the mainframes, but provide the single user with many options.

Now we want the best of both worlds: localized computing and storage on the desktop, as well as the ability to send and receive data from other computers, and do some computing remotely. This can be accomplished with a **network,** a switching system that routes data and messages from one end user to another between computers (fig. 2-29). The telephone system is a classic example of a network—each end user can communicate with any other end user. A computer network is simply a collection of interconnected computers where data can be sent back and forth. The data can include programs, pictures, alphanumeric information and electronic mail. A network is the antithesis of **broadcasting,** where there is a single, one-way source

Function Line (X1, Y1, X2, Y2)

Function Arc (X, Y, BEG, END, RADIUS)

2-25. Functions for drawing a line and an arc between two points.

2-26. The Actor/Scriptor Animation System (ASAS) is an animation language that is an extension of LISP and includes the full programming features of the structured parent language. The original ASAS animation notation (mixed with some LISP) at the left is expanded into LISP by the preprocessor, creating a file that is then either interpreted or compiled (LISP can do either) to produce animated images.

with many receivers, for example, a newspaper or a TV or radio station. Although networks are usually connected with wires, there is an increasing trend toward wireless networks.

A **local area network (LAN)** services a group of computers, usually within the same building. A **wide area network (WAN)** travels longer distances with the data typically traveling over telephone company lines. Often networks enable computers with different operating systems and manufactured by different vendors to talk to each other. Popular networks include Appletalk, used on Apple Macintosh computers; Novell, widely used in corporations

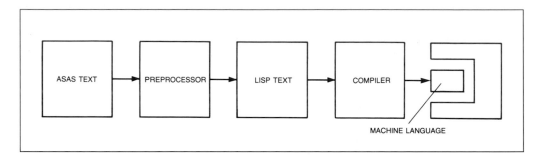

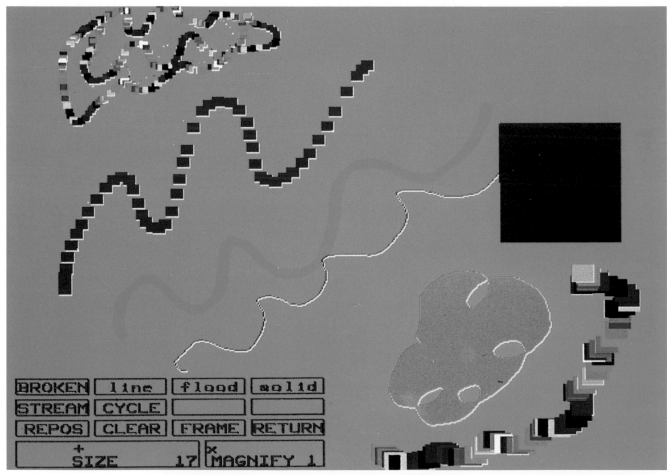

2-27. Graphic languages controlled by menus combine commands selected by touching a menu with an ability to draw interactively. The menu and image illustrate changing line widths, changing colors, and solid versus broken lines. (Courtesy of Digital Effects Inc.)

to network MS-DOS machines like the IBM/PC; and Ethernet, used by PCs and workstations alike.

Aside from the actual physical configuration the most important network parameter is the bandwidth, represented as the baud rate. The **bandwidth** is the number of bits per second that can pass through a channel, be it a phone wire, a network, or a television transmitter. Bandwidth is measured in bits per second, or **baud;** one baud is one bit per second (fig. 2-30). In other words, a 9600-baud channel can

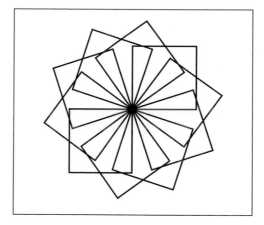

2-28. Program and the resultant drawing. The program, written in Post-Script, defines a function to build a square. The lower left corner of the square is then translated to location 150,150, which is the center of the bounding box. (The bounding box is not drawn by the program.) The "0 setgray 1 set-linewidth" defines the box to have no shade inside it and defines the line width of the box. All the drawing occurs in the next line, which draws the square ten times, rotating it 36° each time.

```
%Rotated Squares

%Program written in the PostScript Language

%%Title:Rotated Squares.eps

%%BoundingBox 0 0 300 300


/square       %this function defines how to build a square

      { 0 0 moveto

      0 50 rlineto

      50 0 rlineto

      0 -50 rlineto

      closepath

      } def


150 150 translate

0 setgray 1 setlinewidth


36 { 10 rotate square stroke} repeat
```

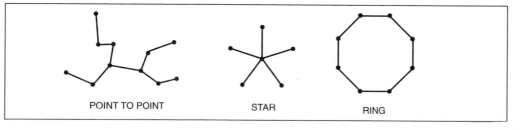

POINT TO POINT   STAR   RING

2-29. Networks include: point-to-point, star, and ring configurations.

transmit 9600 bits per second. The relationship between the baud and the number of data bytes (characters) per second is that the number of bytes per second is typically ⅒ the baud rate. This is because there are eight bits transmitted for each byte, plus a parity bit and a timing bit, for a total of ten bits. Not all networks have the same bandwidth. PC networks like Novell move information at around one megabit per second. Ethernet moves information at around 10 megabits per second. Newer networks, like FDDI, move information at around 100 megabits per second (see fig. 9-22). Given that a full color television frame may contain 6 megabits ($640 \times 480 \times 24$ bits), or 180 megabits per second (30 frames), the importance of faster networks should be evident.

Distributed processing is the connection of a personal computer to a mainframe or to another computer via a network so that the computing is spread between at least two CPUs (fig. 2-31). This combination is truly synergistic; the user is able to locate data in the highly centralized system of the mainframe, bring it into his or her domain, manipulate and analyze the data, and return results to the centralized processor. The centralized processor can still do what it always did best—large batch processing and supporting a network of time-sharing users. But with distributed processing the time-sharing users are not calculating on the mainframe; they are mostly computing on their machines and using the mainframe as an intelligent switch-

2-30. Bandwidth is the number of bits that can pass through a channel during one second, a unit of measurement called baud. Bandwidths have evolved from 150-baud teletype networks to giga-baud transmission cables. Factors that increase bandwidth include whether bits are transmitted in serial or parallel, the kind of cable (or transmission) involved, and the speed at which the bits move.

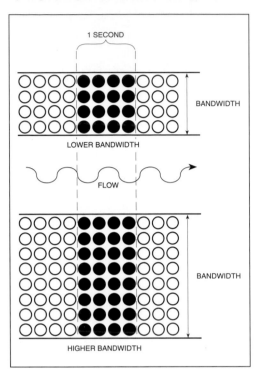

1 SECOND

BANDWIDTH

LOWER BANDWIDTH

FLOW

BANDWIDTH

HIGHER BANDWIDTH

2-31. Distributed processing is a technique for computing problems on more than one computer simultaneously. In this example, a master computer at the far left, complete with a keyboard, disk, and monitor dispatches programs and data to two distributed processors, which also work on the problem at the same time. This architecture can run across a network or internally, where, for example, a distributed processor is used to do such tasks as three-dimensional rendering, color screen calculations, voice analysis, and optical character recognition.

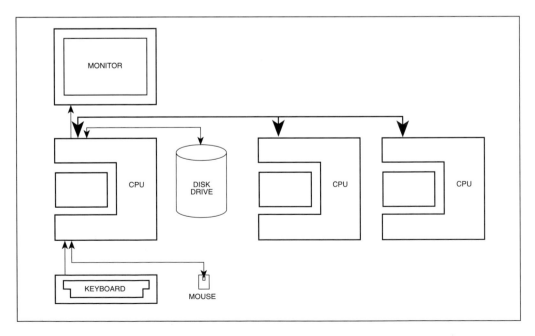

MONITOR

CPU

DISK DRIVE

CPU

CPU

KEYBOARD

MOUSE

ing machine and a coprocessor.

Networks will play an increasing role in all of the graphic arts because so much of what we do professionally involves teamwork among individuals with highly specialized crafts. A network allows an illustrator, a writer, a page makeup artist, and a person who does color correction to contribute to the same **destination document,** each doing their share of the work, despite physical distance.

In the past these destination documents contained copies of their component files; texts, illustrations, and bitmap files were **placed** in the document using copy and paste (fig. 2-32a). The advantage is a complete, integral document; the disadvantage is that the document must be updated if there are changes in any of the component pieces, and everything is stored twice, once in working form and once in the destination document. Another approach is the **embedded document,** in which the component files are copied into the destination document along with a pointer to the source application (fig. 2-32b). In this scenario, each of the component embedded files is "live" and double clicking on them launches their original source application, something that does not occur when a file is placed. A **linked document** behaves much like an embedded document except that the component files are not actually copied to the destination document but rather only a pointer is stored at the destination (fig. 2-32c). These are also called **live links** or **hot links.** The advantage is that changes in any artwork or text in the source documents propagate forward immediately into the destination document. There is no duplication of files. Linked documents vastly facilitate information management, especially when the page components (for example, a photograph, a drawing, a text) are used more than once. Linked documents make possible what is called **publish and subscribe,** where the source document is published and many destination documents can subscribe to it. A disadvantage is that the final document is more volatile because there are more sources

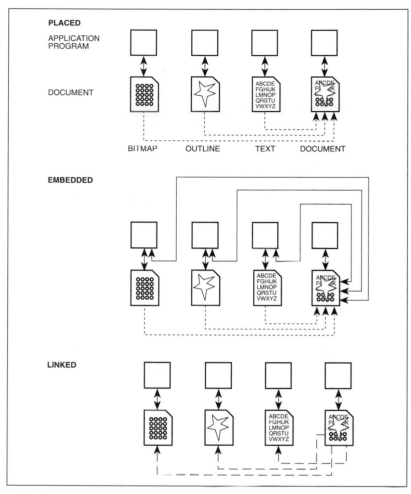

2-32. Placed, embedded, and linked documents are shown here. In all cases the destination document is composed of a bitmap, a line drawing, and a text file, each in a unique format and each created and edited with a unique application program. Another program manages the page creation of the destination document. In the placed document, copies of the three elements are placed in the destination document file, and all connections to the originals and the software used to edit them are severed. In the embedded document, copies are also placed in the page file, but the connections to the source application programs are maintained. Thus, for example, double clicking on the text launches the word processor. In the linked document, no copies of the source document exist in the destination document; when the destination document is viewed you "see through" back to the original documents. With the linked document, the connection with the source application is also maintained; double clicking on the text that appears in the destination document still launches the word processor, but now you are editing the original copy of the text, not a copy of it in the destination document.

for error to creep in. It is usually possible to "fix" a linked document into a placed document, but it may not be possible to rebuild the links that made a destination document. All of these functionalities exist in today's software for personal computers.

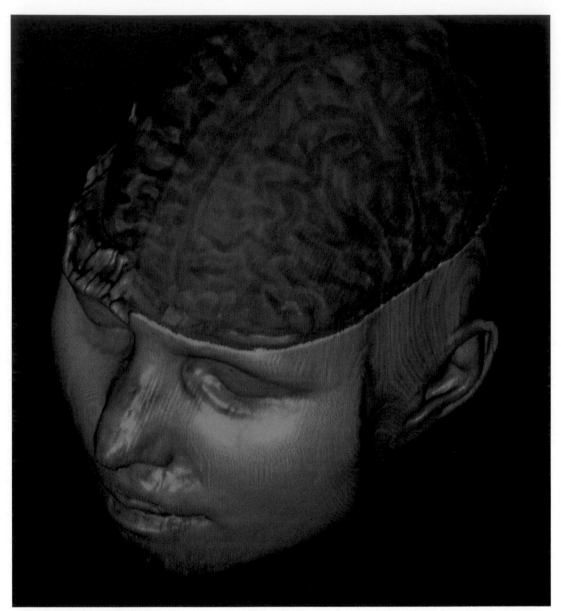

3-0. Volume rendering of a
voxel description. The voxels
show the density for each
quantum cube of volume.
Denser cubes are rendered
with more opacity, enabling
soft shapes to be visualized.
(Image created by Dr. Vin-
cent J. Argiro using Vox-
elView/ULTRA software from
Vital Images.)

PERIPHERAL DEVICES

When we design a building or create an image with a computer-based system, we communicate with the computer through peripherals. Blueprints or instructions are submitted through input peripherals and results (numbers, images, objects) are received from output peripherals. Peripherals include any device that is connected to the computer bus and that the CPU can read or write. Examples include keyboards and printers, the cathode ray tube (CRT) monitor and cameras, tablets, plotters, mice, mechanical equipment, and memories. Peripherals can also be virtual; that is, they may be simulated in software without physically existing.

TOPOLOGIES OF PERIPHERALS

Peripherals can be classified by resolution as well as by dimensionality, point/pixel, input/output, and hard copy/soft copy (fig. 3-1). **Resolution** is a common criterion for classifying input and output peripherals, because all peripherals operate at some spatial, luminance, and often temporal resolution. The luminance resolution is the number of gray levels or colors; the spatial resolution is the number of dots on a screen; the temporal resolution is the number of frames or points the system can display or record per second.

Dimensionality

One way of classifying a peripheral is by the number of dimensions it recognizes or moves. In this regard a peripheral may be zero, one, two, or three dimensional. Zero-dimensional peripherals are switches; they can either be on or off. One-dimensional peripherals let the user communicate with the computer using one-dimensional media, particularly written and spoken language. One-dimensional inputs/outputs include the microphone/speaker, the keyboard/printer and the shaft encoder/stepping motor. (These are all described in more detail below.) Two-dimensional peripherals let the user com-

municate with the computer using two-dimensional (graphic) media and involve the representation of areas. Two-dimensional inputs/outputs include the tablet/plotter and the television camera/monitor. Three-dimensional peripherals let the user communicate with the computer using three-dimensional media. Three-dimensional inputs include feelers, which sense volumetric objects; outputs include robot arms.

Linked to peripheral dimensionality is the **number of degrees of freedom** of a peripheral, that is, the number of ways it can move (fig. 3-2). The number of degrees of freedom is not necessarily equal to the spatial dimensions of the media the peripheral governs. For example, although a plotter makes two-dimensional images, it has three degrees of freedom: the horizontal and vertical movement of the pen, plus an added degree of freedom that moves the pen up and down. A multijointed robot arm may similarly have many degrees of freedom, even though it only moves in three-dimensional space.

A related concept is that of **constraints.** A constraint is a restriction on movement. For example, a human elbow cannot bend in every direction.

Point/Pixel and Line/Area

Lines (made with points) are simple visual elements that represent the basic features—geometry—of an image. Areas (made with pixels) represent other visual elements, such as color, shading, and texture. Lines traditionally have been created with drawing tools, including the pencil, ink pen, ruler, and compass. Continuous tone renderings are created using tools such as paintbrushes, airbrushes, and cameras.

The mechanical art distinction between line art and continuous tone is paralleled in computer graphics. Lines and shapes are drawn on the computer by connecting a sequence of real points with straight lines called *vectors.* Conversely, areas are defined using a discrete matrix of pixels, which often include intensity values.

0D

Input	Output
Button	Solenoid

1D

Input	Output
Microphone	Speaker
Keyboard; OCR	Printer
Magnetic tape	Magnetic tape
Shaft encoder	Stepping motor

2D

POINT

Input	Output
Mouse	HARD COPY
Trackball	Plotter
Joystick	Film recorders
Tablet	
Touch screen	SOFT COPY
Light pen	Refresh CRT
	Storage tube

PIXEL (2D Scanning)

Input	Output
HARD COPY	HARD COPY
Drum scanners	Laser printer
Flying spot scanner	Drum plotter
Flat bed CCD scanner	Ink jet plotter
CCD slide scanner	Dot matrix printer
	Thermal wax plotter
SOFT COPY	Thermal dye (D2T2)
Television camera	Electrostatic plotter
Video still camera	Film recorder
	SOFT COPY
	Video raster CRT

3D

POINT

Input	Output
Sonic digitizer	Laser sculpting tools
Radar; sonar	Robot arms
Laser measuring tools	Multiplex holograms
Photogrammetry	Stepping motor
Gimbled joints	
Data glove; body suit	

ZEL (3D Scanning)

Input	Output
Raster pantograph	Vibrating displays
Raster radar	NC machine tools

VOXEL

Input	Output
CAT, NMR scanners	Stereo lithography

Examples of vector devices include plotters and certain kinds of CRT displays. Pixel displays include dot matrix printers and raster CRT devices, such as a television monitor.

Vector graphics can be approximated on a pixel display, and vice versa, just as type can be screened or a photograph can be displayed as line copy. But interchanging these techniques usually does not produce the best results.

Input/Output (I/O)

Input encompasses the devices and processes for entering information into a computer, and *output* encompasses the

3-1. A classification of peripherals by dimensionality, continuous/discrete, input/output, and hard copy/soft copy.

3-2. A robot arm with six degrees of freedom, indicated by arrows.

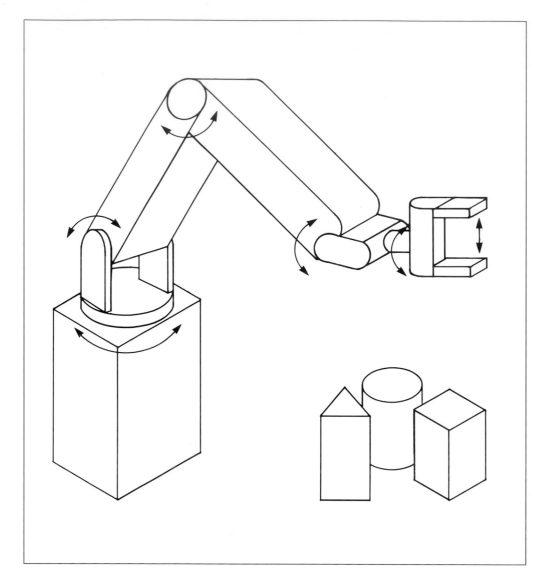

3-3. Input/output—user point of view. An artist uses a computer graphics work station, inputs information through a keyboard and mouse, and views the output of the program on a video monitor.

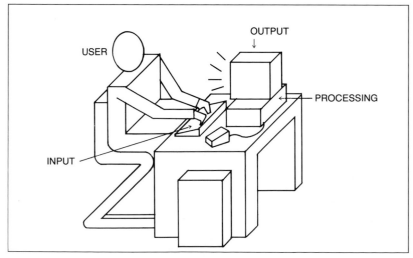

devices that convey the results of calculations to users (fig. 3-3). Input peripherals include the keyboard, microphone, and television camera. Output devices include the line printer, the speaker, and visual displays (fig. 3-4). Although it appears at first glance that some peripherals, for example a teletype, perform both input and output functions, a closer examination reveals two distinct processes; the keyboard on the teletype is the input mechanism and the striker is the output.

Hard Copy/Soft Copy

Output peripherals can also be distinguished by the images they display: **hard** *copy* peripherals produce tangible matter, such as film, prints, and phonograph records; **soft copy** peripherals produce intangible images, such as television monitor displays, which are visible only as long as the display stays on. In the most primitive sense, both hard and soft copy enable a user to *see* results, but only soft copy can be *interactive*—that is, modified more or less immediately. This ability to edit in real time creates what appears to be both an input and output medium (fig. 3-5).

Media produced by a computer often involves hard *and* soft copy. Film itself is hard copy but when projected, the image produced is soft copy. Conversely, film from a computer may be created by exposing it to a soft copy CRT display. Text may be input via a keyboard, displayed and edited on a soft copy CRT, and output using strikers, photographic exposures, or lead cast type (very hard copy).

Soft copy can be distributed faster and easier than hard copy, as soft copy decentralizes the production process by moving information in soft copy form physically closer to the audience. National news magazines and papers, for instance, may be composed, edited, and distributed on soft copy to regional (hard copy) printing centers. Editors, designers, and makeup people work interactively and remotely to construct and preview the paper; the strategy reduces delivery cost and extends the deadline.

ZERO DIMENSIONAL PERIPHERALS (SWITCHES)

The simplest peripherals are devices that have no scale and therefore no dimension, but have two states, on and off. Zero-dimensional devices are not inherently graphic but are used in graphic as well as in three-dimensional applications.

An example of a switch input peripheral is a **button** on a mouse used to, say, flip back and forth between a drawing and a textual mode. An example of an output device is a **solenoid**—a mechanical shaft

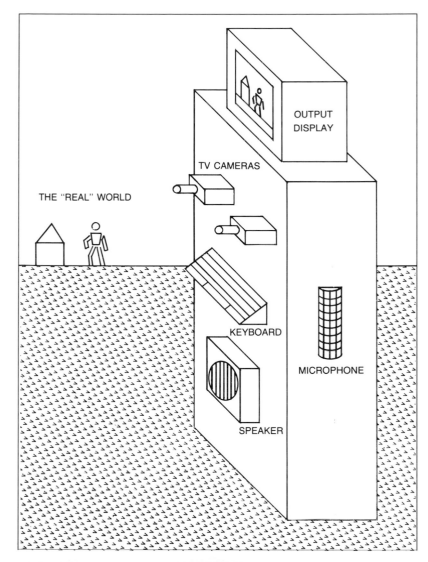

3-4. Input/output from the computer point of view. The input channels are the "senses" of the computer. Shown here are a keyboard, two digitizing cameras, and a microphone. The output includes a speaker and a visual display.

3-5. Visual creation can be interactive using soft copy displays. (Courtesy of Artronics, Inc.)

that is slid back and forth using electric pulses. Solenoids are used to move a pen up and down in a plotter (fig. 3-6). In robotics zero-dimensional devices include

3-6. Switch peripherals include a button on a mouse, used for input, and an electromagnet that pulls a striker to hit the bell for output.

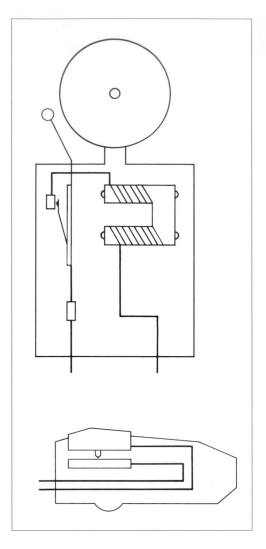

contact switches that enable a robot to "sense" a surface, and electromagnets, which allow it to adhere to and lift metals.

ONE-DIMENSIONAL PERIPHERALS (SPEECH AND TEXT)

Linear peripherals represent written and spoken language, one-dimensional sequential media. They also relate to controls and measurements that involve a single axis—a thermometer or a volume control, for example.

Examples of linear, one-dimensional, inputs include microphones, keyboards, optical character readers, paper and mag-

netic tape and cards, shaft encoders, and potentiometers, another name for knobs and slide scales. Examples of linear outputs include speakers, printers and character displays, paper and magnetic tape and cards, stepping motors and dials (fig. 3-7).

Alphanumeric Text Entry

Alphanumeric data, numbers and text, may be entered into the computer orally, with optical character recognition (OCR), and with keyboard entry. Spoken language systems are very primitive, but vocabulary capabilities are increasing.

Computer peripherals that digitize and synthesize speech employ a *microphone,* an ADC to convert the waveform to a serial string of samples, and a DAC and *speaker* for creating speech. Words and letters—written language—are input via the keyboard and output via a printer in any one of its multiple forms, such as a typewriter, teletype, or CRT display (fig. 3-8).

OCR technologies are well advanced and include readers for magnetic ink, bar codes, multiple-choice forms, standard printed text in a multitude of fonts, and longhand (fig. 3-9). OCR allows whole pages to be entered at once.

A *keyboard* is another efficient input device. The familiar alphanumeric layout is called a QWERTY keyboard after the keys on the top row (fig. 3-10). In addition to keys for letters and numbers, most keyboards include keys for formatting commands, including tabs, line feed, carriage return, and backspace. Another feature is the case key for creating upper- and lowercase letters. Case keys often attach different meanings to the set of punctuation keys.

Function keys are programmable and can represent a sequence of letters, numbers, or commands. These are used by word-processing programs, for example, to insert and delete letters.

Keyboards can be real or virtual and shaped for a specific purpose—music, ballet, and a variety of alphabets, for instance (fig. 3-11).

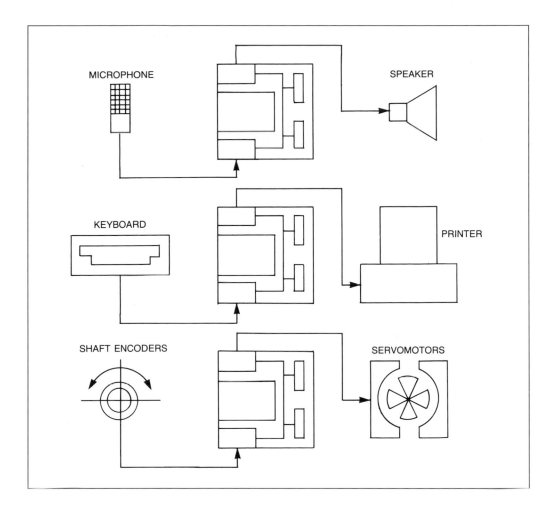

3-7. Input/output pairs of one-dimensional peripherals: microphone and speaker handle spoken words; keyboards and printers handle text. Mechanical connections include shaft encoders and servomotors.

Alphanumeric Text Output

Printers and *CRT* displays are designed to display text as hard and soft copy. Hard copy technologies include *impact strikers* with ink ribbons, such as those in typewriters, and *dot matrix character printers,* where a letter is represented as a small pixel array (fig. 3-12).

The dot matrix letters are usually slightly coarser and harder to read than striker-made letters, unless they are produced at high resolution. When dealing with visual presentations, choosing an output device is important for creating clear images.

Dot matrix fonts are reprogrammable; different fonts can be defined in software as bitmaps. Some character printers allow the dot matrix to be programmed with special-purpose characters or intensity values (fig. 3-13). Programmable dot matrix fonts are often character-oriented displays and have spaces between the individual letters and lines; these should not be confused with the more general-purpose dot matrix printer, which will be discussed in the graphics peripheral section. Halftones can also be approximated on impact printers using normal alphabetic characters, striking over them to create a range of intensities (fig. 3-14).

Shaft Encoders and Stepping Motors

Shaft encoders and stepping motors provide a way to sense and control a rotary shaft, such as a drill. A *shaft encoder* converts a rotary angle to a number and a *stepping motor* converts a number to a physical rotary angle. Shaft encoders are used in photographic systems to record the positions of a camera on a pan-and-tilt tripod head as it is operated by a cameraman (fig. 3-15). The data can then be output to a complementary camera head where the pan and tilt are

3-8. Digitized audio is stored (A) and played back as speech (B), or converted to text (C). It can also be modified or executed as a command (D) or converted back into speech (E).

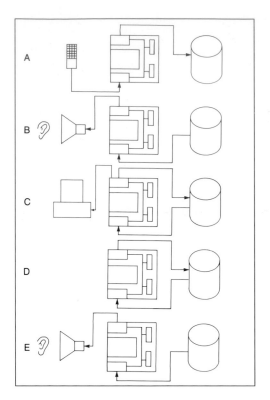

3-9. OCRs accept a variety of input. The most sophisticated systems scan text, recognizing individual letterforms and storing them as character codes.

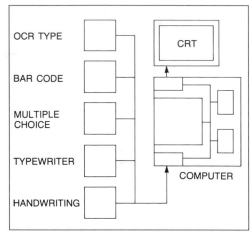

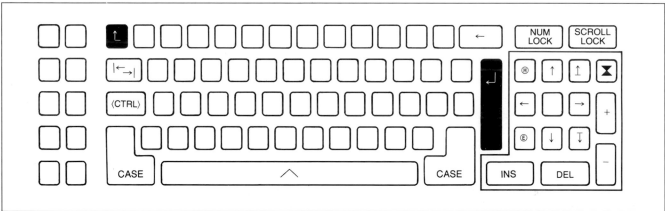

3-10. QWERTY keyboard.

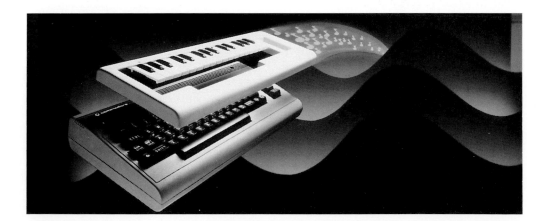

3-11. Music keyboard. (Courtesy of Sight and Sound Music Software, Inc.)

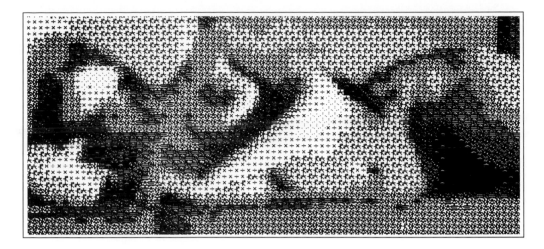

3-12. Striker type is continuous; dot matrix type is made of discrete pixels.

3-13. Dot matrix fonts can be loaded with graphic elements and intensity maps. Although the output images are still character oriented, they have the strong visual texture of computer-generated imagery. (Courtesy of Ken Knowlton.)

controlled by steppers. Thus a scene can first be shot by hand and the camera can then repeat the move independently; or the move could be programmed on the computer.

Stepping motors are widely used in photographic systems, not only for controlling cameras, but for controlling a repertoire of machinery designed to position artwork, models, and lights. Steppers can also control a *platen,* a table for holding and moving artwork (fig. 3-16). Motion-controlled cameras and platens are used together to photograph flat artwork and three-dimensional models as well as to perform multiple exposure and time-lapse photography, such as slit scan and streaking, described in chapter 8.

Potentiometers and Dials

A *potentiometer* is a continuously changing one-dimensional input peripheral. A potentiometer might consist of a knob or slider that is moved by hand and controls, say, the position of an object on a screen. Virtual, soft copy, sliders are controlled with a cursor or touch screen. Physical or virtual, they represent one-dimensional scalar input variables. Their output companions, *dials,* can be either physical meters, like a VU meter, or virtual

3-14. A striker graphic is composed of alphanumeric characters. Striker graphics were one of the first methods for creating images with computers. (Courtesy of Spatial Data Systems, Inc., a DBA Systems Company.)

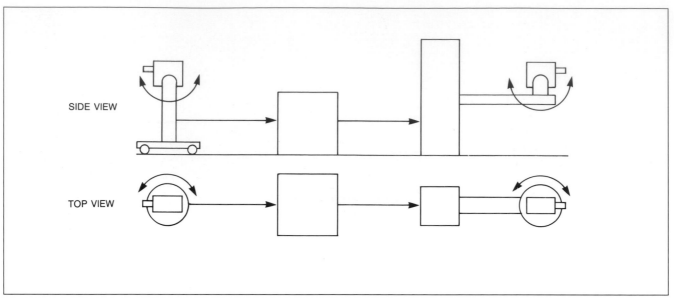

SIDE VIEW

TOP VIEW

3-15. This camera system records and replays the actions of a camera. On the left, a hand-controlled camera may be tilted or panned. Shaft encoders for the tilt and pan record the angular directions and transmit them to the CPU, where they are saved. The CPU then transmits the same positions to a camera that is mechani-cally controlled by stepping motors; this replays the scene. In practice, the moving camera and replay camera might be the same. Furthermore, additional degrees of freedom may be incorporated in the rig, such as the ability to raise and lower the camera and to move it forward and backward.

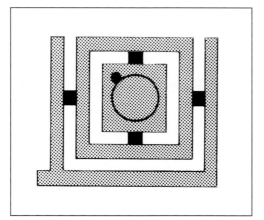

3-16. A three-axis rotating gimballed platen. The square in the middle contains the artwork or model that is manipulated by rotating the parts of the gimballed mount. The sequence of rotations can be changed only by modifying the hardware.

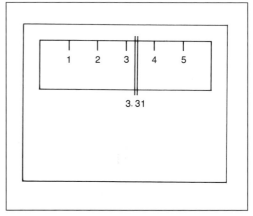

3-17. A combined virtual potentiometer and dial. The operator positions the selector line by moving the mouse that controls the cursor. The insert shows the exact monitored value; should line and monitor deviate, an alarm will sound.

dials, which are only displayed on the CRT (fig. 3-17).

TWO-DIMENSIONAL PERIPHERALS (GRAPHICS)

Two-dimensional input/output devices include devices that are point, or positionally, oriented and devices that are pixel oriented. Point devices locate inputs and outputs on a continuous plane; pixel devices represent each and every cell on a plane. Examples of point input devices include the mouse, trackball, joystick, tablet, touch screen, and light pen. Examples of point output devices include the plotter, the refresh vector CRT, and the storage tube.

Pixel input devices include the laser drum scanner and video camera. The laser drum film plotter, the ink jet and dot matrix plotter, electrostatic plotters, and video CRT raster displays are pixel output devices. In some sense, line printers used to display images (rather than text) fall into this category as well.

As we have suggested before, point devices can approximate pixel representations and pixel devices can approximate point representations. The two kinds of graphics are distinct, however—point graphics depict continuous real numbers whereas pixel graphics depict discrete integer numbers. The internal representation for the two kinds of data are different, but even point devices are eventually digitized at some resolution.

Point Input Peripherals

The *mouse* owes its name to its shape, a small rounded plastic box connected to the computer by a long cable (fig. 3-18). The mouse usually represents and controls the cursor on the screen. A rotating ball on the bottom of the mouse allows it to roll on a smooth surface. The X and Y rotation of the ball allows the computer to locate the mouse at all times. One or several buttons can be pressed on the mouse to execute or choose an operation from a

3-18. A mouse. (Courtesy of Apple Computer, Inc.)

screen menu, or to create and transform images in an interactive fashion. A *trackball* is basically an upside-down mouse with a sphere that is rotated by the palm of the hand.

Joysticks (fig. 3-19) are versatile, as they can be pivoted in two dimensions. Some

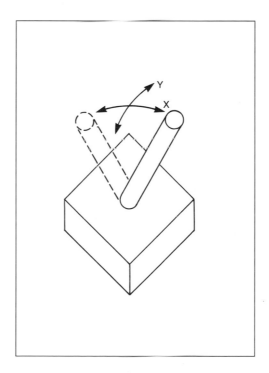

3-19. A joystick can be moved in at least two directions. A joystick with a button performs the same functions as a mouse.

3-20. A graphics tablet can be used to trace and digitize blueprints and drawings and comes with a pen or a crosshair digitizer. (Courtesy of Computervision Corp.)

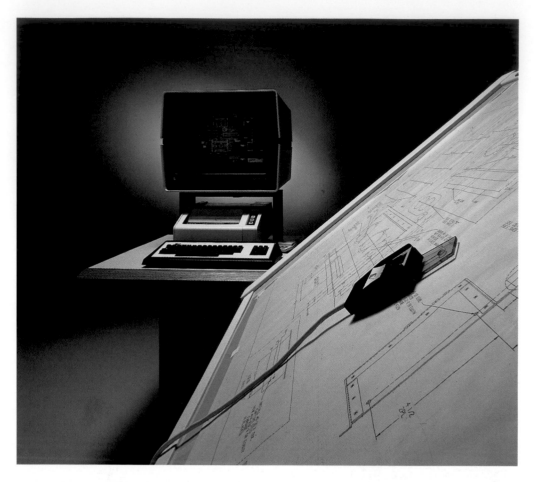

may also be twisted and may contain push-button switches for additional degrees of freedom. The widespread use of joysticks in aviation and in video games demonstrates how useful they are in interactive environments.

The ***graphics tablet,*** or ***digitizing tablet,*** is an electronic drawing pad. It contains a two-dimensional grid of sensors that record the location of an electronic stylus or pen, which is held like a regular drawing tool and moved over the tablet (fig. 3-20). The pen does not draw visible lines on the tablet; rather the grid senses the position of the pen and the computer generates a corresponding image on a screen. Usually the stylus contains a pushbutton microswitch that closes by pushing down on the pen; some styli can sense pressure as well.

The ***touch sensitive screen*** is similar to

a graphics tablet in that it is a positional sensor. It is different, because the touching device does not need to be connected to the computer; a user's finger works well.

Touch screens are fabricated on the surfaces of CRTs and can be programmed to respond in synchronicity with the image displayed (fig. 3-21). Touch screens close the loop of interactive soft copy, because they provide the facility to manipulate the image by touching it.

The pressure-oriented touch sensitive screen consists of a transparent screen overlay that contains a grid of microswitches. The switches, activated by touch, are captured by the CPU. Another way of detecting touch is with an acoustically sensitive screen that uses two long microphones mounted along two of its sides and two long speakers mounted on sides opposite the microphones. An object can be located when it interrupts the flow of sound between a speaker and a microphone.

The ***light pen,*** similar to a touch screen in that it interacts with a CRT screen directly, provides a way to draw and view the results immediately (fig. 3-22). A light pen may also be used to point at the screen and interactively select operations from a menu. The light pen does not emit light but senses and times the light coming from the screen to determine what object is being drawn at that instant.

Point Output Peripherals

Plotters produce hard copy by drawing continuous lines with pens onto paper or another drawing material (fig. 3-23). Flatbed plotters move pens in both directions across a fixed sheet of paper. Drum plotters produce drawings on media fixed to a rotating cylinder. The pen moves along one axis of the drawing, while the cylinder rotates

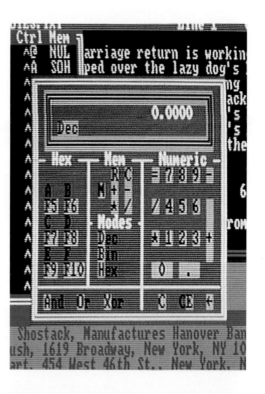

3-21. An interactive virtual calculator can be operated as if it were built out of matter and sitting on a desk. Each button is touch sensitive and changes color when selected. The selected value appears on the numerical readout.

3-22. A light pen is similar to a touch-sensitive screen in that it allows the user to interact with the image directly. (Courtesy of Koala Technologies Corp.)

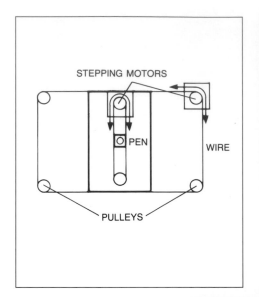

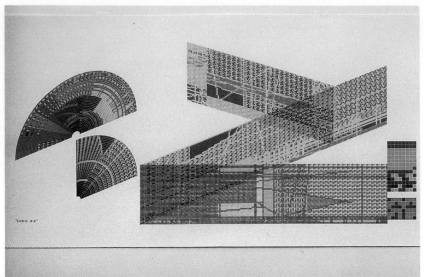

3-23. Flatbed pen plotter and diagram. The position of the pen is controlled by two stepping motors, one that moves in the X and the other in the Y direction. A solonoid moves the pen up and down. (Color plot courtesy of Mark Wilson. © 1983 by Mark Wilson.)

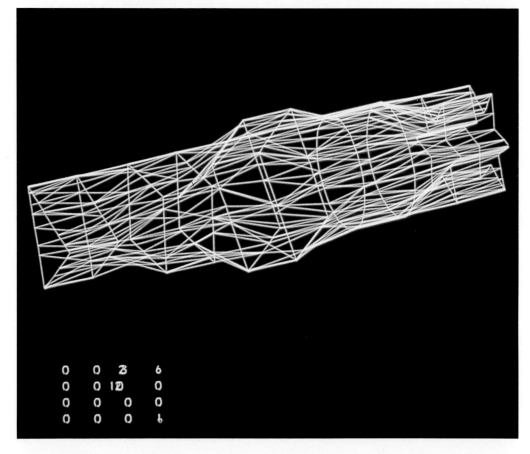

3-24. Image created with a refresh vector CRT. (Provided by Isaac V. Kerlow.)

along the other axis. Some plotters actually draw circles and arcs, but most approximate curves with straight lines.

A plotter can also be equipped with a light instead of a pen and be operated in a black room to expose lines onto photographic film. Colored lines can be drawn by adding filters.

Refresh vector CRT displays draw lines between points on the screen by deflecting

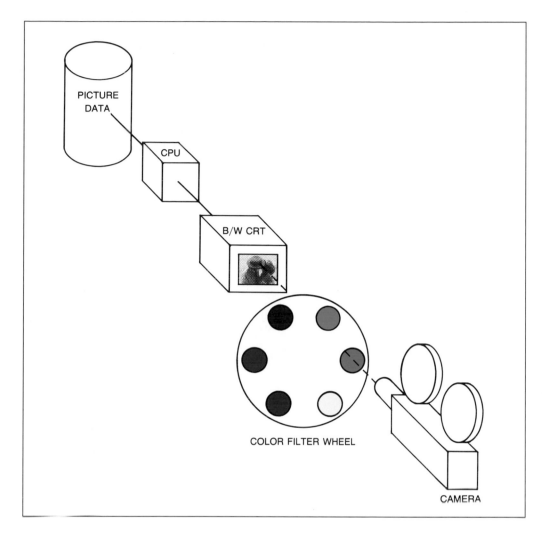

3-25. The illustration depicts the logical and physical conversion of digital data to film. The process begins with pictures stored on a disk, read by a CPU, and output to the computer output microfilm (COM) unit. The COM unit converts the digital data into analog form and displays it on a high-resolution black-and-white CRT. Light rays pass through a color filter wheel and are focused by a lens onto the film plane in the camera.

an electron beam. The beam can be repositioned while it is turned off or it can draw a line when it is moved to another point while turned on. It is similar to a plotter with a light, except that the light or beam is moved electronically (fig. 3-24).

Refresh vector CRTs allow images to be interactively changed. Because the light emitted by the phosphors on the face of the tube decays right after it is hit by the beam, the entire picture must be **refreshed,** or redrawn, many times per second. The image can be redrawn in the same place, or repositioned and redrawn, giving the appearance of a moving image (see fig. 2-7).

Vector displays can only draw with lines and should not be confused with television raster displays, described in more detail later in the chapter. Vector displays are usually monochromatic, but some have colored lines. They also can be commanded to draw in a pseudoraster style by simulating solid areas with a series of parallel lines.

The *direct view storage tube* is a CRT that can display vectors without refreshing them. The technology is cheap but not interactive. The image is stored as a distribution of charges on the inside surface of the screen, written once, and is changed by flashing the screen and drawing a new image.

A **film recorder,** also called a computer output microfilm (COM), utilizes a camera to photograph an image displayed on a CRT. A film recorder usually includes a high-precision monochromatic CRT, color filters mounted in a wheel, and a camera (fig. 3-25). The camera is shutterless and

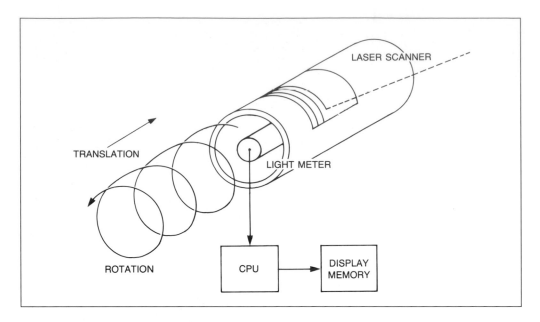

3-26. A color transparency is fastened to a drum scanner—a spinning clearglass rotating drum. A laser attached to a lead screw is slowly translated along the cylinder while the drum is spinning, so the distance transversed during each revolution is one scan line. A light meter in the center of the drum measures the amount of transmitted light. These values are digitized and stored in magnetic memory as an X, Y matrix corresponding to the original image.

housed in a lightproof box. Exposures take from a few seconds to a few minutes, depending on the number of vectors to be drawn. Color is achieved by shooting the image in three passes, for red, green, and blue.

Pixel Input Peripherals

There are a number of technologies for scanning images into the computer so they may be stored as pixels. Scanners may capture color or black-and-white; they may scan reflective or transparent artwork; and they may be low or high resolution.

In a **rotary drum scanner** either transparent or reflective art is attached to the drum. A laser beam translates slowly down the drum while it spins, and a light meter either inside the drum (for transparent art) or just above the drum (for reflective art) captures the data as rows of pixels (fig. 3-26). Laser scanners have resolution upwards of 2000 pixels per inch, and are employed in many high-end electronic publishing applications for image capture.

Flat bed scanners digitize reflective artwork with resolutions upward of 300 DPI and are popular for desktop work (fig. 3-27). This resolution is barely good enough to scan black-and-white pictures for use in electronic publishing, but adequate for

video or desktop media production. Desktop **slide scanners** also utilize a long linear CCD array and move either the array or the slide. These scanners have resolutions as high as 3,000 pixels per inch and are widely used for digitizing color slides.

Video scanners use a color television camera and a video digitizer and can input both single video frames as well as sequences. Video scanners are fast, but limited to the resolution of video, about 640×480 pixels (fig. 3-28). The quality of these images is not good enough for high-quality print production, but may be adequate for newspapers, video production, and multimedia presentations that are displayed on a computer.

Video still cameras record images as pixels directly on a floppy disk. The images are then transmitted via a modem back to the newsroom. The entire scanning process is eliminated because there is never any film in the first place.

Pixel Output Peripherals

Pixel output devices employ a wide range of technologies. As with pixel input devices, they can output black-and-white or color, film or reflective art, and come in a range of resolutions. Whether their output is to be reproduced by printing or

3-27. Desktop flatbed scanner uses a linear CCD array that captures an entire row of pixels at once. It passes underneath the face-down artwork and captures red, green, and blue in three passes. (HP ScanJet IIC scanner courtesy of Hewlett Packard Company.)

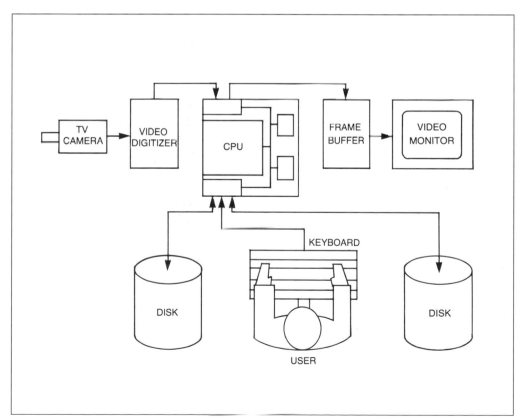

3-28. The interface between computer graphics and video is bidirectional (input/output). The drawing shows an integrated system with a user controlling the computer via a keyboard at its center. The computer contains a television camera and video digitizer to capture images and a frame buffer and a video monitor to output the images. Images can either be stored on a disk for later display or can be immediately output.

3-29. The color separations used to make the plates that printed this image were produced by a laser plotter and calculated directly by the computer. This is quantitatively different from recording the computer-generated image onto photographic film (for instance, 35 mm slides) and then color separating it. (Courtesy of Judson Rosebush and Collier Graphic Co.)

simply distributed directly is another factor also. We have come a long way since we simulated pixel graphics on **alphanumeric printers** (fig. 3-13, 3-14).

Output of pixel printers is expressed in terms of **dots per inch (DPI),** which is the number of distinct pixels for each linear inch of output, be it on paper or a screen. This term should not be confused with the number of halftone dots per inch in a printed picture; these are two different kinds of dots (fig. 6-18)! To keep things separate we will use the term **lines per inch (LPI)** to refer to the number of halftone dots per inch. The printer creates halftone dots (typically in the 53 to 150 LPI range) by composing them out of the higher resolution pixel dot substrate (typically in the 300 to 2,400 DPI range). The total number of intensity levels possible equals $(DPI/LPI)^2$. In other words, the number of intensity levels equals the diameter of each halftone dot measured in pixels times itself (since there are two dimensions). A 300 DPI printer can write 53 LPI with 32 shades of gray, not quite newspaper quality, whereas a 2,400-DPI printer can write 150 LPI halftones with 256 levels, which is the quality of professional color printing.

The most common pixel output peripheral is the **laser printer,** popular on desktops and with black-and-white resolutions upward of 300 DPI (fig. 2-23), and color resolutions upward of 400 DPI. This technology is a variation on xerography: a laser beam scans a rotating drum and deposits an electrostatic charge according to the gray values of the image. Dry toner adheres to the drum where there is a charge; it is then transferred to plain blank paper and fixed with heat. Laser printers can output graphics, variable-sized fonts, and halftones, although not necessarily good ones. Professional typesetting and newspaper-quality halftones require an output upward of 1,200 DPI; these higher-resolution printers can output onto photosensitive paper or film.

Rotary drum plotters are used the same way as drum scanners; in fact, many drum

scanners will also output. Instead of mounting a transparency on the drum, photographic film is mounted and exposed with the laser beam. Output may be in excess of 2,000 DPI on high-contrast black-and-white film as large as 40×60 inches. Color output is produced by making color separations with halftone dots and then printing with process color (fig. 3-29).

The **ink jet plotter** produces color hard copy by spraying three thin streams of ink onto paper, one for each of the subtractive primaries: cyan, yellow, and magenta. On rotary drum units the ink jets move slowly along a track from one end of the drum to the other while the drum spins (fig. 3-30). Resolutions range from low—200 DPI—to very high, and paper size can be large.

Black-and-white or color **dot matrix printers** generate text and images with a grid of dots (fig. 3-31). The dot matrix is formed by striking an inked ribbon against paper; it is much like a typewriter, but instead of individual strikers it uses a small rectangular head with a grid of pins (fig. 3-12). Dot matrix printers simulate halftone printing screens by increasing or decreasing the number of dots in the matrix cell. These printers are inexpensive, low resolution, and slow.

Thermal dye transfer (also known as Dye Diffusion Thermal Transfer D2T2)

3-30. Color ink-jet printer output made on a spinning drum can accommodate large sizes of paper. The design of the machine is similar to the drum scanner/plotter shown in fig. 3-26, except that three ink jets spray ink while the drum spins. (*Manuscript 42* courtesy of John S. Banks, Rising Star Graphics.)

3-31. Color dot matrix printers use striker technology and provide a low-resolution hard copy that many artists like for its texture. (Courtesy of Lauretta Jones.)

3-32. Thermal dye transfer printers currently provide the best direct color output with quality increasingly compared to photographs. (Courtesy of Patty Kulruedee Wongpakdee, Pratt Institute.)

printers also use a color ribbon and can produce full color output almost as good as a photograph, even though their resolutions are upward of 300 DPI (fig. 3-32). They are much more expensive than thermal wax printers. They provide excellent proofs and increas-

ingly function as an alternative to short runs of color photographs.

Thermal wax printers use heat to transfer pigment from a multicolored ribbon to a special, very smooth paper (fig. 3-33). Color requires three passes, and resolutions are upward from 300 DPI. Thermal wax printers are priced to be used on the desktop, and are suitable for proofs and for routine color handouts.

Electrostatic plotters create an image by first depositing a negative electrostatic charge on the paper with a row of very fine electrical contacts, then sending positively charged toner onto the paper so that the particles of toner adhere to the paper where the charges were deposited (fig. 3-34).

Film recorders draw pixels at resolutions in the 500 to 2,000 DPI range onto color film ranging in size from 35 mm to

8 × 10 inches (fig. 3-25). Medium-resolution units are the backbone of computer slide services (for example, figs. 9-29, 9-30, 9-31, 9-35) and cinema output (for example, figs. 7-63 through 7-67).

The **video raster display** couples a video display (possibly a television monitor) with a frame buffer, which stores the contents of all the pixels in video random access memory, or VRAM (see fig. 2-6). VRAM is typically located on a video card (fig. 3-35) and is the basis of almost all computer displays. Unlike a vector CRT, the electron beam of a raster display does not follow a random path to output an image, rather it scans out the image linewise top to bottom. Note that there are many different types of video displays in use in computer graphics, many of them incompatible with each other.

Photographic hard copy of video monitors made by shooting directly from the screen can yield excellent results if care is taken (see fig. 7-20, for example). The camera must be mounted on a solid tripod and be perfectly aligned (horizontally and vertically) to the screen. All the lights in the room should be turned off to avoid light reflection on the screen. The controls of the monitor should be adjusted to optimize the image quality. Take a careful light reading and shoot a roll of film bracketing the exposures to discover the best results empirically. The test shots should include a **step wedge**—at least eight levels of gray color—to assist in evaluation. It is obvious that a good lens and film will produce the best results; a low ASA film offers a very fine grain and good color balance. Exposure times should be under ⅛ of a second to avoid the flicker that comes when the screen is refreshed every ¹⁄₆₀ of a second. Finally, the camera should be activated with a timer to avoid vibrations.

A variety of technologies exist and many are being developed that produce *flat-panel* solid state raster or pixel displays. Existing technologies include liquid

3-33. Thermographic hard copy requires special paper, but produces rich full color. (Courtesy of Seiko Instruments, Graphics Devices and Systems Division.)

3-34. Electrostatic plotters work much like a Xerox copier and come in color and black-and-white models. (Courtesy of Versatec, a Xerox Company, Santa Clara, CA.)

crystals, light emitting diodes, and plasma panels. Respectable black-and-white displays exist, and color units are now being integrated into laptop computers. Like CRTs, solid state displays interface to the computer via a frame buffer. Solid state touch sensitivity displays of arbitrary size and resolution are advantageous, because they are thin and are therefore easily positioned.

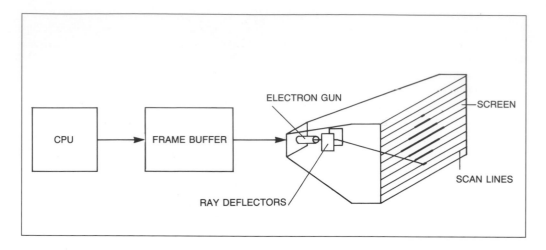

THREE-DIMENSIONAL PERIPHERALS (SPATIAL)

Three-dimensional input and output concerns designers of packages and products and requires a thorough understanding of two-dimensional graphics as well, since three-dimensional objects are often digitized as two or more flat graphics.

Positional three-dimensional I/O is very similar to two-dimensional I/O. In two dimensions a point marks a location in an area, and in three dimensions a point marks a location on a solid, or in space. Positional three-dimensional I/O is used to enter shapes of objects when their boundaries can best be described with corners, or with points that can be used to define edges, surfaces, and solids in space. Examples of positional input devices include three-dimensional stylus digitizers, radars, and shaft encoder systems. Positional output devices include machine tools, intersecting laser beams, and robot arms.

Discrete three-dimensional I/O has several variants, including zel and voxel representations. Examples of discrete zel input devices include the raster pantograph and sideways looking radars. Zel outputs include machine tools that can reproduce the shape of the original in a new material. The CAT scan peripheral is one example of a voxel input device. The closest thing to a voxel output is a specialized replicator

not quite up to Star Trek standards.

Hard copy three-dimensional output is used in product manufacturing, even though the design is usually manipulated on two-dimensional soft copy. Virtual three-dimensional outputs include two-view photographs and holograms, an emerging three-dimensional soft copy. Displays that have color, are touch sensitive, and are tactile will have revolutionary consequences.

Three-dimensional Point Input Peripherals

Three-dimensional digitizers sense points in space or on solid objects and capture a set of XYZ numerical coordinates. These digitizers locate surface points and corners on existing physical models, using a digitizing pen that is sensitive in three dimensions (fig. 3-36). Several technologies are used, including magnetic transducers and sonic sensing.

A *radar* is a three-dimensional point-positioning peripheral that uses electromagnetic waves that travel through the air, hit an object, and return; *sonar* works similarly with acoustics. Both peripherals produce waves that hit the object and bounce back to one or more antennae. Simple triangulation methods, trigonometric calculations, when applied to the radar signals, determine the XYZ location of the object (fig. 3-37).

Point radars are used to locate large objects in large spaces, such as all aircraft or satellites in a sector of space. Radars coupled with interactive soft copy displays are the oldest computer graphics peripherals. Closely allied to radar are *laser measuring* tools, which are widely used in surveying and geological analyses. These tools work by measuring the time it takes light to travel between a transmitter and receiver.

A wide variety of *photogrammetric* techniques exist that analyze two or more images and reconstruct three-dimensional data of objects depicted. These techniques can produce point or zel data depending on the methods used and are discussed in more detail in chapters 6 and 7.

Sensors with *gimbaled joints* (shaft encoders) are also used to determine the location of points in space by measuring the angularity of the articulation. Shaft encoders can be used to determine the positions of equipment and to record human motion, such as the positions of a dancer's joints (fig. 3-38).

Three-dimensional Point Output Peripherals

Three-dimensional *laser sculpting tools* consist of two lasers mounted at right angles to each other, each with two degrees of freedom; one moves on X and Y, the other on Y and Z (fig. 3-39). The space contains three-dimensional photoresist, a volume of light-sensitive material similar, except for the number of dimensions, to photographic paper. Neither laser alone has sufficient energy to expose the resist, but the two beams, when they meet, provide enough light. The exposed resist is then photographically processed, and the result is a three-dimensional transparent solid medium with darkened three-dimensional points.

Laser sculpting tools can also be used in

3-37. A radar can locate objects in three-dimensional space and represent them on a flat display.

3-36. Three-dimensional point and normal digitizing. Some three-dimensional digitizers are able to digitize the spatial XYZ coordinates of the point as well as the direction the stylus is pointing, or its normal. The measurement has six degrees of freedom: three degrees of spatial freedom and three degrees of freedom to show direction. (Courtesy of Polhemus Navigational Sciences Division, McDonnel Douglas Electronics Company.)

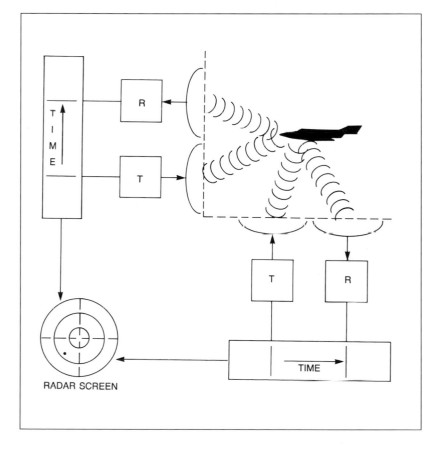

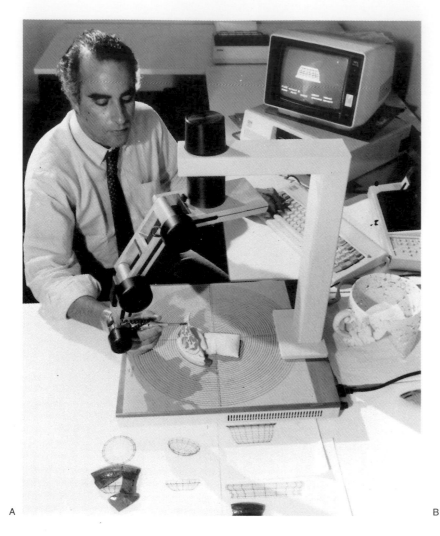

A

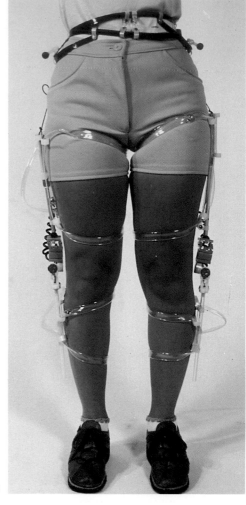

B

3-38. Both these three-dimensional digitizers use shaft encoders. In A, the encoders allow the point on the end of the arm to be accurately tracked. In B, a model is wearing a flexible body brace with angular shaft encoders that measure the amount of rotation in each joint. (Courtesy of Micro Control Systems Inc. [A], and R. Hannah and T.W. Calvert, Medical Engineering Resources Unit, Hospital, Vancouver BC Canada [B]).

the raster mode and produce continuous-tone three-dimensional photoresist displays. The results are three-dimensional blocks of lucite with the density information represented as intensity.

Complementary to volumetric sensors are **robot arms,** volumetric positioners or devices that can mark a position in three-dimensional space. Gimbaled tables are used along with robotlike arms that reach out and position a tool (fig. 3-40). A machine tool is often positioned at a point to complete a specific task, such as drilling or boring into metal. Many of these applications are discussed in chapter 10.

Holography is a medium that can record virtual images in three dimensions; holographic techniques can be used for point or voxel data. One technique employs **multiplex holograms,** which use a sequence of computer-generated perspective views to make a virtual, monochromatic, three-dimensional image (fig. 3-41).

Zel Input Peripherals

A **raster pantograph** measures the depth of an object as a series of sections, parallel contours that describe the

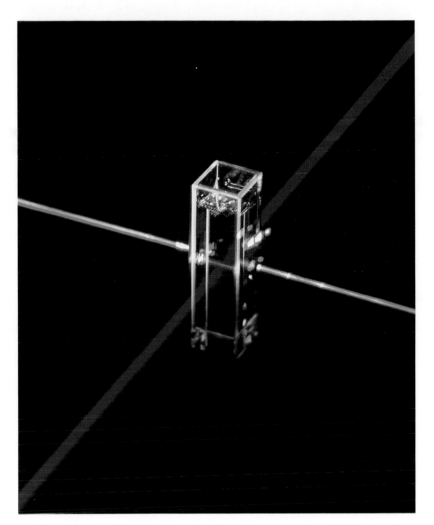

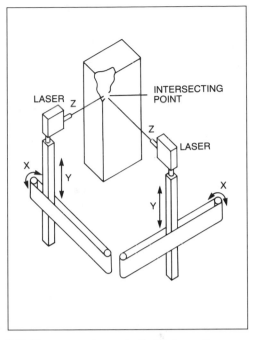

3-39. Two computer-controlled intersecting laser beams can be used to sculpt three-dimensional photoresists. The energy levels must be adjusted so the laser can expose the material only at the intersection points. The laser guns can be translated in two dimensions, so any position in the three-dimensional model can be exposed. (Courtesy of Robert E. Schwerzel/ Batelle Columbus Laboratories.)

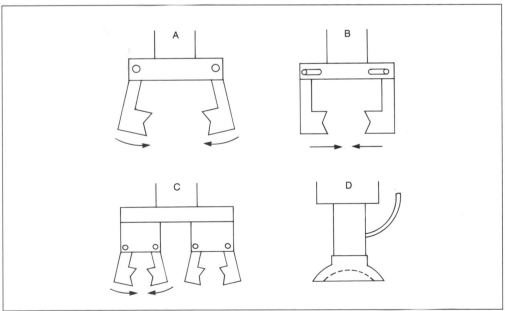

3-40. Computer-controlled mechanical devices include robot arms and even entire assembly lines. Shown here are different types of grippers, each used for a different application: A is a pivoting claw; in B the sides slide horizontally; C contains a double gripper; and D operates with suction.

3-43. Objects with overhangs present problems in pantograph digitizing.

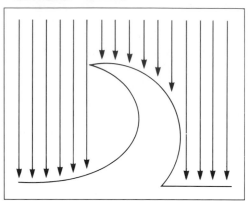

3-41. Direct simulation of holograms using computer graphics is in the experimental stage, but the *multiplex hologram,* made using a sequence of images, is a useful method for displaying synthetic three-dimensional environments. (Courtesy of Holo/CAD.)

3-42. A raster pantograph is a volumetric extension of the raster television digitizer and measures material goods as a series of sections of zels.

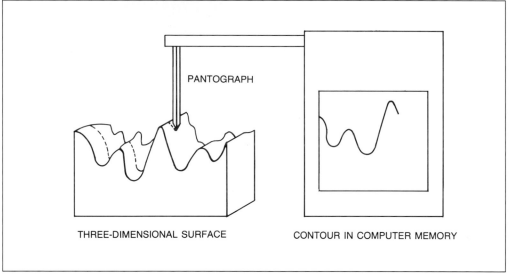

PANTOGRAPH

THREE-DIMENSIONAL SURFACE

CONTOUR IN COMPUTER MEMORY

3-44. A sideways-looking radar is essentially an electronic raster pantograph. Again depth, not luminance, is measured.

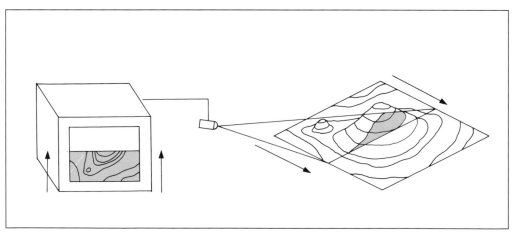

perimeter of the object at equal intervals (fig. 3-42). Mechanical pantographs sense the object with contact feelers; light systems use profile outlines. The output of a pantograph is a matrix of zels. Pantographs, like zels, can digitize with orthogonal or polar coordinates. They measure objects as a series of sections. This process is subject to many of the problems that arise when images are rasterized, such as aliasing. Another problem is that most raster pantographs cannot detect overhangs (fig. 3-43).

Raster radars and ***ultrasound*** scan a focused beam across a volume of space and store the amount of time it takes for each electrical pixel to go out and bounce back, essentially producing a bitmap of zels, or distances, as a result. Raster radars are well suited for digitizing terrain (fig. 3-44); ultrasound effectively digitizes human tissue.

Zel Output Peripherals

Zel output represents the contours of an image. ***Vibrating mirror*** displays that incorporate depth physically modulate the plane of an image in correspondence with the depth of a point (fig. 3-45). Conceptually such displays may be point or raster displays, and the user does not require glasses to see three-dimensional images.

Point as well as zel descriptions can be used to control a machine tool, such as a milling machine, by a process known as

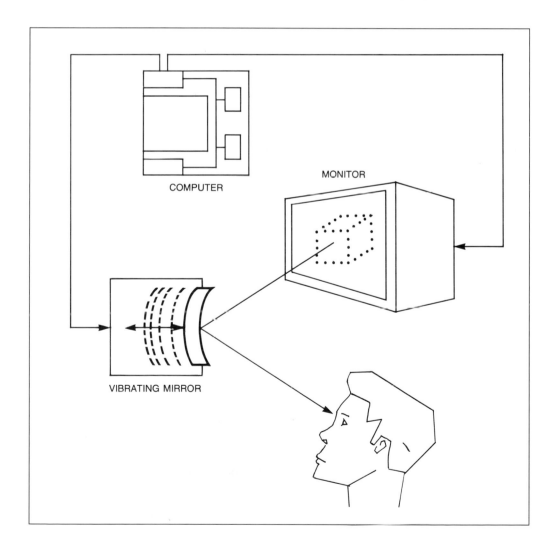

COMPUTER

MONITOR

VIBRATING MIRROR

3-45. A volumetric display is synchronized with an oscillating mirror that vibrates in and out at a fixed frequency. Points, lines, and areas are all quantized and stored as zels. The zels are sorted by depth and then displayed at the exact time the mirror is at the corresponding depth.

3-46. A numerically controlled tool may actually mount its own work, select a grinding or machine tool, and perform an operation. (Courtesy of Kearney & Trecker Corp.)

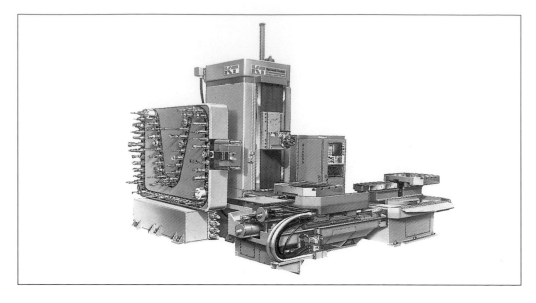

numerical control (NC). NC tools are widely used in the metal machining and toolmaking industries for prototypes as well as for mass production. NC tools include lathes, milling machines, and special cutting and assembly units (fig. 3-46). Indeed, the entire factory is a computer peripheral.

The **depth-cutting milling machine,** the output complement of the raster pantograph, is essentially an X, Y, and Z plotter with a grinding tool instead of a pen, repro-

3-47. The depth-cutting milling machine positions a special grinding machine tool at an X, Y coordinate and cuts down to a certain depth. The depth cut is analogous to the value stored in the zel. It is the complement of the raster pantograph and the three-dimensional version of a television monitor.

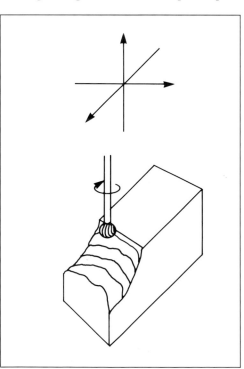

ducing the surface of the object in matter (fig. 3-47). Milling machines also exist that cut around a polar axis and correspond to data bases of polar coordinate zels.

Voxel Input Peripherals

Computer-aided tomography (CAT scan) peripherals use X rays to measure the density of three-dimensional volumes. The X rays are fired from different angles, and the views are computationally integrated to produce a three-dimensional matrix of voxels, each of which stores the densities with a small cubic volume of the interior material. These data do not represent luminance or distance, but the density of matter! If the density is mapped to transparency the entire matrix may be viewed as if you were looking through it (fig. 3-0). If the values of a single slice through this matrix are mapped with gray scales or color, then the image resembles a photographic cross section of the object (see figs. 1-31 and 6-1).

Other technologies use tomography to detect radiation from several angles, including measuring radiation emitted by radioactive isotopes that are ingested by the body, or by using magnets to identify the composition of the component matter.

Voxel Output Peripherals

Voxels provide us with a model to describe, record, and transmit descriptions of complex three-dimensional matter, but peripherals that convert voxel descriptions into physical output are in their infancy. One new technology is **stereo lithography** (fig. 3-48), which works by constructing a three-dimensional object as a series of layers. The layers are "written" or, more correctly, deposited, one voxel at a time, starting at the bottom of the object and working up to the top. The technique makes it possible to output any complex physical object, even an object with hollow spaces inside it. The only requirement is that the resultant object is crafted out of a single plastic material, making it extremely useful for prototypes.

In the future it is possible that voxel output peripherals may be able to exactly reproduce an original object, including its original materials. The good news is that we have a strategy for teleportation, but the bad news is that high-resolution volumetric input and output lie far beyond our capabilities, especially for living matter, which requires atomic scales and very fast scan and reconstruction times. It is interesting to note that nature handles this copying problem not with a voxel solution but with a procedural description, in particular, the DNA amino acid code used to assemble proteins. Learning how to program organisms that grow lies on the near horizon.

Clothing and Multiaxial Peripherals

Finally, let us address three-dimensional peripherals you wear like clothing—getting dressed in our computers, as some people would say. In terms of our previous context, **digital clothing** is simply a collection of **multiaxial point peripherals** that return not just a single point, but typically a single point plus a direction normal and a series of distances and angles relative to the reference point.

The multiaxial peripheral often augments a basic three-dimensional **point and normal digitizer** (fig. 3-36) with a system able to measure the angles of linkages. The three-space point and normal digitizer

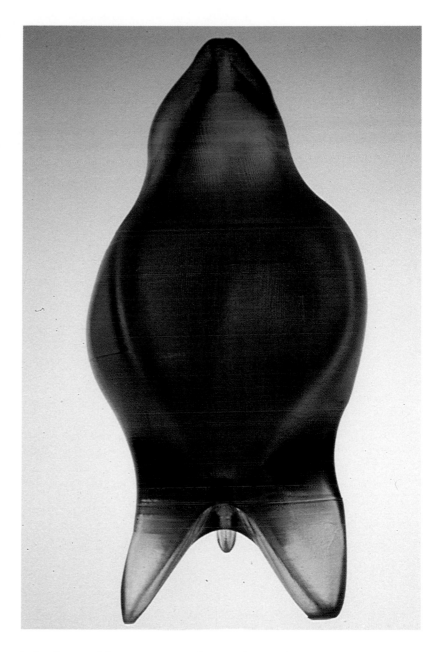

is fundamental because it provides a **point origin** for a part of the body (like the head or the hand), as well as a **direction**—a viewing line, like the direction of one's gaze, or the direction a finger is pointing. In numerical terms, a direction is a normal (see chapter 1), and is described by three numbers that are analogous to a rotation in X, Y, and Z.

In addition to a point and normal digitizer, digital clothing approximates the structure of the body, in particular its rotating joint structure, and employs technology to

3-48. Stereo lithography was used to create *Forbidden Fruits*, a three-dimensional sculpture, by artist Masaki Fujihata. (Courtesy of Masaki Fujihata. Software support: DESIGN BASE by Ricoh Co., Ltd. Stereo Litography: Solid Creator by D-MEC, Inc.)

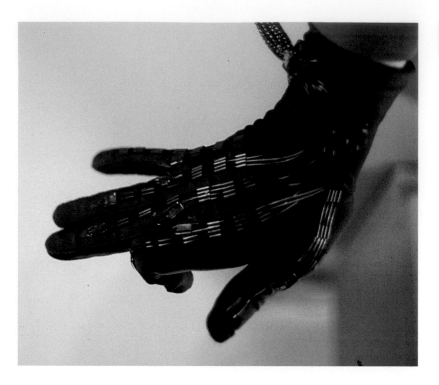

3-49. The data glove is an interface you can wear. (DataGlove™ courtesy of VPL Research, Inc., © 1992.)

measure joint angles. This body tracking can progress from a finger to the whole body. A **data glove** tracks the position and normal of the hand and the joint angles for the fingers (fig. 3-49). A face mask tracks the positions of the jaws, lips, and eyelids—the key communication elements in acting and in animation. And a full **body suit** tracks the position of the head, torso, and the angles of the arms and legs (fig. 3-50).

The data glove enables users to reach into a three-dimensional world and move things around with their hands, instead of with numbers. It enables **gestural communication,** be it pointing, talking in sign language, or conducting an orchestra. The face mask and full body suit provide a way for real actors to control a **waldo,** a computer-generated face or character that is controlled by the digitized actions of a real actor. In a virtual reality mode the properly dressed full body enters a virtual world. The virtual reality is perceived by wearing **eyephones,** full-color binocular displays with stereo sound, in which the computer-mediated environment is updated continuously in real time in reaction to the participant's movements.

FORCE PERIPHERALS

Force Input and Output

Force is the exertion of energy to overcome a resistance or inertia, and it is the most recent way of communicating with a computer. Strictly speaking, force is not graphics. It is neither the X, Y, nor Z dimension, nor is it the time dimension. It is a totally different variable, and it is a variable in how we make art. Drawing is about position, of course, but it is also about force—how hard you push the pencil or pen. And digitizing the forces involved in drawing tools is a new development in graphic peripherals.

Force input peripherals sense and digitize forces. The **pressure-sensitive pen** measures the downward pressure; software translates this into the width of a line, for example. A **squeezeball** is a joystick that also measures squeezing pressure. Again the software can be programmed for a variety of actions to occur.

Force input in three-dimensional space is less familiar to the computer graphics artist. Classically it has been more familiar to the aircraft or spacecraft engineer, where navigation in three-dimensional space often involves an inertial guidance system that measures forces. These inputs include strain gauges, load cells, gyroscopes, velocity sensors, and accelerometers.

Force output peripherals, also called **force feedback peripherals,** communicate forces back to a user. These proactive devices do not simply make images or make sound, they can actually move us around physically. For this reason they can be dangerous. A **force feedback joystick** is a bidirectional communication device that not only senses X and Y direction, but can push back as well. Force output helps when you are controlling a vehicle; for example, a force feedback joystick in an airplane simulator requires the pilot *pull* on the stick and *feel* the resistance of the airplane. Another application enables users to push objects around, but some objects can be heavier than others, or immobile, and some can push back. Still another appli-

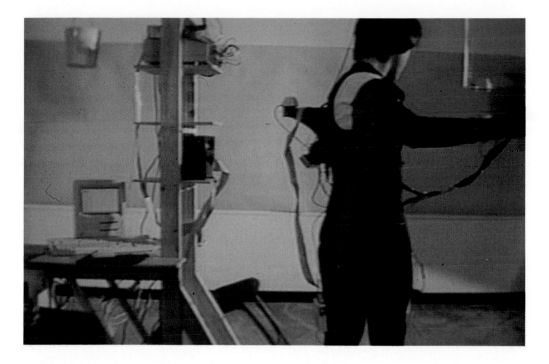

3-50. Body suit together with a pair of data gloves and eyephones. The body suit and gloves track the skeletal position of the participant. The eyephones provide the visual and aural feedback of what he or she sees and hears. (DataSuit™ courtesy of VPL Research, Inc., © 1992.)

cation lets users feel objects in a three-dimensional virtual environment.

Force Feedback Clothing

The ultimate goal in the minds of many researchers is to couple multiaxial clothing peripherals with force feedback. Done safely, this provides the graphics artist, for example, with an interaction paradigm that rivals the real world. Imagine sculpting with virtual clay yet feeling the resistance of the material as you pull it. Imagine rubbing charcoal and feeling the tactile resistance of paper. Or, for the athletic architect, building Chartres and being able to hoist all the stones. These ideas have captured the interest of many researchers. Force feedback gloves exist in the laboratory that enable a user to feel a virtual ball when they squeeze it (fig. 3-51). Tiny motors add resistance at the key pivot points. And many researchers are trying to couple force feedback with visual feedback to heighten the media experience.

When extended to the full body the potential of these peripherals far transcends graphics. But do remember that before the computer, all of the arts involved force in some form or another

to create an image or an object. Since its inception, computer graphics has relied extensively on either textual description and numbers (for instance, computer languages) or graphical descriptions (for instance, via a mouse) to create and manipulate pictures. Computer graphics has been positionally oriented and survived without the integration of force. But now that is changing and force will be increasingly integrated as a creative variable.

3-51. This experimental force feedback glove enables a user to grasp virtual objects and feel them. (Force feedback glove designed and built by Prof. Griore Burdea and graduate students at Rutgers University. Tested in 1991 at the *Virtual Worlds Project* at the IBM T. J. Watson Research Laboratory.)

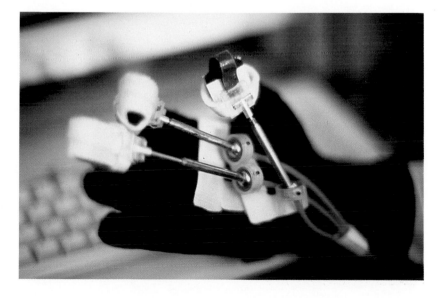

4-0. Graphical user interfaces can take many forms, as with *Tiny Dancer in My Hand* by Myron Krueger, who has pioneered the idea of the image of one's self interacting in real time with a drawing, an image of an object, or the image of another person. (Courtesy of Myron W. Krueger, Artificial Reality Corp.)

INTERFACING
WITH
THE SYSTEM

INTERACTION SOFTWARE
ANATOMY OF THE GUI
INTERACTION HANDLIN
VIRTUAL APPLICATIONS
PROPERTIES OF DIALOGUE
PRODUCING AND DIRECTING
INTERFACE DESIGN CONSIDERATIONS

The *interface* between the user and the computer system—that part of the system that the user tactiletly and semantically controls—is the focus of this chapter. In an automobile the interface devices include the steering wheel, gas pedal, and brake; in a computer graphics system these include keyboards, tablets, and buttons, as well as virtual representations on a screen.

INTERACTION SOFTWARE

4-1. The virtual desktop is represented on the face of a computer screen as a series of windows, buttons, button palettes, sliders, and menus.

The **computer-user interface** is the collection of channels through which the user interacts with the machine. The computer-user interface may exist in many different modalities: by text, by speech, by gesture, or by touch and movement. The interface

has a physical component, it may have a graphical representation, and it also has a conceptual, semantic component.

In an automobile, for example, the physical interface includes the steering wheel, gas pedal, and brake; in a computer graphics system, physical interfaces include light pens, mice, touch screens, graphic tablets, as well as screens and printers, for viewing the image—these physical peripherals were the subject of the last chapter. Here we focus on the **graphical user interface (GUI),** in which the user interacts with the computer via a mouse and a virtual desktop. The graphical user interface is not the only metaphor for communicating with a computer, but it is a powerful one, especially for projects and tasks that employ graphics, and for projects and tasks that can be represented graphically. We will look in detail

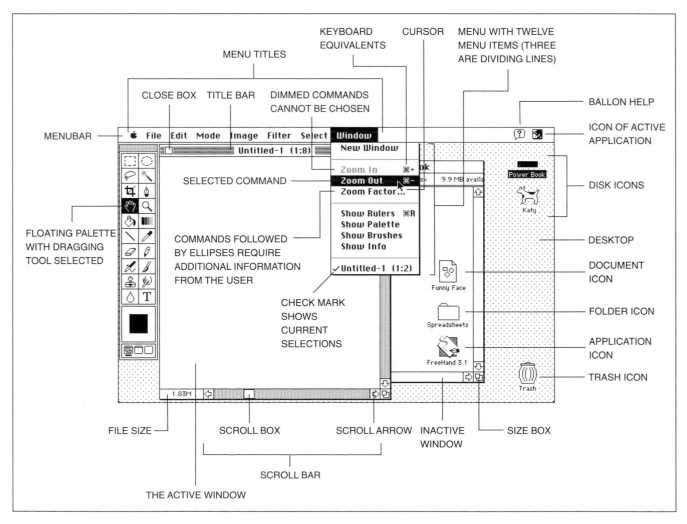

at the anatomy of the graphical user interface not only in terms of its *graphical presentation* (cursors, icons, windows, menus, and so on), but also in terms of its *behavior.*

The behavior of a graphical user interface depends upon a conceptual, logical set of **interaction procedures** that evaluate input and calculate output. To a very large extent, these interaction procedures, often called **handlers,** work irrespective of whether the ialogue between the worker and the machine is textual, vocal, graphical, or gestural. Superior interface designs are usually device-independent, application-independent, and increasingly, computer-independent.

ANATOMY OF THE GUI

GUIs come in all sizes, shapes and colors. Our mission here is to understand some common elements. The highest level of the GUI (pronounced goo-ey) is called the **desktop,** a virtual representation of the computer system and its functionality, typically represented on the screen (fig. 4-1). Let's examine some of the components of the desktop:

The desktop is operated via a **cursor,** a symbol on the screen used for pointing, selecting, drawing, and display that is responsive to the movements of a mouse or other positioning device. In a graphical sense a **cursor** is simply a small bitmap, but because the cursor can take on many different shapes, it is used to communicate to the user (fig. 4-2). The shape of

the cursor often implies information about what is happening in the machine, the "tactility" of the region it is atop of, and what actions it may perform.

At the top of the screen there is usually a **menubar,** a horizontal strip with text and icons that presents the user with one or more pulldown menus. A **pulldown menu** is a list of options or prompts, either implemented as a list of word choices, or as a collection of graphical controls that are displayed on the desktop. A menu selection is activated by positioning a cursor over it and clicking or releasing the mouse button. The menu is then popped off the desktop and disappears, and the system executes the procedure selected, for example, a color change or the filling in of a polygon (fig. 4-3).

Action is also initiated by buttons and sliders. **Buttons** are places on the desktop where a mouse click activates an action of some kind. Buttons are often represented with icons that represent peripherals, programs, and files. When a button is selected, it may highlight or change color. Buttons are elements in larger functionalities; for example, the selection of choices on the pulldown menus are buttons, but buttons are often freestanding on the desktop or within an application window. A group of buttons may be aggregated together into a **button palette** (fig. 4-4), or organized as a table of choices. Two or more buttons may also be programmed to interact; for example, **radio buttons** work like the pushbuttons on a car radio where

4-2. The shape of the cursor communicates information to the user. For example, a vertical I-beam line may indicate textural input, a crosshair may indicate that a user can click and drag a rectangular area, an arrow pointer may indicate that a window can be dragged around, and a hand may indicate that buttons can be selected.

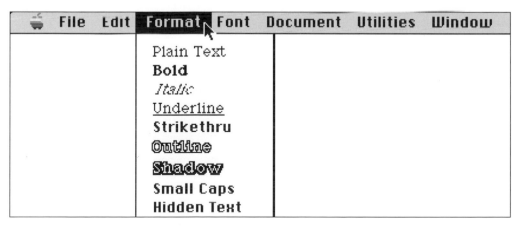

4-3. A pulldown menu is often activated by clicking on the menubar and holding the mouse down. In this example, several different type styles are presented to the user.

4-4. A button palette may include its own dragbar and close box, and be moved around on the screen like a window. This example is a Media Controller, from ADDmotion. The left side is a video player, while the right side contains buttons for placing backgrounds and actors.

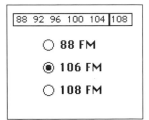

4-5. Radio buttons likely take their name from the pushbuttons on a radio tuner—the radio can only tune in one station at a time. Clicking a new button deactivates the button that was active prior to the click and activates the button clicked.

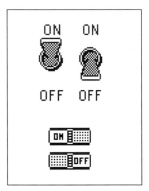

4-6. Toggles found in graphic systems allow an artist to set a behavior pattern, for example, "on" or "off," "outline" or "solid," and so on. (Adapted from *101 Scripts and Buttons* and *Stack Starter*.)

you push click to a station. The action of the radio button deactivates the previously depressed button; only one button can be selected at a time (fig. 4-5). A **toggle** is a button that lets a user choose between two modes, for example, "on" and "off" (fig. 4-6). **Sliders** are used to control range, like volume on an audio system or line width in a graphics system. Like their physical counterparts, they may be implemented either as dials or linear sliders (fig. 4-7), and allow an artist to control graphic variables. Sliders may be *range-bounded* (have minimum and maximum values), or they may be *differential* and adjusted relative to a particular setting.

On the desktop, information is displayed in **windows,** a rectangle of space with its own **titlebar** and **active area.** The window frequently comes equipped with a **cropping control,** which allows the shape of the window to be changed, and with **scrolling controls,** which control the vertical and/or horizontal movement of data inside the window (see also fig. 4-1). Scrolling may also be accomplished using arrow keys on the keyboard.

INTERACTION HANDLING

The Cursor

When you look below the surface of an interface, be it a GUI, a textual interface, or a stereoscopic three-dimensional virtual reality, there are similarities that are useful to know because they provide a way to understand, evaluate, and design systems (should one ever want to build one). In order to look below the surface of the interface, to understand how it behaves, one must shift one's point of view to looking at the screen from the inside out.

Consider the cursor, for example. Graphically it is a small shape that moves around on the screen, but operationally this very basic software unit is more complex. For one thing, the control over the cursor is bidirectional: either the artist moves it under his or her control or the computer application controls and positions it. In general, the cursor is not available while the system is calculating something.

Because its operational characteristics may be determined by the application, the cursor is a very flexible tool. It can be

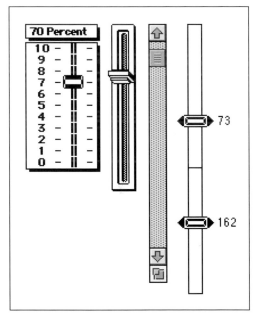

4-7. Sliders can take many forms. A vertical slider is coupled with a digital readout (left), made to look three dimensional (middle left), or used to scroll a Macintosh window (middle right). The right slider contains three controls—the outer two constrain the range of values and the middle control actually sets the value. At the bottom the two outer sliders adjust the range through which the inner slider can move. (Adapted from *101 Scripts and Buttons* and *Stack Starter*.)

used to pick from menus as well as activate graphical processes (fig. 4-8). It can even be used to draw with (fig. 4-9). In text processing the cursor is positioned in the text and clicked, marking an insertion point to indicate the position of the new text (fig. 4-10).

Like the mouse (fig. 3-18), the cursor has two degrees of freedom in location (X and Y) and one degree of freedom in the button click. But the interpretation of cursor movement can be quite sophisticated; for example, GUIs can respond to graphical gestures (fig. 4-11). Another example is making the speeds of virtual events (like scrolling a large window) accelerate or decelerate according to the speed of the movements of the mouse.

There are three important states for cursor input. The first of these is **cursor within,** which means that the position of the cursor is tracked. From a user point of view this is also called **pointing,** and involves moving the cursor around

☞ **RELATED READING**

Cakir, A. D., D. J. Hart, and T. F. M. Stewart. *Visual Display Terminal.* New York: John Wiley & Sons, 1980.

Martin, J. *Design of Man-Computer Dialogues.* Englewood Cliffs, NJ: Prentice-Hall, 1973.

Norman, Donald A. *The Psychology of Everyday Things.* New York: Basic Books, 1988.

Woodson, W. E. *Human Factors Design Handbook.* New York: McGraw-Hill, 1981.

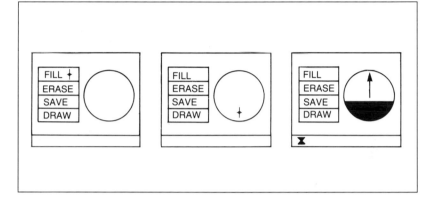

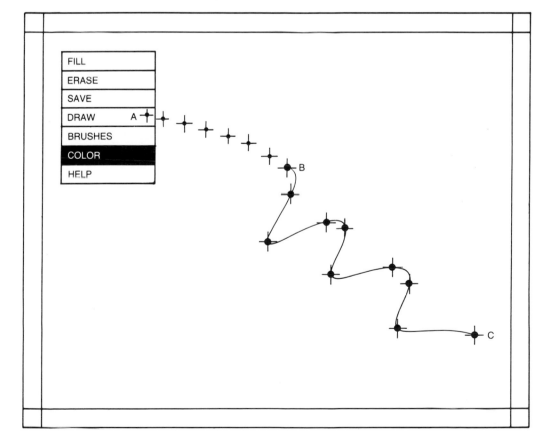

4-8. Cursors are used for input and output operations. First, the mouse is clicked down and up to select the menu function FILL. The cursor is moved within the area of the circle and clicked again. The computer responds by filling in the circle and making it opaque. During this time the cursor appears as a wait symbol, which indicates that the computer is processing.

4-9. The cursor is used to click on a function from the menu (A). It is then moved into the drawing area, the mouse is pushed down (B) and moved while in down position, to draw a line. Releasing the mouse at (C) produces a "cursor up" and terminates the drawing process.

4-10. The insertion point (indicated by the square box) is advanced letter by letter as the user inputs text (A). When a query is entered into the system (B), the wait symbol appears as the computer finds the right answer (C).

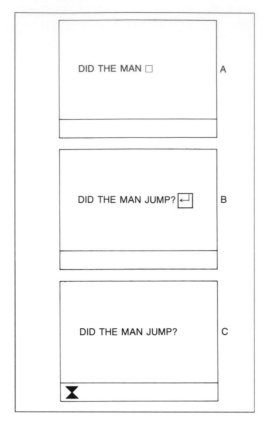

4-11. Gestural commands are implemented using software that recognizes specific movements of the cursor and activates a procedure. For example, a quick rightward stroke might remove the last menu while a left stroke redisplays it, a circular movement might be interpreted as a request for help, and a quick vertical stroke might end the application.

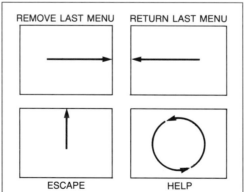

without clicking. Normally the tracking is passive and only involves moving the cursor position on the screen, but it may also involve changing cursors or other actions, like displaying a menu. The **cursor down** handler processes actions when the mouse button is depressed (but not yet released). Cursor down must be followed by a **cursor up,** which occurs when the mouse button is released. Note that other graphics peripherals, like the pen on the

tablet, also have a cursor down and cursor up position. A **click** is defined as a cursor down immediately followed by a cursor up (also fig. 4-8). Note that a click has two explicit directions, and that actions can occur on either or both directions. This cursor down–cursor up combination is a very powerful one, and it is often used in combination: a cursor down, **drag** to a new position, and cursor up make a **selection,** such as highlighting text, framing a graphical area, or drawing (fig. 4-9).

Another propriety of the interface that is translated into graphical behavior is a signal that indicates if the computer is waiting for input or computing. These modes may also be communicated via the cursor. For example, when the machine is awaiting input, or in **ready** state, the insertion point may flash; when the system is computing, the **wait** symbol, a different cursor, is displayed (fig. 4-12). In superior systems, the wait symbol is usually animated or blinks at a different speed, indicating that the computer is still processing as opposed to being frozen or having "crashed." Wait symbols may also be implemented as a separate indicator at the edge of the display.

Many applications provide a way for the user to interrupt the computer processing. This is called **break** and comes in two levels: a **soft break** interrupts a particular task that an application is performing (for example, cancellation of output, terminating a scan, stopping a file copy). A **hard break** interrupts the program and returns the user to the operating system and desktop. Break frequently behaves inconsistently in different applications. Some applications support soft breaks and allow you to restore execution, whereas others don't. Some applications inhibit hard break because it terminates applications without saving work.

Cursors with Text

Text cursors descend from typewriters, teletypes, and linotypes and incorporate some of this heritage into their behavior. The **space** key on the keyboard advances the cursor one charac-

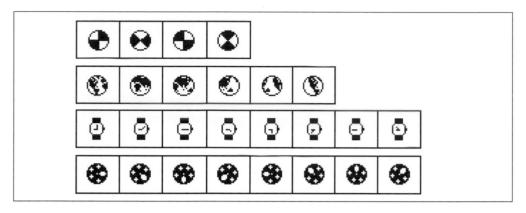

4-12. In most systems a special wait cursor is displayed while the system is processing. An animated wait cursor lets the user know that processing is still in progress and the system has not crashed. The figure depicts four different animating wait cursors: a four-position beach ball, a six-position world, a watch with eight-positions, and an eight-position spinner. When the spinner animates, the big dot appears to rotate clockwise while the little dots appear to rotate counterclockwise. The only user entry the system will accept while in wait mode is a break, which interrupts processing and returns control to the user.

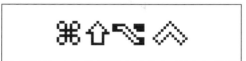

4-13. Symbols for four case keys on an Apple Macintosh. Left to right: command, shift, option, and control case.

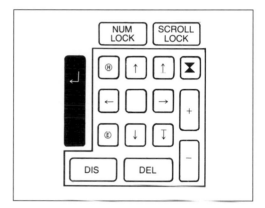

4-14. The four arrow keys move the cursor left, right, up, and down. The enter key picks the position and sends it into the program as input. Holding a cursor key down longer can make the cursor move faster in the direction of the arrow.

ter; **backspace** often deletes text; in fact, it is sometimes called a delete key. The functionality of the **tab** key may vary according to the application; for example, within a word processor it may indent, within a data-base program it may jump to a new field. **Case** keys on a computer keyboard are richer than on a typewriter, and it is common now to find keyboards equipped with four cases (fig 4-13). This allows a wide range of characters to be formed, including not only letters and numbers, but also special symbols and foreign characters with accents. **Arrow keys** may permit the cursor to be directed left, right, up, or down, in lieu of moving the mouse (fig. 4-14).

Do not confuse the **enter** or **return** key with the carriage return (from which it evolved). Early time-sharing computers were line-entry–oriented: a command line was typed on the keyboard and "entered" with a return. The return performed a line feed, returned the carriage to the

left, and performed the "enter," that is, activated the computational process (fig. 4-15). In fact, a carriage return and a line feed are actually text-formatting characters, whereas an "enter" or [RETURN] submits input to the CPU.

A Transaction Dialogue

A **dialogue** is an interaction, constrained by rules, between a user and a machine. It is made up of a prompt, a response, a validation, and a result, very likely preceded by process, and returned as

GREETINGS, ARE YOU DR. CHANDLER?

ANSWER YES OR NO PLEASE: NO ☐

4-15. Enter is not the same thing as line feed/carriage return. In this example, a user's response to a prompt has been typed in but not entered. The cursor remains at the end of the line for the next character input. Will it be a space, another letter, or an enter? Until the enter key is pressed, the computer cannot respond. The entry can therefore be edited before it is submitted.

4-16. A dialogue interaction at an ATM (automated teller machine) contains numbered prompts and responses. Line one validates a response ("Horace Williams") and formats it into the next question, which validates the password. Question three requires one of two table selections for a response, and question four validates the response against the balance and the limit of cash in the machine. After dispensing cash, the machine displays data from memory (line five) and reprompts. The transaction is terminated with BYE, and the system prompts for and awaits next user.

Prompt	Response
1 YOUR NAME PLEASE?	HORACE WILLIAMS
2 HELLO MR. WILLIAMS, YOUR PASSWORD?	NMS924
3 DO YOU WANT CASH, DEPOSIT, OR BYE?	CASH
4 HOW MUCH?	$50.00
5 DONE. YOUR BALANCE IS $768.00	
6 DO YOU WANT CASH, DEPOSIT, OR BYE?	BYE
7 YOUR NAME?	

text or a picture. A **prompt** is a textual or iconographic message issued by the CPU that requires some response from the operator or artist, also known as the user entry (fig. 4-16). The user's response may involve clicking or text entry. The **validation** (fig. 4-17) indicates whether this response is a valid word, a meaningful number, or in the right position. The computer program validates the user's input by comparing it to predefined tables of valid choices, or checking numerical boundaries (fig. 4-18). If this response is valid, the computer saves the data or executes a procedure associated with the response and returns a result (the answer).

If the response is invalid, or meaningless, the system issues an **error message,** advising the user of the mistake, assisting if possible, and reprompting for a response.

A prompt should also have an **escape,** or a way to sidestep the question without answering it, by returning to the procedure (prompt) that invoked the prompt in question. Escape is sometimes activated by a special key, or special symbols entered into the response, such as a space followed by a carriage return. Note that escape and break are two different functions: escape stays within the confines of the program (going up one menu), whereas break interrupts the machine's processing.

VIRTUAL APPLICATIONS

Handles and Widgets

All the elementary components of a GUI may be aggregated into applications. In many cases a virtual two-dimensional representation of the application, and how it performs, is implemented on the desktop. For example, a pocket calculator, a telephone touch-tone pad, a control panel, or a keyboard may be represented on a CRT and used interactively (fig. 4-19).

Virtual applications may simulate graphic design processes such as painting and drawing, page makeup, textile design, and pattern layout. Music notation, circuit designs, and even abstract flow diagrams also lend themselves to virtual representation. In all of these cases, the real-world process may be manipulated experimentally, yet with "handles" that resemble how we interact with the real world (fig. 4-20). The subtlety of this interface is very important, and our culture is in the midst of discovery about how to design and attach control to virtual applications. These interface handlers are sometimes called **widgets** because they provide a generalized flexibility to do a specific task (fig. 4-21).

Even our most familiar companion, the

Properties of Individual Prompts	Prompt #3	Prompt #4

Input Datatype
    Binary Toggle
    Numerical
    Text
	Text	Numerical

Text of Prompt	`DO YOU WANT`
	`CASH, DEPOSIT,`
	`OR BYE?`
		`HOW MUCH?`

Validation Table or Range
    if Boolean, 0 or 1
    if Numerical, Either a Table of Permitted Numbers or a Minimum and Maximum Value
    if Text, a Table of Proper Choices
	`TEXT:`
	`    CASH`
	`    DEPOSIT`
	`    BYE`
		`NUMERICAL:`
		`    0 ≤ BALANCE`
		`    AND 0 ≤ CASH`
		`    IN MONEY`
		`    MACHINE`

Procedure Table
    List of Procedures to Execute
      upon Proper Responses
	`GOTO PROMPT #4`
	`GOTO PROMPT #4`
	`GOTO PROMPT #7`
		`ACTIVATE MONEY`
		`MACHINE AND`
		`OUTPUT MONEY`
		`GOTO PROMPT #5`

Escape Procedure to Return to if User Exits	`GOTO PROMPT #1`	`GOTO PROMPT #3`
Default Value Predefined Selection	`BYE`	`0`

Error Message	`INVALID`
	`RESPONSE TRY`
	`AGAIN`
		`TOO MUCH MONEY`
		`REQUESTED`

book, has undergone a virtual transformation. Word processing, font management, typesetting, and page definition are functions that permeate graphical applications. A **page,** also called a card, is one of a series of two-dimensional areas, much like the pages of a book, or the frames of film or video. Like a paper book, a computer page can mix together text and pictures, but it can also incorporate buttons, as well as things that change, like animation, video, or interactive windows (fig. 4-22).

A complicated graphics system should behave in a logical manner—in other words, users who make requests should find themselves presented with choices. For example, in a painting program (fig. 4-23), clicking on the "COLOR PALETTE" button displays a color-mixing window. From a system point of view the hierarchy of overlaid menus corresponds to the structure of the procedures in the system (fig. 4-24).

Virtual keyboards can simulate the familiar QWERTY keyboard and work by using a mouse to click the keys, but these prove to be slower for most people than typing. Another interface strategy is to display a

4-17. Properties of a prompt. The second and third columns correspond to and illustrate prompts three and four of fig. 4-16.

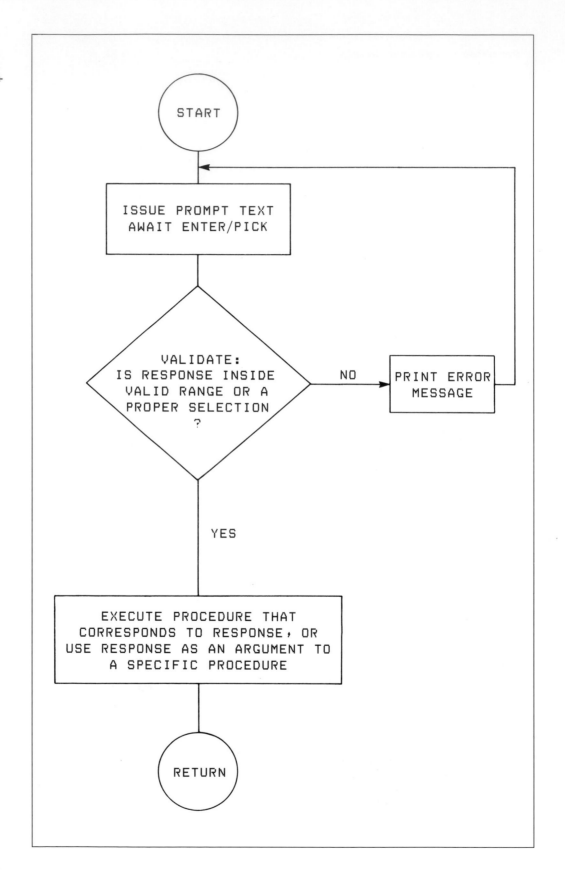

4-18. This flowchart illustrates the main steps that take place in the dialogue between designer and computer.

START

ISSUE PROMPT TEXT
AWAIT ENTER/PICK

VALIDATE:
IS RESPONSE INSIDE
VALID RANGE OR A
PROPER SELECTION
?

NO → PRINT ERROR MESSAGE

YES

EXECUTE PROCEDURE THAT
CORRESPONDS TO RESPONSE, OR
USE RESPONSE AS AN ARGUMENT TO
A SPECIFIC PROCEDURE

RETURN

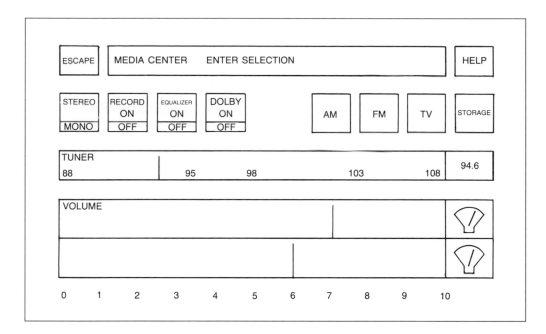

| ESCAPE | MEDIA CENTER   ENTER SELECTION | | HELP |

STEREO	RECORD	EQUALIZER	DOLBY		AM	FM	TV	STORAGE
MONO	ON	ON	ON
	OFF	OFF	OFF

TUNER

88   95   98   103   108   94.6

VOLUME

0   1   2   3   4   5   6   7   8   9   10

4-19. This virtual media center is built out of the elementary parts (buttons, toggles, and sliders) and it behaves like a real one. Radio buttons select one of four sources (AM, FM, TV, or from library storage). Several toggles define global variables (stereo/mono, record on/off, equalizer on/off, Dolby on/off). Sliders adjust the tuning scale and volume controls, which also contain readouts (the channel tuner displays the channel frequency, and the VU meters show the sound volume).

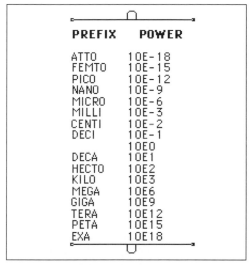

PREFIX	POWER
ATTO	10E-18
FEMTO	10E-15
PICO	10E-12
NANO	10E-9
MICRO	10E-6
MILLI	10E-3
CENTI	10E-2
DECI	10E-1
	10E0
DECA	10E1
HECTO	10E2
KILO	10E3
MEGA	10E6
GIGA	10E9
TERA	10E12
PETA	10E15
EXA	10E18

4-20. Handles on a column of text are indicated by the horizontal line and shield at the top and bottom of the text. Manipulation of the handles allows the text to be positioned, and the height and width of the column to be adjusted. (Drawing adapted from *Pagemaker*.)

4-22. A Page Navigation Panel is displayed with a five-page document. The current position of the user is on the third page. BEGINNING goes to the first page; END to the last. BACKWARD goes back one page; and FORWARD advances one page.

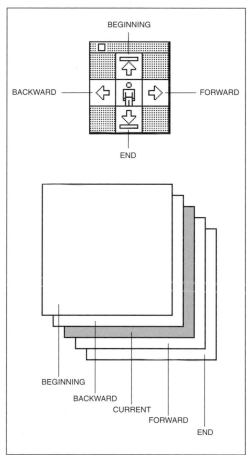

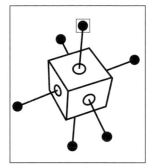

4-21. A three-dimensional widget can rotate a cube on any of its three axes uses only a two-dimensional interface device (a mouse). The image of a three-dimensional cube is displayed on the screen along with three handles, which are essentially levers connected to each axis. When the handle is dragged by the mouse the software calculates the rotation and redisplays the cube. The handle with the rectangle around it is currently selected.

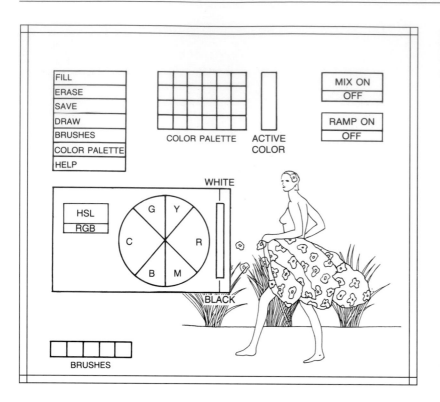

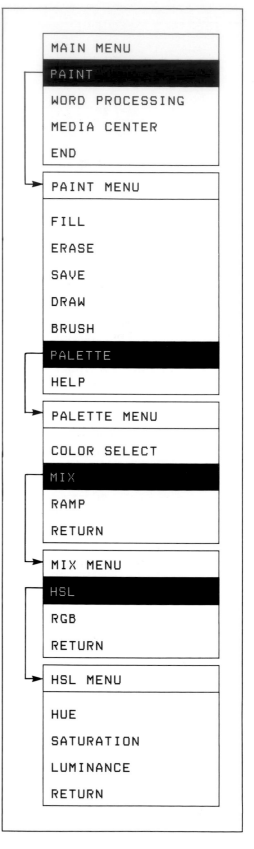

4-23. Selecting the mix color mode *pushes* a color mix menu onto the screen. Toggling from HSL in the mix color menu will bring up the RGB menu. Escape *pops* the mix menu off the screen.

4-24. The selection made in figure 4-23 from the point of view of the system structure parallels the graphic presentation.

virtual control board that aligns to a physical keyboard; the keyboard is operated normally with all fingers, but the keystrokes have specialized meanings (fig. 4-25).

Text Manipulation

Word processing allows a user to format text and to combine *text*—letters, numbers, and punctuation—with *formatting commands,* which shape and manipulate the text to form lines, columns, and pages.

A simple word processor can do everything a typewriter can do, as well as change, insert, delete, and rearrange letters, words, paragraphs, sections, and chapters. More sophisticated software will indent, center, format tabular data, justify, number pages, and index (fig. 4-26). At their most sophisticated they become typesetters with a selection of point sizes, faces, and proportional letter spacing. Format commands also control colors and case. On interactive video displays they allow a user to make letters or words blink or to display them in reverse video, that is, in negative—

4-25. Virtual keyboards allow text to be input in different languages and alphabets. Variations in diacritical marks and ligatures can be implemented.

a black letter surrounded by a white box.

Forms entry is an interactive textual method that displays multiple prompts on the screen and provides spaces for responses (fig. 4-27). The user is able to respond to prompts, review the entire form, then enter it. With this method a user gains perspective on his or her work; especially when different entries are related, mistakes in a single answer are more likely to stand out given this broader view.

Forms entry systems, in addition to performing individual prompt validations, also perform ***transaction validations,*** which ensure internal consistencies among groups of prompts, for example, that a state and zip code correspond. Fields that fail to validate are reprompted, and the user corrects the erroneous responses, then reenters.

PROPERTIES OF DIALOGUE

When using a computer graphics system for the first time, communications must be presented in detail. Once a working dialogue is established, shortcuts are employed—abbreviations and acronyms, default behaviors, and gestures that signify an entire sequence of commands.

Communications can be expressed using a languagelike syntax, such as

4-26. Formatting command ('$', F6.2) prints a $ followed by six columns of numerical information, containing a decimal point and two decimal places.

$ 142.43

16.21

1.28

$ 159.92

| ↳ | DEFINE | DISPLAY | EDIT | ☞ |

SLIDENO 36

CLIENT VAN NOSTRAND REINHOLD

COPYLINE1 NEW BOOKS

COPYLINE2 SPRING COMPUTER SERIES

TYPESTYLE `GOTHIC` ROMAN

TYPECOLOR RED `BLACK`

| ↳ | DEFINE | DISPLAY | EDIT | ☞ |

NEW BOOKS

SPRING COMPUTER SERIES

4-27. In this forms entry template for making up word slides, the system positions the cursor at the first input field, here SLIDE-NO, and the user enters a valid response. The cursor advances to CLIENT, COPY-LINE1, and COPYLINE2, with the user entering the appropriate information for each of these fields. At the prompt TYPESTYLE and TYPECOLOR the system allows two choices for each, and the user selects between them by moving the cursor right (or left) using the cursor control keys. The entire form is submitted to the system by pressing ENTER. Moving the cursor to DISPLAY and entering causes the formatted text to appear. Adjustments are made by moving the cursor to EDIT and entering; the filled-in form reappears and the user can edit the entries, enter, and redisplay them. The space to the right of the hourglass displays error messages.

"enlarge that picture 133 percent," or they can be graphically expressed by touching the screen and sliding the picture into position. In textual, aural, gestural, or graphic communications, expressions are bound by rules of syntax and the limitations of the machine.

Command language interpreters are interaction systems that involve a collection of standardized prompts with a consistent syntax. These interpreters are widely used and examples include operating systems like UNIX or CP/M, languages like BASIC or APL, and virtually all interactive graphics systems. Command language interpreters have a variety of features that enable a user to select predefined ***defaults*** (responses to prompts), ***truncate*** responses (type only a few letters of a command), cancel selections, backspace, ***backup*** (undo what was just done), and ***type ahead*** (respond to the next prompt before it appears).

Many command language interpreters

provide a way for a user to proceed if an error message appears. Still others will avoid prompts when they are unnecessary; almost all allow a user to configure his or her own system; for example, how long a cursor has to be pressed to detect a pick.

Indirect command files are interactive sequences that can be recorded or composed and replayed; they essentially enable a user to write a program, and like programs, indirect command files can be given parameters, or arguments. Thus indirect command files are one way to routinize redundant tasks and define graphic templates—for example, a standard business graph format developed for many applications (fig. 8-33). The designer creates and modifies the template, and the graphs produced maintain all the constraints chosen by the designer. The unchanging parameters, such as the font, the chart type, and the layout for these formats would be built into the indirect command file; whereas the parameters that are always unique, such as the actual data to be plotted, would be passed as parameters to the indirect command file at the time the picture was to be made.

A particular command language interpreter, like any other computing language or procedure, is part of a ***computing environment,*** a conceptual location with constant syntax and language (fig. 4-28). Different environments often employ different syntax, but all, including command language interpreters, procedures, and menus, have a beginning—a place they start when invoked—as well as an end, often activated by escape. Knowing what environment is active as well as knowing how to make the transition between environments is essential for using computers and navigating the system. You generally invoke lower-level environments by issuing commands, either via words or buttons, and exit an environment using an escape, or a "quit."

Good systems harmonize the stylistic design of prompt behavior throughout a system, even between environments. This

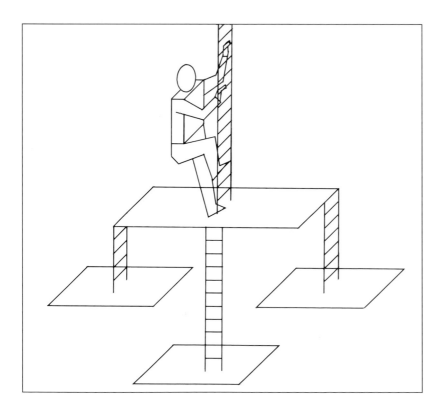

4-28. A particular computing environment is usually invoked by a higher-level environment and may in turn call lower-level environments.

requires a clear definition of the prompt parameters, plus consistent implementation. Command language interpreters should facilitate the way in which both experienced and inexperienced users operate the system. Redundant systems are easier to learn, but the experienced user wants shortcuts like type ahead and truncated response. A well-designed system should let you do both. A system should be simple and have features that will not get in the way. But the system should not be too simple, since graphic artists seem to quickly want to devise their own shortcuts; and you should not underestimate your own ability or that of your staff to develop more sophisticated commands, or to escalate the demands upon the services a system provides. Finally, a system should be fun to use, efficient, and should foster creativity.

PRODUCING AND DIRECTING COMPUTER GRAPHICS

In computer graphics, as in graphic arts in general, a designer may directly or indirectly manipulate a system. The former situation is typical when an artist works on a system, the latter is more common in commercial production.

Management Systems

Much of what the designer, producer, director, and art director do involves managing information, budgeting, scheduling, and contracting work. A *data-base system,* which includes files of names and addresses, budgets, schedules, and rate cards, is one tool available to the art director. Data bases can include photographs, drawings, and moving pictures in addition to alphanumeric material.

A data base is often designed for a particular purpose. A casting director, for instance, can compile a list of actors and actresses, and then search the system for only those who fulfill a set of criteria (see fig. 9-6). A video camera is used to capture

data and the pictures are then indexed according to specific parameters. Once selected, the pictures are displayed along with the textual information.

Budgeting systems can use preformatted spread sheets (discussed in more detail in chapter 9). Often the spread sheet is tailored to a specific activity, such as the American Independent Commercial Producers' live-action budget form. ***Production scheduling and monitoring systems*** track schedules, manage a staff's time, and analyze the fastest ways to do things. Production variables, such as the hours expended and costs, can be graphically plotted, as can more abstract concepts like readability, visibility, or the percent of pictures in a publication.

Computer systems are not significantly different from systems in general. The introduction of a computer into an established organization may represent a radical change in the way information is stored and retrieved, but it does not modify the basic management process. Even in computer facilities salaries constitute the greatest expense and individuals are the most important part of an operation. Their basic skills, knowledge, experience, and creativity determine the success of the organization. Computer systems are not substitutes for human creativity, initiative, or style, but facilitate the expression of these.

Conversions from traditional to electronic media will be fraught with anxiety until workers and managers understand that the value of good retouchers, for example, is their ability to select and position the appropriate color; they need not put color on a brush and touch it to a photograph. These creative acts can be executed after one has enough experience to smooth a wrinkle, or accelerate the flow of a line. The goal is to make the picture read more clearly, which is a skill that is completely transferable to electronic media.

Contracting with Production Units

When considering computer graphics as a solution to a particular design problem, it is best to begin by simply and specifically describing your needs to members of a production unit. If the production unit's personnel say that they cannot execute your designs the way they are drawn, perhaps they can adapt your designs and propose a better solution. Alternate sources of supply should be considered if an absolute requirement cannot be realized.

Contracting for computer graphic production begins with a producer (or client) issuing a request for a quotation, which consists of a drawing or storyboard and a written description of the work to be performed.

The production unit responds with a quotation, which includes a written description of the solution, a timetable, and a price. The producer evaluates the quotation, negotiates the fine points, and issues a purchase order before the production unit begins work. This work is reviewed by the client at predefined intervals and approved before the production unit completes it to spec and delivers it along with an invoice (fig. 4-29).

The **contract** defines the terms of sale and conditions of production; in fact, this can actually be the quotation or purchase order, or even a letter of agreement. This document includes a written description, the number of pieces or the running time, the delivery medium, delivery date, price, terms of payment, and point of delivery. It may also contain credits, rights of resale, and additional conditions (fig. 4-30).

The **written description** provides a clear, technical description of the production. It might describe the visual contents—"a picture showing a three-dimensional robot juggling three colored balls; the robot is inside a house." The written description should indicate whether the design is to be rendered as a pixel image or a vector image, whether the image is described in a two-dimensional or three-dimensional environment, and how the image is to be rendered. If the image depicts a three-dimensional environment, the description should say if shading or lighting are to be used. If the image is wire frame, the description should indicate if hidden lines are to be removed. Descriptions may even include the number of points or polygons used in a picture, the resolution of the image, and its finished size.

Written descriptions often reference storyboards, drawings, and blueprints, but no computer graphic is going to look exactly like a hand-drawn illustration. Clarifications between sketches and desired results are essential to avoid misunderstandings.

The number of pieces should be expressed as a count: "thirteen slides, two copies each for a total of twenty-six slides," for instance. Running times are best expressed in seconds and could include the number of frames per second that are being delivered. "Twos," for example, means each frame is repeated twice, and has half the production value of "ones," where every frame is unique.

4-29. Interactions between a client and production unit in contracting computer graphics.

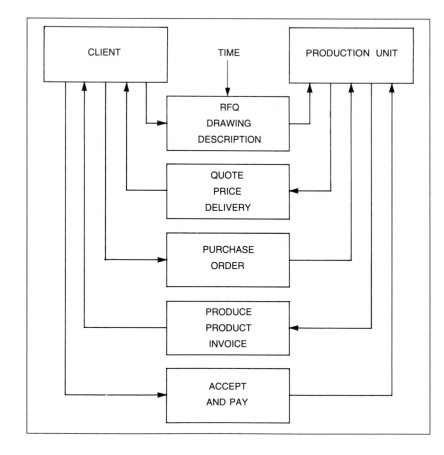

QUOTATION

FROM:

TO _____

_____

_____

QUOTATION NO. _____

QUOTATION DATE _____

YOUR INQUIRY NO. _____

QUOTE VALID FOR _____ DAYS

QUANTITY	UNITS	DESCRIPTION	UNIT PRICE	AMOUNT

TERMS	F.O.B.	ESTIMATED SHIPPING DATE	DELIVERY MEDIUM

PROVIDED BY CLIENT _____

_____

Submitted
by _____

Accepted
by _____

4-30. Quotation or contract.

The delivery medium might specify 35 mm or 16 mm film, ¾-inch or 1-inch videotape, 35 mm slides, 4 × 5-inch color transparencies, color separation sets, paper plots, ink jet color plots, or even images in digital form, such as a floppy disk.

A fixed price is a firm bid to do the entire job. Quantity price depends on the number of pieces and the length or running time. Cost-plus-markup pricing specifies that price is equal to the costs of raw materials and services, plus a fixed markup.

Terms dictate when money is paid and how much is paid at each time. Terms might specify one-half in advance and one-half cash on delivery, or 100 percent net thirty days. Contracts spread out over long periods of time often specify monthly payments tied to performance milestones.

The *point of delivery,* or F.O.B., specifies the point of delivery, usually the manufacturing site of the production unit. The issue involved is who pays for shipping and sales taxes—these together can account for as much as 10 percent of the cost.

Often clients request that the production unit alter the images in one way or another. The unit pays if the changes are modifications and within the domain of the contract, and the client pays if the changes are revisions, which alter the intent of the original description. There is a fine line distinguishing a modification from a revision, and it is only when both parties are sensitive to each other's economic and visual needs that an acceptable solution can be reached.

Rules of Thumb

Production takes time. Graphic artists at work stations take time. Indecision, committees, rather than an individual, giving and receiving directions, and the "let's hurry up and wait" scenario waste time and money. Lack of direction, lack of planning, and indecision are often as responsible for cost overruns and late deliveries as are technical malfunctions, artistic misunderstandings, and the simple grind of production. Poor planning is not easily remedied in the production stage.

A few rule-of-thumb statistics, mostly applying to animation, involving cost and time are useful. The *production time ratio* is the relationship between the wall-clock time required to design and produce a product, and the running time of the finished work. The *production cost ratio* is the average cost of producing a single frame or page (cost/frame). The *CPU time ratio* is the ratio between the computing or console time to produce a product, and its actual screen running time.

In practical terms, it is not unusual to spend two to three weeks and $10,000 to $25,000 making a five-second logo, six weeks and $30,000 to $100,000 to make a thirty-second or one-minute commercial, and three years and $5 million to $15 million to make a ninety-minute movie. Smaller units of work cost more because the costs of data bases cannot be amortized. It may be wise to begin a project with a price in mind and try to design with that price as a constraint, as computer graphics, like anything else, have a wide price range.

The size of the data base (doubling the size of the data base, for instance, more than doubles the complexity of the project), the number of views produced, the amount of action, and the rendering method chosen all affect the cost of a project. Building a data base is a one-time expense but one that can be amortized when the data is used to generate many frames. The computer, after all, is a machine that works well in a repetitive mode, and graphics are no exception.

There is a joke in the animation industry that says all computer-generated movie frames take twenty minutes to compute, regardless of the speed and cost of the computer on which the computation is being performed. Faster CPUs do not necessarily produce faster throughput, only more complicated images. The twenty-minute frame seems to be bounded primarily by the limits of practicality—a thirty-second commercial computing at twenty minutes a frame requires ten days to compute.

Of course one can design an image that could take longer to compute than the universe has been in existence, no matter how fast the computer runs. The pragmatics of performing a calculation on an existing computer inside an existing time frame require planning from both a business and a production point of view. These "limits of computability calculations" are perhaps the most basic considerations in computer graphics, and they are integrally related to all creative decisions.

INTERFACE DESIGN CONSIDERATIONS

Computer graphics systems are objects of design as well as being tools for designing images, objects, and environments. Three major considerations that pertain to the design of computer graphic systems include ergonomics, man-machine interfaces, and system selection. These considerations involve the designer, who brings to the project a sense of style and direction, as well as the human factors engineer, who evaluates strategies by testing them on people.

Ergonomic Considerations

Ergonomics, the technology concerned with the application of engineering data to problems relating to man and the machine, is applied to instrumentation displays, especially in industrial applications where health and safety must be considered. In a computer graphics work station this includes not only the dimensions of the physical components of a system, but also the *visibility* of an image (visibility is to a picture what legibility is to text) and features of the work station itself, such as lighting.

The designs of these tools and environments are directly related to a worker's performance. Well-designed tools improve creativity and productivity, give people pride,

and reduce health and psychological problems, including eye strain, muscular pain, and stress. The work station must be used by a large variety of people, and its components—monitor, keyboard, seat, and table—should therefore be adaptable (fig. 4-31).

Since most of a designer's contact with the system takes place through the monitor, it should not be too small, and the user should be able to tilt it to avoid light reflections and muscular discomfort. The overall quality of the image should not flicker. When color monitors are used, they should be RGB monitors, which have separate channels for red, green, and blue, and not NTSC, or composite, monitors. Image resolution should exceed seventy dots per inch so that the image is legible.

Monitors and television screens are known to emit X-ray, ultraviolet, near-infrared, radio-frequency, extremely low-frequency, and ultrasonic radiation. The long-term effects of these on an individual's health are not yet known. If health problems are suspected, the amount of radiation emitted can be measured and compared to existing occupational exposure standards. Corrective measures, like lead glass and shielding, can also be taken.

The position of the keyboard should be low enough to avoid wrist tension. Detachable keyboards allow users to reposition them. Keys should be clearly labeled and should follow one of the standard arrangements such as QWERTY. The cursor keys, numerical keys, scrolling keys, and editing keys should be separate from the alphanumeric keys. A well-designed keyboard will have a recognizable touch, so a user can feel whether a key was struck.

The design of the rest of the input and output peripherals should also conform to the best ergonomic standards available. The digitizing tablet should not be so sensitive that it registers unintended signals from mechanical vibrations. A designer should be able to adjust the tracking speed of the light pen or mouse.

The layout of the room should be considered when installing a computer work

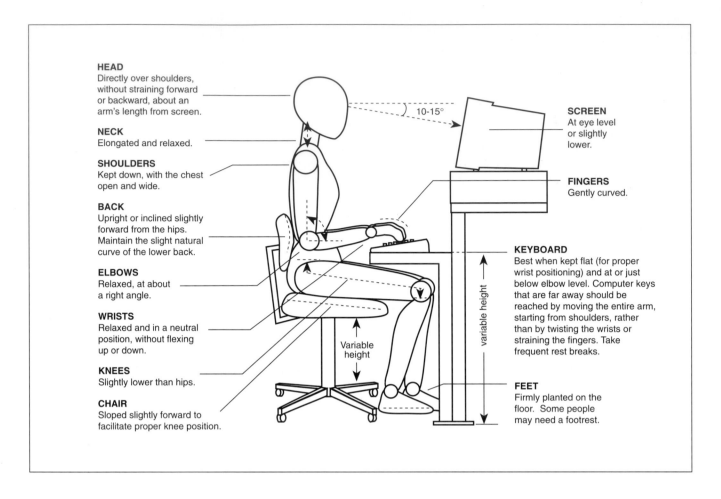

HEAD
Directly over shoulders, without straining forward or backward, about an arm's length from screen.

NECK
Elongated and relaxed.

SHOULDERS
Kept down, with the chest open and wide.

BACK
Upright or inclined slightly forward from the hips. Maintain the slight natural curve of the lower back.

ELBOWS
Relaxed, at about a right angle.

WRISTS
Relaxed and in a neutral position, without flexing up or down.

KNEES
Slightly lower than hips.

CHAIR
Sloped slightly forward to facilitate proper knee position.

10-15°

SCREEN
At eye level or slightly lower.

FINGERS
Gently curved.

KEYBOARD
Best when kept flat (for proper wrist positioning) and at or just below elbow level. Computer keys that are far away should be reached by moving the entire arm, starting from shoulders, rather than by twisting the wrists or straining the fingers. Take frequent rest breaks.

FEET
Firmly planted on the floor. Some people may need a footrest.

Variable height

variable height

4-31. This drawing provides pointers to avoid injury while using computers for extended periods of time. (Based on material provided by Dr. Emil Pascarelli, The Miller Health Care Institute for Performing Artists, Saint Luke's-Roosevelt Hospital, New York City.)

station. Light should illuminate the keyboard and work space but never fall directly on the monitor. Noisy components and those requiring air conditioning should be in a separate room from the work stations. Printers, CPUs, and disk drives usually perform better if isolated from dust, extremes in temperature and humidity, and magnetic fields.

Man-Machine Interface

Man-machine interface refers to the channels (software and hardware) and their operational characteristics that affect the communication between the system and the user. The implementation of interactive techniques and the clear display of information are two man-machine interface issues especially relevant to the design of a computer-based imaging work

station. Interactive techniques are the most direct methods of controlling the computer, based on action and response operations such as picking an item from a menu or hitting a key. A quick response from the computer, even if the action is incorrect, makes the user or designer feel in control and promotes a relaxed work atmosphere.

Interaction techniques are designed to give the user control over the system, so such tasks should be made as easy as possible. Function keys allow the user to keep the number of keystrokes to a minimum. Dialogue should be structured so the user can choose options in any order. The system should also indicate where a user is in a sequence of events, possibly by displaying messages in selected parts of the screen, using split-screen techniques or multiwindow displays (see fig. 4-23). A user-friendly system allows the designer to recover gracefully from mistakes and to correct errors.

Effective information displays require consistency and legibility. *Design standards* include the careful organization of information, orderly color coding, alphanumeric and symbolic information, and positioning to ensure visual consistency and implies predetermined general guidelines or design standards. Visual information that conforms to design standards incorporates well-established graphic design principles and tests for comprehension. For example, color-coding systems operate best when the number of colors used is kept to a minimum; most people can distinguish between four to eight colors without confusion. In cases where the response to color messages is critical (a process control application, for instance), users should be given color blindness tests.

Alphanumeric coding should use very common words or acronyms. Textual messages should be short, so users can remember them without difficulty, but may refer to detailed and up-to-date manuals that contain the appropriate explanations in nontechnical language. Such manuals can be printed documents or on-line documents that can be called by pressing the HELP key. In the case of symbolic or iconic coding, the symbols must be carefully and clearly designed. Tests should be conducted to ensure that symbols are self-explanatory (understandable without the aid of a code list reference). The legibility of type varies widely on computer displays and must be tailored to the resolution of the display.

System Selection

The enormous variety of tasks in the fields of design, animation, and imaging cannot be performed by a single computer system. Therefore, when selecting a computer system, the first step is to define its central application. Computer systems can be divided into several groups according

to the general tasks they perform—systems usually perform a specific group of tasks best, though they often include secondary features (fig. 4-32). It is important, therefore, to base the selection decision on the single most important application.

The second step is to consider what components it needs (both hardware and software), its size, power, and functions (fig. 4-33). Resolution, the number of colors, the syntax of dialogues, and versatility are features that must be considered, as are speed, reliability, response time, and price. These may be compared in cross-reference tables (fig. 4-34).

Computer systems can either be microcomputers (the smallest systems), minicomputers (the medium-sized systems), or mainframe or supercomputers (the largest systems). The number of designers using the system determines which of these is appropriate. A microcomputer-based system should support a single user, whereas a minicomputer system, depending on its capacity, may be shared by several users. A mainframe or a supercomputer is only cost-effective for applications that require teams of designers working on a project, or on a group of related projects.

Another consideration is whether the system should be a ***turnkey*** system, a fin-

A	B	C
TYPE DESIGN	PROCESS CONTROL	ARCHITECTURE
ILLUSTRATION	INFORMATION SYSTEMS	INDUSTRIAL DESIGN
COLOR CORRECTION	CARTOGRAPHY	INTERIOR DESIGN
COLOR SEPARATION	BUSINESS GRAPHICS	PACKAGE DESIGN
PAGINATION	VIDEO GAMES	CLOTHING
ANIMATION	SIMULATORS	TEXTILE DESIGN

4-32. Two-dimensional systems for applications that require extensive manipulation of images and text in a flat, two-dimensional space. Such applications include type design, illustration, color correction, pagination, and animation (A). Interactive two-dimensional systems for applications that require the visual display of data bases and processes. Such applications include process control, information systems, cartography, business graphics, and video games (B). Three-dimensional systems for applications that are based on the representation and manipulation of three-dimensional structures. Such applications include industrial design, architecture, interior design, packaging design, and clothing and textile design. Most of these systems have tools for building and rendering three-dimensional solid objects in a schematic or realistic manner (C).

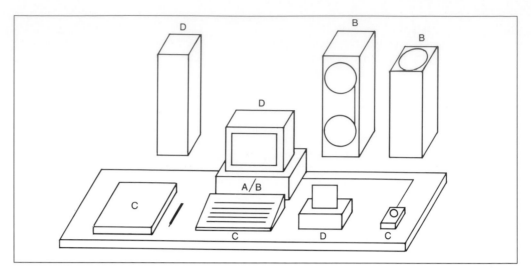

4-33. Components of a computer graphics system include the CPU or main computer (A). Memory sizes can range from a couple of kilobytes to thousands of megabytes, and memory devices include RAM, hard and floppy magnetic disks, and tapes (B). Input devices include digitizing tablets, keyboards, mice, and light pens (C), and output devices include terminals, plotters, printers, and film recorders (D). Resolution and color quality differ from one output system to the other; these may be point or pixel, refresh or static. Software is made up of systems and applications programs and is often the decisive factor in the success or failure of a computer-aided design system. Analyzing functions offered by similar programs is often a good method of choosing which program performs the operations best for a specific application.

ished product that is produced, integrated, delivered, installed, tested, and maintained by the vendor, or a system that can be developed and enhanced in-house. The software package in the turnkey system can only be implemented on specific equipment and leaves very little room for changes. Because it is mass-produced and marketed, it should be relatively bug-free, and may incorporate many features. On the other hand, a system assembled in-house can be tailored to specific needs. Successful in-house development requires a great deal of responsibility and expertise from the buyer as well as a programming staff. These systems usually require constant technical support that can only be provided by full-time systems and applications programmers.

Product evaluation should be made by the people who will use the system as well as by those who will be affected by its operation. Such a group includes designers, data processors, engineers, managers, and administrators. If a limited number of experts are available within the company, an outside consultant could help research the optimum choice.

Installations that already have and use a system similar to the one being considered should be visited; experienced users can provide nonbiased, detailed insights about the systems that they have been using every day in their professional lives. Basing such a decision on the information printed in glossy brochures is no substitution for first-hand observations.

In order to avoid major disruptions in the production process, it is necessary to slowly move applications to a new computer system, maintaining traditional production procedures until the new system, and methods for solving design problems, are firmly in place. Diagrams of restructured design and production flow can help those involved to adjust to the new procedures.

Systems Operation and Staffs
Once the computer system is installed, special attention must be given to training personnel. Staffs in a typical system are

	On-line Help	Number of Colors	Price
Vendor 1	YES	8	2,000
Vendor 2	NO	64	6,000
Vendor 3	YES	16	5,000

made up of **systems programmers,** who design, repair, and maintain the operating system, languages, and application programs. Since software is complex, modifications are best made by the people who define and write the systems. (In a turnkey application, the systems programmers may all work for the vendor.)

Staffs also include a **steward,** who is responsible for configuring a system. The steward does not design or use the system, but tailors its use at a particular site— enrolls users, defines their privileges, and configures the constraints or boundaries to be imposed. A system for newspaper layout, for example, should be able to accommodate many newspapers with different page sizes, numbers of columns, and column widths; a steward sets parameters and configures the system to allow some degree of flexibility. He or she therefore must know more about the overall sys-

tem than a user and must be able to communicate with the systems programmers.

Users employ the capabilities of the system to typeset, create graphics, and paste-up electronically. Like the systems programmer, the user is a programmer in that he or she interacts with the system, issues commands, enters data, and checks the results. A user operates the system that a programmer constructs.

The **operator,** found in large multiuser systems, supervises the computer system and runs it or operates it on a minute-to-minute basis.

Finally, computer data is volatile, easily damaged, and can be financially devastating if lost. Backup and archival procedures are essential and require advanced planning. Backups should be done daily or weekly. Though they take time and are almost always unnecessary, they are a required precaution.

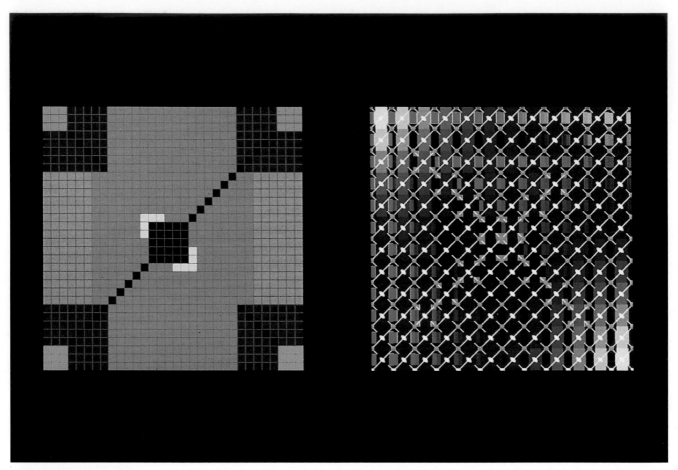

5-0. This image was created on the Bucolic System, which allows users to practice color theory interactively. The simple geometrical module on the left is colored by using RGB and HSV controls. The module is repeated on a 12 × 12 grid at the right to produce a pattern. The colors in the basic module are interpolated according to where the module is positioned on the 12 × 12 grid. (Courtesy of Barbara Meier and Diana Rathborne, Brown University.)

5

COLOR
AND
BLACK-AND-
WHITE

COLOR SYSTEMS
LUMINANCE CONTROLS
COLOR CONTROLS
COLOR CALIBRATION AND MATCHING

One of the main themes of computer graphics is image manipulation, whether the manipulation is done on a computer or not. Some computer graphics techniques emulate traditional imaging techniques that are exclusive to a particular medium. Other techniques are unique and exclusive to the computer graphics medium. For example, a computer system not only makes the negative of an image—an emulation of a traditional method—but it can pixelate the image as well, something that would prove extremely time consuming using a traditional method. The computer is very much a medium of manipulation; it can also serve as a tool and "amplifier" of existing approaches.

Computers, as procedural machines, require routinized methods for creating and manipulating pictures. These methods constitute a **visual language**—a formal notational system used by a graphic artist to create and communicate ideas and emotions. Visual language is a modern label for a very old concept; indeed, most graphic artists already use visual language commands, like "enlarge picture 133 percent." Visual language can be textual and command driven, or graphical and interactive, such as on a computerized paint box. It is irrelevant whether the directions are executed by a worker or a machine. The key idea is not so much how, but the fact that graphical tasks can be broken down into a finite number of individual steps and executed in a predictable manner (an algorithm).

This chapter explores one of the fundamental variables of visual language: the color of things. There are many approaches to this in both the traditional and the digital world. **Color** is the mixture of three different wavelengths of light as perceived by the eye, and it may be associated with a wide variety of visual things: a point, a polygon or an object (for example, a cube), or a pixel, voxel, temperature, light source, atmosphere, or expression. To some extent the world of black-and-white is a subset of color. One difference is that **black-and-white** processing implies a single channel of brightness information, whereas color implies at least two, typically three, and sometimes four or more channels of information.

In the real world, that is, in nature, the domain of brightness and color is effectively infinite, from as dark as a black hole to as bright as the big bang. Imaging media (film, tape, even digital data) record brightness only within a finite range, and the issues of digitization apply here (see chapter 1). Color may be expressed with real numbers, ranging, for example, from zero to one, or as a sampled number of integer steps, ranging, for example, from 0 to 255 (fig. 5-1). Thus the sampling problem is analogous to spatial or temporal sampling, only instead of expressing resolution as pixels or frames per second, color resolution is expressed as the number of color steps from black to media white.

5-1. Color systems can be expressed in both integer and real notation and converted from one notation to the other. Integer notation, on the left, uses whole numbers (0 to 255 in this case). Real notation uses fractional numbers (zero to one). In this case, the formula INTEGER = 255 × REAL converts one to the other.

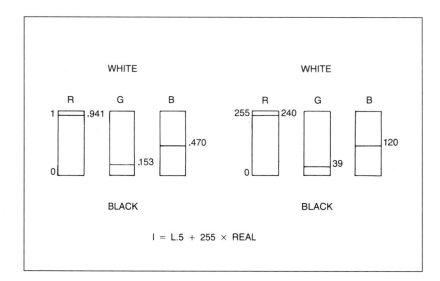

☞ **RELATED READING**

Gerritsen, Frans. *Theory and Practice of Color.* New York: Van Nostrand Reinhold, 1975.

Hurvich, L. M. *Color Vision.* Sunderland, MA: Sinauer Assoc., 1981.

Judd, D. B., and G. Wyszecki. *Color in Business, Science and Industry.* 3d ed. New York: John Wiley & Sons, 1975.

Marx, Ellen. *Optical Color and Simultaneity.* New York: Van Nostrand Reinhold, 1983.

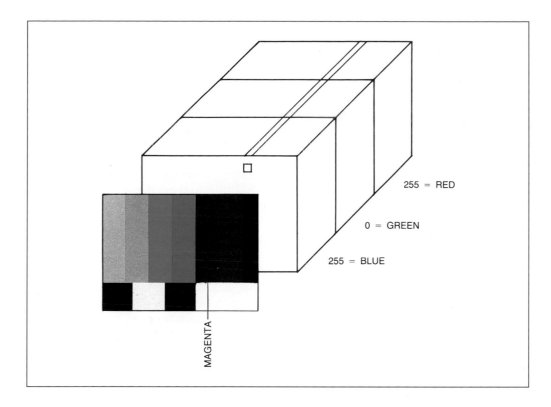

5-2. Three bitplanes are needed to represent the color value of a single pixel in a tristimulus gamut. Each colored polygon (in this case, each one of the color bars) is composed of hundreds of pixels with the same value. The red, green, blue values of a magenta pixel are 255, 0, 255, respectively.

255 = RED

0 = GREEN

255 = BLUE

MAGENTA

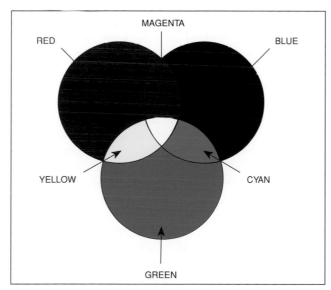

5-3. The RGB color gamut can be visualized as three circles of colored light that overlap in pairs to produce three areas bounded by arcs of secondary colors; the three overlap together in the center to produce white. Black is the absence of any light whatsoever.

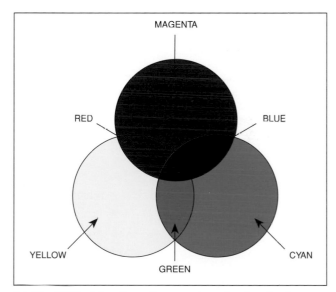

5-4. The CYM subtractive color gamut can be visualized as three circles of colored pigment that overlap in pairs to produce three areas bounded by arcs of secondary colors; the three overlap together in the center to produce black. White is the absence of any pigment whatsoever.

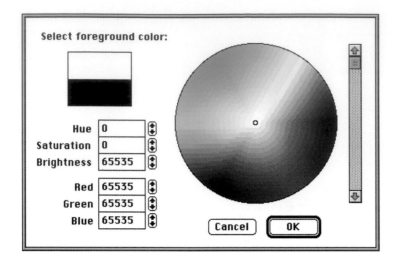

color in a tristimulus gamut, three sets of bitplanes are used—one for each channel of color (fig. 5-2).

The most common variables used to represent color are the **red-green-blue (RGB)** gamut, where the variables represent the brightness of the three additive primary lights. Separate red, green, and blue colored lights shining on a surface become white where they overlay and are said to be additive (fig. 5-3). This is how a CRT works also.

Pigment-oriented systems work with the subtractive primaries, **cyan, yellow, and magenta (CYM),** and are used in printing and painting. The CYM gamut absorbs light, and the mixture of cyan, yellow, and magenta pigments in equal proportions produces black (fig. 5-4).

The **hue-lightness-saturation (HLS)** gamut is expressed as a double cone space that contains hue, luminance, and saturation values (fig. 5-5). The HLS model is useful because it permits luminance to be manipulated as a variable independent of the hue and saturation. Likewise lightness can be held constant while varying the hue or saturation—in other words, the gray level doesn't change.

Four-variable Color Models

Color representation in computer graphics is not limited to three-variable representations, but can include four or more variables. Four-variable systems require four numbers, or four channels of bitmap memory.

The most common four-color model is **process color,** which uses **cyan, magenta, yellow, and black (CMYK)** inks, and is used for offset printing. Although theoretically not necessary, black is used in addition to the three subtractive primaries to improve contrast and decrease the amount of the more expensive colored inks (fig. 5-6). The black represents the darker shades common to the cyan, magenta, and yellow components.

A fourth channel may also be used to complement RGB or CYM images in order to store a **matte,** which is a bitmap that

5-5. The hue-lightness-saturation (HLS) color gamut is expressed as a double cone (or sometimes a cylinder) where luminance extends from black to white up the vertical axis. Hue is the color and is represented as the angle around the vertical axis. Saturation is the radius, or distance from the vertical axis, and represents how much of the color's complement makes up the color. This color gamut may be represented as a circular cross section and slider, where the cross section is used to pick hue and saturation and the slider controls brightness. (Color Picker is from the Apple Computer Macintosh desktop.)

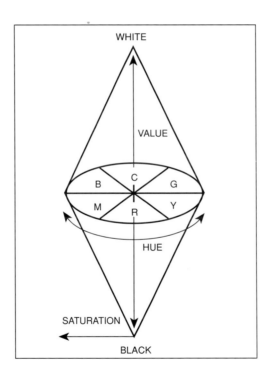

COLOR SYSTEMS

Tristimulus Color Gamuts

The predominant method of implementing color on a computer employs a **tristimulus representation,** or a three-variable model in which color is described by three channels of information represented by three numbers. When a pixel represents

records the opacity/transparency of an image at each pixel. This fourth channel is called an **alpha channel,** and it facilitates the compositing of an image over a background, for example, and allows the scene behind a semitransparent object to show through. The alpha channel also aids in compositing situations where edges are diffuse and soft, and objects are in motion (the blurring makes them transparent). These matting techniques and applications are discussed in greater detail in chapter 6.

Multispectral imaging provides luminance information at many different frequencies of light, including not only the visible frequencies but also at infrared, ultraviolet, ultrasound, X-ray, and radio frequencies. By displaying these extra channels with color, we essentially translate nonvisual information into images we can perceive and understand (fig. 5-7). Multispectral imaging also allows us to superimpose image data with other data that are geographically distributed, for exam-

ple, automobile emissions of pollutants, so that we can study relationships.

Video Color Gamuts

Color in television is represented several ways. The purest is **component color,** in which red, green, and blue are represented and transmitted as three separate, synchronous, and parallel channels. In an analog studio, three wires are used for component color (and sometimes a fourth for a synchronization channel). An alternative approach is called **composite color,** in which the red, green, and blue information is converted to a single channel containing what is essentially a low-resolution color signal laid over a higher-resolution luminance (black-and-white) signal. The NTSC, PAL, and SECAM television formats all accomplish this. The process of converting component color signals to a composite color signal is called **encoding,** and the hardware or software that does this is called an encoder. The inverse process is

5-6. This image shows the four components of the CMYK gamut and all the basic combinations. (From Gerritsen, *Theory and Practice of Color,* p. 81.)

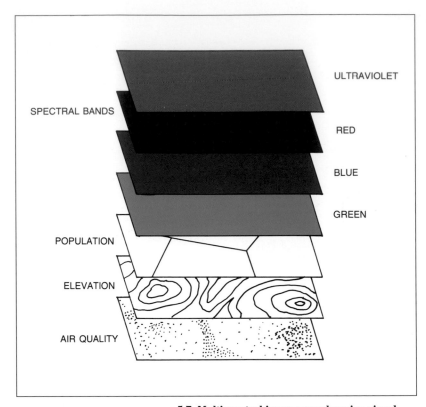

SPECTRAL BANDS

ULTRAVIOLET

RED

BLUE

GREEN

POPULATION

ELEVATION

AIR QUALITY

5-7. Multispectral images synchronize visual channels (like red, green, and blue), nonvisual channels (like ultraviolet), and often topographic and sociological channels where the information is also represented with pixels.

5-8. Three separate red, green, and blue component signals plus a separate sync signal are encoded into a single composite NTSC video waveform, which can in turn be decoded back into the component red, green, blue, and sync signals. Note that the individual component signals do not contain a sync pulse but that the composite waveform does; note also the presence of the color burst in the composite signal, which contains information about the encoded color.

called **decoding** (fig. 5-8). The advantage of composite color is that the color signal travels on a single wire (or transmitter); the disadvantage is that it has less color information than a component color signal. When a component color signal is first encoded to composite color and then decoded again the result has less information than the original signal. All off-air and cable television is composite color, as are the VHS, ¾″ U-matic, 1″ C, and D2 videotape recording formats. But there are some videotape formats that record component color (Hi8, Betacam, and D1), and virtually all computer screens use component color.

LUMINANCE CONTROLS

Histogramming

A *histogram* of an image is an inventory of the image, the number of pixels at each intensity value presented in graphic form (fig. 5-9). Color images require three (or four) histograms.

In an image that contains luminance values, one can readily determine from the histogram whether the pixel values in the image are evenly distributed in terms of light and dark, or if they are clustered, for example mostly in the middle grays in a picture lacking contrast. The information revealed in the histogram may be used to improve the visibility of an image by redistributing the pixel values and improving contrast.

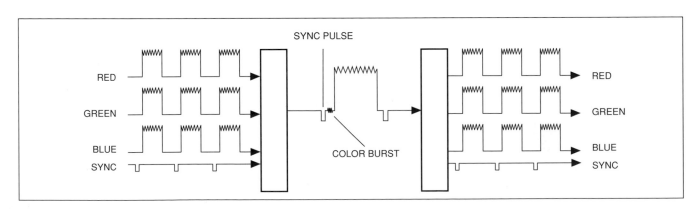

SYNC PULSE

RED

GREEN

BLUE

SYNC

COLOR BURST

RED

GREEN

BLUE

SYNC

Look-up Tables and Palettes

A **look-up table,** or **palette,** is a matrix of one or more columns with as many rows as there are intensity levels in an image. You will recall this number is determined by two raised to the power of the number of bitplanes—if there are three bitplanes, then there are 2^3 or eight rows in the look-up table. The number of columns corresponds to the number of color channels and would be one for black-and-white, or three for RGB color.

A look-up table is used by taking the numerical value stored in a pixel and using that value as a pointer, or index, into the look-up table memory. The value stored in the contents of that particular look-up table location is then used as the actual luminance value (fig. 5-10).

Look-up tables are often implemented as part of the frame buffer hardware, where they translate the value in each pixel at the time of image display. The hardware look-up table is loaded once at the beginning by copying a specific look-up table from a disk into the look-up table

memory. There are many different palettes, and they are used by loading them into the frame buffer look-up table memory. But only one palette can be used at a time.

Look-up tables are very much a part of graphic arts computer systems; in an **identity look-up table** each row is loaded with its own address. The identity table contains

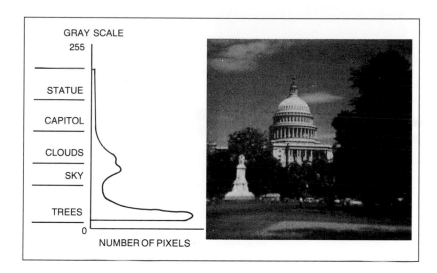

5-9. An image and its histogram. The vertical scale of the histogram represents the luminance of the image, with black at the bottom and white at the top. The horizontal scale indicates the number of pixels at each intensity level. The histogram reveals that most of the pixels are low values and make up the trees. (Courtesy of Spatial Data Systems, Inc.; a DBA Systems Company.)

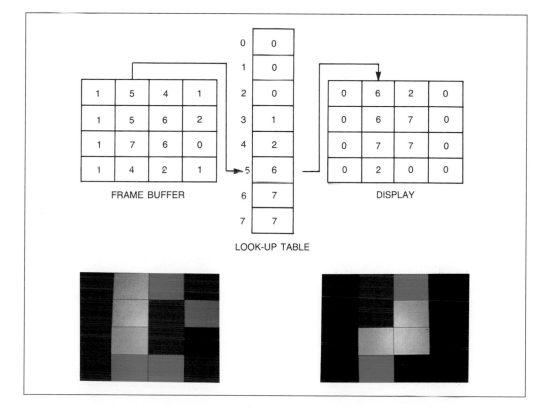

5-10. The numerical values of the pixels that configure the image (five in this example) point the display processor to a color look-up table address. The address contains a luminance value (six) that is used to specify the brightness of the corresponding pixel in the final image.

5-11. The value in an identity look-up table is equal to its address, so the resulting picture intensity is identical to the input pixel array.

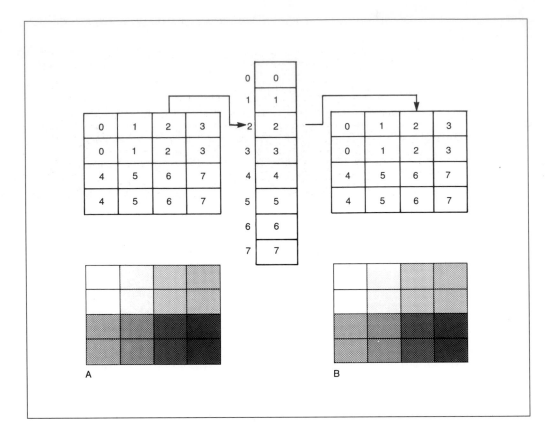

5-12. A negative look-up table reverses the luminance of the image by inverting the contents of the table. A three-bit look-up table is depicted in the illustration. At the zero address, the value seven is stored, and so on. Pixels with low values (like two) get translated to a high-intensity value (like five), and high-intensity values (like six) get translated to low-intensity values (like one).

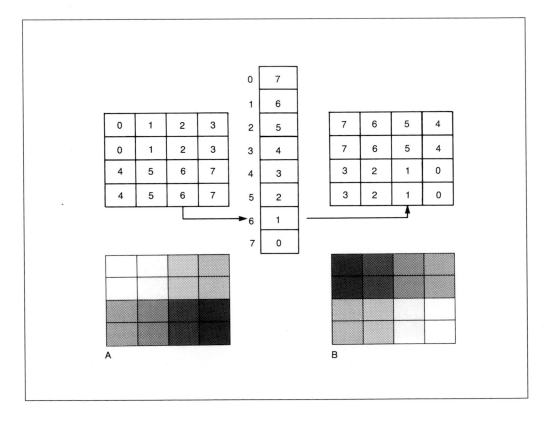

A   B   C

	32 Gray Levels (A)	16 Gray Levels (B)	8 Gray Levels (C)
0	0	0	0
1	1	0	0
2	2	2	0
3	3	2	0
4	4	4	4
5	5	4	4
6	6	6	4
7	7	6	4
8	8	8	8
9	9	8	8
10	10	10	8
11	11	10	8
12	12	12	12
13	13	12	12
14	14	14	12
15	15	14	12
16	16	16	16
17	17	16	16
18	18	18	16
19	19	18	16
20	20	20	20
21	21	20	20
22	22	22	20
23	23	22	20
24	24	24	24
25	25	24	24
26	26	26	24
27	27	26	24
28	28	28	28
29	29	28	28
30	30	30	28
31	31	30	28

5-13. Reducing gray levels. The illustration shows an image containing thirty-two gray levels and three look-up tables, each with thirty-two rows of five bits each. The first look-up table is an identity table and reproduces all the gray levels in the picture. The second look-up table uses only half the luminance values and replicates them in adjacent rows. The third look-up table is constructed in a similar manner, except it uses only eight distinct gray levels and copies each one four times. In other words, in the last look-up table, gray values of 20, 21, 22, and 23 will be reproduced as a luminance value of 20. The last look-up table maintains a dynamic range between black and white; only the number of gray levels has been reduced. (Courtesy of Spatial Data Systems, Inc.; a DBA Systems Company.)

0		0
1		0
2		0
3		0
4		0
5		0
6		0
7		0
8		31
9		31
10		31
11		31
12		31
13		31
14		31
15		31

THRESHOLD

5-14. In a high-contrast image, the look-up table contains only luminance values for black and white. The level or row address that determines where on the gray scale the distinction is made between black and white is called the threshold. (Courtesy of Spatial Data Systems, Inc.; a DBA Systems Company.)

the value of the pixel, so that when a pointer is indexed into this table, the result extracted is the same as the original number, and the picture looks as if no look-up table were involved whatsoever (fig. 5-11).

A *negative look-up table* reverses the luminance of the image by inverting the contents of the table. This is the equivalent of subtracting each pixel value from the brightest value (fig. 5-12). Pixels with low-intensity values get translated to high-intensity values and vice versa, forming a negative of the picture.

Look-up tables are useful for reducing gray levels in a picture. This is accomplished by using a look-up table that contains multiple rows with the same value (fig. 5-13). The extreme case reduces the number of gray levels to two and makes a *high-contrast* black-and-white matte element. The luminance value that determines the break between black and white is called the *threshold* (fig. 5-14).

Remember that modifying the contents of the look-up table modifies the display but not the contents of the image. Thus, look-up tables provide a method to nondestructively preview images and are useful to correct colors, among other things. If one wants to actually change the contents of image memory, the calculation performed by the look-up table must be applied to the image itself (fig. 5-15). For example, to fix the negative of an image in frame buffer memory, one can

make each pixel in the bitmap equal to the value output by the look-up table and then replace the table with an identity table. The visual results of manipulating either the look-up table or pixels are identical. The pixel method requires more computing and may not be reversible, whereas the look-up table method only requires modification of its contents.

Contrast and Color Correction

Look-up tables are especially useful for increasing and decreasing contrast as well as for correcting the color of images. *Contrast,* the ratio of black to white pixels in an image, is adjusted by redistributing black and white values to increase visibility. *Color correction* is a similar process that alters each color to create a balance. Histograms often provide a basis for enhancing contrast and colors. The histogram provides a diagram of the intensity levels of pixels; in an image where most of the pixels have a narrow range of intensity values, the visibility of the picture can be improved by assigning a wider dynamic range of intensity to those pixels (fig. 5-16).

Color correction on a computer system is a much more elastic process than in traditional analog electronic or photographic media, because the color look-up tables provide a wide potential for variation. In a color correction system there is one look-up table for each primary, and each is individually controlled (fig. 5-17).

COLOR CONTROLS

The techniques in this section involve methods of manipulating color. These have practical and artistic applications not only on low-resolution systems, but on full-color, high-resolution systems as well.

Color Codes and Color Mixing

In addition to representing luminance values, pixels can contain *color codes,* or numbers representing colors. Color names and codes have been widely used in the

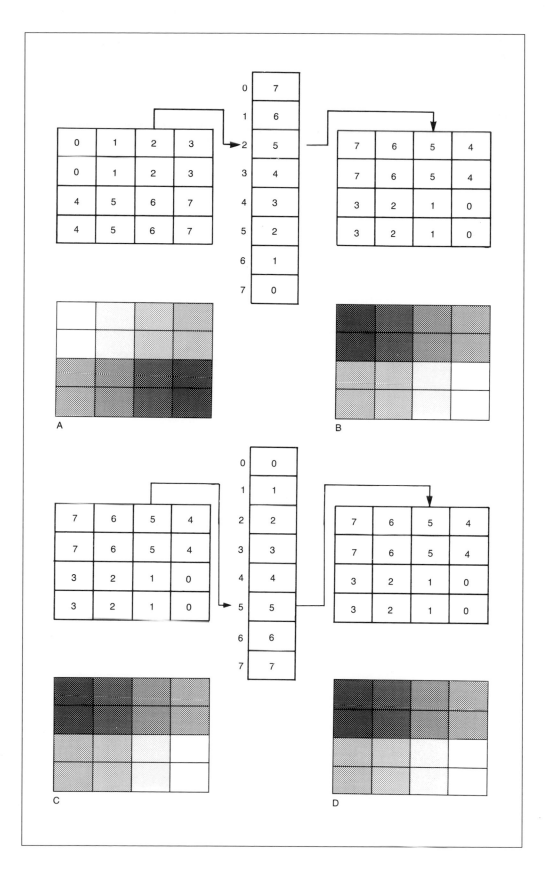

5-15. Modifying bitmap versus modifying palette. In the top illustration, a look-up table translates the original image into its negative. In the bottom, the original image has been modified to incorporate the result of the look-up table manipulation. This image must now be read into an identity look-up table if it is to be output as a negative.

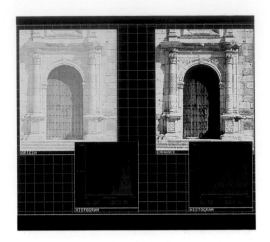

5-16. In the image on the left, most details are lost in shadows; very few of the pixels are dark grays. By distributing the pixels more evenly along the histogram—adjusting contrast—we can expand the dynamic range of the look-up table. The middle-gray values are spread out in the range of the highlights and blacks, increasing the visibility of the image (right). (Courtesy of the University of Massachusetts.)

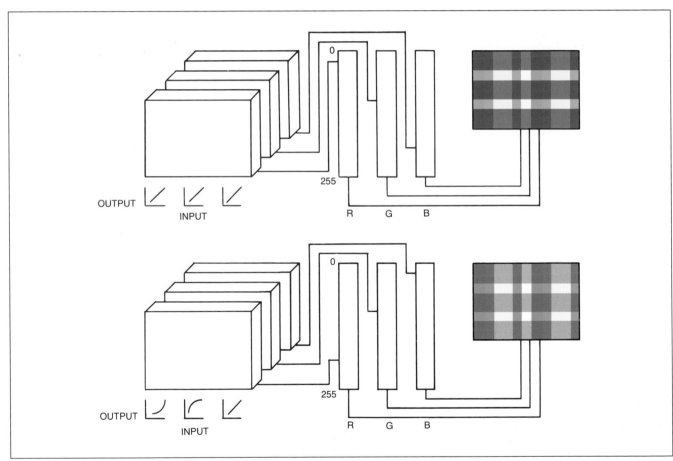

5-17. Shown here is the original image to be corrected. Each set of bitplanes points to one column in the look-up table. The output of the look-up table controls the RGB values on the monitor. A line graph depicts the relation between input and output. Because each look-up table is an identity table, the lines are straight. By altering the contents of the look-up tables, the linear color relationships can be changed so the intensity values of the original image are converted to new values that alter the color balance.

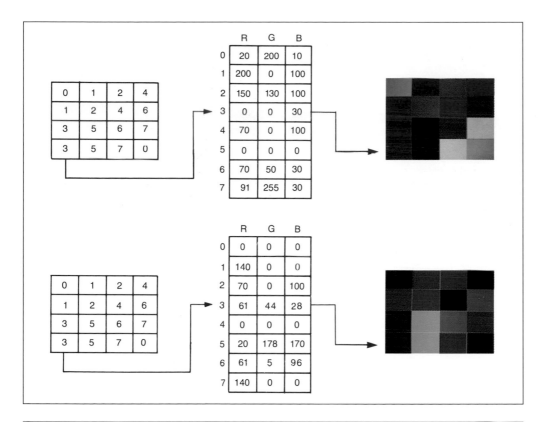

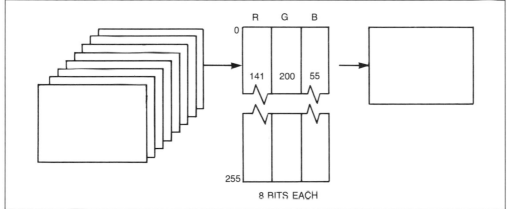

5-18. An image created with color codes and two color look-up tables. The image is colored by indexing each color code into a row in the look-up table and then reading and displaying the corresponding red, green, and blue values. The two look-up tables, or palettes, each define a unique set of color combinations. Displaying an image with alternate palettes is the software equivalent of printing a silkscreen with different color combinations.

5-19. In a system with eight bitplanes of memory, there are 256 possible color codes, and any of the 256 different rows in a look-up table can be indexed. Since each of those rows can contain an eight-bit value for red, green, and blue, the system at large can display 16 million different colors, though it can display only 256 of them at once.

graphic arts industries, such as Pantone numbers in printing, color names in painting, and Wratten numbers for filters. The strategy in all of these cases is to identify a color by a name or number, then use a look-up table to specify the mix of ingredients.

In a computer system a color code is a number stored in a pixel that in turn points to a look-up table containing the actual RGB color. This look-up table has three columns, containing red, green, and blue color values (fig. 5-18), and it has as many rows as there are color codes.

Look-up tables expand the capability of frame buffers with only a few bitplanes of memory, because extra columns can be added to the table to provide a limited number of full colors (fig. 5-19). Because the pixel color code points to a row in the look-up table, and thus to an RGB triplet, a single color may be interactively mixed. When colors in the look-up table are manipulated, all occurrences of that color on the screen are affected, because all the values pointing to that color are being translated in the look-up table.

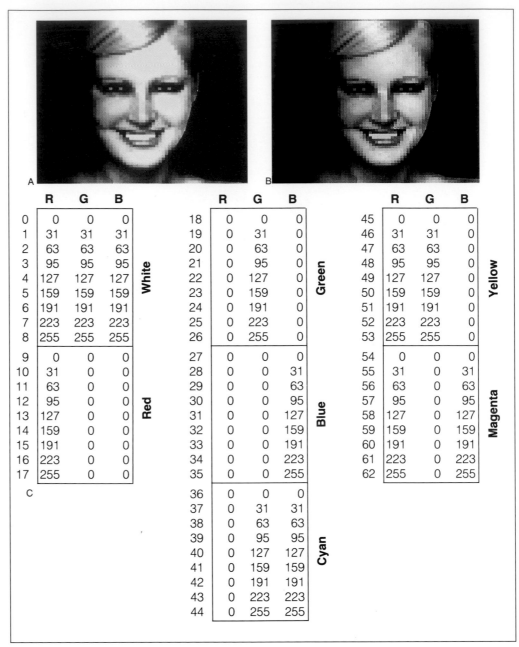

#	R	G	B		#	R	G	B		#	R	G	B	
0	0	0	0	White	18	0	0	0	Green	45	0	0	0	Yellow
1	31	31	31		19	0	31	0		46	31	31	0	
2	63	63	63		20	0	63	0		47	63	63	0	
3	95	95	95		21	0	95	0		48	95	95	0	
4	127	127	127		22	0	127	0		49	127	127	0	
5	159	159	159		23	0	159	0		50	159	159	0	
6	191	191	191		24	0	191	0		51	191	191	0	
7	223	223	223		25	0	223	0		52	223	223	0	
8	255	255	255		26	0	255	0		53	255	255	0	
9	0	0	0	Red	27	0	0	0	Blue	54	0	0	0	Magenta
10	31	0	0		28	0	0	31		55	31	0	31	
11	63	0	0		29	0	0	63		56	63	0	63	
12	95	0	0		30	0	0	95		57	95	0	95	
13	127	0	0		31	0	0	127		58	127	0	127	
14	159	0	0		32	0	0	159		59	159	0	159	
15	191	0	0		33	0	0	191		60	191	0	191	
16	223	0	0		34	0	0	223		61	223	0	223	
17	255	0	0		35	0	0	255		62	255	0	255	
					36	0	0	0	Cyan					
					37	0	31	31						
					38	0	63	63						
					39	0	95	95						
					40	0	127	127						
					41	0	159	159						
					42	0	191	191						
					43	0	223	223						
					44	0	255	255						

5-20. The illustration shows an original black-and-white image (A) containing nine gray levels, ranging from black to white. The nine levels are stored in an eight-bit (256-level) frame buffer and point to rows zero through eight in a special look-up table (C). The "color values" in these rows depict a range of intensities from black to white. The look-up table continues with additional colors, each with nine intensity levels. For example, look-up table positions nine through seventeen contain a full range of reds from dark red to a fully saturated red. Other sections contain a range of blues, greens, cyans, yellows, and magentas. The colors do not have to be primaries or secondaries, each must simply have an equal range of intensity levels. Tinting the picture (B) involves substituting pointers in the image. Thus, to tint a part of the image that is 50 percent gray to the corresponding 50 percent red, the program replaces all pixels with a value of four (the look-up table pointer for medium gray) with a value of thirteen, the pointer to medium red. (Courtesy of Digital Effects Inc.)

Tint Color

Tint color, created with a special look-up table, simulates the technique of coloring black-and-white photographs by painting over them with a color wash.

Tint coloring begins by quantifying a digitized black-and-white image with a limited number of luminance values. A special look-up table is then constructed that contains this same number of limited values, but in ranges of color as well as black-and-white (fig. 5-20). The process of tinting the picture replaces the pixel value in the image with a corresponding pointer to the look-up table value for a different color and the same intensity. Thus, to tint a part of the image that is 50 percent gray to the corresponding 50 percent red, the program replaces all pixel values pointing to medium gray with pixel values pointing to medium red.

Tint color can be used in many different configurations. A 256-row by 3-column look-up table can have sixteen levels of gray and sixteen different colors, or eight levels of gray and thirty-two different colors, or sixty-four levels of gray and four different colors, and so forth.

Pseudocolor

Pseudocolor is similar to posterization and is another effect that can be simulated with look-up tables. Each pixel intensity value is pointed to a red, green, and blue color triplet. Pseudocolor is really a variation on color codes, except that the bitmap image actually has luminance information, not just color numbers (fig. 5-21). The visual effect of pseudocolor is contour areas of color in what was originally a black-and-white image, either for a graphic effect or to make them more comprehensible. The use of pseudocolor is not limited to pixel matrices of luminance, however, and is also used to view matrices of zels and voxels, coloring them according to their depth or density. Pseudocolor is usually interactively controlled and is an incisive tool.

Dithered Color

Dithering is a technique used to maintain the total color information of an image while representing it with fewer colors; it is especially useful when displaying full-color pictures on displays with only eight or ten bits per pixel—for example, only three bits each for red, green, and blue, as opposed to eight bits each in an image with high color resolution.

5-21. Pseudocolor assigns colors to a continuous-tone image. (Courtesy of Digital Effects Inc. and Andrea D'Amico.)

5-22. Dithered color. (Courtesy of Digital Effects

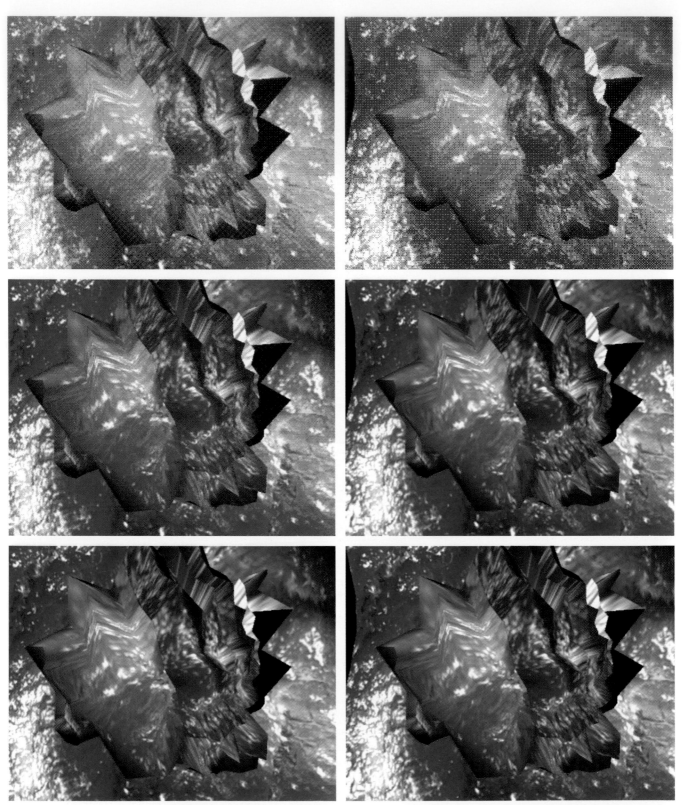

5-23. Color resolution variations of a digital image are shown. From left to right, top to bottom, the resolutions are 2, 4, 8, 16, 24, and 32 bits. (*Second Torso and Crystal* courtesy of Isaac Victor Kerlow.

The difference between a low- and high-resolution color space is not the dynamic range of the colors from brightest to darkest, but the number of intermediate values. Dithering compensates for the fewer number of colors first by approximating the high-resolution pixel with a low-resolution one, and by adding any surplus or deficit color into the adjacent pixel when it is computed. Thus, while the number of different colors in the image has been substantially reduced, the total representation of color in the picture is equal to the total color overall at high resolution (fig. 5-22).

COLOR CALIBRATION AND MATCHING

Because there are so many different color spaces, so many different technologies to create color hard and soft copy, and because the eye is so sensitive, color fidelity is a critical issue in computer graphics.

Color Resolution Requirements

The exact number of colors used to represent a picture can range from two (black and white) to the millions (fig. 5-23). Low-resolution full-color schemes that use eight bits (one byte) per pixel often assign three bits for red, three bits for green, and two bits for blue. Ten-bit-per-pixel approximations often use three bits for red, four bits for green, and three bits for blue. Green is given more color resolution because it provides the most luminance information to the eye; blue is less easily perceived, especially in the subtle flesh tones.

Low-resolution HLS gamuts concentrate more bits into luminance than hue or saturation, a matter somewhat analogous to NTSC color television. One scenario might reserve six bits for luminance and two bits each for hue and saturation.

The most common high-resolution color uses **one-byte-per-pixel-per-primary.** This allows for 256 intensity levels in each of three primaries, or a total color spectrum in excess of sixteen million colors (2^{24}).

CMY to RGB

$$\begin{bmatrix} C \\ M \\ Y \end{bmatrix} - \begin{bmatrix} 1 \\ 1 \\ 1 \end{bmatrix} = \begin{bmatrix} R \\ G \\ B \end{bmatrix}$$

RGB to CMY

$$\begin{bmatrix} R \\ G \\ B \end{bmatrix} - \begin{bmatrix} 1 \\ 1 \\ 1 \end{bmatrix} = \begin{bmatrix} C \\ M \\ Y \end{bmatrix}$$

5-24. Simple color gamut conversion formulas convert between RGB and CYM. 1 1 1 represents white in the RGB color system and black in CMY. In the example, green subtracts magenta from reflected white light.

Resolutions in excess of twelve bits per primary provide a dynamic range in excess of most modern output media, including photography, video, and offset printing, but less than the dynamic range of the eye or daylight.

Color Conversions and Matching

Color conversion software respecifies one color gamut into another; this is often a significant challenge. Media that involve emitted additive light—like television—are best commanded using additive colors, whereas systems that are subtractive—like print—are best commanded using subtractive colors. Color gamuts such as RGB, CYM, and HLS are easily converted from one into another using programs that allow an artist to work with alternate color gamuts (fig. 5-24). But not all conversions between color spaces are reversible without some loss of information (component to composite video color, for example).

A related problem is that different output media may have unique subsets of a total color space, as with a printer or video. **Color-matching** software addresses

5-25. Color-matching software allows the color domain of a specific peripheral to be compared to an idealized color space. Only the area inside the curved space is visible by the human eye.

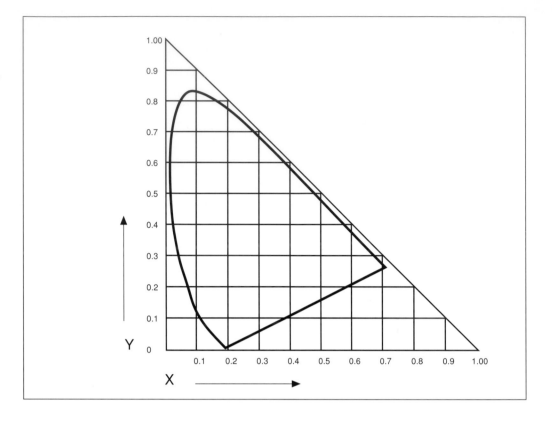

5-26. Pantone color-matching software displays a Pantone swatch on the CRT screen. A designer is provided with the best representation of the printing ink mixture on the screen and can also refer to a physical Pantone book for comparison. (Adapted from the Pantone dialog box in the Quark Xpress program.)

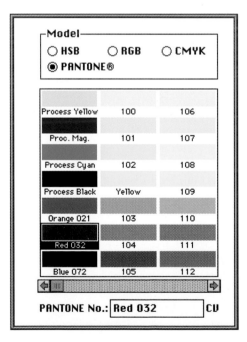

these problems and enables a user to pick colors in one color gamut that will be used in a different gamut, such as picking colors on a CRT screen that will appear in a printed brochure. One tool relates the displayable colors of the computer monitor to the producible color gamut of different output devices and shows the range of allowable colors inside an area (fig 5-25). Color-matching systems like Pantone display swatches of color on the CRT that correspond to their printed blends of mixed inks (fig. 5-26).

Digital standards, which define portable color spaces that are device- and media-independent, are expected to help solve the current limitations and provide greater integration of the production process across different media.

Color Calibration

Color calibration involves aligning a particular scanner, monitor, or hard copy output device to a standard color gamut. All the color correction and matching software in the world won't help adjust the color if the monitor is maladjusted. Scanners are calibrated by scanning reference images, such as a step chart of gray values, patches of well-defined color, and a human face. Printers are calibrated by outputting reference images, and then adjusting the hardware or lookup tables to compensate. Television monitors are calibrated by displaying color bars (fig. 5-27) and adjusting the position of the reference colors on a vectorscope (fig. 5-28). The color bars are also essential to include with any video that is recorded from the computer, because they in turn provide a calibration reference for adjusting a videotape recorder or television monitor on subsequent playback. A more sophisticated method of calibrating a monitor is to attach a sensor to the monitor, and then display a set of reference color patches that it senses. The software then adjusts the frame buffer lookup tables in a closed feedback loop to optimize the color fidelity (fig. 5-29).

	GREY	YELLOW	CYAN	GREEN	MAGENTA	RED	BLUE
R	.7	.7	0	0	.7	.7	0
G	.7	.7	.7	.7	0	0	0
B	.7	0	.7	0	.7	0	.7
	0	1	0				
	0	1	0				
	.4	1	.4				

5-27. Television color bars are a standard set of color stripes defined for color television calibration. This illustration shows the numerical values of the various colors on a scale of 0 to 1. Note the colors are not fully saturated! Multiply values by 255 and round to convert to integer.

5-28. A video signal is calibrated by examining the color bars as they appear on a vectorscope. The vectorscope is laid out like a color wheel, with hues around the circumference and saturation on the radius. The signal is adjusted so that the six primary colors fall into the six target rectangles on the screen. (Photograph of Tektronix vectorscope courtesy of Tektronix Inc.)

5-29. The calibration sensor reads the luminance of the screen and a software program compares the value read to the ideal value, and, if necessary, adjusts the screen. (Scanmatch courtesy of Super-Mac Technology Inc.)

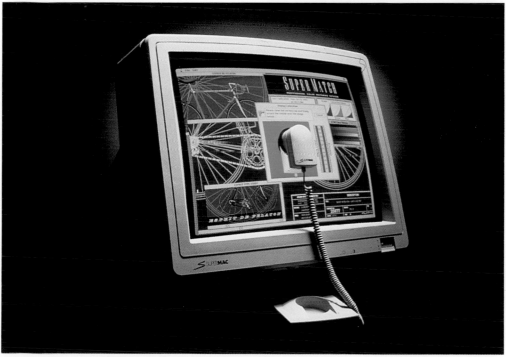

6-0. Digitized images enable artists to combine picture fragments together to improve composition, reorganize images, and create new realities. (Courtesy of Ryszard Horowitz and R/GA Print.)

TWO-DIMENSIONAL IMAGING PROCESSES

MONADIC IMAGE PROCESSES
POINT TO PIXEL TECHNIQUES
DYADIC IMAGE PROCESSES
LOCAL AND GLOBAL OPERATORS
IMAGE ENHANCEMENT
COMPUTER VISION AND IMAGE ANALYSIS

Image-processing techniques are procedures that modify images, both to enhance their visibility and to creatively alter them. Images can be photographic in origin and represent a pixel array of intensity values. They can also be synthetically generated and approximate a photographic perspective.

Bitmaps can represent natural measurements with no intensity variations; zels or a cross section of CAT scan voxels are two examples (fig. 6-1). Images may even be graphs of mathematical equations plotted in a two-dimensional space. The image is really the solution space, the contour of the equation (fig. 6-2).

Image-processing systems manipulate images rather than create them. An image to be processed is first digitized by sampling its levels of brightness, then storing them as pixels in a bitmap. (Television cameras, flying spot scanners, and laser drum scanners all can digitize images, as is discussed in chapter 3.) Image processing is often viewed interactively on soft copy displays.

6-1. A CAT scan cross section of the brain. The picture is pseudocolored so that different densities become different colors. It thus looks photographic, though it is not. (Courtesy of Digital Effects Inc.)

MONADIC IMAGE PROCESSES

Monadic image processes, functions with one input and one output image, include the traditional photographic procedures of sizing, cropping, flipping, repositioning, and mapping. The most primitive image operation, the basic method for altering a picture, is the pixel *read* and *write.* This involves reading a pixel from the frame buffer memory, modifying its contents in the CPU, and writing the new value either back into the same frame buffer memory, or into a second one (fig. 6-3).

Some monadic image processes may be implemented as part of the frame buffer hardware. These modify the display but do not permanently alter the frame buffer memory. Look-up tables are one such feature and are discussed at length in chapter 5.

Scroll, Scale, Rotation

Scroll is the translation of the image left or right, up or down. It is computationally performed by reading a pixel and then displaying it at a different XY screen position. This is usually done with special hardware scroll registers, one for the horizontal offset and one for the vertical displacement. The part of the scrolled picture offset is usually wrapped around the image plane (fig. 6-4).

Scrolling is also used to create *pattern repeats,* repetitive areas that form a continuum (fig. 6-5). Standard repeats include half and full drops, and flips.

Scaling enlarges or reduces the number of pixels that define an image in order to change its size. Scalings can be either discrete, even pixel quantities, or continuous.

Scaling a picture larger by an integer amount involves simple pixel replication, since there is no new information to be added (fig. 6-6). But scaling a picture smaller by integers is not as easy. In a picture that is reduced by one-fourth its pixels, selecting every other pixel would create aliasing, because the final image would only incorporate one-fourth the information of the original picture (fig. 6-7). A proper solution is to average groups of four pixels together and store the average in the remaining pixel

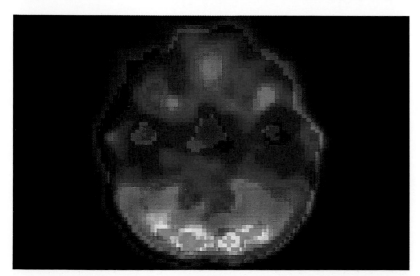

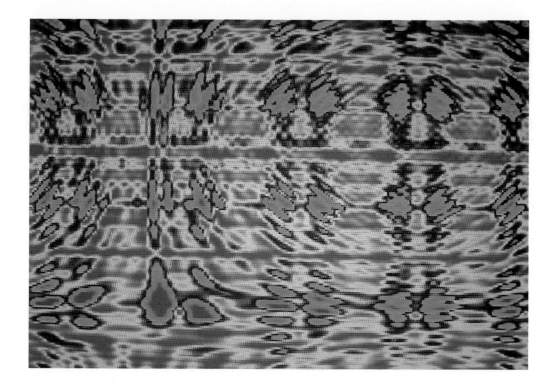

6-2. Images can represent the contour of equations in two-dimensional space. (Courtesy of Don Leich.)

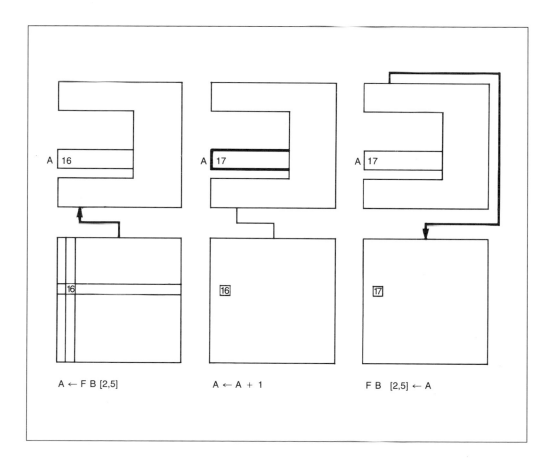

A ← F B [2,5]   A ← A + 1   F B [2,5] ← A

6-3. In this image the numerical value (16) contained in frame buffer location (2, 5) is *read* into main memory. The CPU then performs an operation and *modifies* it, in this case increasing it by one. Finally, the new value (17) is *written* back onto the frame buffer.

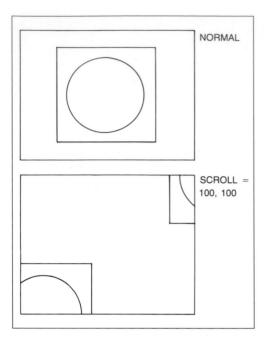

NORMAL

SCROLL = 100, 100

Scaling is often accomplished using hardware scale registers that specify the number of times the pixel is to be replicated in the X and Y directions on the screen. Scale registers control how the hardware indexes the picture when it displays it on the monitor; they do not actually affect the bitmap memory. If a bitmap is scaled up by showing each pixel four times using a hardware scale register, it can be scaled back to the original. But if the image is altered, the higher-resolution data is gone and cannot be recovered (fig. 6-10).

Scaling registers are often called *zoom* registers, but strictly speaking, a zoom pertains to the focal length of a lens. Although it appears to enlarge the picture, a zoom actually narrows the field of view; it is not a two-dimensional effect. Scroll and scale registers may be used together for many purposes, including animation (fig. 6-11) and the positioning and cropping of pictures.

Rotation is the pivoting of an image about a central point, usually the origin of the coordinate system (fig. 6-12). It is usually continuous and expressed as a positive or negative angle along with the address of a pixel around which the rotation should occur. Hardware rotation also exists, although it sometimes only rotates a picture in even multiples of 90 degrees.

Flips are 90-degree and 180-degree rotations that reorient the picture and provide mirror views. Flips can transpose the left side to right, the top to bottom, and one corner to the other that is diagonally opposite (fig. 6-13). *Three-axis rotation* allows an image to be pivoted anywhere in space (see chapter 7).

Image Warping and Mapping

Image warping and mapping are techniques for stretching images in nonlinear ways, much as if the image were rubber. *Image warping* is two-dimensional and is accomplished by either mathematically distorting the image (fig. 6-14) or by identifying key pixels in an image

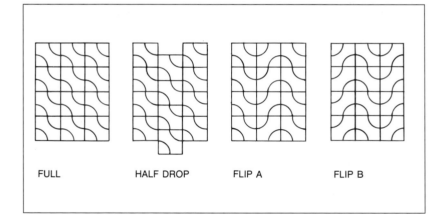

FULL   HALF DROP   FLIP A   FLIP B

6-5. Many different patterns can be created by manipulating simple modules. Basic manipulations include constant repetition at regular intervals, repetition at offset intervals, and flipping.

(fig. 6-8). This would eliminate aliasing, and although the image is only one-fourth the spatial resolution, it preserves the total luminance information.

Enlarging and reducing by noninteger amounts is also accomplished by averaging. Each pixel is treated as if it were a tiny area, a floating point domain. When the scaling process calculates averages it averages not only whole pixels but parts of pixels as well (fig. 6-9). Again, this is a technique that retains total luminance information, but changes spatial resolution.

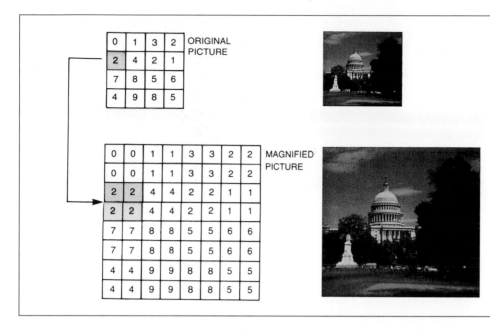

6-6. Scaling, 2 × integer enlargement—each pixel in the input image is repeated four times. A 3 × scaling would repeat each pixel nine times. (Courtesy of Spatial Data Systems, Inc.; a DBA Systems Company.)

ORIGINAL PICTURE

MAGNIFIED PICTURE

MAGNIFIED PICTURE

1	2	5	6	9	10	13	15
3	4	7	8	11	12	14	16
2	3	7	8	10	11	15	16
5	6	9	10	11	12	13	14
4	5	6	7	11	12	13	15
1	2	8	9	13	14	15	16
3	4	5	6	9	10	14	15
2	3	4	5	7	8	9	10

6-7. Integer reduction with point sampling. Scaling down the original picture by half will actually reduce the number of original pixels by three-fourths. In this example, the original image (sixty-four pixels) was reduced by half and only one-fourth of the original number of pixels remained (sixteen pixels).

ORIGINAL PICTURE

1	5	9	13
2	7	10	15
4	6	11	13
3	5	9	14

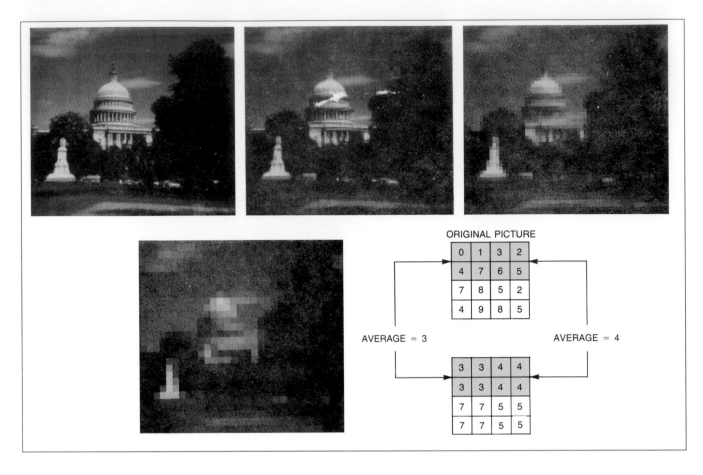

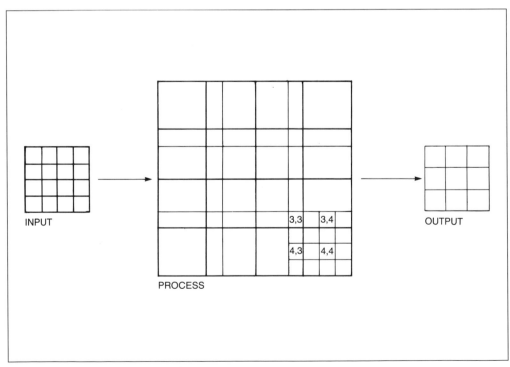

6-8. Integer reduction with image averaging. The diagram shows a 2 × 2 average. The images illustrate averages at different factors of reduction. (Courtesy of Spatial Data Systems, Inc.; a DBA Systems Company.)

6-9. Scaling with continuous reduction. The input picture is a 4 × 4 matrix, the output picture is a 3 × 3 matrix. Each new resultant pixel contains parts of one or more pixels from the original image. For example, the output pixel (3, 3) is a composite of input pixels 3, 3; 3, 4; 4, 3; 4, 4.

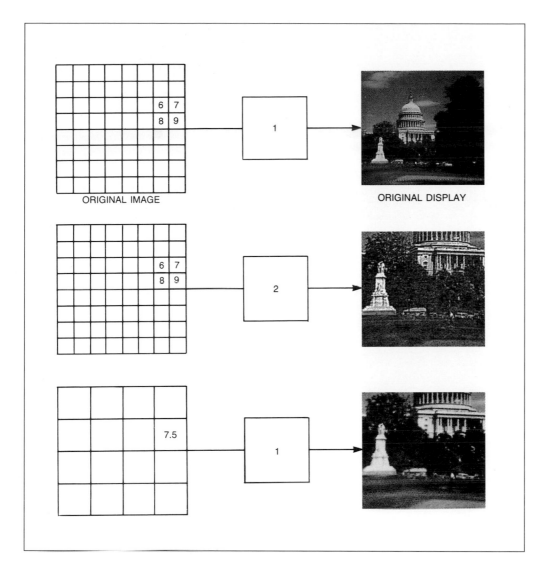

ORIGINAL IMAGE

ORIGINAL DISPLAY

6-10. Hardware and software scaling. The top row illustrates a bitmap and the corresponding picture, with the scaling registers set to identity, or one. The scale registers in the center row are equal to two, and the display of the picture is enlarged 200 percent, although the data remains untouched. On the other hand, if the bitplane itself has been enlarged then the finer resolution of the data would have been lost, and the scale registers are set to identity (bottom row). (Courtesy of Spatial Data Systems, Inc.; a DBA Systems Company.)

associated with specific features (fig. 6-15). Biologists use warping techniques to study growth and evolutionary patterns in an organism, and plastic surgeons use the technique to study aging.

Image mapping is a similar technique that wraps two-dimensional pixel arrays around the surface of three-dimensional objects in perspective. Image mapping is discussed in detail in chapter 7.

POINT TO PIXEL TECHNIQUES

Line Representation

On bitmap displays lines are represented as a sequence of adjacent pixels. Horizontal or vertical lines are represented by rows or columns of pixels, but diagonal lines are represented by a staircase of pixels, and the steepness

6-11. The picture contains sixteen subframes, each 128 pixels square. Each sub-frame contains one frame of action in a real-time cycle sixteen frames long. The CPU can quickly change the address of the scroll and zoom register, thus cycling all the subpictures to a zoomed-up, full-screen animation. The resolution admittedly is rather coarse, but the animation contains all action. (Animated by Eric Ladd. Courtesy of Omnibus Computer Graphics Center.)

6-12. A rotation of 45 degrees about the center of the picture. (Courtesy of Spatial Data Systems, Inc.; a DBA Systems Company.)

6-13. New images can be obtained by flipping the original image (top left) three ways: from left to right, from top to bottom, and across the diagonal.

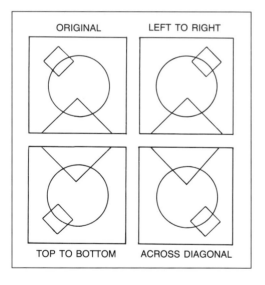

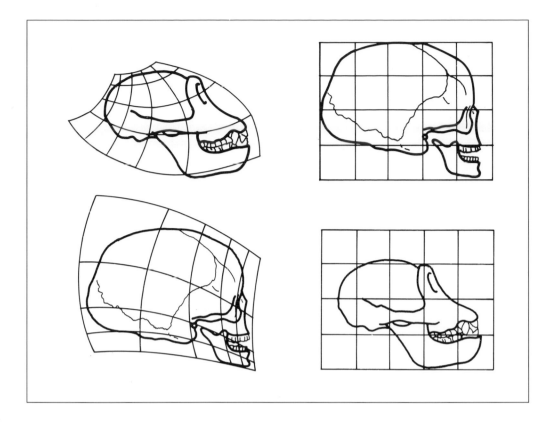

6-14. This classical illustration, from D'Arcy Thompson's *On Growth and Form*, suggests a continuity in the evolution of a chimpanzee's skull to that of a man, which may be simulated by mathematically warping the coordinate system of one to the other.

6-15. Warping aligns two or more similar images. The line drawing depicts three different faces; the grid lines, calculated by digitizing key features on each face (nose, mouth, chin, and face contour, for example), show the warping necessary to transform each face to the final composite below. The photograph is a composite image of twelve faces (six men and six women). (Photo courtesy of Nancy Burson.)

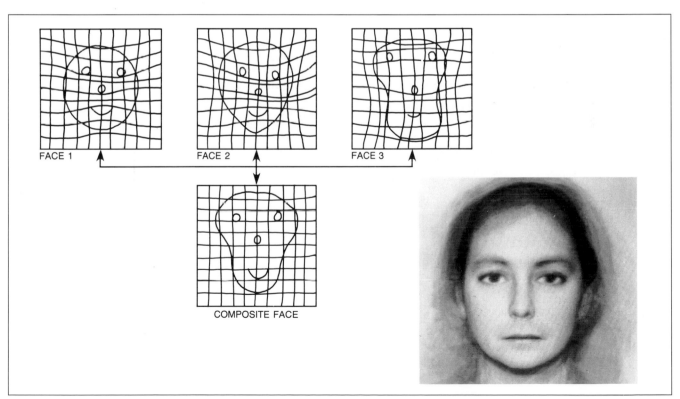

FACE 1 FACE 2 FACE 3

COMPOSITE FACE

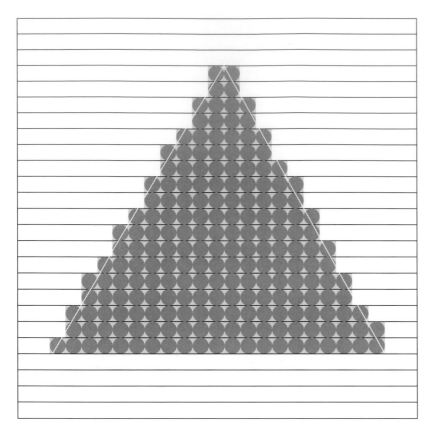

Area Fill Methods

Areas are shapes bounded either by vectors or pixels. Scan conversions and fills are two methods used in computer graphics to create areas. **Scan conversion** converts a polygon area, bounded by vectors, into a series of horizontal lines usually represented by pixels. Scan conversion techniques work with real, floating point numbers. However, if we scan convert a polygon into pixel memory, the process essentially involves integer numbers, since there is a one-to-one correspondence between the number of scan lines and the resolution of the bitmap (fig. 6-16). Many algorithms perform this function, some with anti-aliased edges.

A **fill** is similar to a scan conversion in that it converts the pixels within a boundary to a certain intensity value or number. The boundary is defined by pixels already existing in bitplane memory; furthermore, the boundary must completely surround the area to be filled (fig. 6-17).

Both methods are found in illustration and paint systems. The scan convert is used to draw solid shapes, whereas the fill is used to change the value of an already-existing patch of equal intensity pixels on a screen.

Halftoning

Most two-dimensional pixel images that have a wide luminance range require several bitplanes to contain the luminance values of each pixel. An image with 256 light-intensity levels, for example, requires eight bitplanes. The process of converting a two-dimensional image with a wide range of luminance values to a matrix containing only black-and-white is known as **halftoning.** This process is very similar to the conversion of photographs to a halftone (black-and-white) screen for printing.

Halftoning represents different luminance values not as an array of pixels of constant area and varying intensity, but

6-16. A scan conversion algorithm converts the outline of a triangle (outlined in white) into a series of horizontal lines (light gray) described by pixels (dark gray). There are twenty-five scan lines in the drawing from top to bottom; these are the horizontal white areas between the black lines; in other words, the scan lines have a height equal to the diameter of the pixels. The scan conversion algorithm determines the left and right edge of a polygon at each scan line and draws a parallel horizontal line from the left to right edge. These horizontal lines can be converted to pixels and represented on a bitmap display.

of the staircase is analogous to the steepness of the line.

The conversion from a line defined by its two end points into pixels is performed on the computer with a program called a **digital differential algorithm (DDA).** Several techniques for doing this implement the program in hardware. Unfortunately, if the lines are represented with only one bit per pixel, they appear aliased.

In bitmap memories that contain more than one bit per pixel, lines and edges can be anti-aliased using pixels with shades of gray adjacent to the completely dark pixels that make up the main body of the line. The pixel is really a small square of area, and it is intensified in direct proportion to what percentage of it is intersected by the line. The resulting line appears smoother and more continuous (see fig. 1-45).

as an array with constant intensity (black/white) and varying area. For an image to be "halftoned," a higher spatial resolution matrix is needed, that is, more pixels in X and Y. The intensity information of each pixel is converted to and contained in several pixels. For example, a pixel with a low intensity will be equivalent to a halftone array with very few pixels turned on; a pixel with a very high intensity (white) will turn on many of the pixels in the halftone array (fig. 6-18).

6-17. A flood algorithm changes the value of all connected pixels that are of identical color or intensity.

DYADIC IMAGE PROCESSES

A dyadic image process involves two input images and one resultant image. The resultant image consists either of one image partly overlaying another, or of the two images combined.

Matte Compositing

Matting is a process used to lay one image over another. (In the television industry, mattes are called *keys;* in the print industry they are called *holdbacks* and *knockouts.*) Two input bitmaps include elements to be composited, such as a set of bitplanes defining a background and a set defining a foreground. A third bitplane contains the **matte,** or logical operator, which specifies which pixels from each image will be used to form the composited image.

A high-contrast matte contains only zeros and ones; the output is determined on an either/or basis (fig. 6-19). Self-mattes, or **keys,** are mattes that are shaped by the foreground object. The foreground components are placed against a flat field of black or of color, often a bright blue, which is easily referenced by the computer, that replaces the background color pixels with black pixels. Next, all the remaining pixels, depicting the objects in the foreground, are changed to white, producing a high-contrast matte (fig. 6-20). The two

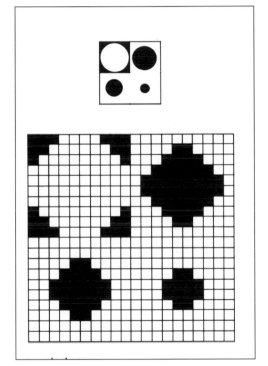

6-18. A very bright pixel is represented by many pixels in the higher spatial frequency halftone array; a dim pixel is approximated by a smaller area. In the figure there are 10 × 10 subpixels in the halftone array for each pixel; therefore, 100 levels of gray are possible.

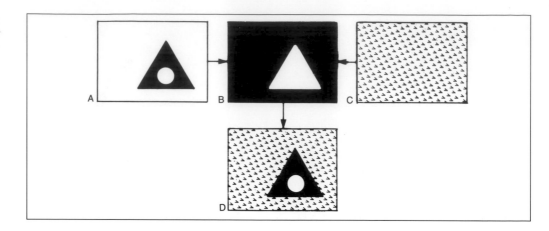

6-19. This figure shows foreground and background elements (A, C), the matte (B), and the final composite (D). For each zero pixel in the matte, the resultant pixel is taken from the background; for each one pixel in the matte the resultant pixel is taken from the foreground.

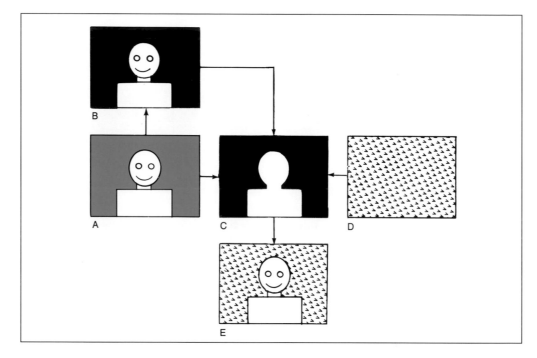

6-20. Creating a key matte. The foreground, here a headshot, is placed in front of a blue background (A). The blue background is converted to black (B) and all other colors become white, creating a matte (C). The original foreground image is then composited with a new background (D), yielding a composite (E).

images are then composited in the manner just described (see fig. 6-19). Given two input images, each of which could self-matte, there are twelve ways the images could be composited (fig. 6-21).

Continuous contrast mattes represent not high-contrast black-and-white, but continuous gradation of gray (6-22), often eight bits deep and stored in an **alpha channel,** a fourth image channel along with RGB. Continuous contrast mattes permit two images to be blended and for transparent objects, like a glass of water, to be matted over a back-

ground. When the inputs are composited, instead of each resultant pixel being from either one image or the other, the matte determines a blend of the two at each pixel. The blend, obviously, is defined as the percentage of gray in each matte pixel.

Continuous contrast mattes allow objects with soft edges or objects in motion to be combined without hard matte lines dividing the foreground and background. Hair, for example, has a soft, fuzzy edge that is difficult to matte without some degree of quantization to

OPERATION

A   A IN B   A ATOP B

B   B IN A   B ATOP A

A OVER B   A OUT B   A XOR B

B OVER A   B OUT A   CLEAR

6-21. Compositing operators illustrate all possible combinations between images.

A

B

C

D

6-22. Continuous-tone mattes are employed in film and video as well as digital media. In this illustration, the background is a color sea scene (A); the foreground element is a transparent glass placed in front of a black background (B). A continuous-tone matte is formed next (C). The foreground and background images are then composited (D) by weighting their proportions according to the variable density matte. (Courtesy of Steve Borowski and R. Globus, Globus Brothers Studios.)

6-23. Static matte selections.

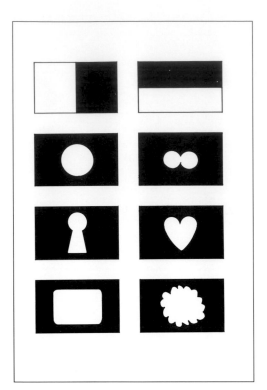

determine what is and is not part of the hair, but when the matte has a degree of transparency to it, the soft edges of the foreground hair blend into the background.

Static mattes are often empirically determined, as in a split screen. Here the matte specifies that the left half of the picture is to come from one input image and the right half from another. Mattes can be rectangular, square, triangular, or be shaped like binoculars, keyholes, or hearts (fig. 6-23). They can also effectively crop a picture—essentially the part of the image that corresponds to the black pixels in the matte is not reproduced.

Overlays are another form of static mattes used for field guides, safety grids, registration (fig. 6-24). Overlays can also be implemented with special look-up tables and as an extra bitplane that can be turned on and off by the graphic artist.

6-24. A twelve-field overlay is used to locate objects in images. A safety grid determines the limits in which to place an image or title for film projection or television broadcasting. Registration marks are used to match different images. Counting reticules are used to count sample elements in the image.

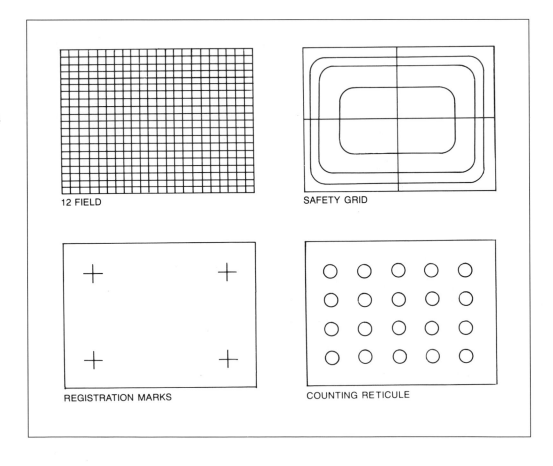

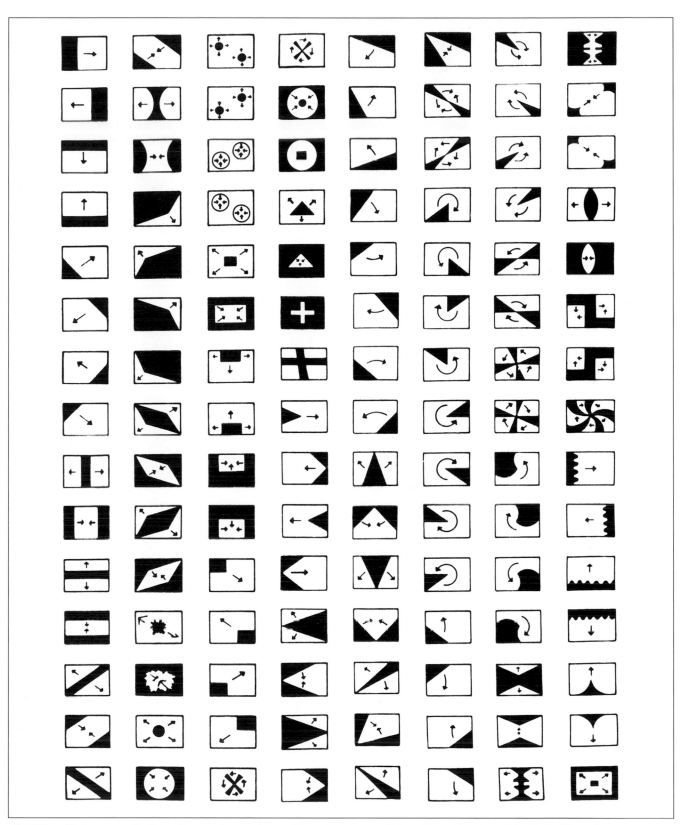

6-25. Wipe effects are used in film, video, and computer graphic systems to smooth transitions. (Courtesy of the Optical House.)

6-26. The diagram shows a virtual switching system where an input image and a black field are combined at different proportions with a fade slider that is operated at a certain speed (number of frames/length of time). The resulting image will be equal to the input image multiplied by the fade factor: RESULT ← (FADE VALUE × INPUT).

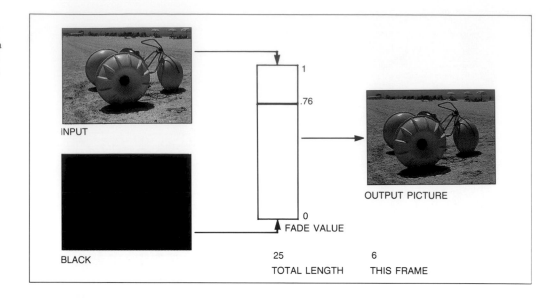

6-27. The dissolve from input image A to B is controlled with a dissolve slider. The final result is expressed as: RESULT ← (INPUT A × DISSOLVE FACTOR) + (INPUT B × (1 − DISSOLVE FACTOR)). (Provided by Isaac V. Kerlow.)

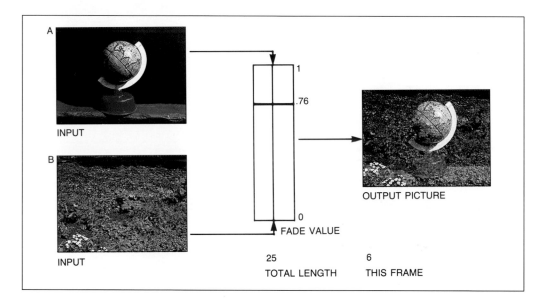

Traveling mattes are sequences of mattes applied to a series of frames and are used in motion pictures and television. Animated traveling mattes or ***wipes*** are used to create a transition between two scenes (fig. 6-25). A wipe is identified by a name or number and its duration. Traveling mattes can also be prepared from a sequence of live action, where the foreground self-keys the background.

Matting and compositing processes that involve more than two input images are reduced to a sequence of individual composites, each with two inputs, a matte, and an output. One of the main advantages of computer graphics methods is that there is no generation loss or image degradation through the succession of composites.

Fades, Dissolves, Double Exposures

Fades, dissolves, and double exposures are all operations between pairs of digital images that are arithmetically combined. (Arithmetic operations are different from logical operations in that

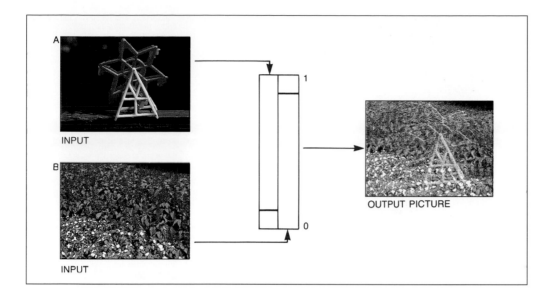

**6-28. Double exposure.
(Provided by Isaac V.
Kerlow.)**

A

INPUT

B

INPUT

1

0

OUTPUT PICTURE

each resultant pixel is an arithmetic combination of two input pixels, rather than a logical choice between them.) A *fade* is a traditional arithmetic operation in which a variable between zero and one is multiplied by each pixel, producing less exposure as a result (fig. 6-26). A fade usually occurs across a sequence of frames, causing them to become black.

A *dissolve* is actually two fades combined; an image fading out is added to the image fading in (fig. 6-27), creating a transition between the shots. Fades and dissolves are nonlinear; the manner by which the individual increments are determined is discussed in chapter 7.

Another arithmetic operation, the *double exposure (DX)*, combines two images (fig. 6-28). If the dynamic range of the output image, that is, the number of luminance levels between black and white, is equal to the input image, adding the images together would produce very bright, overexposed values, as does shooting two exposures on one frame; a computer, like film, has a finite dynamic range and thus a maximum value beyond which no value may be brighter. A better strategy would be to add the two pictures and divide by two. The resultant image would not overflow the

dynamic range and would appear much the same as a frame in the middle of a dissolve, where the output frame has one-half the exposure from each incoming scene. The total exposure will not exceed the total brightness permitted in the medium.

Double exposures work well to superimpose type and logos over backgrounds. The type must be completely white in order to burn out, or double expose, any background image.

Double exposures are used to make *glows,* a double exposure with a soft edge, *streaks,* traveling elements that make a motion smear, and *strobes,* which are discrete streaks (fig. 6-29).

Cells and Sprites

Cells are objects built out of polygons and recorded in a display list. *Sprites* are pixel arrays that are smaller than the total area of the picture and function as submodules. Sprites include type characters, brushes, stamps, and cursors. These small pixel arrays vary in size from less than ten squared and one bit deep, to full-color areas hundreds or thousands of pixels square. Sprites may be rectangular as well as square in shape and incorporate transparency as well as luminance information.

6-29. Glows are created by double exposing the recording medium—first with the artwork in focus and then with the artwork diffused. (Courtesy of Animotion.)

6-30. A sprite two bits deep can be three colors and transparent. Like acetate cartoon cells, sprites self-matte the background. The colored bits are overlaid, the zero bits are transparent, and the corresponding pixels on the image are unchanged. Here we see the original sprite and background separately and the overlaid result.

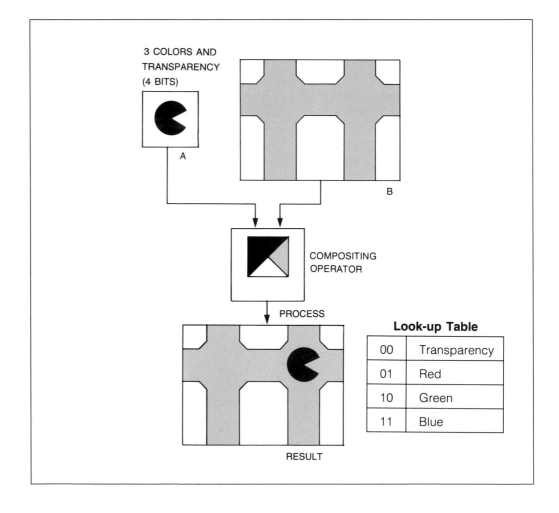

In **dot matrix type,** the raw sprite letter is stored in a character generator chip as a table of zeros and ones. Bitmapped characters are often defined in ROM; they can be plugged in and out of a computer to provide different fonts, characters, sets, and patterns. The letters are indexed by the American Standard Code for Information Interchange (ASCII) code.

In the sprite, the bits of value one are part of the letter; zero bits are transparent. When the sprite is matted over a corresponding set of pixels in an image, the bits in the image that correspond to the ones are made a color, while the zero transparent bits do not alter the image (fig. 6-30).

Cells, because they are stored on a display list, may be repositioned and rescaled interactively and then scan converted and displayed. Sprites too often reside in special memories structured much like frame buffers. Sprites are positioned and sized using registers that specify the XY location on the screen and the size. Sprites can be more flexibly positioned in a graphics system than in a dot matrix character display, which simply shows a fixed number of dot matrix letters per line and a fixed number of lines. Often the sprite location is interactively determined using a graphics peripheral, like a joystick in a video game. This hardware permits the sprite to be positioned anywhere over the image without being written or fixed into the bitmap.

Cursors essentially are cells or sprites that can be moved around on an image and that are controlled by a pen, mouse, or joystick. Because the system knows the location of the cursor, it can identify the object to which it is pointing. Blinking cursors are simply cursors that are alternately displayed and blanked.

Sprites are easily animated and are ideal for creating limited real-time computer animation. First, a cycle of action, such as the cells that animate a PAC-MAN running or the position of talking

☛ **RELATED READING**

Gardner, Martin. "Mathematical Games." *Scientific American* (October 1970, February 1971).

Knowlton, Ken. *EXPLOR*. Murray Hill, NJ: Bell Laboratories, 1974.

lips, is defined as sprites. Second, the cells are defined in sequence (fig. 6-31). The animation is either interactively composed or composed using a scripting system much like an animation sheet, which specifies a sequence of cells and positions. Once the preview is complete, a second process composites the animation, fixes each sprite into the background, then stores the composite image for future playback.

A **brush** is a sprite that can be fixed into the image immediately and is used for painting digital pictures as well as for retouching. Brushes often function in a preview or movable mode, so they may be positioned correctly, and then entered, or fixed into the image (fig. 6-32). Brushes, like sprites in general, can be solid as well as transparent and can paint over images as a wash. A **stamp** is a sprite, or brush, formed by excising a rectangular matrix of pixels from an image. This is then positioned and drawn somewhere else in the picture.

LOCAL AND GLOBAL OPERATORS

An image-processing function is designated either as local or global. This distinction is subtle, and depends on how the resultant image is calculated. **Global operators** are functions applied to each pixel independently of the other pixels in the image. For example, the process of making a negative reads each pixel in the image, uses each in a calculation, and replaces each with a result. Almost all of the processes that we have discussed so far involve global operators.

Local operators are also procedures applied to each pixel, but the result of the calculation incorporates information

6-31. Sprites (or cells) can be animated by displaying them in sequence over the background image. The position of the sprite can be controlled either by the program or with a joystick. In this case, eight sprites represent the shapes of the lips effected by pronouncing different combinations of letters. The sequence of sprites is controlled by a sequence of numbers fed into the computer. (Courtesy of Jan Svochaak and Susan Bickford.)

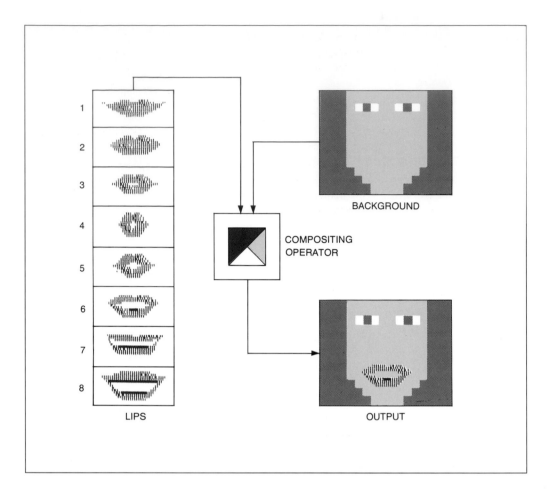

6-32. A *line-drawing brush* can create strokes of varying thicknesses (as used to create the sailor holding the telescope). A *blending brush* mixes the colors of the pixels it overlays (as in the violet waves). An *airbrush* deposits a solid central spot of color, which fans out to transparency. A *stencil* is an area of the screen that cannot be affected by a brush—like a frisket, it allows colors to surround an object without damaging it (as on the boat), protecting it from the blending brush that creates waves. (Courtesy of New York Institute of Technology.)

about the pixels that surround and touch it (fig. 6-33). In a local operation, changes to a pixel are affected by the values of adjacent pixels.

A local operator can be visualized by thinking of a theater audience with people sitting in rows of seats. The occupied seats equal one, and the empty seats zero. The audience is told: "Look to your right and if the seat to your right is empty, move into it." Each member of the audience does this simultaneously, as if it were one iteration of a machine. The people with empty seats to their right move over, while everyone else remains stationary.

Computer language would state that each pixel with a value of one in the bitplane should examine the value of the pixel immediately to its right, and if the value of that pixel is one, do nothing,

but if the value of that pixel is zero, set it to one and set the original pixel to zero (fig. 6-34).

A program called *Life* (fig. 6-35) is one example of a local operator in computer graphics and was invented by John Conley. Another illustration of local operators is the language *Explor*, written by Ken Knowlton of Bell Labs (fig. 6-36). Explor is a collection of FORTRAN subroutines and has been widely circulated as a teaching tool. It also allows artists to define local operators.

Another kind of local operation is **image averaging** (also called *pixelation, block pix, mosaic*), the averaging of small areas of an image to reduce picture resolution (see fig. 6-6). This can be a creative method, one that aggregates areas of pixels into patterns or shapes (fig. 6-37) and at different resolutions in either

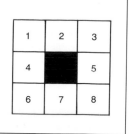

6-33. A pixel and its eight neighbors.

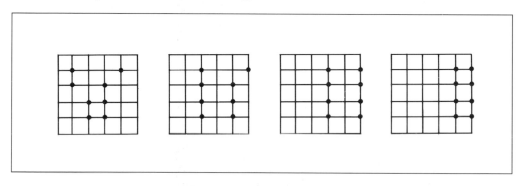

6-34. Local operator animation. Each member of the theater audience changes position depending on surrounding seat availability. Repeating the procedure described in the text eventually stacks everyone to the right of the theater—the result of successive iterations depends on previous ones.

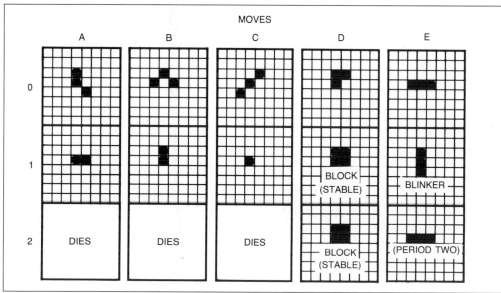

6-35. The game of *Life* is played on a one-bitplane matrix and has three rules for turning bits on and off. The rules are based on neighborhood conditions and simulate the conditions and patterns necessary to create colonies of pixels that are stable, divide, reproduce, and die. The three rules are: (1) every pixel with two or three neighboring pixels survives for the next move; (2) each pixel with four or more neighbors dies from overpopulation, and each with one or no neighbor dies from isolation; (3) each empty cell adjacent to exactly three neighbors will generate a new pixel on it at the next move.

6-36. Ken Knowlton may have been inspired to write *Explor* by his research on growing silicon chip wafers. In Knowlton's model—an example of how pixel graphics can represent things other than images—the bitplane represents a molecular array of silicon and each pixel represents one atom. The pixel value describes how many atoms deep the layer of silicon was (essentially a zel). Growing the crystal begins with a layer that is one atom thick; each atom has a random chance that an atom will stick on top of it. The growth simulation hypothesis states, however, that (for each discrete moment in time of the process) this chance is increased if the value of the neighboring pixels is greater, because the pocket or shoulder attracts the atom from the side. (Courtesy of Ken Knowlton.)

6-37. Image averaging is performed by reading the values inside each diamond, adding them, and dividing them by the number of pixels in the diamond. The result is the average intensity value, which is written back out to each pixel. (Courtesy of Digital Effects Inc.)

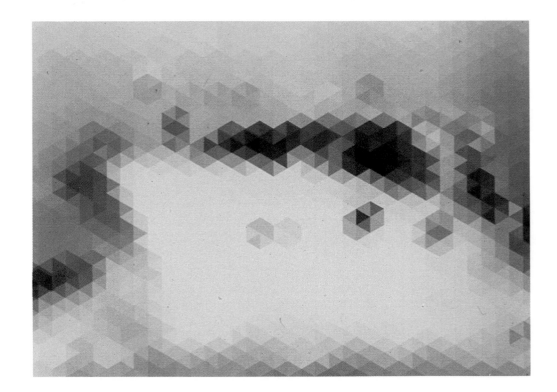

black-and-white or color. The procedure involves reading a group of pixels, calculating an average, then writing the average back out to each pixel in the pattern.

Brushes that blend colors in an image and simulated air brushes also involve local operators.

IMAGE ENHANCEMENT

Numerous digital techniques are unavailable using optical, photographic, or analog electronic methods. Many of these techniques originated in the field of image processing. *Image enhancement* techniques are used to improve the visibility of images, bringing out details that would otherwise remain latent. These include diffusion and sharpening filters, noise reduction methods, and spatial frequency techniques, which are becoming part of the graphic artists' vocabulary. (Many of the techniques described in the section on color in chapter 7 also involve enhancement.)

Diffusion Filters

A *low-pass,* or *diffusion, filter* softens an image. The procedure works locally by averaging each pixel and its eight neighbors, then writing that average value back in the pixel (fig. 6-38). This is somewhat similar to image averaging, except that the average is only written back into the central pixel of the resultant image. This moving average essentially blends areas of the picture and is often used in interactive paint systems to meld colors and retouch.

The amount of blurring in a diffusion filter depends on the size of the sampled neighborhood and can vary in width as well as height. The minimum (and identity case) is a one-pixel region that simply averages the pixel and replaces it with its own contents. A wider filter might sample a 3×3 matrix of pixels (see fig. 6-38), 5×5 pixels, 7×7

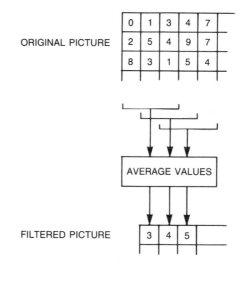

6-38. A low-pass filter calculates a moving average that blurs and smooths the image. (Courtesy of Spatial Data Systems, Inc.; a DBA Systems Company.)

6-39. Weighted average. In the 3 × 3 pixel array illustrated, the central pixel accounts for 50 percent of the value of the result, whereas the eight surrounding pixels each account for one-eighth of the remaining 50 percent of the averaged value, or 6.25 percent each.

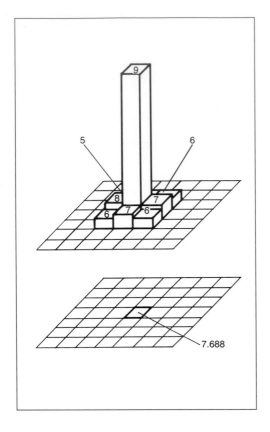

9 × .5	=	4.5
6 × .0625	=	.375
7 × .0625	=	.4375
6 × .0625	=	.375
7 × .0625	=	.4375
6 × .0625	=	.375
8 × .0625	=	.5
5 × .0625	=	.3125
6 × .0625	=	.375
		7.688

6-40. A high-pass filter sharpens an image. (Courtesy of Spatial Data Systems, Inc.; a DBA Systems Company.)

pixels, or larger areas, producing increasingly blurred pictures. The average can also be *weighted;* this means that the value of the central pixel affects the resultant value more than the value of the surrounding pixels (fig. 6-39).

Sharpening Filters

The opposite of a low-pass filter is a *high-pass* or *sharpening* filter, which reveals details only. High-pass filtering subtracts the low-pass filter from the original image, leaving only details (fig. 6-40).

Noise Reduction

Noise reduction in digital pictures uses a collection of ad hoc procedures and subjective evaluations to increase visibility. *Noise* in a picture refers to spurious, abnormal pixel values, whatever their source (fig. 6-41). Noise reduction is seldom completely effective—for example, a low-pass filter can smooth out noise, but it smooths out details, as well.

Distortions resulting from camera lenses, time smears, or movements of the camera during an exposure can sometimes be corrected with *restoration techniques,* which use facts about the defect to improve picture quality (fig. 6-42).

Spatial Frequency Processing

Pixels describe an image in terms of its luminance, but images can also be represented and perceived in other ways. We suggested that horizontal resolution is one kind of *spatial frequency,* or the number of samples across the space of the picture.

The contents of an image also exhibit spatial frequencies, which appear as changes in luminance across a scan line. For example, a photograph of a picket fence contains a spatial frequency roughly equal to the number of pixels from the center of one picket to the center of the next (fig. 6-43). Spatial frequency in an image is associated with the perception of the degree of detail. The more detailed an image, the higher its spatial frequency (fig. 6-44).

The spatial frequencies of an image

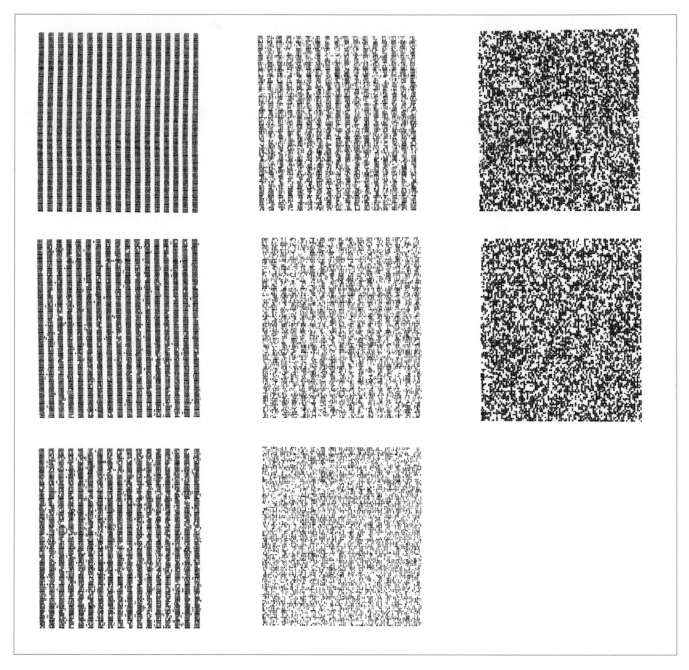

may be analyzed to discover latent properties and to provide quantitive measures of its contents. Spatial frequency analysis begins by taking inventory of all the spatial frequencies in the image. For example, a picture of a picket fence will have a spatial frequency that is quite different from the spatial frequency of a picture of rain. A picture of a picket fence in the rain will contain both; the sharp spatial frequencies associated with a picket fence can be isolated from the lower spatial frequencies of the rain, and the frequency of the rain removed. The result is a picture where the picket fence is more visible and the rain is gone (fig. 6-45).

This approach can also be used to search images and identify objects associated with specific spatial frequencies. For example, satellite images of the ocean can be searched for ships by

6-41. Noise mixed with a set of vertical bars in various percentages. (Provided by Isaac V. Kerlow.)

6-42. Image-processing techniques can restore the blurred image by eliminating the original movement.

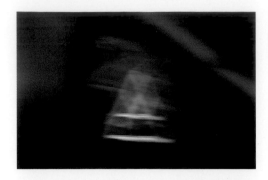

6-43. Spatial-frequency analysis can be used to detect and remove regular interference patterns, such as the out-of-focus bars in the illustration on the left.

6-44. A gothic image is very detailed and has a high spatial frequency (right). A Renaissance image (left) has less detail, smoother edges, and a lower spatial frequency.

establishing the background frequencies for waves, then flagging images with dramatically different frequencies.

COMPUTER VISION AND IMAGE ANALYSIS

Computer vision systems are concerned with the perception of images and with identifying objects and physical features such as shapes and volumes. Computer vision not only converts pixels into lines and shapes, but determines the relation of shapes and what they signify. Computer vision is the opposite of computer graphics and is closely related to *perception,* the science and art of forming mental constructs of the world and then navigating in that volumetric space.

Computer vision is a prerequisite for machines that navigate, and its widespread applications complement the graphic arts. These include the development of measures that relate to visibility. Computer vision is used to read typographic characters and bar codes, recognize faces, signatures, or thumbprints, and inspect parts on an assembly line. Image analysis is used in medicine, where CAT scan data is reconstructed into volumetric organs and X rays are analyzed for tumors.

Inputs to computer vision systems include a variety of light and imaging devices, which are often complemented with pressure, molecular, and temperature sensors, as well as with a range of electronic extensions, such as radar, ultrasound, and sonar.

Edge and Boundary Determination

Edge detection and boundary determination are used to assist in converting pixel images back into point and polygon representations; they are the opposite of scan conversion and DDAs. An *edge* is a sharp distinction in color or intensity values between adjacent pixels. Edges are keys to finding surfaces that intersect should the image depict a three-dimensional environment. Long straight edges often mark intersections of ceilings and walls, corners of rooms, or outlines of furniture.

In its most primitive form, an edge is simply the difference in value between two adjacent pixels; an edge detection algorithm subtracts the value of each pixel from the value of its neighbor and stores the results in a bitmap (fig. 6-46). The result looks much like a bas-relief image.

Edges imply a structural bias in an image and are a first step in finding polygons; an edge is essentially one side of a polygon, a vector between two points. Different algorithms produce different kinds of edges and are worth creatively exploring (fig. 6-47). An edge matrix added back into an original image sharpens it by enhancing the shapes of things, making the image more distinct (fig. 6-48).

More sophisticated software can convert a gradient of pixels, adjacent pixels that have similar intensity and slope, into lines in the point/vector domain. A *boundary* is similar to an edge, but is a contour, formed by pixels that can be converted into a curving line or a polygon. Boundary determination works by

6-45. Spatial frequency enhancement can reduce irregular picture noise, such as lens glare, provided the noise has spatial frequencies different from the rest of the image. (Courtesy of Isaac Victor Kerlow.)

6-46. Edges are depicted with a matrix that shows the difference between the value of a pixel and its horizontal or vertical neighbor. This resultant bitmap is a matrix of changes and is called the *first derivative* of the image. (Courtesy of Spatial Data Systems, Inc.; a DBA Systems Company.)

6-47. Gradient edge detection. (Courtesy of Spatial Data Systems, Inc.; a DBA Systems Company.)

6-48. Laplacian edge detection plus original image. (Courtesy of Spatial Data Systems, Inc.; a DBA Systems Company.)

identifying a contour of pixels and then converting it into a series of floating point numbers that define a polygon outline (fig. 6-49).

Matching

Template matching compares preexisting shape definitions, usually a small pixel array, to an input image, in order to identify specific details or features (fig. 6-50). It is used for quality control on assembly lines, in surveillance (computerized searches for missile silos in satellite images and for tumors in X rays) and for robotic vision. Computerized matching systems do not necessarily work if the object being matched is viewed at a different size, from a different angle, or with different lighting. This problem is now being actively researched for artificial intelligence purposes.

Reconstruction

Bitmap images that depict three-dimensional spatial environments, such as a digitized photograph of a house, are analyzed and possibly reconstructed into three-dimensional environments using a variety of procedures (fig. 6-51).

Three-dimensional reconstruction often uses edge and boundary detectors to discern shapes, and ***normal determination,*** which evaluates information about the location of light, the comparative color of the surfaces, reflected brightness, foreshortening, and texture patterns, in order to ascertain surface orientation (fig. 6-52). One normal is calculated for each pixel, and stored in a bitplane memory. When associated with contours, normals assist in locating surfaces in a three-dimensional spatial environment, because they indicate their orientation.

Another tool for three-dimensional reconstruction is ***photogrammetry,*** a method that correlates two perspective views of a scene and derives three-dimensional spatial locations (see fig. 7-10). The two-view technique requires some knowledge of points in the three-dimensional environment in order to yield a proper result, because apparent

6-49. The same image before and after boundaries have been determined. The top illustration shows the original continuous-tone image. The bottom shows the result of a process that determines the boundaries between sharp distinctions of gray levels. (Courtesy of Allen R. Hanson, Edward M. Riseman, and members of the VISIONS research group at the University of Massachusetts.)

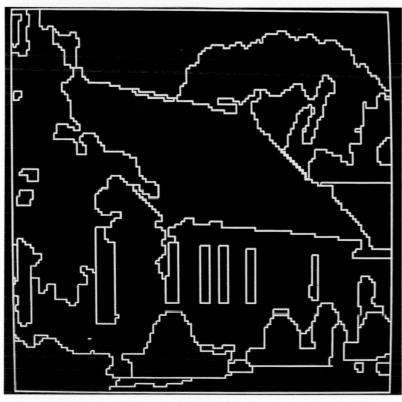

6-50. Pattern matching uses a template for hexagonal nut against which it will be matched. Photograph by Dana H. Ballard and Chris M. Brown, *Computer Vision.* © 1982, p. 67. Reprinted by permission of Prentice-Hall, Inc.

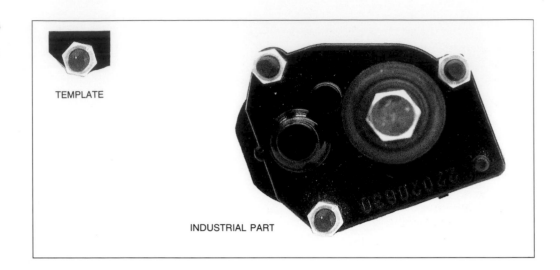

TEMPLATE

INDUSTRIAL PART

6-51. In three-dimensional reconstruction, the general features of landscape and object are extracted from a photograph (see fig. 6-49) and reconstructed in three dimensions. The spatial relationships between them are established in the form of a relational data base. (Courtesy of Allen R. Hanson, Edward M. Riseman, and members of the VISIONS research group at the University of Massachusetts.)

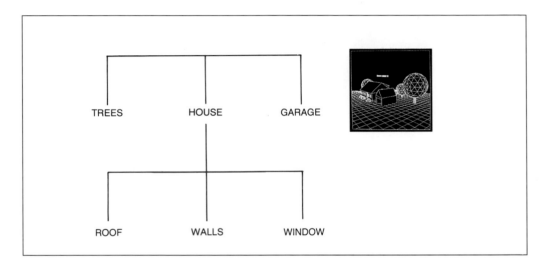

TREES   HOUSE   GARAGE

ROOF   WALLS   WINDOW

6-52. Characteristics of a surface depicted in an image may be used to determine the orientation of the surface in space (normal determination). These techniques include perspective (A) and foreshortening texture patterns (B).

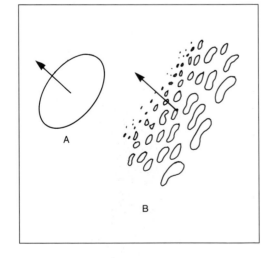

A

B

two-dimensional size depends on both object size and its distance from the observer.

Computerized three-dimensional reconstruction, like an individual's perception, is not always perfect. Accurate interpretations require some preexisting data structure and memory on the part of the observer (fig. 6-53). The Necker cubes and the Rubin vase (fig. 6-54) are examples of failed psychological "algorithms," because they yield two solutions, or multistable images.

☞ **RELATED READING**

Ballard, Dana H., and Christopher M. Brown. *Computer Vision.* Englewood Cliffs, NJ: Prentice-Hall, 1982.

Gregory, Richard L. *Eye and Brain, The Psychology of Seeing.* 3d ed. New York: McGraw-Hill, 1978.

Harmon, Leon. "The Recognition of Faces." *Scientific American* (November 1973).

Hubel, David H. *Eye, Brain and Vision.* New York: W. H. Freeman, 1988.

Poggio, Tomaso. "Vision by Man and Machine." *Scientific American* (April 1984).

Rock, Irvin. *Perception.* New York: W. H. Freeman, 1984.

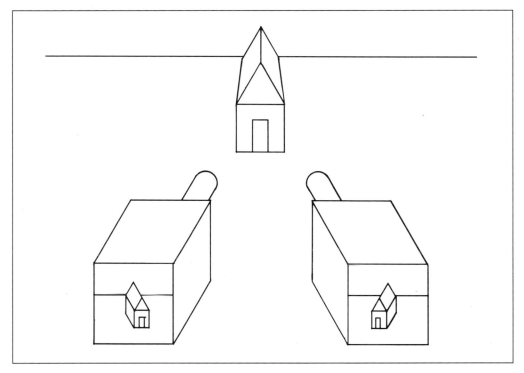

6-53. Three-dimensional reconstruction based on two-view photogrammetry.

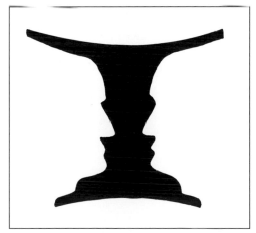

6-54. A Rubin vase—a multistable image—can be seen as the silhouette of a vase or as two faces.

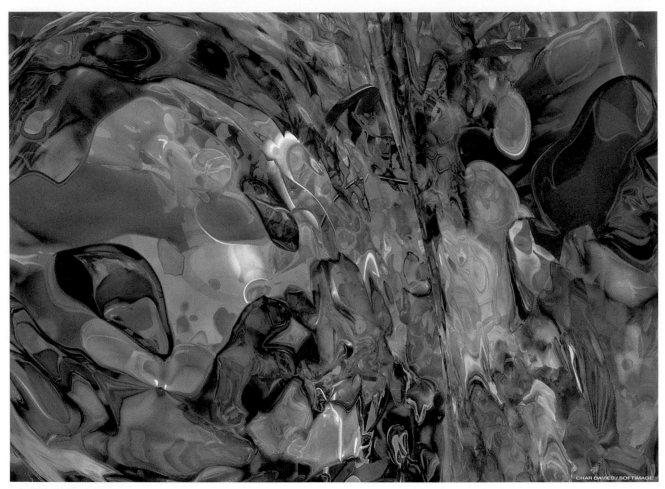

CHAR DAVIES/SOFTIMAGE

7-0. The ability to construct and represent an imaginary yet realistic world is the lure of computer graphics. This skill has progressed from simple geometries to being able to represent complex environments with curving surfaces, organic forms, and subtle properties of natural phenomena such as water, mist, fog, and fire. (*Stream*, © Char Davies/SOFTIMAGE 1991. Artist: Char Davies. Software: SOFTIMAGE Creative Environment.)

7

THREE-DIMENSIONAL MODELING

MODEL CONSTRUCTION
COMBINATORIAL GEOMETRY
PRIMITIVE TRANSFORMATIONS
PERSPECTIVE, WINDOWS, AND PORTS
SURFACE ATTRIBUTES
LIGHTS AND LIGHTING
RENDERING

Visual language as it applies to three-dimensional graphics, particularly points, lines, planes, and volumes, is considerably different from the pixel representational form and includes objects as opposed to images. ***Objects*** are virtual entities in a continuous environment, whereas images are discrete picture areas. Objects include points, lines, and shapes in two-dimensional space as well as three-dimensional volumes. The principles are basically the same. The focus of this chapter is to define, position, manipulate, light, and render objects in three-dimensional graphics.

In many respects three-dimensional solid modeling is a lot like constructing theater props. Positioning models in the imaginary computer space is analogous to classical set design. Action, characterization, and lighting are all comparable, but rendering and visualization apply only to graphics.

7-1. Summary of modeling techniques shows several basic primitive objects at the top, and multidimensional construction techniques at the bottom. (From top left to bottom right: sphere, cube, cylinder, cone, torus, icosahedron, dodecahedron, lathe, rounding, bevelling, slicing, skin, mesh surfaces (2), and Boolean operations (2). (Diagram by Isaac V. Kerlow, illustrated by Andrew Holdun.)

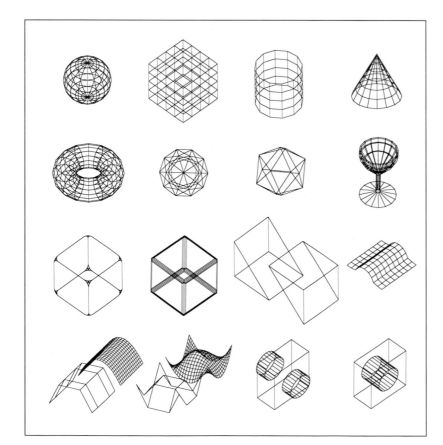

Shape and Volume Representation and Digitization

Objects that are stored in a computer can either be concrete—a tape recorder or a building—or abstractions—a model of an atom, a subatomic particle, or a psychological variable. Objects, static or mobile, can be geometrically built or composed freehand. Very basic objects, like stars, are represented as points. A list of points can be connected with lines and can define a surface or the edge of a volume (fig. 7-1). All objects are represented as numbers, but they are often composed and manipulated using commands or procedures, which address them using a variable name.

The definition of objects in a computer, whether they are simple lines bounded by two points, or complicated shapes, requires that the objects be stored in the machine. Digitization and procedural descriptions are two ways of inputting that information. Both techniques can be controlled either explicitly or interactively.

Objects are digitized using a keyboard, tablet, camera, or special measuring device. Extrusion is a technique that turns two-dimensional inputs into three-dimensional objects; three-dimensional objects are also digitized from serial sections and coplanar blueprints. Photogrammetry is used to reconstruct three-dimensional objects from photographic images; and spatial measuring tools specify either points, zels, or voxels that are already three dimensional.

Objects are also described using predefined computer programs. Procedural descriptions include geometric figures such as boxes, cylinders, doughnuts, surfaces, such as those in an automobile fender, and irregular forms, such as trees. The graphic artist controls the position, size, and shape of these objects with simple commands and arguments.

Closely allied to the object definition methods in this section are combinational methods such as clipping and unions, and animation techniques such as in-betweening and interpolation.

Point Digitizing

The most basic way to enter points into a computer is on a keyboard. This is essential in situations where the data exists at higher resolutions than the digitizer. Regular shapes, such as rectangles, can easily be entered on a keyboard, because only a few points need to be defined (fig. 7-2).

Objects that are more irregular—the outline of a letter or logo—are usually digitized by placing the artwork on a digitizing tablet and picking points or tracing around the perimeter with a stylus. Another strategy is to redraw the object onto graph paper, identify key coordinates and curves such as arcs, then enter them via a keyboard. This is often best, because the lines produced are smoother (fig. 7-3), and because many objects, for example, type, often have a geometric basis.

Extrusion

Extrusion is used to convert a two-dimensional outline into a three-dimensional space and defines the sides of the object (fig. 7-4). The term comes from machinery containing dies through which metal or plastic is pulled. Computationally, it is a procedure that translates a copy of the front surface back into Z space and then connects sides between the front and back edges, creating a three-dimensional shape.

Objects of Revolution

Another model-constructing technique is used to make symmetrical surfaces of revolution, such as a bell (fig. 7-5). **Objects of revolution** begin by digitizing only a cross section of the object. The cross section only consists of X and Y data and is centered around the Y axis. A computer program then spins, or rotates, this line around the central axis to make a solid object, either a mesh of polygons or a continuous surface. Objects of revolution need very little data to construct complicated objects and work much like a vase that is thrown on a potter's wheel or turned on a lathe.

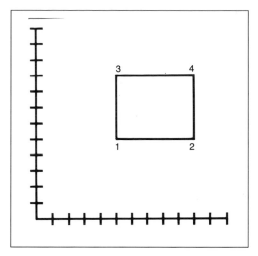

7-2. Only two points, opposite corners, must be entered to point digitize a rectangle. The computer recombines the X and Y values for the other two points—the lower left corner and the lower right corner have the same Y value, and the lower right corner and the upper right corner have the same X value.

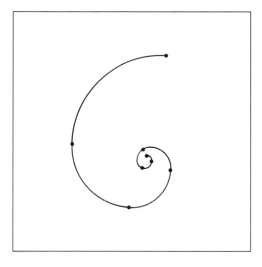

7-3. When digitizing objects the number of points needed depends on the rate of change. It is useful to enter more points for a rapidly curving line, and fewer points for a slowly curving line. This makes the sharp curves smoother without wasting points.

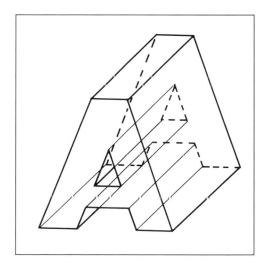

7-4. Extrusion of an alphanumeric letter into a three-dimensional volumetric representation.

**7-5. Surfaces of revolution
are created by spinning a
curved line about an axis.**

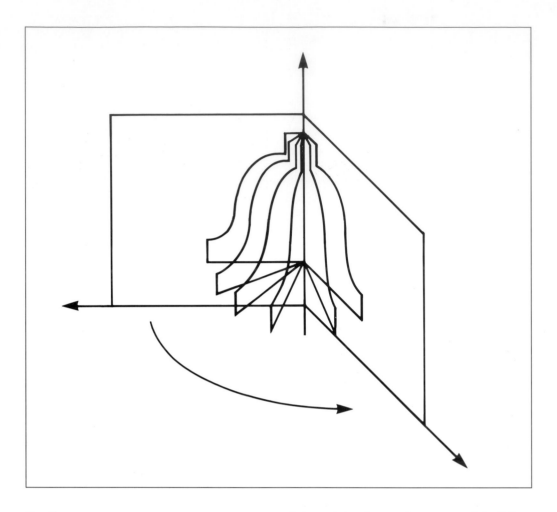

Sections

Another way to build three-dimensional objects with a computer is to construct a series of sections that are lifted into position (fig. 7-6). A ***section*** is a cross section of an object, a contour line of a quantized elevation, and allows organic, nongeometric shapes such as a biological organ or topographic terrain contours to be digitized.

Contour perimeters are digitized one at a time by picking points on a tablet, or by typing numerical coordinates on the keyboard. Each contour is assigned a layer number. After all layers have been digitized, a computer program constructs a surface mesh by automatically constructing polygons that connect each contour to the contour above and below it, creating a solid object (fig. 7-7).

Using a polar coordinate scheme and digitizing a data point at a constant angular interval is the easiest way of building objects with contours. Thus sections are easily connected, because each section point can be connected to the section point directly above (and below) it, forming planar triangular facets. The disadvantage of this method is that it does not compensate for quickly curving places in the contour (which require additional points in order to appear smooth), places where a section may curve back on itself and form an overhang, or holes (fig. 7-8). In these situations, a more sophisticated surface-meshing algorithm is required, one that is able to build a mesh surface when the points are not evenly distributed along each contour.

Coplanar Technique

The coplanar technique of building models is used to create three-dimensional

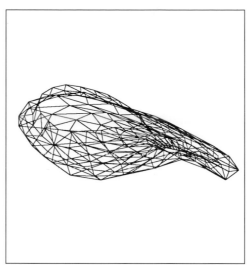

objects from blueprints. **Coplanar** signifies two planar views, a plan and an elevation, both two dimensional (fig. 7-9). The elevation, or front view, contains X and Y data. The plan, or top view, contains X and Z data. Each data point—for example, each corner—appears in both views and is assigned a point number—its address in a point list.

The two drawings are digitized by being taped to a digitizing tablet, and a graphic artist first digitizes a point from the plan and then the corresponding point from the elevation. A computer program merges the X and Y value digitized from the first view with the Z value digitized from the second view into a single three-dimensional point stored in computer memory. (The second Y value is discarded.)

A **point list table** results from this process and has as many rows as there are points, and three columns, one for X, Y, and Z. The table contains no connectivity information between the points; that is, there is no indication of what points together form polygons or polyhedra. This information is contained in **connect lists,** which define the sequences of point numbers that form a boundary of an object. In defining a cube, for example, the point list will consist of eight points, each point representing one vertex of the cube. There will then be six connect lists, each con-

taining the four points needed to describe one of the polygons that make up the surface of the cube. Each point in the cube will appear in three different connect lists—the three surfaces that connect at that corner.

The coplanar method is efficient in computer memory because points are only stored once, yet may be used in multiple connect lists. If a point needs to be repositioned, then all the polygons that use it automatically incorporate the change. Usually the process begins by digitizing **rectification points,** or registration marks, in the two views. These points permit the program to relate the position of the drawings on the tablet with the internal data base and provide a way to correctly reposition artwork, for example, so new points can be added in the future.

Point and connect lists do not necessarily require blueprints beforehand. They can also be captured with XYZ stylus digitizers and can be explicitly declared.

Photogrammetry

Surfaces can also be defined with **photogrammetry** techniques that project a grid onto an actor or scene and then digitize the grid points as they appear in perspective photography, which uses two cameras (fig. 7-10). Single points appearing in both views are merged into

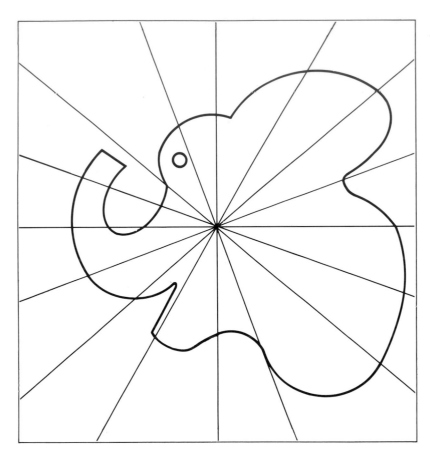

Procedural Methods

Another way of defining objects is to use the computer to calculate the sequence of points rather than directly digitizing the objects. This is done with a command that activates the procedure. A circle, for example, is best defined using a procedure, or formula, that determines the X and Y positions for each angular distance about the circle. This method can calculate extremely accurate circles with an arbitrary number of points or sides. This is quicker than digitizing the circle using a tablet and stylus, and the result is more uniformly round. By using a procedural method to construct a circle, we can calculate a circle with ten points, one hundred points, a thousand points, or a million points. The circle is not a predefined object, but is created whenever it is needed, and at whatever resolution is needed.

In a vector graphics system a circle is represented as a series of straight sides. In order to make a circle look round, the number of sides needed depends on the size of the circle in the field of view; as little as two dozen or as many as a few hundred sides may be required. Because the circle is calculated using a procedure, one can calculate the number of points needed (fig. 7-13).

Circles are not the only objects that can be procedurally built and parametrically controlled. Most computer graphics systems come with a fairly rich set of *primitive functions,* including a circle, rectangle, box (defined by its length, width, height, and center position), sphere (defined by its center position and radius), cylinder, doughnut (or torus), prism, and other basic geometric figures (fig. 7-14).

Statistical Distributions and Fractals

Procedurally defined parametrically controlled objects do not have to be regular; they can include irregular, bloblike volumes, irregular treelike shapes, statistical distributions, and flowing surfaces (fig. 7-15). **Particle systems** manipulate thousands of pointlike objects and are used to represent fireworks, explosions, fire, and fluid flows

7-8. When a curve is changing gradually, as on the right, a sample point is taken at even angular intervals. Here 5 degrees approximate the contour. Contours that change quickly or curve back on themselves, as on the left, cannot be meaningfully sampled using the even-angular technique. Holes and overhangs are particularly problematic.

three-dimensional points using a reconstruction technique; the point mesh is then replicated in the machine. Photogrammetry is useful for objects that cannot be sectioned or are in motion.

Zels

Another digitizing technique represents an object or a surface as a matrix of depth values called *zels.* The depth matrix may be orthogonal, or cylindrical (fig. 7-11). The matrices of zels can be converted from polar to Cartesian forms; they can also be converted to mesh surface representations as well as to contours.

Voxels

Voxels are digitized by hardware such as a CAT scanner and provide a discrete approximation of densities of space. Voxels can be organized in many ways and, like zels, may be converted to and from polygon surface meshes (fig. 7-12).

(fig. 7-16). **Fractal** objects have irregular, but self-similar properties, so that when their scale is magnified or reduced the computer is able to calculate the appropriate level of detail (fig. 7-17). Because many natural and organic objects are better described with fractals than with primitive geometric shapes, they are widely used to model objects such as clouds, mountains, rivers, and coastlines.

Parametric Surface Patches

Parametric surface patches describe three-dimensional objects in terms of equations that define four edges of the patch. Often the equations are defined by control points at the four corners of the patch; these control points, or parameters, may be thought of as a normal (see fig. 1-33) with a magnitude, and are what give the patch its name (parametric). Given these four control points, an algorithm is used to calculate

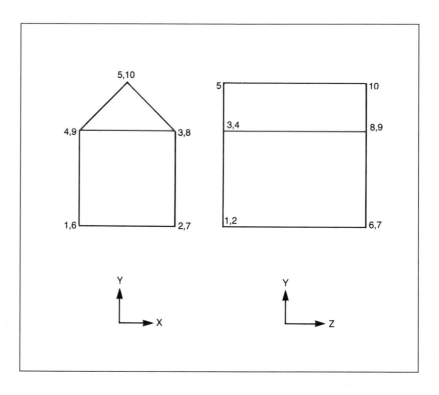

POINT LIST

	X	Y	Z
1	0	0	15
2	10	0	15
3	10	10	15
4	0	10	15
5	5	15	15
6	0	0	0
7	10	0	0
8	10	10	0
9	0	10	0
10	5	15	0

CONNECT LIST

1, 2, 3, 5, 4, 1

6, 7, 8, 10, 9, 6

5, 10, 9, 4, 5

5, 10, 8, 3, 5

2, 7, 8, 3, 2

6, 1, 4, 9, 6

7-9. This drawing depicts the side and front views of a house. Each point is assigned a number common to both views; this number is not a spatial coordinate but an identifying number. Many points in each elevation actually represent two points (one in front and one behind) and therefore have two identification numbers associated with them. The three-dimensional coordinates of each point are determined by merging an X, Y coordinate from the left drawing and a Y, Z coordinate from the right drawing. The list of points and the spatial coordinates are shown in the point list, and a separate connect list defines the boundaries of each polygon in the structure.

7-10. Three-dimensional reconstruction using two-view photogrammetry. A grid is drawn or projected onto a three-dimensional object, which is in turn photographed using two cameras (see fig. 6-53). The camera positions and focal lengths are known. Each point in both photographed grids is assigned a number and then separately digitized. The two sets of points are mathematically merged creating a three-dimensional data base.

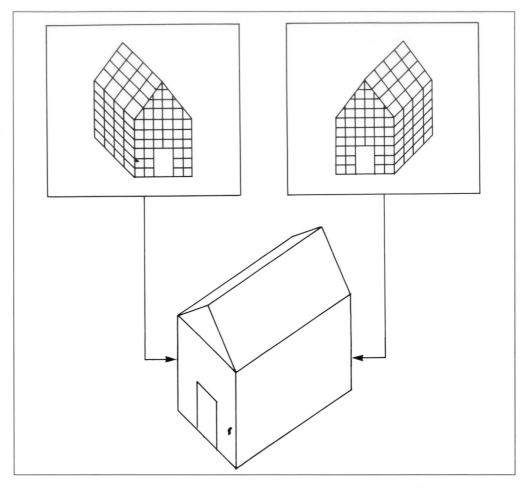

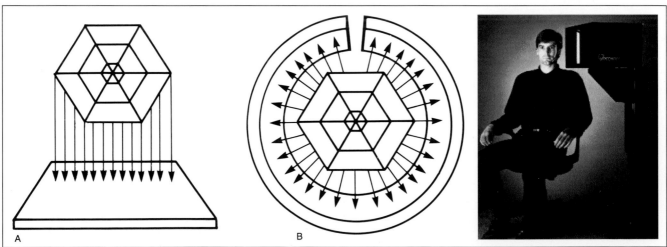

7-11. Orthogonal and polar zels are matrices of depth values. Orthogonal zels (A) are the distances from a plane in space to the surface of a reference plane; the illustration shows one row. Polar zels (B) are the radial distances from an object to a surrounding cylinder; again one row is shown. The photograph shows a machine that measures polar zels of human-sized subjects. The mechanical assembly at the right of the picture rotates around the subject. The measurement is done by shining a laser beam, which can be seen on the left cheek of the subject. (Photograph of the Cyberware 3030/PS 3D Laser Scanner courtesy of Cyberware, Monterey, CA.)

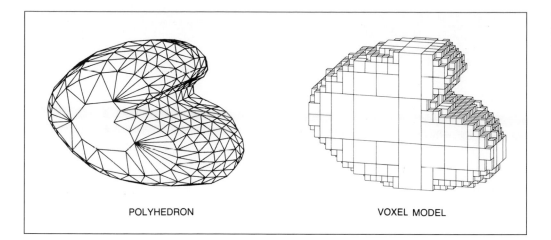

7-12. Voxels are volumetric, not surface, representations.

POLYHEDRON

VOXEL MODEL

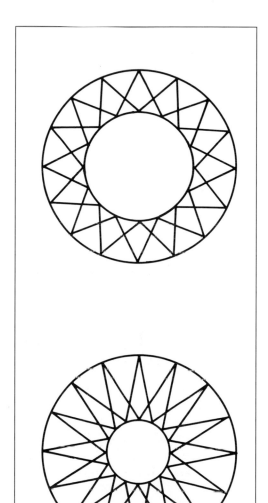

```
10      REM   KR.CIRCLE
20      REM   DRAWS CIRCLE USING
             ANGULAR INCREMENTS
30      CX = 140:CY = 96
40      TH = 0
50      DTH = 6.2832 / 40
60      DIM SX(40),SY(40)
70      RADIUS = 90
80      FOR I = 1 TO 40
90      X = RADIUS * COS (TH)
100     Y = RADIUS * SIN (TH)
110     SX(I) = X + CX
120     SY(I) = Y + CY
130     TH = DTH * I
140     NEXT I
150     HGR2 : HCOLOR= 3:PEN = 0
160     FOR I = 1 TO 40
170     IF PEN = 1 THEN GOTO 190
180     HPLOT SX(I),SY(I):PEN = 1
190     HPLOT  TO SX(I),SY(I)
200     NEXT I
210     END
```

7-14. Procedurally defined objects also include complicated models such as the eye and the iris. A single parameter controls the opening and closing of the iris, and the procedure might be called by typing "EYE .5," where the argument is the percentage of the opening of the iris.

7-13. In a computer graphics system, procedures are invoked by calling them by name. Arguments for a circle include the number of sides, the X and Y coordinates for the center, and the radius. The command might be: "90 Circle 140 96 40."

7-15. Growth simulation
defines objects by imple-
menting rules about how
natural plants and ani-
mals grow, for example,
how a tree branch subdi-
vides. Additional rules,
such as maximizing the
exposure to light, or not
penetrating other objects,
may also be incorporated
in the calculations.
(Frame from *Panspermia*
courtesy of Karl Sims,
Thinking Machines Corp.,
1990.)

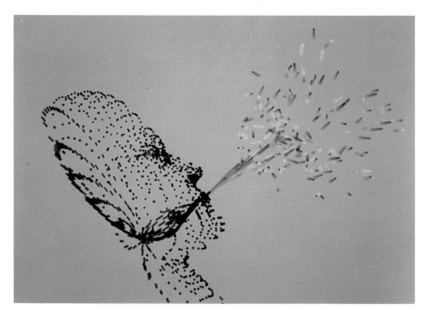

**7-16. Particle systems encompass a variety of
techniques for determining the location and
movement of vast collection of pointlike
objects. The rules can be rather simple, like a
starburst explosion, or infinitely complex, like
the single frame shown here, in which a face
made of particles is turning itself inside out
and blowing the particles out of the mouth.
Note how the particles in motion are elongated. (Frame from *Particle Dreams* courtesy of
Karl Sims, Thinking Machines Corp., 1988.)**

an XYZ coordinate anywhere within the
patch (fig. 7-18). The advantage of patches is
that large, continuously curving surfaces
can be defined with very few points. Furthermore, the shape of the surface can be
manipulated by changing only the control
points. Patches are widely used in applications such as automobile and aircraft design
as well as in sculpture that involves complex
surfaces.

SET CONSTRUCTION: COMBINATORIAL GEOMETRY

Union Operators

Chapter 6 inventoried a collection of matting operations between pictures—logical
operators like AND or OR that specify how
images are combined (see fig. 6-21). This
same concept can be used three dimensionally on solid models. In three-dimensional space, these logical combinations are
called ***union operators*** and combine two
volumetric shapes to form a new shape (fig.
7-19).

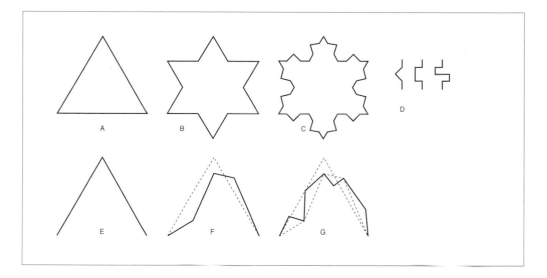

This is easiest to conceptualize if the three-dimensional objects are made up of voxels and are compared voxel by voxel, using logical operators. Unions not only provide a way to aggregate primitive objects into more complicated ones, but also subtract parts from the whole.

Clipping and Capping

Clipping is a process that slices an object into two parts as if cut with a knife. A fundamental tool for objects in three-dimensional space, clipping is used to eliminate objects that are outside the field of view as well as to chop objects into pieces (fig. 7-20).

Clipping defines a plane in space (essentially a giant rectangle) and then sorts the objects between the two sides of the plane. Where a line or edge crosses the clipped plane, the procedure calculates a new point at that location (fig. 7-21).

Capping is a process that defines new surfaces formed where a clipping plane truncates an object (fig. 7-22). This prevents an object from appearing hollow; capping constructs a new side so the polyhedron looks opaque or solid. Clipping is

7-18. The key idea behind parametric surfaces is that they are defined by only the control points at the corners of the patch, here indicated by the colored normals. The surface of the patch is calculated by interpolating the curves the control points define. (Courtesy of Michael DiComo, Pratt Institute.)

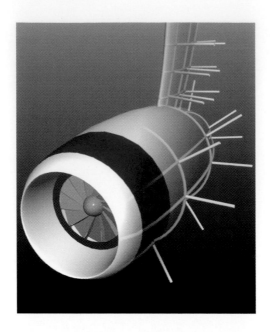

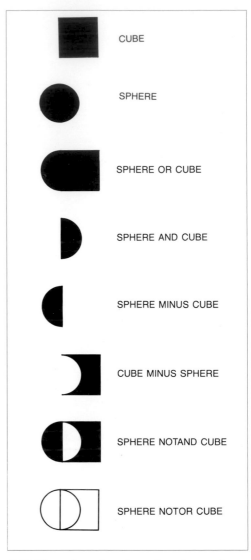

much like unions; clipping, however, involves an intersection between a plane and a volume, while unions involve the intersection of two volumes.

Geometric transformations are operations that move and position objects in either two- or three-dimensional spaces. Translate, size, rotate, and shear are four primitive computer graphics transformations.

These transformations describe the ways in which a rigid object can be manipulated in space. Primitive transformations can always be undone or combined to describe a single position that includes more than one primitive transformation, such as rotation and size.

PRIMITIVE TRANSFORMATIONS

Transformational functions use arguments to specify the magnitude of the transformation and store the result as data, much as an object is stored—positions and motions are entities just as objects are entities. Transformational data is independent of the data of the object being positioned. For example, a transformation specifies the *position* of an aircraft, but not any informa-

7-19. The union of a cube and a sphere, where the sphere has a diameter equal to the width of the cube and bisects its circumference. The OR union results in a volume that contains both the cube and the sphere. The logical AND union produces a resultant volume that is common to both volumes. The NOTAND operator produces the volume of the cube and the sphere that are not common, or shared. The NOTOR union eliminates everything. The sphere MINUS the cube produces a hemisphere, and the cube MINUS the sphere results in a box with a depression.

tion as to what kind of aircraft is at that location.

Translation

Translation, or offsetting, is a transformation that moves an object left or right, up or down, or in or out in three-dimensional space. A translation of some combination of X, Y, and Z repositions an object anywhere in space by adding the amount of the displacement to each point in the object to be transformed (fig. 7-23).

An *identity translation,* a translation of 0, describes a situation in which an object is not to be moved. Positive number translations displace objects along the corresponding positive axis; in other words, right, up, or toward the viewer. Negative values move the object to the left, down, or away from the viewer.

Sizing

Sizing transformation either reduces or enlarges objects. By definition, sizing always occurs around the origin, which is one reason why objects tend to be defined with the origin at their center. Sizing transformations change the size of an object, multiplying their coordinates by the scaling factor(s) (fig. 7-24).

As in translation, there are three sizing transformations, one for X, Y, and Z, and it is not necessary to size an object equally in all three dimensions. Sizing a sphere in X and Y, but not Z, will create an ellipsoidal shape, for example. Sizing a letter in X, but not Y, will condense or expand it.

An *identity sizing* (leaving the size of an object unchanged) is a sizing of 1. Scaling factors greater than 1 enlarge the object; scaling factors between 0 and 1 reduce it. A sizing of 0 reduces the entire object to a point, and negative numbers flip the object into mirror image positions.

Sizing should not be confused with *zooming,* which changes the focal length of a lens and does not make an object larger or smaller. Nor should sizing be confused with *dollying,* which translates a camera closer to an object. Sizing, zooming, and

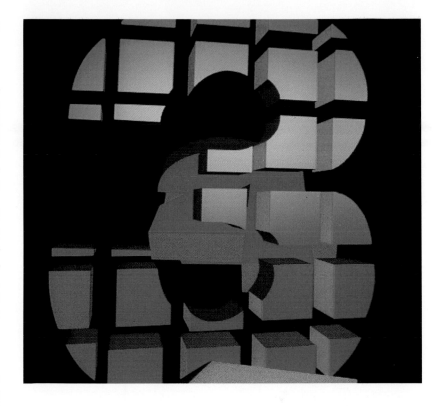

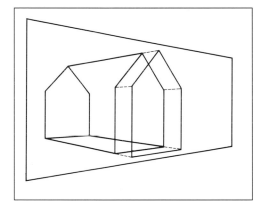

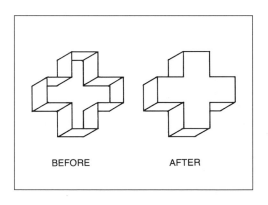

BEFORE AFTER

7-20. The "3" has been clipped in X, Y, and Z to create smaller cubes, which are then translated away from the center. (Provided by Judson Rosebush.)

7-21. This clipping diagram shows how a single clipping plane intersects a three-dimensional house. The part of the house outside the field of vision is eliminated.

7-22. An extruded cross before and after capping.

7-23. Adding three horizontal units to a point located at 6, 5, 1 will translate that point to location 9, 5 1. The displacement must be added to each and every point that describes a shape in order to translate a shape or a group of shapes.

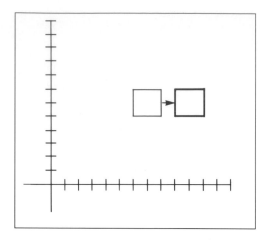

7-24. A letter T sized by a factor of two would become twice as large. But the same letter sized by two in the X dimension, and three in the Y dimension, will result in a larger letter with different proportions. In either case, each of the eight coordinates that describe the letter are multiplied by the scaling factor and result in a new set of coordinates.

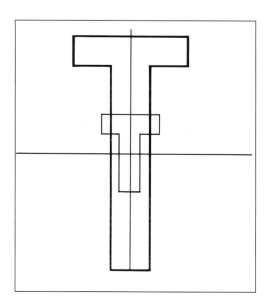

7-25. Two-dimensional rotation of 310 degrees about the origin.

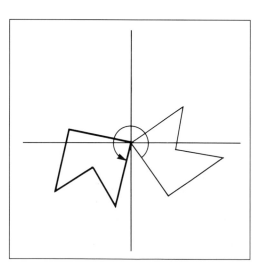

dollying all affect the apparent size of an object on a screen, but only sizing affects its actual dimensions.

Rotation

A *rotation* specifies a pivoting, or angular, displacement about an axis. In two-dimensional computer graphics rotations only occur around the origin (fig. 7-25). An example of two-dimensional rotation is the movement of the hands of a clock. In three-dimensional graphics there are three rotations, one each around the X, Y, and Z axes (fig. 7-26).

Objects are rotated by specifying an angle of rotation and using trigonometric functions to determine the new position. Rotation angles are usually expressed in degrees; but they can also be in other rotary measures, such as radians. These angles can be positive or negative; the identity rotation is 0 degrees (or any multiple of 360 degrees).

Rotations are said to be either *left-handed* or *right-handed*, specifying whether a positive angle rotates clockwise or counterclockwise. The handedness rule is based on the curl of fingers, on either hand, around into a fist with the thumb pointing out. The fingers curl in the direction of a positive angle rotation (fig. 7-27).

Remember that rotations, like sizings, always occur around an axis, and this is different from rotating a figure around its own center (fig. 7-28).

Shear

The *shear transformation* displaces points relative to the origin. Shear is similar to italicization and can work forward or backward (fig. 7-29). A shear involves the displacement of two axes against a third, and although there is only one way to shear in two-dimensional graphics, there are six different ways to shear in three-dimensional space.

Inverse Transformation

All primitive transformations can be *inverted*, for example, the inverse of a

10-degree positive rotation is a 10-degree negative transformation, and inversion is a common command in three-dimensional systems (fig. 7-30). Inverting a transformation is simple, as it is not necessary to know how the transformation was made, but only to have the transformation as data, in order to invert it.

Concatenation of Transformations

The four primitive, singular transformations, position, size, rotate, and shear, are not only methods for representing single positions, but can be combined, or **concatenated,** to specify a position that incorporates a sequence of two or more individual, primitive transformations (fig. 7-31). The sequence of transformations affects the result. Rotations and sizings are especially sensitive to sequence, because

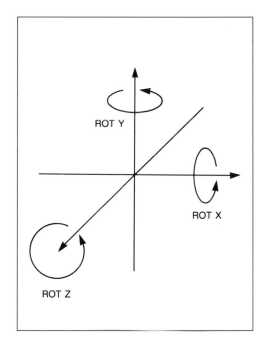

7-26. Right-handed rotations in three-dimensional graphics.

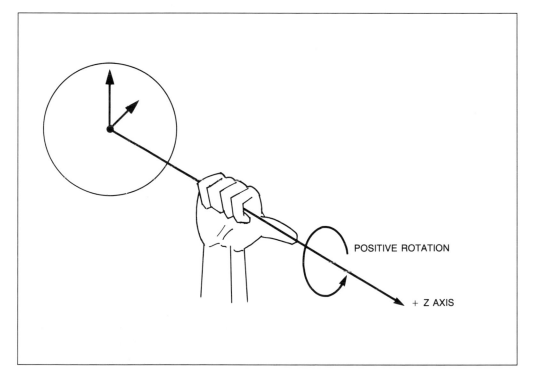

7-27. Left-handed rotations specify a positive angle rotation that goes clockwise when viewed from the positive axes. On the clock illustrated, the X axis is right, Y up, and Z toward you. If you curled the fingers of your left hand around the Z axis, your thumb will point toward you, in the positive Z direction, and your fingers would curl clockwise. Positive Z angle rotation would make the clock go forward in time. With a right-handed system, positive angles would go counterclockwise, and negative rotation angles would have to be used to make time go forward.

7-28. Rotation and size occur around an origin. A Z rotation of a rectangle (A) pivots the rectangle around the origin, not its own center. A rotation around its own center is accomplished first by translating the center of the rectangle to the origin (B). The rectangle is then rotated (C) and translated back to its original position (D).

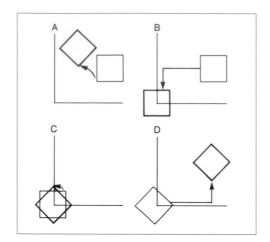

7-29. Identity shears have a value of 0. Positive number shears make objects lean forward, in the positive direction. Negative number shears make objects lean backward, like backward-slanting letters. Shears are sometimes used in animation to "race" type into a scene horizontally, and as the type comes to a rest, it relaxes, shears backward, and then returns to normal.

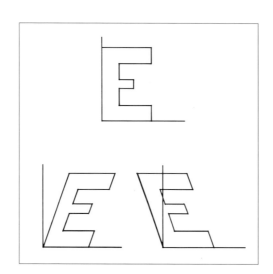

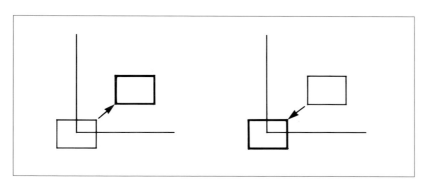

7-30. The drawing on the left shows the translation of a rectangle from its initial position at the origin to a new location. The second drawing shows an inverse transformation, the translation of a new rectangle located at 4, 3, 0 back to the origin.

they occur around an axis (fig. 7-32). The proper sequence of transformations can only be achieved after the location of the origin is identified, without confusing it with the center of the object.

Transformations can be concatenated ad infinitum and result in a single transformation. Often functions exist or can be written that describe complex transformations yet only require simple arguments. For example, a command ZCENTEROTAT with arguments XPOS, YPOS, and ANGLE might describe a rotation about an arbitrary point. In this case, three transformations are combined—a translation from XPOS, YPOS to the origin, the rotation of ANGLE degrees, and the translation back.

Many applications require that a single object be repeated in many positions. This is accomplished with a technique called ***instancing,*** which uses a model object only, but defines a series of transformations that represent all the positions. Examples of instancing include multiple columns on a building, the location of houses in a subdivision, the position of trees in a forest, and textile pattern repeats (fig. 7-33).

Transformations may also represent serial events or ***animation,*** a pathway of motion or a sequence of positions across time, like the position of hands on a clock, a turning water wheel, or a falling rock. Transformations merely specify the position and do not specify what is at the position.

PERSPECTIVE, WINDOWS, AND PORTS

Perspective is a technique for representing three-dimensional environments on two-dimensional surfaces, such as the surface of a monitor or a sheet of paper. Perspective is related to point of view and to a window, or frame. Together these function like an eye or camera. Computer graphics can model many kinds of perspective, but this discussion will center on the single-vanishing-point perspective evolved during the Renaissance.

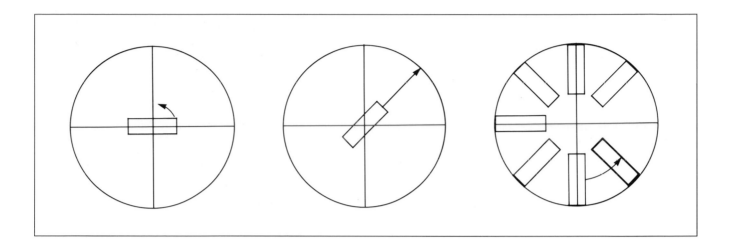

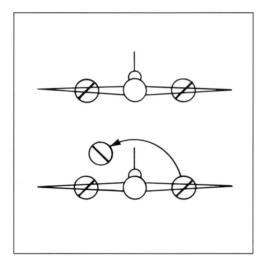

7-32. This figure shows a propeller, centered at the origin and translated to an engine shaft on a wing. If the propeller is rotated and then translated, the result is a spinning propeller sitting on the engine. But should the translation precede the rotation, then the propeller would orbit around a central axis of the aircraft.

7-31. Concatenated transformations involve a sequence of transformations: a paddle on a water wheel is positioned using two successive transformations, one that rotates the paddle, and a second that translates the paddle onto the circumference of the wheel.

7-33. Instancing a single object, in this case a column, repeatedly translates it to create a pattern.

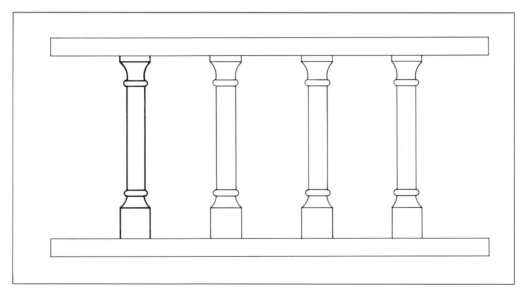

☛ **RELATED READING**

Glassner, Andrew S. *3D Computer Graphics, A User's Guide for Artists and Designers.* 2d ed. New York: Design Press, 1989.

Hall, Roy. *Illumination and Color in Computer Generated Imagery.* Monographs in Visual Communication. New York: Springer-Verlag, 1989.

Mandelbrot, Benoit B. *The Fractal Geometry of Nature.* New York: W. H. Freeman, 1983.

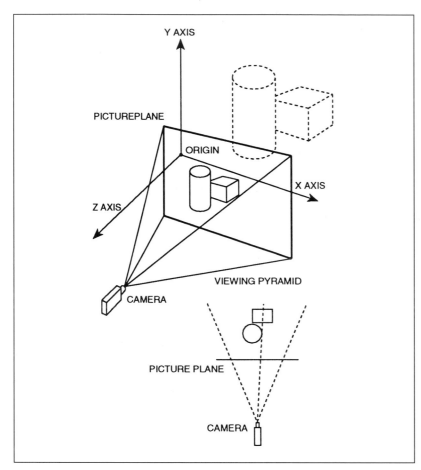

7-34. A three-dimensional environment can be viewed from a point of view, located anywhere in space, through a window connected to the point of view by a viewing pyramid (the pyramid of vision), which defines an expanding field of view. Rays drawn between a point in the environment and the point of view intersect the window, or image plane, and form a perspective projection of the environment.

The Point of View and the Window

The *point of view (POV)* is the position in space from which a three-dimensional environment is viewed. It is defined by an XYZ point analogous to the location of a camera or an eye. The viewing point is the location at which all perspective lines converge.

Along with the **POV** is the *aim point,* which is the point that the camera or eye is looking toward. The **aim point** lies on the *window,* a rectangular image plane perpendicular to the viewing point and located between it and the viewing environment (fig. 7-34). The window is analogous to the film in a camera or the retina of an eye, except it is located in front of the POV instead of behind it.

A perspective view is created by projecting each point of an object onto the window by drawing a ray between the point and the POV, and determining where that ray intersects the window. Thus the points in the object coordinate system are transformed to the window coordinate system. A *lens* is the aggregation of a window and POV, and the *focal length* of the lens is the distance between the window and the POV. For a normal lens, the distance between the POV and the window is equal to the diagonal of the window. A POV that is close to the window functions like a wide-angle lens, and a POV that is far away functions like a telephoto lens.

As the POV pulls away from the window, the perspective gets flatter. When the POV is at infinity, points orthogonally project, that is, the XY location of a point in the window is the same as the XY location in the environment—the depth (or Z value) is not represented (fig. 7-35).

Distortions that accompany increasingly wide-angle glass lenses, such as curved lines, or barrelhousing, and fish eye, do not occur in computerized perspective, although these effects can be created. Many other kinds of perspective, including isometrics, sphericals, anamorphics, and even the unreal imaginings of M. C. Escher, or the formal but pre-Renaissance perspective of Pompeii, can be generated with computer graphics.

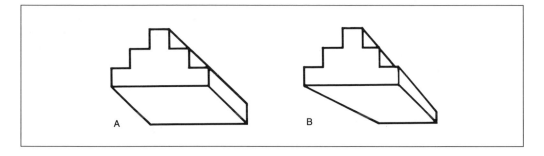

7-35. Orthogonal and van-
ishing-point perspectives
create different images
and have different purposes. Orthogonal perspec-
tives are used in
blueprints (A); vanishing-
point perspectives are
used to create the illusion
of depth (B).

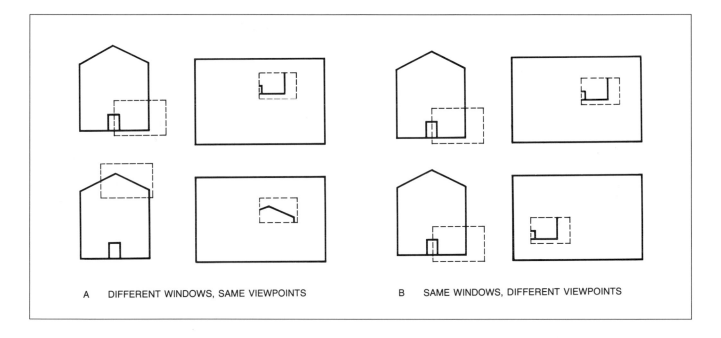

A   DIFFERENT WINDOWS, SAME VIEWPOINTS   B   SAME WINDOWS, DIFFERENT VIEWPOINTS

A *zoom* is a change in the focal length of the lens during a shot. Pivoting the POV is akin to a *pan;* and translating the POV during a shot is called a *dolly.* The window, like the eye, may be moved; it may also be scaled bigger or smaller so that the imaginary computer camera can look at things on an atomic or interplanetary scale. One can even tip a window to reduce keystoning, the apparent distortion of parallel lines.

The point of view is connected to the four sides of the window to form a perspective pyramid. All the objects that are outside this pyramid are clipped and excluded from the final image.

Windows and Ports

A window corresponds to what we see on a screen; but a window and screen usu-ally have different coordinate systems. The coordinate system of the window is related to the size of the data; the coordinate system of a screen is described by hardware. It is thus necessary to scale the image window into the address space of the device itself (fig. 7-36).

A *port,* usually rectangular, is that part of the display screen where the window is presented. A port may be the full resolution of the display; thus, a port on a frame buffer might be 0, 640 in X and 0, 480 in Y. Or, a port may be smaller than the total area of the display. In a newspaper, for example, the full port is the total area of the newspaper with smaller ports used to display pictures. A traditional window-to-port conversion is done by cropping a photograph and scaling it. The activity is no different in

7-36. A window exists in
the coordinate system of
the environment and its
units of measurement are
changeable. A port exists
in the coordinate system
of the display and its units
of measurement are
defined by the hardware.
Windows and ports
together provide a way to
represent environments
of arbitrary scale on displays of arbitrary scale on
displays of arbitrary resolution by freeing the
mechanics of the virtual
environment from the
mechanics of the display.

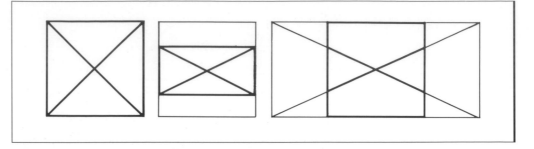

computers—the crop is the window and the scaling is the ratio between the width of the window and the width of the port.

The three window-to-port conversion methods are illustrated in figure 7-37. Remember that the computer is an elastic machine, and that a window and its port need not have the same aspect ratio. Ports are a fundamental element in the graphic arts, and have their own variables.

Stereopsis

Stereopsis, the dimensional perception provided by two different views of the same scene—such as the two eyes of a human being—can be simulated in computer graphics by calculating two slightly different views of the same scene. The two are then independently viewed by each eye using a simple viewer or with crosseyes (fig. 7-39).

Three-dimensional computer graphics deals not only with the geometry of objects, their position and size, but also with the properties of their surface. Indeed,

the description and treatment of the surface of an object are as complex as the geometric description of the object itself. Surface attributes include color, transparency, pattern, and a host of properties that determine how the surface reflects light (fig. 7-38).

SURFACE ATTRIBUTES

Color

The **color** of a surface is usually represented as a red, green, and blue triplet (RGB), but it can also be described with subtractive primaries: cyan, yellow, and magenta (CYM). Colors are often represented as real numbers between zero and one, rather than as integers, allowing for greater resolution and easier manipulation. Low-resolution color gamuts are more limited in three-dimensional graphics where a full range of continuously vary-

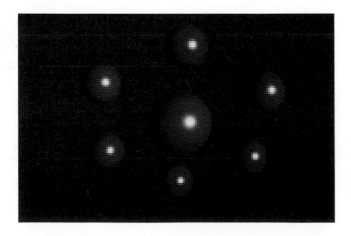
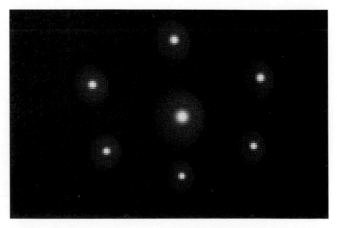

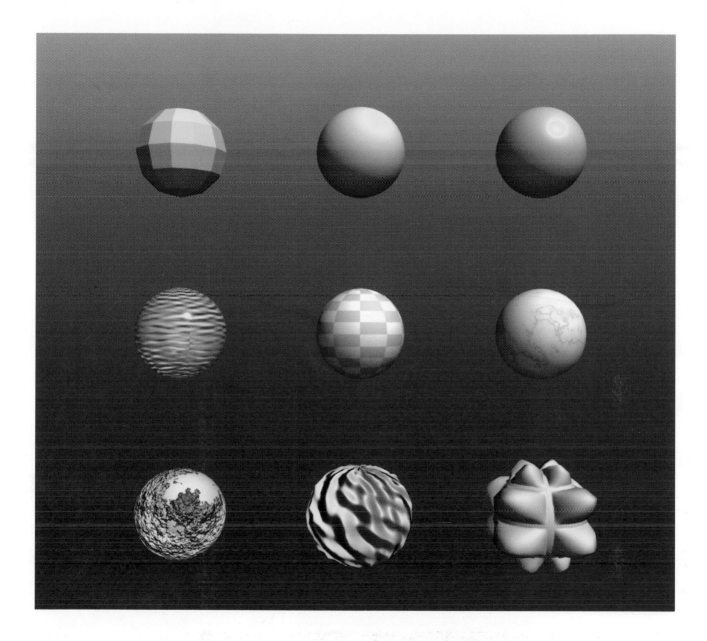

ing color is essential for **chiaroscuro,** the pictorial representation of light and shade (see chapter 5 for an extensive treatment of color).

Luminescence

Luminescence is the amount of light a surface emits, without reflecting light from an outside source. In other words, if you were to look at a surface in a totally dark room, the luminescence would be the color that glows. The luminescence property of a

7-39. This cross-reference table shows various surface and rendering attributes applied to a single sphere. The top row shows flat (Lambert), continuous (Gouraud), and specular (Phong) shading. The middle row shows transparency mapping, image mapping, and a procedural texture. The bottom row shows a bump map, a wave displacement map, and a displacement map. The transparency map defines how transparent an object is at a certain point on its surface. The displacement maps define actual surface deformation. (Courtesy of Michael DiComo, Pratt Institute.)

surface is usually not considered a light source; it is used with lighting to ensure that certain surfaces of objects will not get too dark. In situations where lighting is not used, luminescence is the same as color, and, like color, it is an RGB triplet with a range from zero to one.

Transparency and Filters

Transparency describes the amount of light that passes through a surface. A transparent surface transmits light without appreciable scattering, so that surfaces behind it are partially visible (fig. 7-40). Transparency is expressed as a real value between zero and one. A transparency value of zero describes an opaque surface. A surface with a transparency value of one is fully transparent and therefore invisible.

Transparency is usually represented as an RGB triplet so that different colors can have different degrees of transparency, permitting the implementation of colored filters. Thus, while a value of 0, 0, 0 indicates that the surface is completely opaque, a value of 0.7, 0.7, 0.5 indicates that red and green are 70 percent transparent, but blue is 50 percent transparent.

Transparent surfaces also have color, and the two attributes should not be confused. For example, a blue filter might have a *color* of 0, 0, 0 and a *transparency* of 0, 0, 0.5. A blue filter that was colored yellow might have a color of 1, 1, 0 and a transparency of 0, 0, 0.5. Again, there is a world of strange creative nooks here for anyone wishing to explore them.

Pattern and Image Mapping

Mapping takes an image, a two-dimensional bitplane memory, and treats it as if it were a surface in three-dimensional space. Images and patterns can be mapped onto surfaces with color, or onto transparent or reflective surfaces.

At its simplest, mapping places a flat image in perspective (fig. 7-41). More sophisticated methods wrap an image onto curved surfaces, much as a label is wrapped around a can (fig. 7-42). In the

7-40. The extent to which an object is transparent depends on how much light can pass through it. Fully transparent objects transmit light, so bodies lying beyond them are visible. (Courtesy of Intelligent Light.)

7-41. Planar mapping pivots a bitmap image in three-dimensional space. (Courtesy of Digital Effects Inc.)

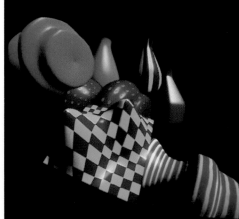

7-42. Curved mapping takes a two-dimensional bitmap image and wraps it onto a three-dimensional curved surface. (Image by Brian A. Barsky, Tony D. DeRose and Mark D. Dippé. Courtesy of University of California at Berkeley, Computer Graphics Lab.)

case of the can or cylinder, the image is not distorted, but an image mapped onto a sphere or parametric surface needs to be distorted or stretched to fit—much like a map of the earth, which needs to be distorted at the poles.

Mapping provides a way to define massive amounts of photographlike detail, such as a brick wall or water, without resorting to geometric objects. Rather than creating a data base for a brick wall, the graphic artist need only create a data base for an image of a brick wall and them map it onto a polygon.

Pixel images are not the only kinds of bitplane memory that can be mapped. Normals are mapped using a technique called bump mapping described in the texture section. A reflection map, which is a spherical projection of an environment around a point, is used to make objects seem reflective.

Luster

Luster is the property of a surface that determines how shiny it is. Shiny objects, like chrome, reflect sharp highlights and have high luster. Objects with low luster, like newsprint, are dull and scatter light (fig. 7-43).

Luster can be defined as a RGB triplet with a range from zero to one, allowing different lusters to be set for each primary. Lusters of zero have no specular reflection whatsoever; lusters of one are completely shiny like mirrors.

7-43. Luster refers to the reflecting qualities of a surface. (*Artist's Table* by Glenn Entis for Pacific Data Image, Inc.)

7-44. Bump mapping is a technique that creates surface texture, not by altering the geometric integrity of the object, but by wrapping a two-dimensional matrix of normals onto a surface. Texture can also be simulated by perturbing the normals of the objects in a random or constant fashion. (Courtesy of Digital Effects Inc.)

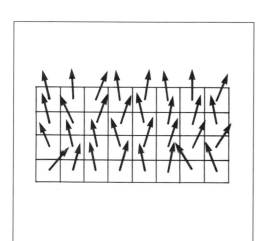

7-45. A bump map is a matrix of normals that can be randomly directed or follow a pattern. Surface normals represent the orientation of a surface, the direction the surface is pointing, and determine reflected light. When a bump map is wrapped onto a surface, the original surface normals are modified, which affects the lighting calculation, as the surface no longer uniformly reflects light. Bump maps will reflect light in many different directions and can therefore approximate the way light is microscopically reflected by materials such as cotton, silk, rayon, or linen.

7-46. Omnidirectional light is emitted in all directions equally.

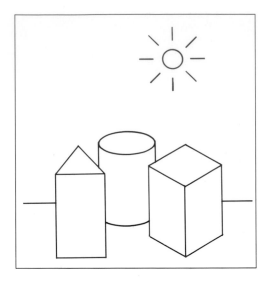

Texture

A **texture** is a flat representation of an uneven surface that is created by manipulating the reflection of light (fig. 7-44).

Texture mapping, like image mapping, does not alter the actual geometry of the surface. The texture, like an image, is defined by a two-dimensional bitmap matrix of values; but whereas the image-mapping matrix contains pixels with luminance values, the texture matrix contains elements with normals. The normals have subtle deviations that are either patterned or random and that microscopically recreate the way light is reflected, causing an object to look smooth or rough (fig. 7-45).

Texture is similar to shine or luster, but luster applies to the entire surface, whereas texture supplies a "grain" to the surface.

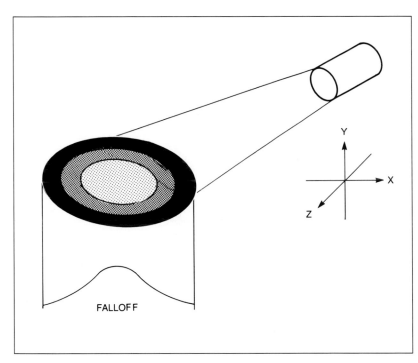

FALLOFF

LIGHTS AND LIGHTING

Lighting is a subtle art and requires perception, technical skill, and sensitivity. Lighting in computer graphics is in many ways analogous to lighting for theater or film, and, like model building or action, is responsive to the touch of a creative artist.

A **light** is a source of illumination. Lights interact with a surface and determine the chiaroscuro, the amount of light that a surface reflects, as well as cast **shadows,** volumes of space where light has been removed. In computer graphics, lighting can be controlled using English language-like commands that specify the position of lights and their properties.

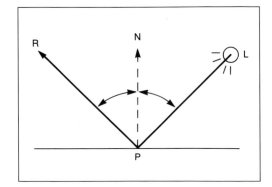

7-47. Spotlights are like omnidirectional lights— they have a position and brightness—but they emit light in one direction, specified by a normal. Spotlights can usually be focused on an area or flooded out, and their brightness relative to their normal can be defined.

7-48. The angle of incidence (LPN) is the angle between a light source (L) and the surface normal (PN). The angle of reflection (NPR) is the angle between the normal and a perfectly reflected ray (R) and is equal to the angle of incidence.

Properties of Lights

Lights have a number of properties. First, like objects they have **position,** an XYZ location in space. Lights may be located at infinity (like the sun) and behave like point sources, or they may be located outside or within the field of view. Second, the **brightness,** or quantity of light emitted, is expressed as an RBG triplet, usually on a scale of zero to one or infinity, which determines the color of light.

An **omnidirectional** light radiates equally in all directions (fig. 7-46). A **spotlight** radiates in a single direction, which is expressed as a normal (fig. 7-47). Spotlights can have a **fall-off** parameter, which controls the brightness of light relative to the axis of directionality. **Barn doors** may be used to control where light falls, and **cookies** cause the light to fall in patterns.

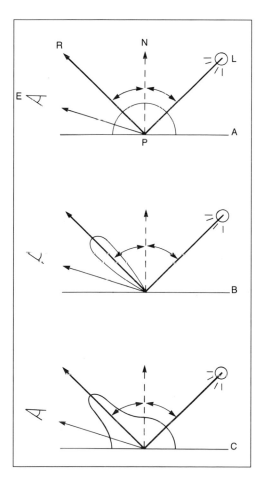

Reflection: Interaction of Lights and Surfaces

Reflection is the bouncing of light waves from a surface back to the environment and the POV. Light is not always modeled in computer graphics; when it is not, the color of a surface is the color recorded on the image. When lighting is employed, the reflective properties of the surface as well as the color of the lights determine the imaged surface color; this is the color of the light reflected to the camera lens.

Reflection calculations involve surface normals, because the normal specifies the directionality of a surface, and the amount of reflected light varies according to the relationship between the **angle of incidence**—the angle between the light source and the normal—and the **angle of view**—the angle between the normal and a camera or eye (fig. 7-48).

A **diffuse,** or matte, surface is one that reflects light randomly and evenly in all directions; the surface appears as a dull, flat color, like the felt on a pool table (fig. 7-49). Diffuse reflection scatters light equally in all directions and depends solely on the angle of incidence; the smaller this angle, that is the more directly above the surface the light is, the more light is reflected. Different surfaces reflect different percentages of light, but the diffuse reflection remains unaffected by the viewing angle.

7-49. A matte or diffuse surface reflects light in all directions, signified by the hemisphere in the diagram (A). The amount of light reflected to an eye or camera is a function of the angle of incidence and has nothing to do with the location of the eye, since light is reflected in all directions. The amount of diffuse reflection is also called the coefficient of diffuse reflection and is essentially the radius of the hemisphere. Specular reflection (B) is the tendency of some surfaces to reflect light only in the direction of the angle of reflection. The specular light reflected to the eye is a function of both the angle of incidence as well as the location of the eye. In a perfectly reflecting surface, one with very high luster, the reflected light is concentrated only on the angle of reflection and the surface becomes a mirror. But surfaces with lower luster cause some spreading of light, as in this diagram with its teardroplike reflection. Luster adjusts the width of the teardrop, and the magnitude of the teardrop along the angle of reflection is controlled by the quantity of specular reflection, also called the coefficient of specular reflection. When diffuse and specular reflection are combined (C), the result is a composite curve. Changing the two coefficients alters the ratios between the hemisphere and teardrop shape and provides a way to mix varying amounts of diffuse and specular components. The relation between diffuse and specular reflection, the luster, and the amount of light reflected in red, green, and blue for each, provide important visual clues about the composition of objects.

7-50. Shadows are cast by light sources onto other objects in the scene; multiple lights cast multiple shadows. (Courtesy of Raster Technologies, Inc.)

Specular reflections are not uniformly distributed; they are concentrated around the **angle of reflection**—the angle between the surface normal and a perfectly reflected light ray. In the shiniest case the surface functions like a mirror. Specular reflections create highlights on an object; the concentration of the highlight depends on the luster of the object. Objects with high luster reflect pinpoint highlights; objects with lower luster create more softened highlights (fig. 7-49). Specular reflections tend to be the color of the lights; diffuse reflections are the color of the surface. Different surfaces have different amounts of specular reflection.

A lighting calculation involving both diffuse and specular reflection requires infor-

mation about the color, luster, position of the surface, the proportions of diffuse and specular reflection, a point of view, and the position, color, and brightness of the light(s). These are then manipulated to simulate surfaces ranging from metals like gold and aluminum, to plastics, glass, paper, and paint (fig. 7-49).

Surfaces with texture, or bumpmaps, are calculated in a similar way to surfaces with properties of diffuse and specular reflection. The reflection properties do not change, but the calculation uses the mapped normals instead of a single normal when calculating lighting, which gives the surface more life.

Shadows

Shadows, areas of an environment that are blocked from light by other objects, provide important depth cues and heighten realism. Multiple lights, of course, produce multiple shadows, which are automatically calculated by programs in most computer systems. Shadows in computer graphics may be hard edged, or they may have an umber or penumbra to them (fig. 7-50). Transparent surfaces cast shadows that are not completely black, and when superimposed create deeper, blacker shadows.

Images can be drawn with or without shadows. Specific lights in a scene may be designated to cast shadows just as some objects can be designated to cast shadows, depending on whether or not the goal in a particular application is realistic simulation. The designer creatively and imaginatively tells stories and communicates ideas either by simulating reality or by mixing the components of reality and surreality to create visually striking effects.

Refraction

Light not only interacts with surfaces but with volumes as well. One volumetric light property is **refraction,** which causes light to bend or change direction whenever it travels from one medium to another, for example, from air into glass into water. Refraction can be modeled in computer

☞ **RELATED READING**

Barnhill, Robert E., and Richard F. Reisenfeld. *Computer Aided Geometric Design.* New York: Academic Press, 1984.

Chasen, Sylvan H. *Geometric Principles and Procedures for Computer Graphic Applications.* Englewood Cliffs, NJ: Prentice-Hall, 1978.

Gasson, Peter C. *Geometry of Spatial Forms.* New York: John Wiley & Sons, 1983.

Mortenson, Michael E. *Geometric Modeling.* New York: John Wiley & Sons, 1985.

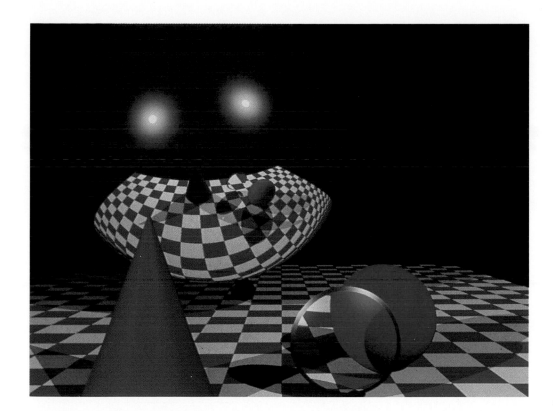

7-51. The refraction in this image was computed using a technique called *ray tracing.* (Courtesy of Intelligent Light and Todd Rodgers.)

graphics as a single constant, the refractivity of the material (fig. 7-51), and is used to model curved surfaces such as lenses, crystal balls, and gem cuts.

Atmospherics and Translucency

Light is affected when it passes through volumes that contain air, glass, fog, and water; the changes it undergoes are sometimes called *atmospherics,* similar to what Leonardo da Vinci called aerial perspective.

The atmospheric effects that can be created in a computer include haze, fog, rain, clouds, and translucent substances that are not appropriately represented as opaque surfaces, such as quartz (fig. 7-52). Atmospherics often involve an uneven absorption of light, and a softening of edges, and produce effects such as depth in a landscape by graying areas that are farther away.

Rendering refers to the way objects are actually represented or drawn on a screen: is a cube drawn as a wire frame skeleton or as a solid object; do lights cast shadows; by what rules do lights and surfaces interact?

RENDERING

The rendering or viewing algorithm is fundamentally concerned not with what objects are but with how they are drawn. Rendering is a tool of the graphic artist, and, though renderings sometimes model our physical world, they often involve ad hoc procedures to improve visibility—how effectively pictures communicate.

Points

The most basic rendering involves drawing points, which can describe things inherently pointlike, such as atoms or stars (fig. 7-53), as well as surfaces, such as a rippling flag.

In addition to having alterable spatial positions, points can also have a variety of intensities, colors, and sizes.

Often, because of their small size and

7-52. Atmospheric effects simulate the absorption of light as it passes through air, smoke, water. (Courtesy of the Mathematical Applications Group, Inc.)

tendency to get lost in transmission, points are drawn with a surrounding glow that makes them seem larger.

Wire Frame or Line Rendering

The simplest way to represent an object is with lines (fig. 7-54). These **wire frame,** or vector graphic, displays are the most economical ways to display data and are the stock and trade of plotters and storage tubes.

Wire frame renderings may be monochromatic (black-and-white), colored, or even shaded. In addition to intensity and color, lines may have variable width and a dot or dashing pattern (fig. 7-55).

Because they show the backs as well as the fronts of objects, wire frame renderings are often difficult to comprehend and make it hard to distinguish between objects that are closer and those that are farther away. One technique to improve visibility is **depth cueing,** which, with a simple calculation, draws lines that are farther away with a dot pattern, a darker value, or a narrower width (fig. 7-56). Depth cueing is also used to color elevations, like those found in contour maps (fig. 7-57).

Line does not necessarily bound and define surface; it can exist in very free forms and imply surface without actually enclosing an area (fig. 7-58).

Occultation

Often, especially when lines are being used to represent the outlines of volumes, it is desirable to draw only the lines that would be visible to a viewer, and to omit the lines that would be obscured by solid objects. **Occultation** is the determination of the edges and surfaces that would be visible from the observer's point of view. Only visible surfaces are drawn, and all occulted, or hidden, ones are removed (fig. 7-59). This is also called *hidden line* or *hidden surface removal*.

Renderings with occultation are much more complex computationally than simply wire frames, and, depending on the application, may or may not be worth the added expense.

Opaque Surface Rendering

Surfaces can be represented not only by their outlines or edges, but as **opaque** solid areas of color (fig. 7-60). Renderings with occulted, opaque surfaces are often called *solid renderings*. **Scan conversion,** one method of creating an opaque area of color, draws many touching parallel lines inside the surface or superimposes the surface over a bitmap and changes the value of all the pixels that lie within the surface (fig. 7-61).

Another method involves **crosshatching,** diagonal lines or a pattern drawn on the surface. Like scan conversion, crosshatching is done at screen, not data, resolution. **Close-packed vectors** (CPV) draw a series of parallel lines from one side of a polygon to the other (fig. 7-62). CPVs are different from the scan conversion method, because scan conversion works at screen resolution, whereas the CPVs are part of the data and get bigger or smaller as the data gets bigger or smaller. These provide a dynamic graphic feel and are often used to simulate streak photography.

Chiaroscuro (Shading)

Chiaroscuro, or shading, is the representation of opaque surfaces with a range of dark to light values, as if they are illuminated by lights. Chiaroscuro is computed after visible surface determination; it is the result of the surface orientation, color, and luster and the light color, position, and brightness.

7-53. The stars in this universe have been created with point-rendering techniques and diffusion filters. (Courtesy of Digital Effects Inc.)

The simplest chiaroscuro technique is called constant value face shading, or polygonal shading. **Polygonal shading** performs a single calculation for each polygonal surface and renders the entire surface of each polygon with a single intensity of light (fig. 7-63). Polygonal shading makes each polygon easily distinguishable from the others, causing objects like spheres to look faceted. If a smoother figure is required, one solution is to add more facets. This is

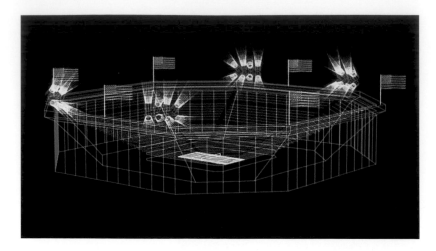

7-54. Wire frame rendering of the National Tennis Center in Flushing. (Courtesy of Digital Effects, Inc.)

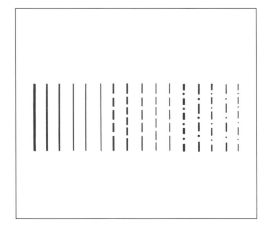

7-55. Line widths and dashing patterns provide graphic variety and improve clarity in computer-generated images.

not the best approach, however, because a very large number of facets must be added to make the object appear smooth.

A better solution is to employ intensity interpolation, or **continuous shading** (fig. 7-64). Continuous shaded surfaces may also have luster and highlight as well as texture or image maps. Continuous shading produces a more realistic result, but takes longer to compute than polygonal shading. A still better but even more computationally intensive approach is **ray tracing,** in which a ray of light is traced from the point of view through each pixel on the screen to whatever object it intersects (fig. 7-51). One advantage of ray tracing is that if the object is transparent, refractive, or reflective, the new direction of the ray can be computed and further traced until it intersects with another object. This provides a way to create very realistic images and incorporate objects like reflective spheres into a

7-56. Depth cueing draws lines that are farther away with either different line widths (A) or darker values (B). (Courtesy of Digital Effects Inc.)

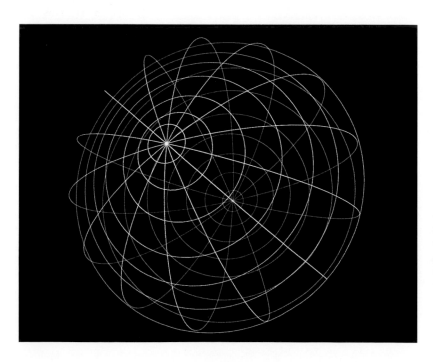

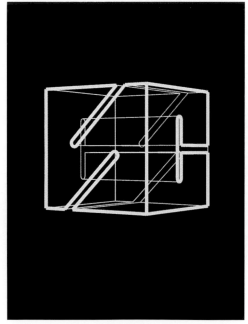

7-57. Different elevations have different colors; the higher the elevation, the lighter the color. (Courtesy of Digital Effects Inc.)

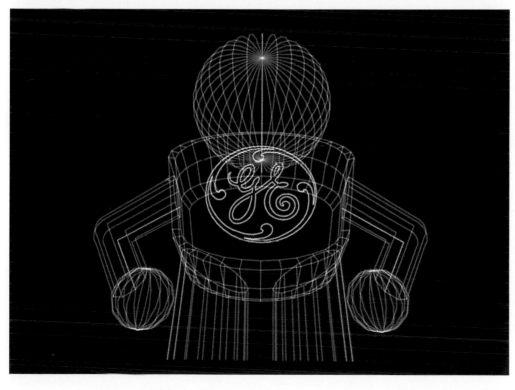

7-58. Lines can suggest surface without actually defining a closed, bounded, area. Compare this to figure 7-66, where the lines define edges that bound a surface. (Courtesy of Digital Effects Inc.)

7-59. Occultation systematically sorts the data base and displays only the edges and surfaces of an object that are visible. (Courtesy of Pixel, Inc. Software written and designed by Manuel de Landa.)

scene. Another approach to illumination utilizes **radiosity,** in which the amount of light reflecting off each object in the scene is added back into all the other objects. This provides a calculation of ambient light that is closer to the natural laws of physics (fig. 7-65).

A surface may also be created with a gradation of color that is not determined by lighting sources. The simplest way to do this is with **color-graduated** or **color-ramp** surfaces in which each corner of a polygon is assigned a color. The software then interpolates a color for each pixel of the resultant image in a manner similar to interpolating a shading value. This is a common technique for graphically creating a sky or background, where color must vary from one hue to another (fig. 7-66).

Procedural Texture

Procedural texture techniques simulate the texture of objects using algorithms that are often executed at rendering time and that may be a function of rendering parameters, such as the location of lights. Procedural textures are like procedural objects in that they are

☞ **RELATED READING**

Holden, Alan. *Shapes, Space, and Symmetry.* New York: Columbia University Press, 1971.

Jankel, Annabel, and Rocky Morton. *Creative Computer Graphics.* Cambridge, England: Cambridge University Press, 1984.

Pearce, Peter. *Structure in Nature as a Strategy for Design.* Cambridge, MA: The MIT Press, 1978.

Thompson, D'Arcy. *On Growth and Form.* London: Cambridge University Press, 1971.

Wong, Wucius. *Principles of Three-Dimensional Design.* New York: Van Nostrand Reinhold, 1977.

7-60. In solid surface rendering, the hidden surfaces are occulted and the objects are rendered with opaque surfaces using scan conversion. (Courtesy of Digital Effects Inc.)

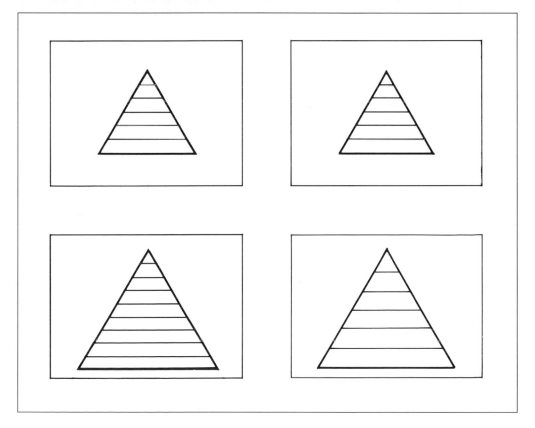

7-61. Scan conversion (left) opaques a surface at the screen resolution. Thus, if the object gets bigger or smaller, it will still be evenly colored. Close packed vectors (right) are parallel lines drawn on the face of a surface and are part of the object. When an object gets bigger, smaller, or rotates, the closed packed vectors change accordingly.

7-62. Close-packed vectors
have many artistic uses
and produce lightweight,
semi-transparent surfaces.
(Courtesy of Walt Disney
Productions and Robert
Abel Associates. © The
Walt Disney Company.)

defined by parameters to a program; the difference is that these programs define texture, not geometry. Procedural textures can be two- or three-dimensional, for example, the pattern of a zebra (2D), or the inside of a block of quartz (3D), that is calculated as one passes a cross section through it (fig. 7-67). Although a procedural texture is part of the object description, and not a rendering parameter, it is really only evaluated for a specific rendering situation.

Drafting

There are also rendering techniques that go beyond the representation of a virtual world. Oftentimes it is important to supplement rendered images with additional information. This may include names and

labels of persons, places, and things, as well as additional line and artwork (for example, routes of travel, motion pathways, safety guidelines). A simple example of these many cases is **drafting,** a specialized rendering technique that augments two- or three-dimensional graphics with information about the product. Drafting often provides several different specialized views of the object. **Dimension drawings** include measurements, dimension lines, and arrows, and often centerlines and tolerances (fig. 7-68). **Assembly drawings** show how the components of an assembled mechanism fit together; they may also specify surface-finishing properties (fig. 7-69). **Exploded views** show parts and dimensions in perspective and method of assembly (fig. 7-70).

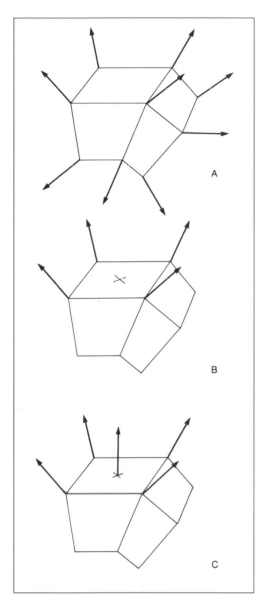

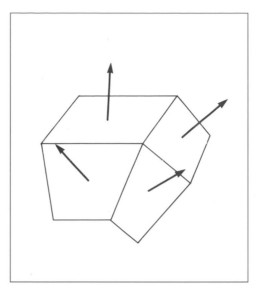

7-63. Polygons are *shaded* by calculating one normal per polygon and then using that normal to calculate a single reflected light value to opaque the polygon. The lighting calculation can employ diffuse as well as spectral reflection, although it is normally only done with diffuse reflection, because highlights simply do not show up unless there are a large number of polygons. (Courtesy of Digital Effects Inc.)

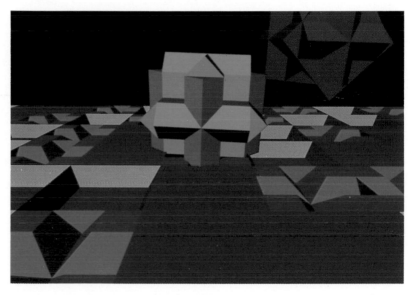

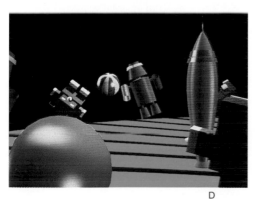

7-64. Continuous-shading techniques calculate many shading values for each polygon—essentially, one shading value is computed for each pixel in the display. Two methods, Gouraud and Phong, average the surface normals for adjacent polygons and associate these average normals with the corners of each polygon (A). For a rectangular mesh, each polygon is represented by four corner normals; adjacent polygons share corner normals. In Gouraud shading, a lighting calculation is then performed for each corner normal, and the shading values are interpolated across the surface of each polygon, creating a smoothly changing surface (B). Phong shading is similar, except the normals themselves are interpolated across the surface, and a shading value is calculated for each pixel (C). Both methods can incorporate diffuse and specular reflection, but Phong shading produces a more realistic approximation, particularly when highlights are involved. Continuous-shading methods require skill and a knowledge of the construction of the data base—for instance, normals should not be averaged if the object contains creases or folds that must be preserved. In objects with texture, the bump map normal is combined with the interpolated surface normal when the intensity is calculated (D). (Photo courtesy of Pacific Data Images and Glenn Entis.)

7-65. Radiosity is a lighting technique that calculates the amount of light reflected back into the scene from all the surfaces. The image of this *Simulated Steel Mill* was created using a modified version of the hemi-cube radiosity algorithm, computed on a DEC VAX 8700 and displayed on a Hewlett-Packard Renaissance Display. The environment consisted of approximately 55,000 elements, and was one of the most complex environments computed at that time. The research was part of a National Science Foundation grant entitled "Interactive Computer Graphics Input and Display Techniques," directed by Prof. Donald P. Greenberg. (Courtesy of Stuart Feldman, John Wallace, and Donald P. Greenberg, Program of Computer Graphics, Cornell University.)

Specialized renderings also often use special perspectives. In drafting these include the **orthogonal, axonometric,** and **oblique projections.** The orthogonal projection is where an object is viewed dead on (lower left of fig. 7-70), and the axonometric and oblique projections are used instead of the more familiar perspective projection because they employ true distances along two or three axes (fig. 7-71).

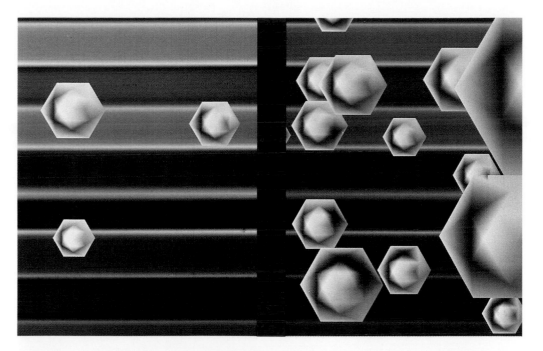

7-66. The color-interpolated surface begins by assigning different colors to different vertex of the polygon, and then interpolating the colors across the face of the polygon. (Courtesy of Digital Effects Inc.)

7-67. Procedural texture calculates the skin or surface appearance of an object according to a set of program rules. (Courtesy of Isaac Victor Kerlow.)

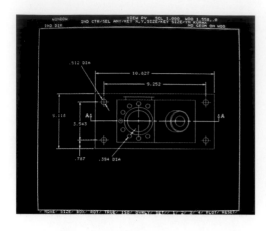

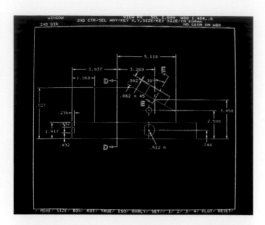

7-68. Dimension drawings incorporate measurements and tolerance information, centerlines, and radius information. (Courtesy of the Mathematical Applications Group, Inc.)

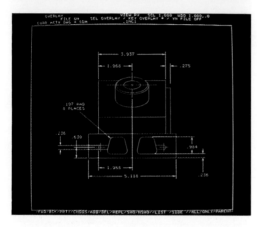

7-69. Assembly drawings show parts, cross sections, and details (Courtesy of Jean-Paul Peretz.)

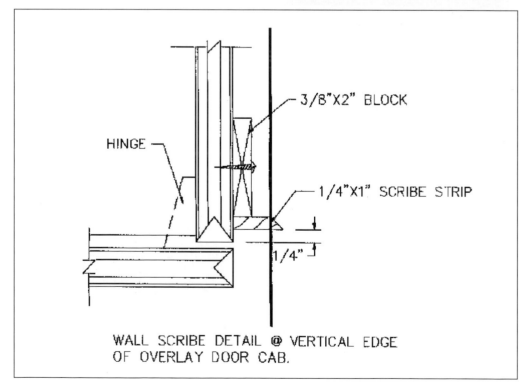

WALL SCRIBE DETAIL @ VERTICAL EDGE
OF OVERLAY DOOR CAB.

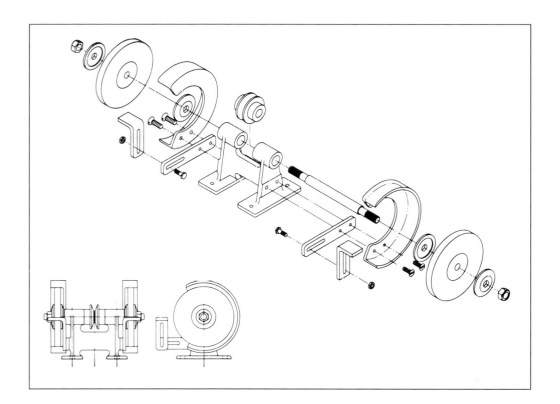

7-70. Multiview perspectives let us view an object from different points of view. In the center the exploded drawing relates the parts to the whole; we can visualize how this electric grinder comes apart (or together). The exploded rendering is an isometric perspective; the two coplanar views in the lower left arc orthographic projections of the grinder assembled. (Courtesy of International Business Machines Corp.)

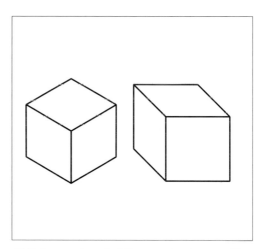

7-71. Isometric and oblique projections enable measurements to be made on certain axes. In the isometric perspective, the distances along the edges of the cube in the drawing are equal for all three axes. In the oblique perspective, distances on the X and Y axes of the cube correspond to distances on the X and Y axes of the paper, but the Z axis is not equally scaled.

8-0. Digital media combines technical advantages with creative benefits. Designers can bring their best ideas to a concept and not be concerned about technological limitations. (*Beautiful World* design by Margo Chase.)

8

TWO-DIMENSIONAL MEDIA APPLICATIONS

DIGITAL TYPOGRAPHY
ILLUSTRATION SYSTEMS
COLOR CORRECTION AND SEPARATION
PAGINATION
FINE ARTS

Digital computers have revolutionized the production of two-dimensional media, be it newspapers, magazines, presentation slides, or a simple business card. Primary processes involved in the production of two-dimensional media include typesetting, painting, illustration, pattern design, chart makeup, photography, color correction, pagination, compositing, and cel animation. A **desktop publishing** system consolidates all these different steps into a single system in which all the component functionalities operate on common data formats and employ a consistent set of GUI rules (fig. 8-1). It is also true that a desktop publishing system can also incorporate some nongraphic functions, such as scheduling, production run control, accounting, and analysis of distribution, sales, and surveys. Synonyms for desktop publishing include *integrated publishing* and *digital prepress*. The latter term perhaps best captures the spirit of the movement, except that today's two-dimensional publishing world also encompasses presentations on television and film, on slides and overheads, and, increasingly, directly on computer screens to the end user. All digital computer data are media-independent, so in a general sense, media-specific tools are slowly disappearing. A graphmaker that can be used to assemble slides can also assemble TV frames or newspaper halftones. This is not to say that con-

☞ **RELATED READING**

Bigelow, Charles, and Donald Day. "Digital Typography." *Scientific American* (August 1983).

Cavuoto, James, and Stephen Beale. *Linotronic Imaging Handbook.* Torrance, CA: Micro Publishing Press, 1990.

Gottschall, Edward M. *Typographic Communications Today.* Cambridge, MA: The MIT Press, 1989.

Hiebert, Kenneth. *Graphic Design Processes, . . . Universal to Unique.* New York: Van Nostrand Reinhold, 1992.

Kim, Scott. *Inversions.* New York: W. H. Freeman, 1989.

Stone, Sumner. *On Stone, The Art and Use of Typography on the Personal Computer.* San Francisco: Bedford Arts, 1991.

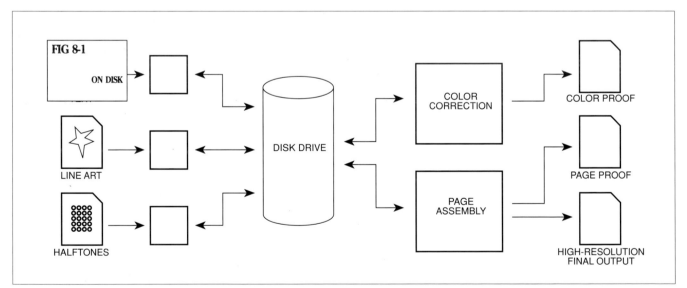

8-1. An electronic prepress system enables a user to incorporate text, line art, continuous tone, and color images into a single document that can be printed on paper or distributed electronically. Text is incorporated as ASCII files, line art as vector graphics, and continuous tone as bitmaps. A color correction system can modify image files and save them back to disk, where they are stored with all other files. The page makeup system can paginate and position all of the elements as they are to appear on the final printed piece. Output can be in the form of low-resolution page proofs or high-resolution press-ready film negatives.

tent is composed identically for all distribution media—it isn't—only to say that the tool set is the same. The designer of the future will be expected to think about making media at some resolution. Even the printing press is becoming a digital output device.

Today almost all publishing is done on soft copy WYSIWYG desktop computers. Text, pictures, and page descriptions are fully digital. Virtual pages are edited with cut-copy-paste technique. Finished pages are transmitted by networks and satellites, making it practical to migrate the printing and distribution of published materials to locations that are remote from the production center. Newspapers, for instance, may be composed in a central location, then facsimiles are transmitted to multiple printing plants via satellite (fig. 8-2). This decreases shipping costs, while expediting product distribution.

Electronic publishing provides alternatives to plate making and printing. Hard copy, should it be desired, can be created by consumers at their homes or offices.

The basic components of integrated publishing systems are terminals for text input and editing and stations for graphic illustration, photographic digitization, color correction and separation, and page make-up. The output devices include laser scanners, plate-making equipment, impact printers, and television.

DIGITAL TYPOGRAPHY

Type is one of the fundamental tools of the graphic artist, a tool that the graphic artist has in common with the writer. ***Digital typography*** involves not only typesetting, but the design and creation of type as well. Whether type is ideographical, as in Chinese, or phonetic, as in Western languages, word processing and typesetting specify how letters and ligatures are positioned, and how lines are organized and graphically formatted.

Type Creation and Design

The design and creation of type is a specialized field that employs computer-assisted techniques. The shape of digital type, like the shape of type through history, is influenced not only by the designer but by design and reproduction technologies as well. Effective type requires accurate transcriptions of traditional typefaces and type designs that are tailored to the new medium.

Digital type design must consider leading, justification, letter spacing, and kerning, as well as features that are unique to the new media, such as data storage, portability, and anti-aliasing.

As we suggested before, ***type*** is a one-dimensional sequence of symbols each of which is visually represented as a

8-2. A centralized factory transmits to remote printing and distribution centers (left). A centralized facility transmits directly to the consumer (right). Computerizing the production process and transmitting to remote sites for printing and distribution is becoming a common method for newspaper and magazine circulation.

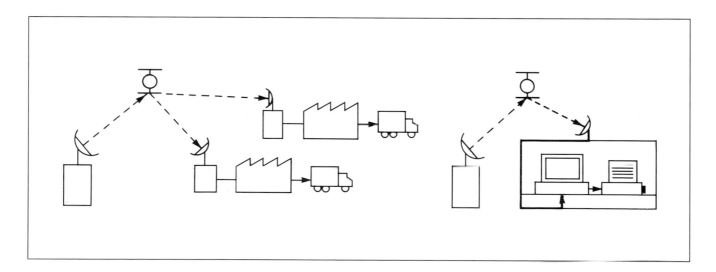

8-3. Letterforms can be represented with codes, contours, and bitmaps.

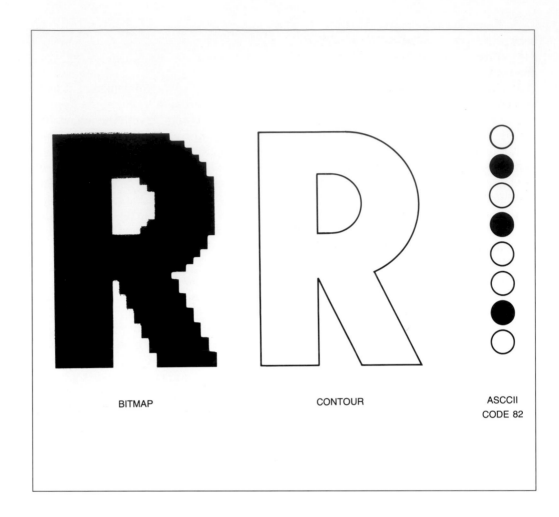

BITMAP

CONTOUR

ASCCII
CODE 82

8-4. Building a character with points and arcs.

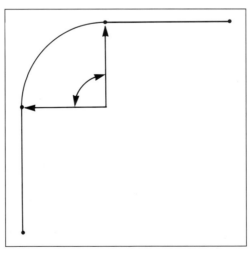

two-dimensional graphic element. Each symbol can be encoded either as a polygon outline or as a bitmap. All three representations are used in computer graphics hardware (fig. 8-3).

Typewriter displays use a code number to cause a striker to impact the paper. Vector displays, and applications that need to scale type, represent letters as polygon outlines. Video displays and many pixel displays use bitmaps.

The vertices that describe the contour of a character can be digitized on an electronic tablet or geometrically constructed by digitizing only critical points and then connecting them with straight lines, arcs (fig. 8-4), or curve-fitting equations (fig. 8-5).

Procedural methods, whether plane geometry or brush-stroke simulation, are harder to use at first but often produce smoother, faster results, especially when the letter shapes are complex or must have dynamic range in scale.

Computer technology can foster innovations in type design. Interpolation techniques make it possible to derive hybrid typefaces from two existing styles. Although thousands of variations can be generated using this method, it is up to the designer to select those that can be worked and refined into a consistent alphabet (fig. 8-6).

An alphabet can also be drawn with different computer-simulated pen tips, which is especially useful for alphabets where stroke direction and sequence are important. The characters in figure 8-7 were created by specifying key points, describing the paths of the strokes, and choosing the shape of the pen. Describing letterforms with a program allows the designer to explore systematic variations by just altering one or two variables.

Mathematical distortions of type designs can also be easily achieved with computer-based design systems (fig. 8-8). These possibilities include the simulation of effects and distortions traditionally realized with lenses and mechanical apparatuses.

The conversion of polygon type into bitmaps is accomplished by positioning and sizing the polygon outline and then scan converting it to pixels (fig. 8-9). The results, however, often leave much to be desired, as problems include not only aliasing, but uneven weight that results from subtle changes in alignment and resolution. Anti-aliasing, higher pixel resolutions, and adequate planning in the design stage lead to satisfactory results.

Overstriking, variable intensity pixels, and careful alignment are techniques for enhancing the visibility of bitmap typography, especially in low-resolution output devices (fig. 8-10). Bitmaps may also be manually created, which is a preferred method for low-resolution bitmaps used in dot matrix printers and video display terminals (fig. 8-11). The designer's role is not to design at high resolution regardless of what becomes of the design in the

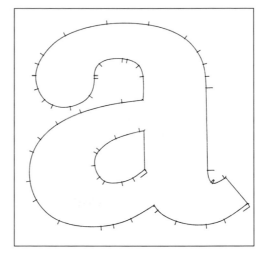

8-5. Building a character with curve-fitting equations. (Courtesy of URW Unternehmensberatung.)

8-6. Interpolation between serif and sans serif typefaces. (Courtesy of URW Unternehmensberatung.)

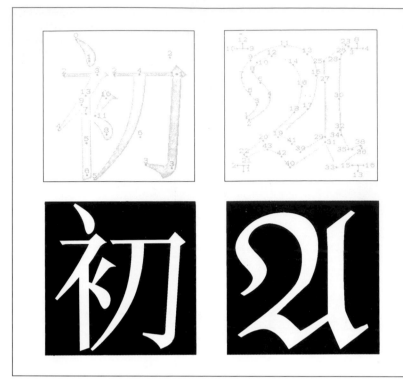

transmission process, but to understand that communication involves many resolutions, and to design at the resolution that suits the message space.

Although a polygon letterform contour can be sized to a small or large point size, the two must be different shapes. Smaller type, for example, is proportionally thicker than larger type and is designed to be easily read at some real world size. Traditional lead and phototypography therefore design different type for each point size. Computerized type defines a series of contours for each letter in a font. For example, three different contours might be made for each letter, one for normal book size type (9-14 points), one for smaller sizes (4-8 points), and one for headlines and display type (16-64 points).

Typesetting

Typesetting, or the placement of letters and words on a page to compose legible

8-7. Stroke simulation. Variables describe the finished character; an experimental Chinese font by Go Guoan and John Hobby (left); AMS Euler Fraktur by Hermann Zapf and The Stanford Digital Typography Group (right). Both characters were created using the Metafont program. (Courtesy of Scott Kim.)

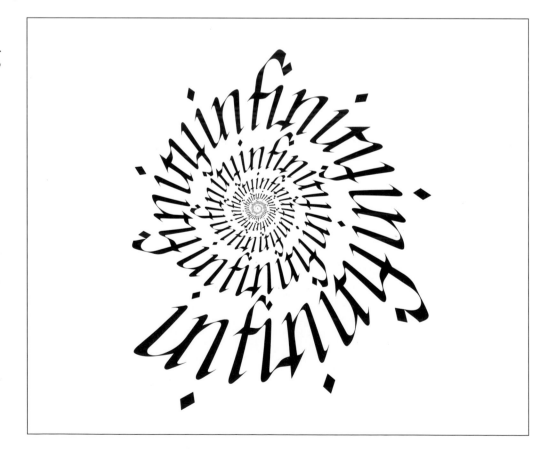

8-8. The calligraphic module has been digitized and arranged in a spiral with a special program. (Courtesy of Scott Kim.)

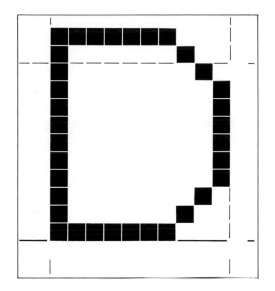

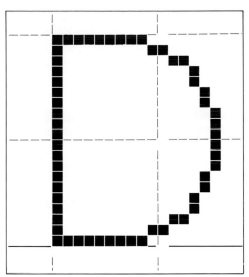

8-9. Type in a polygon format can be converted to bitmaps at different resolutions. (Courtesy of URW Unternehmensberatung.)

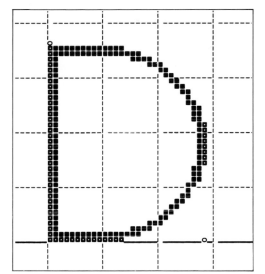

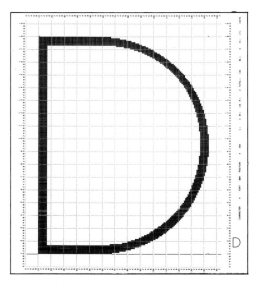

8-10. The legibility of low-resolution bitmaps is enhanced with anti-aliasing techniques—even four levels of gray provide a significant improvement. (Provided by Isaac V. Kerlow.)

Mexican Market

8-11. The legibility of a low-resolution typeface can be greatly improved by designing the face at a specific resolution. Alphabet A is too schematic, B is too bold, but C reads easily. (Courtesy of Janice Hillman.)

The Real Hawkeye Pierce
"What city?" inquired the operator for Maine Information.
"Crabapple Cove," replied the magazine writer.
"Oh, that's where Hawkeye lives," came her quick response. "You know, the guy in 'MASH'."

A

The Real Hawkeye Pierce
"What city?" inquired the operator for Maine Information.
"Crabapple Cove," replied the magazine writer.
"Oh, that's where Hawkeye lives," came her quick response. You know, the guy in 'MASH'."

B

The Real Hawkeye Pierce
"What city?" inquired the operator for Maine Information.
"Crabapple Cove," replied the magazine writer.
"Oh, that's where Hawkeye lives," came her quick response. "You know, the guy in 'MASH'."
We know, and it's also the name of the inlet where the real Hawkeye

C

Body Type

DISPLAY TYPE

8-12. Text and display typefaces.

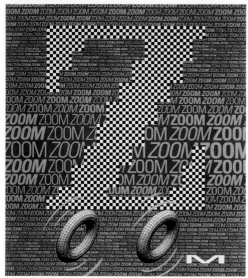

8-13. By creating fonts that are polygons and not bitmaps, it is possible to output type in many different sizes and weights, like the ZOOMs in the background of *Type on Wheels*. The device-independent language used to describe these letter forms is Postscript, also described in chapter 2. (Courtesy of Mark Anderson Design. Designer/Illustrator: Earl Gee.)

text, is a command-oriented process with a rich historical tradition. **Body type,** used to set text that will be read as a linear continuum, tends to be used in fixed integer sizes. **Display** or headline type is used for larger copy and is often sized to fit; it is continuously scalable (fig. 8-12).

Typesetting production involves the **input text,** a string of letters, numbers, and punctuation, and **formatting** commands, which specify how the text is to be justified, tabulated, and letter spaced (fig. 8-13). Text is entered into a computer

either with a keyboard or an optical character reader (OCR). The text and commands are edited using a **word processor,** a program that allows the text to be modified, augmented, and cut; it also allows the integration of the formatting commands. After the text is edited, it is saved on a digital disk or output as a formatted file that contains the input text interspersed with **control characters** (special characters that are recognized by the typesetting system and control indents, tabs, carriage returns, letter spacing, and justification). This formatted file is input to a typesetter, which outputs either film galleys or soft copy type that is displayed on a screen or forwarded to a pagination system (fig. 8-14).

Typesetting systems are related to other computerized procedures that can index, correct spelling errors, hyphenate, and analyze readability. The ability to input ASCII text files to a typesetting system makes typesetting more accessible to authors with personal computers, by eliminating a whole series of intermediate production steps (fig. 8-15).

Typesetting variables can be controlled and adjusted, often on a letter by letter basis, with contemporary digital typesetters. The visual language variables that are involved in typesetting include font name, case, boldness or weight, italicization, color, drop shadows, point size, letter spacing, leading line width, column depth, and justification.

The face, or **font,** is a collection of characters and special symbols in a particular size and style (fig. 8-16). Thousands of fonts exist in script, serif, and sans serif styles. Fonts may be condensed, regular, or extended; bold or italic; solid or outline.

Case, as in upper- and lowercase, distinguishes capital and "small" letters. Many fonts also have a control case, which contains punctuation, numerals, and special characters. Case is usually controlled by a key on a keyboard, just as it is on a typewriter (fig. 8-17). **Drop shadows** give the illusion of depth, but are actually two dimensional, whereas **extruded sides** do extend into space and are three dimensional (fig. 8-18).

The **type size** of a font is determined by measuring the font from the lowest to the highest extension of a letter, from the bottom of a lowercase g to the top of a capital M, for instance. Type size is specified in *points*—seventy-two points equal one inch. Type size created with digital media generally range from six to seventy-two points in increments of one-half point.

Leading is the vertical distance in points between lines of text; this book is set in

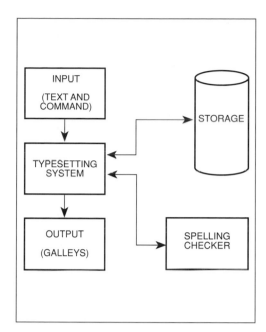

INPUT
(TEXT AND COMMAND)

STORAGE

TYPESETTING SYSTEM

OUTPUT
(GALLEYS)

SPELLING CHECKER

8-14. This block diagram shows a digital word processing and typesetting system. Text, sometimes embedded with control codes, is input via a word processor. A spelling checker may examine the text file and output a corrected version. The typesetting software letter spaces, kerns, and justifies the text, and formats it into a bitmap file that can be output on a printer.

8-15. Text and graphics files are combined and output to a Postscript-driven imagesetter. (*Columbus Page* design by John Weber.)

SERIF

SANS SERIF

Script

CONDENSED

NORMAL

EXPANDED

BOLD

BLACK

ITALIC

OUTLINE

8-16. A variety of fonts.

**8-17. Uppercase, lower-
case, and pi case.**

UPPERCASE
lowercase
!#$&*''¢@[]( )

**8-18. Drop shadow and
extrusion.**

DROP SHADOW

EXTRUSION

**8-19. Leading, width, and
depth. Twelve points
equal one pica and six
picas equal one inch.**

ten-point type with two points of lead. Line *length* refers to the width of a line measured in *picas.* Approximately six picas equal one inch and this copy is fifteen picas wide. *Depth* is the length of a column from top to bottom and is measured in inches (fig. 8-19).

Systems tailored to hard copy display often use windows that contain real world coordinates. But points, picas, and inches are all measures that have less meaning in soft copy displays where the screen can vary in size. In these situations type size is either measured relative to an arbitrary window or by predefined, fixed sizes referred to by number or name.

Letter spacing is the space between individual characters, or how closely they butt up against each other, and is regulated to enhance the aesthetic qualities or to improve the readability of text (fig. 8-20). Letter spacing should not be confused with condensation or extension, which makes the actual letters wider or narrower. Nor should it be confused with *kerning,* which adjusts the space between individual letters for differences in their width and relationship (fig. 8-21).

Justification, or the fitting of type into lines of equal length, proportionally spaces letters, giving different characters more

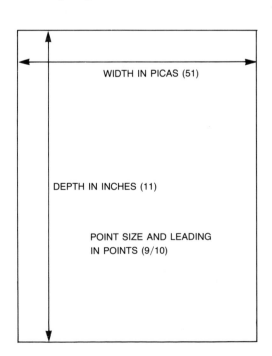

WIDTH IN PICAS (51)

DEPTH IN INCHES (11)

POINT SIZE AND LEADING
IN POINTS (9/10)

or less space according to their width to flush out the surplus width in the line.

In addition to being justified (left and right), type can be left justified (ragged right), right justified (ragged left), or centered (fig. 8-22). Paragraph indents and tab settings are additional parameters usually specified as a number of spaces.

ILLUSTRATION SYSTEMS

Computerized paint and makeup systems complement and, to some degree, approximate traditional methods, though computer systems have unique benefits and liabilities (fig. 8-23).

Interactive illustration systems allow color mixing, freehand drawing, and the sizing and positioning of shapes. Many include type display and image digitizing capabilities. Most systems are operated by selecting options, in any order, from a soft copy menu (fig. 8-24); these often call other menus that offer further options.

Much of the "brainstorming" involved in the design process can be easily implemented on a computer design station. For example, the technique of interpolation can be very effective for generating

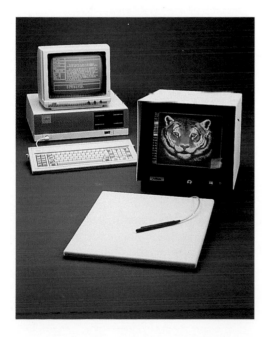

TOUCHING
TIGHT
NORMAL
LOOSE

8-20. Letter spacing: tight, touching, normal, loose.

WOLVES

WOLVES

8-21. Kerning tailors the space between individual letters, so it varies from combination to combination. In a word set without kerning all letters are evenly spaced. Kerning tightens up spaces and makes combinations such as "wo" tighter than combinations such as "ol."

Computer graphics are expanding the role of graphic designers beyond the traditional imaging media. The future is open for designers who know how to combine the structuring of information with effective visual design.

Computer graphics are expanding the role of graphic designers beyond the traditional imaging media. The future is open for designers who know how to combine the structuring of information with effective visual design.

Computer graphics are expanding the role of graphic designers beyond the traditional imaging media. The future is open for designers who know how to combine the structuring of information with effective visual design.

Computer graphics are expanding the role of graphic designers beyond the traditional imaging media. The future is open for designers who know how to combine the structuring of information with effective visual design.

8-22. Justification: both sides justified, flush left, flush right, and centered copy.

8-23. An illustration system comprises a computer with memory, a color monitor, one or more input peripherals (a mouse or a graphics tablet), and sometimes a hard copy device. (Courtesy of Artronics, Inc.)

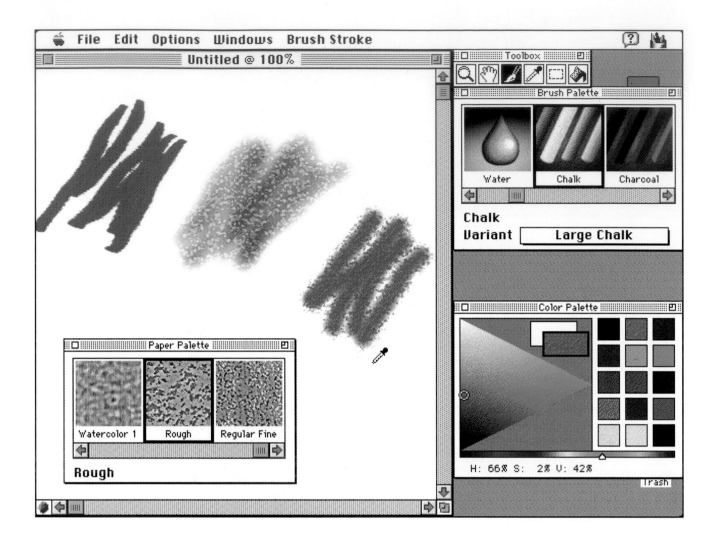

8-24. A WYSIWYG display (pronounced wiz-i-wig), short for what-you-see-is-what-you-get, allows text to be mixed with lines and graphics. Fonts appear realistic and virtual tools perform virtual illustration and painting tasks. (Screenshot of *Painter* courtesy of Fractal Software.)

variations of a seed idea by changing one shape into another (fig. 8-25). Color variations, label and copy positions, and bottle shapes can also be explored.

In addition to designs, news graphics for television, audiovisual slides, industrial illustrations, limited animation, and charts and graphs are produced at a computer design station.

Computer-generated business graphics are very accurate and significantly reduce the time involved in creating presentation art. The graphic work stations can format raw data that is downloaded from mainframes as well as data directly keyed in. These data can then be displayed on computer monitors, recorded on video-

tape, plotted or printed onto paper or overhead transparencies, or recorded as a 35mm slide. As we have discussed before, there is a wide choice in outputting hard and soft copy, with a varying number of colors and spatial resolutions (fig. 8-26).

The resolution and features of a computer graphics workstation are not entirely independent of the underlying hardware. Two hardware technologies are critical here: workstations with raster bitmap pixel displays and polygon refresh display lists. The difference is comparable to the distinction between line copy and continuous tone; the features and functionality of the two technologies vary substantially, and although both technologies

8-25. This 5 × 5 matrix interpolates a different design variable in each axis to create a cross-reference table of symbol variation. A similar strategy, called multimasters, may be used with fonts to create variations associated with point size and with boldface. (Courtesy of Scott Kim.)

can coexist in a machine, this is often not the case.

Color Features

Color is associated with polygons as well as pixels, often in conjunction with look-up tables, for both display list and bitplane architectures. As explained in chapter 5, the maximum number of colors is related to the width of the look-up table, and the total number of colors that can be simultaneously displayed is related to the number of bits/pixel.

Other features most illustration stations support include the ***mixing*** of primary or secondary colors and ***ramping,*** the ability to create all the shades of color that exist between two extreme colors using interpolation (fig. 8-27). Colors can be picked up and moved, and some illustration systems also have limited animation capabilities based on color table animation, described later in this chapter.

Display List Features

Display list machines are well suited for the makeup of business charts and graphics, because the graphic elements can be manipulated and positioned individually or in groups. Polygons do not, however, describe continuous tone images like photographs and paintings; these need a pixel display. Software that utilizes a display list is often called ***draw software.***

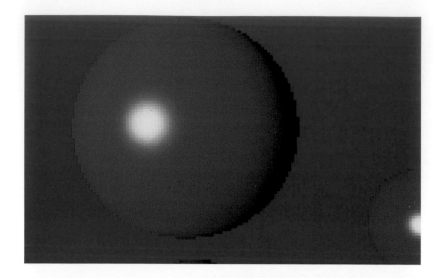

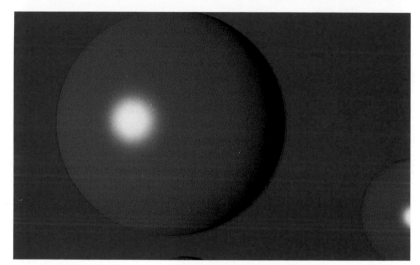

With faster computers it is not essential for draw programs to have special hardware and many "run" on raster bitmap displays. The key difference is how the data are stored.

The role of the display list is to store and organize polygonal objects, typically described with vertex of real numbers and continuously scalable. Types of objects stored in display lists include the outlines of letterforms, logos, circles, cartoon characters, or anything else that may be described with an outline and filled in (fig. 8-28). The critical advantage of the display list is that the individual polygons may be repositioned, sized, rotated, and assigned priorities (which objects appear in front of others). Because the polygons on the display list are stored as real numbers if they are not grounded in the resolution of the display. Thus when a polygon gets bigger we do not see a small area of pixels magnified larger; instead, the polygon is enlarged before it is scan-converted to pixels. It appears smooth no matter how big or small it is. Because the display list keeps track of objects, it does not matter if the object is hidden on the screen (perhaps behind a larger object) and not present in the bitmapped pixel display; it is still pre-

8-26. A medium-low-resolution image preview and a finished color graphic. Color and spatial resolution are inferior in the preview image, though the preview image may be suitable for certain applications. (Courtesy of Judson Rosebush and Atlantic Motion Pictures.)

8-27. The user selects and mixes two end colors in color ramping, and the system calculates a series of colors between the two by interpolating each primary.

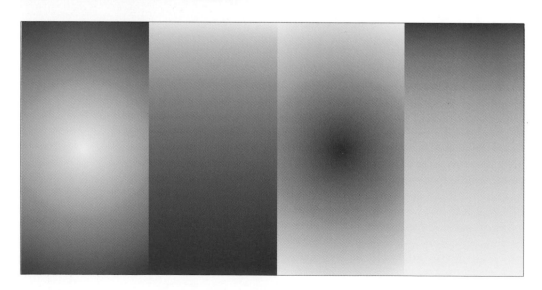

sent in the display list and can be redrawn if needed.

Bitmap Pixel Features

But not all illustration is done using lines or hard-edged shapes, and so we also need tools to work with images in the pixel domain. **Paint software** allows us to draw and paint directly into the pixel bitmap, just as if we were painting on canvas. Ingenious software simulates the effects of techniques like airbrush, charcoal, drawing on roughened surfaces, and rubbing colors together (fig. 8-29). A paint system can crop out a block of pixels from an image, reposition it, and then use it like a colorful rubber stamp. Paint systems are also widely used to retouch and color correct digitized photographs.

One thing a paint system can't do is separate out the individual objects of a scene; this is because the image in the paint system is simply a matrix of pixels and there is no knowledge about the individual objects. This is why paint systems are sometimes combined with draw software and its underlying display list. In the past, resolutions of a paint system were limited to the number of pixels visible on the screen, but now most software permits a user to scroll around inside images that are much bigger than the screen. Scaling of bitmap images is problematic, especially enlargement, since it only makes the individual pixels bigger.

8-28. Although this image—display list output—appears to be three dimensional, it comprises only two-dimensional elements. The rivets, the door, and handle are all created with circles. The inside of the safe door is made of three concentric circles, one overlaying the other, and colored with different shades of gray to approximate shading. The tubular components of the safe door, as well as the locking pins, are similarly composed of two-dimensional rectangles carefully spaced and color ramped. Color ramping was also used in the pathway leading into the safe, in the clouds, and in the background. The software permits individual objects, such as a cloud, or assemblages of objects to be repositioned. (Provided by Judson Rosebush.)

☞ **RELATED READING**

Black, Roger, *Roger Black's Desktop Design Power.* New York: Bantam Books, 1991.

Greiman, April. *Hybrid Imagery, The Fusion of Technology and Graphic Design.* New York: Watson-Guptill, 1990.

8-29. Image created on a paint system. (Courtesy of Mark Lindquist at Digital Effects, Inc.)

COLOR CORRECTION AND SEPARATION

Color correction is the process of adjusting the color balance of an image. Transparent or reflective art is first scanned into the machine and stored as the three additive primaries, red, green, and blue. The color values are interactively manipulated and balanced on the screen, with corresponding graphic readouts showing the correction curves (see fig. 5-17).

In color printing, the RGB components are converted into subtractive pigment colors, cyan, magenta, yellow, and black. The black channel is biased to accentuate the deep tones and shadows and was originally produced with a special amber filter that extracted luminance common to the CMY. Color and image processing are discussed in more detail in chapters 5 and 7.

Color separations are separate high-contrast, or halftone, images composed of variable area dots, with one separation for each of the four colors. The outputs vary in the number of dots per inch, the shape of the dots, and rotary screen offsets. The four separations can be represented as one-bit-deep bitplanes, but at a spatial resolution substantially higher than the original pixel resolution or the number of dots per inch. In fact the resolution is high enough so that each dot of the halftone is actually made up of many pixels (fig. 6-18). This is then output to a laser plotter for hard copy black-and-white high-contrast film negatives; these are used to create printing plates, one for each of the four colors (CMYK).

PAGINATION

Pagination is the integration of text, illustrations, and pictures into a whole page. A pagination system is essentially a digital pasteup and stripping machine (fig. 8-30). In addition to coordinating the placement of the integral elements of the page, such as headlines, subheads, type, photographs, illustrations, captions, and rules, pagination assists in managing *jumps,* the flow of copy and graphics from page to page. Many systems can display *folios,* a whole sequence of pages where each page is viewed at a smaller than actual size (fig. 8-31), especially useful in newspaper or magazine makeup.

Interactive work stations paginate by previewing the assembled page, so that type can be directed to a specific page and column, justified, and hyphenated to fit. Pictures, drawings, and graphs are assigned cropping information and ports.

Shorter lead times, faster assembly, soft copy preview, digital data management, and archiving are the benefits of computerized pagination, which renders the production aspects of publishing more

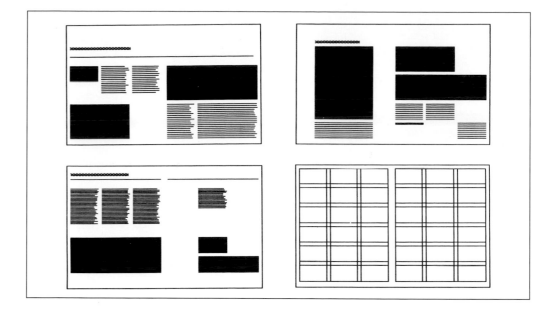

8-30. Layout grid used in a low-resolution pagination system, and three double spreads indicating positions of images and headlines. (Courtesy of James ver Hague, Rochester Institute of Technology.)

accessible to the writer, editor, illustrator, and graphic designer. Changes such as a spelling correction propagate forward into the final assembly electronically, not mechanically. All parties, therefore, can better coordinate their efforts, as each is aware of last-minute changes that affect the final product.

Inputs to pagination systems include formatted type files, illustrations, graphics, and digitized photographs. The graphic artist assembles the page interactively, directing the various inputs to specific ports on the page. Many pagination systems allow the artist to composite with mattes, lay down flat areas of color, and perform a number of the imaging techniques discussed in chapter 6. The paginator coordinates the output from many different graphics systems. The typical output from a pagination system is a digital file, usually an extremely high-resolution, possibly color, bitmap that is either digitally transmitted or converted to hard copy, often with a laser scanner or plate maker. A detailed pagination strategy is presented in figure 8-1.

Design parameters in computer systems can be implemented as permanent specifications in the pagination system, indicating general format guidelines for

8-31. Eight pages of a classified ad section are displayed on the screen at once. (Courtesy of Atex, Inc.)

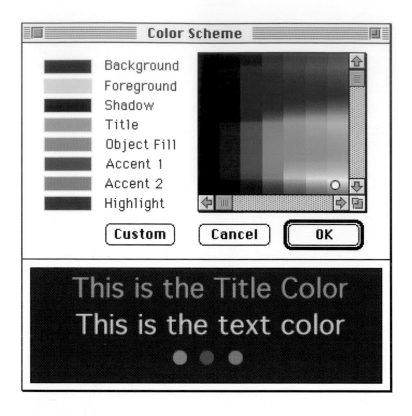

This is the Title Color
This is the text color

8-32. Design standards for a business graphic define several ports where the various components of a business graphic slide are displayed. Type, sizes, lengths, leading, and color constraints can be stored along with the text in the source file. The design standards may also specify graphic parameters like the maximum number of slices in a pie chart.

preferred composition and layout schemes. Specific variables include column widths, typefaces and point sizes, headline grids, margins, and safety areas (areas that will always be visible regardless of the format). In a computerized pagination system, these design standards may conform to rigid formats, or they may be flexible, allowing greater visual variety (fig. 8-32).

Pagination systems offer a wide range of capabilities: some display true typefaces, others simulate type; some allow for the integrated display of image and text, and others use boxes to indicate position (fig. 8-33). These systems are evolving and have only recently approached their full capacity.

Microcomputer-based pagination systems that can illustrate, create business graphics, and do page makeup are becoming common for smaller publishing environments. Many of these systems offer integrated software packages to handle accounting, telecommunications, word processing, data-base management, and image scanning. Color graphics work stations with more powerful computers and high resolution require a large memory capacity, wide communication bandwidths (the ability to move data), and sophisticated input-output capabilities.

Most integrated publishing systems allow a variety of hard copy output resolutions. Proofing printers are available that can output text and images at 240 lines per inch. More expensive photo-typesetting systems can output to plate-making equipment at 1,000 lines per inch.

8-33. Text and image integrated. (Courtesy of Atex, Inc.)

FINE ARTS

Computer graphics introduces a wide range of techniques that lead our imagination down artistic paths never before explored. Computers are used not only to create new imagery and interactive works, but also in conjunction with traditional painting, sculpture, and conceptual art. Computer-generated images can be created by modeling concepts and events in the form of a computer program, a script, or a score, and the result can then be visualized. This creative process, called **proceduralism,** allows the artist to produce a concrete image based on a series of written operations and variables. One of the hallmarks of proceduralism is that the artist manipulates the parameters of the artwork rather than manipulating the artwork directly.

Artists have been using computers as creative tools since the 1960s. Early computer-generated art was predominantly two-dimensional with a focus on geometric patterns, drawings using interpolation, and randomness (fig. 8-34). Many early computer artists used programming languages as their sole creative and expressive tool, partly out of interest and partly out of need: user-friendly hardware and software were not common before the late 1970s. Artists also sought ways to use computer technology without learning how to program, by collaborating with professional programmers or by using the available systems.

The development of interactive paint and illustration systems beginning in the mid-1970s has provided opportunities for skillful artists to discover new ways to paint and draw (fig. 8-35). The development of three-dimensional techniques during the late 1970s, and their refine-

8-34. This piece was created in the 1980s with a computer-controlled pen plotter and custom software written by the artists. (*Système Lunaire* courtesy of Jean-Pierre Hébert.)

☞ **RELATED READING**

Burson, Nancy, Richard Carling, and David Kramlich. *Composites, Computer Generated Portraits.* New York: Beech Tree Books, 1986.

Deken, Joseph. *Computer Images.* New York: Stewart, Tabori & Chang, 1983.

Franke, Herbert W. *Computer Graphics—Computer Art.* 2d ed. Berlin: Springer-Verlag, 1985.

Goodman, Cynthia. *Digital Visions, Computers and Art.* New York: Harry N. Abrams, 1987.

Kerlow, Isaac Victor, ed. *Computers in Art and Design, SIGGRAPH '91 Art and Design Show.* New York: Association for Computing Machinery, 1991.

Reichardt, Jasia. *Cybernetic Serendipity.* New York: Praeger, 1969.

8-35. This ink jet printout is not a digitally processed photograph, but rather an image created from scratch using a paint system and a mirror. (*Self-Portrait* courtesy of Erol Otus. Giant Paint software by Island Graphics, TARGA 32 graphics board by Truevision Corp.)

ment during the 1980s, focused attention on both the simulation of reality and the creation of a new breed of abstract and surrealistic imagery (fig. 8-36). But not all artists utilize the computer as an instru-

ment of direct product, many simply use the technology to aid the traditional creative process. In such cases, the computer is utilized as a sketching or design tool (for designing templates and patterns, or for creating paint-mixing formulas), or as a generator of concepts.

Original two-dimensional hard copy output is produced with printers and plotters using a variety of techniques unique to computers. Contrary to popular belief, large hard copy originals can be extremely tedious to produce and, aside from their statements of content, also provide milestones of our technological evolution. Recent advances in advanced image-processing techniques, like compositing several images into one, provide new ways to present visual information and search for new styles and messages. Com-

puters are also being used to create sculptures (fig. 8-37), and installations that interact with participants (fig. 8-38 and 8-39). Animation, spurred by more affordable modeling and rendering systems and by advanced motion simulation techniques, has also enjoyed a popular resurgence.

Whereas early computer artists could gain access to the technology only through research or educational institutions, today's desktop computers provide artists with powerful processing and a wide variety of software for their personal expression. The technical possibilities for computer-generated art continue to evolve, thus attracting artists who see its great potential for esthetic expression and who are, in turn, finding new ways to extend this capacity.

8-36. This rendering of a three-dimensional environment resembles the abstract compositions painted in Europe during the 1950s. But this work, entitled *Inscape #11,* was not created with a paint system. Instead, it was created by applying color, transparency, bump, and displacement mappings to simple three-dimensional objects. (Courtesy of Hye-Kyung Kim, Pratt Institute.)

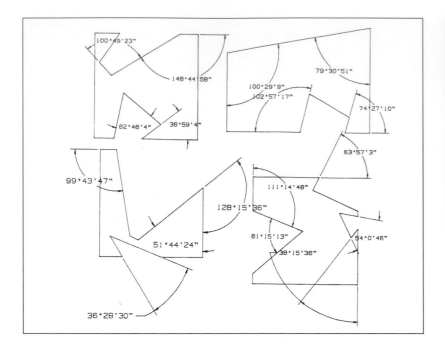

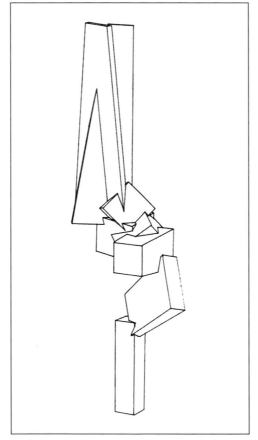

8-37. The bronze sculpture shown above was designed with a CAD system that generated line drawings like the one shown on the left. (Courtesy of Bruce Beasley.)

8-38. *Paradise Tossed* is an interactive animated survey of technological terrain, idealism, and design from a woman's point of view. In the installation, participants can travel through and interact with four time zones: Interactivity offers a new perspective about the changing nature of roles and workplaces. (Courtesy of Jill Scott, 1992. Funded by The Australian Film Commission and Mikros Image/Paris.)

8-39. *Phage* is a computer-based installation that displays in real time a series of constantly changing images. (Courtesy of Michael Tolson.)

9-0. Interactive techniques can be combined with real three-dimensional rendering and very fast hardware to give the user unparalleled power. The dragon in this experimental videogame is controlled by the player with a joystick, and the computer system displays very realistic shaded images in real time (Courtesy of Evans & Sutherland Computer Corporation, Kellan Hatch, and Michael Jackson.)

9

TWO-DIMENSIONAL INTERACTIVE SYSTEMS

DIGITAL UNIFIED MULTIMEDIA
MULTIMEDIA SYSTEMS
MULTIMEDIA APPLICATIONS
INTERACTIVE VIDEO INSTRUMENTS AND GAMES
EDUCATION AND TRAINING
VIRTUAL REALITY

DIGITAL UNIFIED MULTIMEDIA

It is now evident that in the future computer graphics will be increasingly involved with many media, not only text and pictures, but also sound, moving pictures (for example, video), animation, and interactive buttons.

The driving force behind this media revolution is the desktop computer that can digitally represent any and all media. But the implications of this are more profound than simply a conversion from analog to digital technologies. The new **digital unified multimedia** technologies unify different media by representing all information in a common format (digital data), manipulating it in a single machine (the computer), distributing it on a single carrier (for instance, a CD-ROM), and perceiving it via digital peripherals (for instance, a screen and speakers) (fig. 9-1).

For example, what were previously different media, like books and movies, that were produced in very different ways may now be produced using a single language-machine-recording-transmission/distribution-playback technology. This is an awesome piece of cultural consolidation. It simplifies many aspects of the creative production process, and enables some new possibilities.

Virtual Media

One of the hallmarks of the new age is that media is represented and manipulated virtually on the screen, rather than handled physically. This **virtual media** has all the flexibility of computer files: it may be organized, sorted, indexed, displayed in thumbnail form, easily copied without loss, dispatched over networks, and so on. Furthermore, because it has a virtual representation, it may be manipulated and edited virtually as well, on the screen. In fact, all different kinds of media may be crafted with a simple, unified tool paradigm: **cut-copy-paste** (fig. 9-2). We can cut, copy, and paste fonts, text, columns of text, pages, sound waves, music notation, pictures, icons, video clips, and buttons (fig. 9-3). There are, of course, specialized processes unique to each medium, but at a strategic level, however, it is easy to intuitively figure out how to cut-copy-paste just about anything.

Another characteristic of the new age is that there are new media forms that augment classical media like text, sound, images, and moving pictures. The most obvious of these is the **button,** an instigator of process and the primary tool of **interaction,** the ability of a system to respond to user input. Buttons are computational "objects" that activate processes; buttons do something when you click on them. Buttons are not entirely new in computing and we discussed them in chapter 4 in their functional, software context (see also figs. 4-4 through 4-7). Buttons are media, that is, information that gets recorded and transmitted, and they retain their functionality when the media are

9-1. Digital unified media fuses text (words, books, literature, word processing, E-mail), sound (voice, music, music notation, telephony), images (graphics, photographs, prepress, fax), moving images (video, QuickTime, videophone), and the button (the mediation of interactivity, process) into a single production, distribution, and playback system.

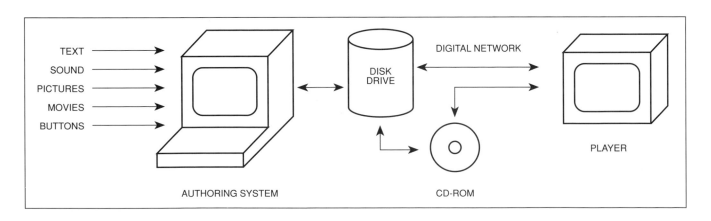

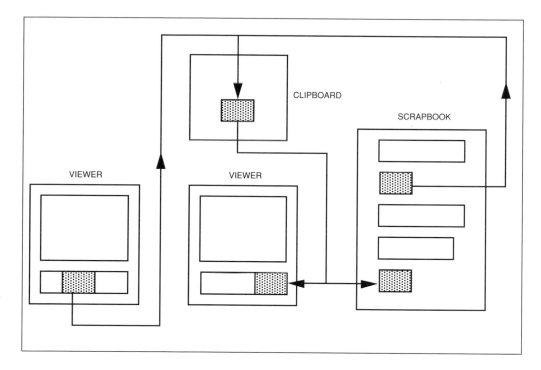

9-2. A block diagram of the cut-copy-paste paradigm includes the concept of a *selection,* here a sequence of frames highlighted by the slider in VIEWER A. The selection may be *copied* from the application to a *clipboard,* a temporary storage, and from there it may be *pasted* to another application, like VIEWER B, or to a *file.* Data from the file may also be copied to the clipboard and pasted to an application. A *cut* is like a copy in that the selection is copied to the clipboard, but it is different in that the selection is excised from the application.

read, listened to, seen, or watched. The button also employs the same unified cut-copy-paste tool paradigm as all other media.

When several kinds of virtual media (for instance, text, sound, images, or moving pictures) are combined with buttons into a single document the result is called a **compound document.** An example is an "electronic book" that augments text with sound, moving pictures, or interactive illustrations and diagrams that are clickable and navigable using a mouse. More sophisticated documents can incorporate complex procedures, for example, a toolkit that comes equipped with rules about gravity that lets a student perform what-if experiments (fig. 9-4).

Hypermedia Authoring

The creation of multimedia documents poses special challenges and requires that we organize information in new ways. Information is no longer organized as a serial stream, but rather as "chunks" and links. A **chunk** is a block of information that functions as a nucleus item (for example, a glossary definition, or the spoken pronunciation of a word). A **link** is a point-

er to a chunk of information (fig. 9-5). **Hypermedia** enables us to access chunks of information many different ways, and to relate chunks of information in one medium with chunks in another, for example, a spoken pronunciation of a word with a glossary definition (fig. 9-5). Hypermedia allows users to navigate a data world in their own unique way and at their own pace. Good interface designs allow users to glimpse lower-level data through the interface, and to go get more detail (fig. 9-6).

Authoring systems assist in constructing hypermedia and provide specialized tools to organize, sequence, and present multimedia data, and to construct links. These languages, such as *HyperTalk, Lingo,* and *Authorware,* let an author construct scripts that control the system's behavior. Besides the graphical design of the interface, the creator must also decide how the system *behaves.*

Multimedia systems may be used over networks and employ features like **publish and subscribe** (described in chapter 2 and fig. 2-32), whereby chunks are assembled into final documents only at the moment the document is actually used. This allows information workers in differ-

9-3. The concept of the selection and cut-copy-paste applied to six different media: in text, words are highlighted (A); in sound, a waveform is highlighted (B); in a picture, a portion of the picture is outlined with a mousedown and drag (C); in a video, a selection is made on a horizontal dragbar (D); in an animation, frames and tracks may be selected (E); and in a button, the entire button is selected along with its script and icon (F).

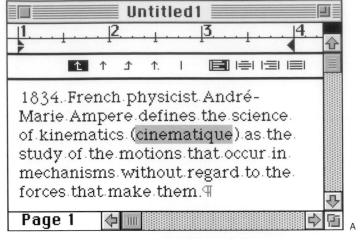

Untitled1

1834. French physicist André-Marie Ampere defines the science of kinematics (cinematique) as the study of the motions that occur in mechanisms without regard to the forces that make them. ¶

Page 1

A

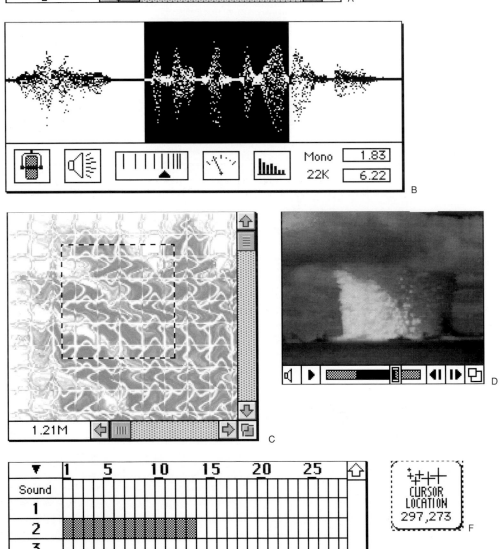

Mono 1.83
22K   6.22

B

1.21M

C

D

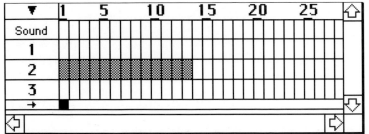

Sound
1
2
3

E

CURSOR LOCATION 297,273

F

ent graphical locations to independently prepare different components of a document that is assembled at "run time." **Conditional text** is a feature that allows several versions of a document to be stored concurrently, and different versions to be displayed to different users (fig. 9-7). Chunks of text and other hypermedia need to be independent of any particular system, and so developers are turning to **rich text format (RTF),** a portable text format that includes control characters for font specification, bold and italic styles, and tabular tables. There is also a trend toward a **standard generalized markup language (SGML),** which provides a portable description of page layouts that contain text, sound, pictures, movies, and buttons.

MULTIMEDIA SYSTEMS

The Basic Platform

Multimedia represents a giant fusion of the "three Cs": computers, consumer electronics (especially audio and television), and communications (publishing companies as well as broadcasters). The hardware components include a computer with RAM and a disk, an 8- or 24-bit color card and monitor, digital sound and speakers, and a hard disk that is big enough and fast enough to play back movies. Thus the software (the "entertainment," the "education," the "video game") is sold

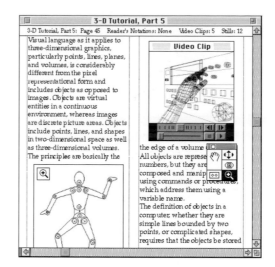

9-4. A compound document is like a letter or a page from a book except that it may also contain sound, video, buttons, and interactive experiments.

9-5. Links in a smart document point to chunks of media that can be invoked from many places. Clicking on the word "robot" pops a glossary definition up on the screen and pronounces a word. Clicking the word as it appears in the glossary definition also plays the sound file.

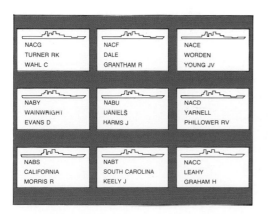

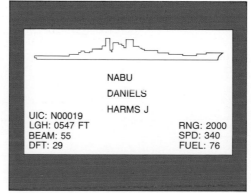

9-6. The spatial data-base manager organizes information in a logical manner. The first illustration depicts a collection of ships in a task force, including the name of the ship, its commanding officer and profile. Selecting any one ship zooms it up to full screen and expands the amount of information displayed. (This drawing is based on material created by Computer Corporation of America, 1969.)

☞ **RELATED READING**

Apple Computer, Inc. *Apple CD-ROM Handbook: A Guide to Planning, Creating and Producing a CD-ROM.* Reading, MA: Addison-Wesley, 1992.

Apple Computer, Inc. *Apple Human Interface Guidelines. The Apple Desktop Interface.* Cupertino, CA: Apple Computer, 1987.

Crawford, Chris. *The Art of Computer Game Design.* Berkeley, CA: Osborne/McGraw-Hill, 1984.

Sherman, Chris. *The CD ROM Handbook.* New York:McGraw-Hill, 1988.

Tognazzini, Bruce. *TOG on Interface.* Reading, MA: Addison-Wesley, 1992.

Wilson, Stephen. *Multimedia Design with Hypercard.* Englewood Cliffs, NJ: Prentice-Hall, 1991.

9-7. Conditional text and conditional graphics allow a multimedia producer/ director to embed different levels of detail into multimedia documents. For example, a virtual repair manual for a machine may include details about both the entry-level model and the deluxe version. The appropriate directions are presented in response to the user entering the serial number of the problem machine. This eliminates redundant documents.

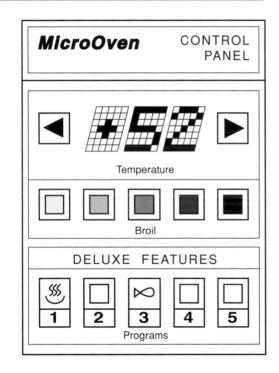

and distributed on media such as a compact disk, just as music is today. Except that this **CD-ROM** is digital unified multimedia: it is a mechanically stamped, and laminated optical read-only disk, currently with 600 megabytes of storage (fig. 9-8). The disk is prepared using an authoring system, it is about some interesting topic or reference or activity, it is mass produced, and it is sold to the public, who uses it in their players.

From a consumer electronics perspective, multimedia hardware resembles a television receiver with a built-in computer able to play back CD-ROM cartridges (like Nintendo videogames), and videocassettes. From a desktop computer perspective, it is a system that can also do authoring, and includes a video digitizer, a sound digitizer, a scanner, keyboard, and mouse. This is envisioned to be notebook-sized, with color flat-panel displays, or be box-sized, with an external bus and modem. Because it allows for the creative use of media tools, and because it affords more variation than the packaged CD-ROM, this is a machine for students and knowledge industry workers.

An emerging requirement is that multimedia be **portable media.** Not only must different programs operate on common data formats, but different programs on different machines must operate on common data formats. Convergence is slow, but it is happening. Another trend is **interoperability** (fig. 9-9), the ability of software to run on different kinds of

9-8. The CD-ROM combines high volumes of data storage with an attractive package. It has a low manufacturing cost and uses the same manufacturing technology as the audio CD.

computers. Digital multimedia is also **scalable media,** that is, the textual, sonic, spatial, temporal, chromatic, functional, and baud resolutions can be varied on an application by application basis, as well as on a price-performance spectrum of players and distribution media.

Compression

A key technology that advances these goals is **compression,** algorithms that reduce file size (fig. 9-10). Compression enables smaller files to be stored, smaller files to be transferred from the disk to the CPU, and scalable displays. The opposite of compression is **decompression,** which unpacks the file and displays it. The **compression ratio** is the ratio between the original file size and the compressed file size. There is often a trade-off between the compression ratio and the quality of the picture.

Lossless compression schemes compress and decompress the original data perfectly; the result is identical to the original. **Lossy** compression schemes, especially when applied to still or moving pictures, do not reconstruct the original data perfectly, but seek to reconstruct the original appearance. Lossy compression involves understanding just what the eye actually perceived and, in theory, throws away what you can't see. Both kinds of compression have their uses, and many systems support user-selectable compression schemes.

Two compression standards important to multimedia are JPEG and MPEG. Both are lossy standards. **JPEG** is an example of **spatial compression;** all compression occurs **intraframe** and involves reducing redundancies within a single frame. **MPEG** is an example of **temporal compression,** in which **interframe** redundancies and motion predictability between sequential frames are used to reduce the data. It is believed that the human has different receptors that perceive static images and that perceive motion; in static images the eye looks at details, in moving images the eye perceives the structure of the motion.

9-9. Three levels of interoperability in the computer world are presented: different chip CPUs can support different operating systems that can support different GUIs. The lines show ways in which systems can mix and match and are by no means exhaustive. (From Herr and Rosebush, *Visualization Software,* 1992.)

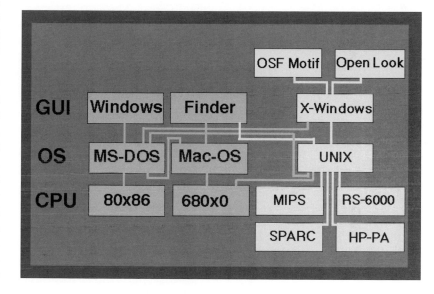

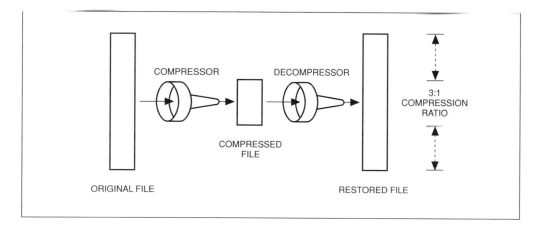

9-10. The amount of storage of an original file is reduced by a compression program and can be subsequently re-expanded by decompression. The drawing implies a lossless scenario because all the data are recovered. The more duplication and redundancy in the data the more it can be compressed.

☞ **RELATED READING/VIEWING/INTERACTING**

Educorp. *Educorp CD ROM 2.0.* Solana Beach, CA: Educorp Computer Services, 1990.

Greenblat, Rodney A. *Rodney's Wonder Window.* Santa Monica, CA: The Voyager Company, 1992.

Nautilus CD ROMS. Dublin, OH: 1990–1992.

Spaceship Warlock. Vancouver: Reactor, 1991.

The Voyager Company. *The Complete Annotated Alice.* Santa Monica, CA: The Voyager Company, 1992.

Time Table of History. Novato, CA: The Software Toolworks, 1991.

Time/Warner New Media. *Desert Storm, The War in the Persian Gulf.* Burbank, CA: Warner New Media, 1991.

Verbum Interactive. San Diego, CA: Verbum, Inc., 1991.

You Can't Get There From Here: Ephemeral Films 1946–1960. Santa Monica, CA: The Voyager Company, 1992.

MULTIMEDIA APPLICATIONS

Interactive Navigation

Multimedia is many things and has many purposes. Some of the applications we have shown or implied include an **interactive databank** information sourcing and distribution technology, and reference materials such as encyclopedias, timetables, and atlases have been initial best sellers (fig. 9-11). Multimedia also makes sense when there is an advantage in coupling two or more media, for example, the playback of music and the animation of the score. (fig. 9-12).

The ability to manage video and audio on the desktop makes practical nonlinear editing of time-variant media. These can

9-11. Data bases of pictures and movies are best accessed graphically, using icons for the pictures or video clips. Often this accompanied by information about the picture, including its name, keywords that reference it, a short textual description, the date, and the photographer. (Screen shot of The Image Bank Visual Catalog 1.)

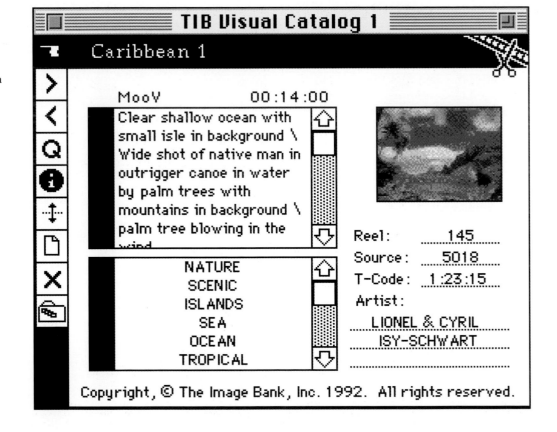

include process control, but most practically for the graphic artist, sound and video. A **nonlinear editor** digitizes all the sound and video (or film) scenes and stores them on a disk drive. Virtual clips of picture and sound can now be cut-copy-pasted to edit a movie (fig.9-13).

Another direction of multimedia is **process control,** the real-time operation of a real-world task via a computer screen interface (fig. 9-14). Sensors connect to real-world machinery and return data that are formatted into the graphics display. The multimedia aspect includes sounds, moving pictures, and of course, buttons, sliders, and menus to aid the control (fig. 9-15). A virtual control screen can be implemented on any computer and can replace traditional physical controls (fig.

9-16). One of the roles of the designer is to help facilitate the process of transforming the monitoring and control of complex processes into simplified diagrams that can be more efficiently manipulated than the actual machine or process.

Communications Issues

Communications is another theme of multimedia, especially in the **paperless office. Virtual calendars** assist scheduling. **Electronic mail** routes text, voice, and picture. **Ticklers** and face-animated **agents** interrupt us at predetermined times and suggest behavior changes (fig. 9-17). **Electronic publishing** sends digital data out onto local or wide area networks. This is a somewhat different distribution strategy than CD-ROM. **Videotex** and **teletext** per-

9-12. Multimedia creates new possibilities, like highlighting the score of a symphony while it plays. (From *The Art of Listening* courtesy of The Voyager Company.)

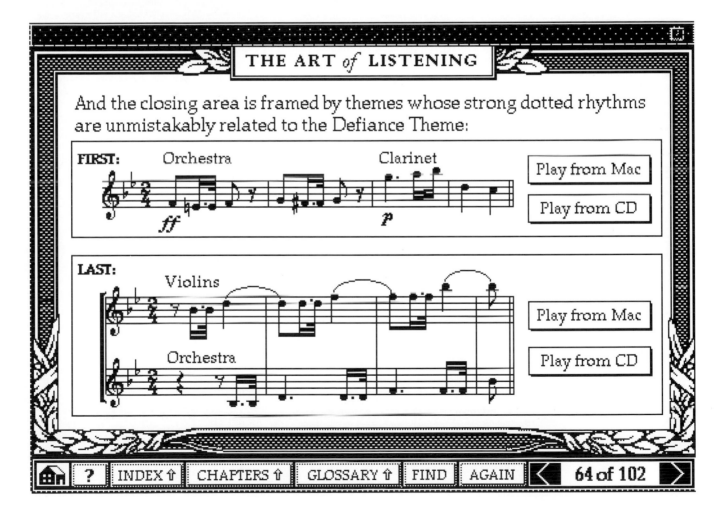

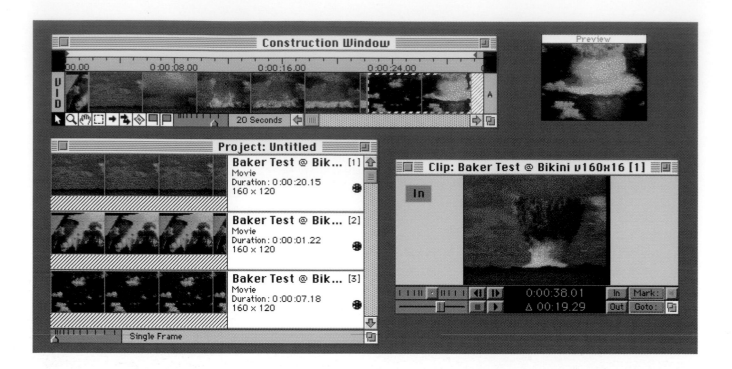

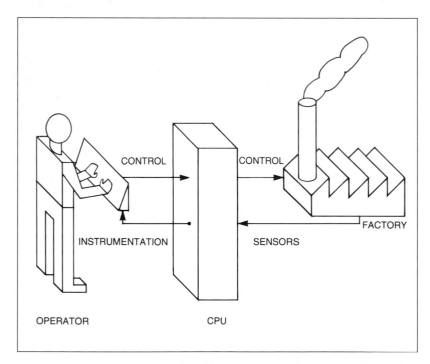

9-13. A nonlinear video editor includes bins, which hold the individual shots (lower left), a clip window to preview individual shots and set trims (lower right), a workprint, in which the shots are arranged sequentially (top left, note the rightmost shot is selected), and a preview window (upper right), which previews the current frame in the workprint. (Screen shot of *Premiere* software by Adobe Corp.)

9-14. The components of a process control system include a computer and data base, input sensors that are evaluated by the computer and displayed on a control console, an operator who controls the process, and the process itself.

mit textual data, icons, and formatting information to be transmitted via an ordinary phone line and played on a desktop computer (see fig. 9-21). **Videophones** use compression technology to transmit low-resolution video, also over ordinary phone lines. **Teleconferences** combine video and sound with additional instruments of communication, like **shared drawing tools,** which allow two users to view a common drawing window and draw back and forth into it, each seeing what the other is doing (fig. 9-18).

Communication bandwidth is one of the driving forces behind multimedia. More bandwidth implies higher resolutions and

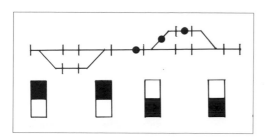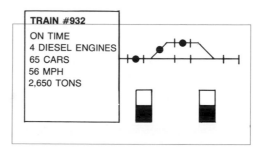

9-15. This process control board is used to operate four switches along a section of railroad track. The GUI shows a track diagram with dots superimposed to show the location of a train (left). This information is obtained from sensors on the physical tracks. The hatchmarks represent signal blocks. The operator can click on the train dots and a submenu displays train status information (right). If the conditions permit it, the operator can use the buttons at the bottom to set the position of the railroad switches.

less need to compress the data. The most common low-bandwidth multimedia is the telephone line, at about 9600 baud. This is totally adequate for applications like **tickers** (fig. 9-19), where a steady stream of numerical data is stored and displayed on a screen. In order to send images over a telephone line they must either be compressed or encoded into a graphical protocol such as **NAPLPS,** the **North American Presentation Level Protocol Standard** that is used for encoding and transmitting videotex in North America. NAPLPS uses ASCII codes for text augmented with Picture Description Instructions (PDI) for the image description (fig. 9-20). The PDIs represent the graphic as polygons, not pixels, so the transmission is efficient; furthermore, the data are device-independent and scalable to different resolution displays (fig. 9-21). The designer must be sensitive to the fact that layouts and designs must be planned with a resolution or, more particularly, a range of resolutions in mind.

Communication bandwidths that are faster than plain old telephone service include faster digital telephone lines, local area networks, and busses. Currently there is a struggle to apply compression to higher-resolution data such as television so they might flow through lower-resolution channels such as CD-ROM and digital disks (fig. 9-22).

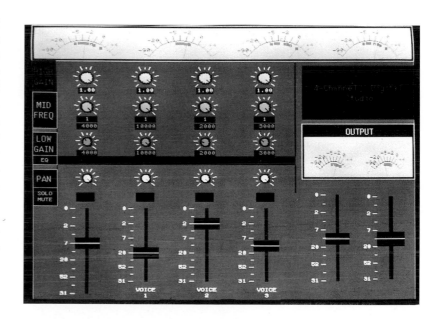

INTERACTIVE VIDEO INSTRUMENTS AND GAMES

The marriage between video and interactive computer graphics is a profound and serendipitous one. Video, after all, is a real time picture-processing system with medium resolution and is a dominant distribution medium in our culture. With computer graphics, video becomes an interactive medium.

The **Video synthesizer,** an instrument that allows a "visual musician" to form

9-16. This virtual recording console simulates a traditional audio mixing board. A user can select and mix inputs, and see volume levels on VU meters, all in real time. (Courtesy of Visual Intelligence Corporation.)

9-17. Agents are digital assistants who pop onto the screen to remind one of appointments or incoming mail, aid in searching information, or reprimand one for marginal behavior. One trend in computing is that agents are getting a lot smarter.

INCOMING MAIL

From: Explorer
Subject: Hot Tips

Read Now

Read Later

9-18. The three users of this teleconferencing system shared a common drawing window; they also see each other on the screen and can talk back and forth.

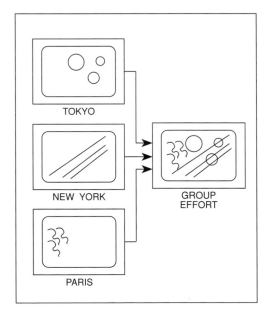

TOKYO

NEW YORK

PARIS

GROUP
EFFORT

and modify images in real time—often in conjunction with music (fig. 9-23)—s one such interactive system that is controlled with knobs, piano-styled keyboards, and typewriter keyboards.

The *interactive video game,* which has brought computers closer to more people than any other technology to date, is a closed system with interactive computer graphics displayed on a color screen. These games require cognitive skills, strategy, and fast reflexes.

Video games both educate and entertain. A highly participatory medium that relies on a variety of graphic techniques, the game is based on either a conflict between the player and the machine—a skill and action game—or a problem posed by the machine for the player to solve—a strategy game.

The skill and action video game is reflex oriented and pits the player against an antagonist—often in an unfriendly environment. Played by the computer, the antagonist becomes increasingly fiendish as the player's skills improve (fig. 9-24). Examples include Pong (the first computer

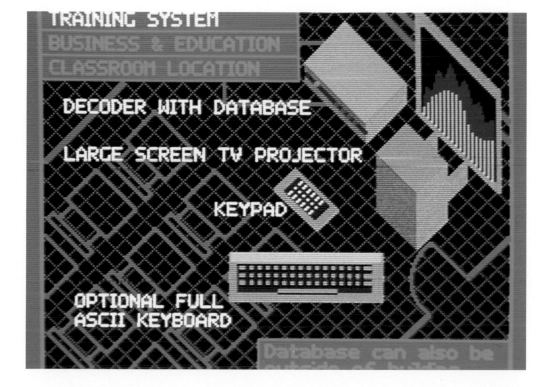

```
1114            SPOT CURRENCIES - 24 HR WORLD INPUT            WRLD
TIME CY   PAGE   SOURCE      LATEST        PREV    HIGH    LOW
                                                 N.AMERICA HI/LO
1114 DMK  RBCM   ROYAL BK    3.0540/50     40/55   3.0585  3.0480
1113 STG  MHTN   MAN HAN     1.2700/10     00/10   1.2720  1.2680
1114 SFR  UBZA   U B S       2.5660/80     60/80   2.5700  2.5625
1111 YEN  MHTN   MAN HAN     247.95/05     95/05   248.50  247.30
1111 FFR  BMMA   BK MTL      9.3125/75     30/80   9.3250  9.3000
1058 GLD  UBZB   U B S       315.00/315.50 00/50
--------------------------------------------------------------------
1058 SIL  UBZB   6.14/6.16        0723  3 MTH EUR EDLR  7.50-.62
0828 FED  PREB   7 11/16 3/4      1113  T BND CGO JUN     79%16


             S1-K1-1        REUTER MONITOR      0355
```

9-19. Exchange tickers are used in electronic publishing, because a computer can be programmed to pick off pertinent information, for example, the transactions in certain currencies or commodities. The role of the graphic designer is to assist in displaying this information in a meaningful way. The figure illustrates a system that displays information on spot currency prices. (Courtesy of Reuters Limited.)

Escape	32	15	45	31	52	27
Graphics mode		Start line	X coordinates		Y coordinates	

9-20. Table shows numerical codes that represent commands.

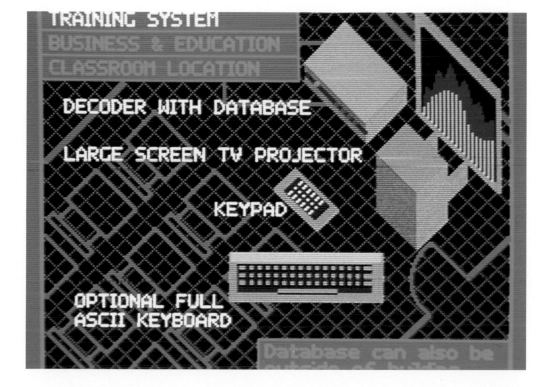

9-21. Bold graphic design and clear typography, as in this videotex page, are essential for successful medium-resolution graphics. (Courtesy of Stanley Bernesche, Office of External Affairs, Canada.)

9-22. Baud rates of some common computer busses, communication networks, and televisions.

Description	Megabits/sec	Comments
Bandwidths		
Foot Messenger	0.000,003	For 25 mile distance @ 10 mph and 30,000 bit (~1000 words) message
Telegraph	0.000,030	70 wpm @ 5 characters/word @ 5 bits/character = 30 baud
Teletype	0.000,050	@ 500 characters/minute @ 6 bits per character = 50 baud
2400 baud modum	0.002,400	One ordinary (POTS) telephone line
Plain Old Telephone Service (today)	0.064,000	Maximum capacity POTS 64 kbps, voice, fax, modem, SSTV, ARPANET
DS-0 Data Channel	0.064,000	Digital Signal Level Zero, this channels nets out 56kbps to the user
Basic ISDN	0.144,000	Integrated Services Digital Network, uses 2 DS-0's plus a 16 kbps data channel
Switched 384	0.384,000	Also called Fractional T-1, this is used for videoconferencing
Audio CD-DA	1.200,000	Two 20,000 hertz channels sampled 40,000 times per second at 16 bits
DS-1 (aka T-1, Primary ISDN)	1.544,000	Equals 24 DS-0's, may connect to PBX; NSNET uses this
DS-2	6.312,000	98 DS-0's or 4 DS-1's
Xerox Ethernet	10.000,000	Popular local area network (LAN)
IBM Token Ring	16.000,000	Local area computer network
NTSC Broadcast TV	24.000,000	Broadcast television bandwidth
DS-3 (aka T-3)	44.600,000	672 DS-0's, 28 DS-1's or 7 DS-2's; used by the telephone company
FDDI LAN	100.000,000	Fiber Distributed Data Interface
D2 Videotape Recorder	114.000,000	Digital NTSC composite television
Broadband ISDN	135.000,000	Telephone Company Service
Compressed HDTV	140.000,000	NHK MUSE format
Asynchronous Transfer Mode (ATM)	154.000,000	Packetized switched mixed data wide area network, also faster modes
D1 Videotape Recorder	214.000,000	Digital NTSC component television
Multi Bus 2	256.000,000	For workstation computers
EISA Bus	264.000,000	Computer bus
VME Bus	320.000,000	Computer bus
HPPI channel	800.000,000	High Performance Parallel Interface
HDTV Digital Recorder	1,180.000,000	Lossy SMPTE 240M HDTV, by Sony
AT&T Sonet	2,400.000,000	AT&T Long lines fiber trunk capacity
Human Visual Systems	5,600.000,000	Estimate eye to brain data rate
Fiber Optic Capacity	16,000.000,000	Experimental capacity, Bell Labs
Fiber Optic Capacity	64,000.000,000	Theoretical fiber capacity
Human Visual System	6,168,960.000,000	36,000 x 28,000 pixels x 17 bits per pixel x 3 colors x 2 eyes x 60 frame/sec. (per Seth Shostack)

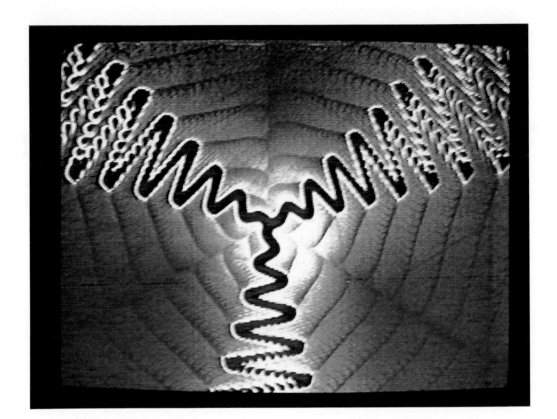

game), PAC-MAN, and sports contests.

The strategy game involves thinking and cognitive skills; it is less action and reflex oriented. Examples include Adventure, which involves a search or a quest through a complex spatial world (fig. 9-25), and Star Trek, a war game that creates environments, shows the status of deployments, and offers options displayed on a command-and-control panel.

Video game design incorporates graphic technologies that range from sprites to the integration of on-line videodiscs that store still frames and animated sequences (fig. 9-26). Graphic design requires an understanding of characterization, action, and environment, and progresses from storyboards to flowcharts that contain alternate pathways and show visual style.

EDUCATION AND TRAINING

Teaching and training systems can incorporate process control, data-base retrieval, cartography, and interactive game playing, but focus on education. Applications include console training and practice, drill skills like typing, and organized curriculums for learning, which can incorporate a mixture of cognitive and reflex skills. Programmed learning systems involve interactive interface between trainers and trainees, plus a program of instruction.

From the point of view of the trainee, the system presents an interactive network that the student can explore at his or her own pace. This system must anticipate how a student learns the correct information and must recognize when a student is confused or using incorrect methods. The system presents the information again with more precise examples and retests the student.

The system permits instructors to monitor the individual student as well as the teaching algorithm. They can thus tailor the curriculum to stress a student's problem areas or analyze the entire educational process. Both teacher and student

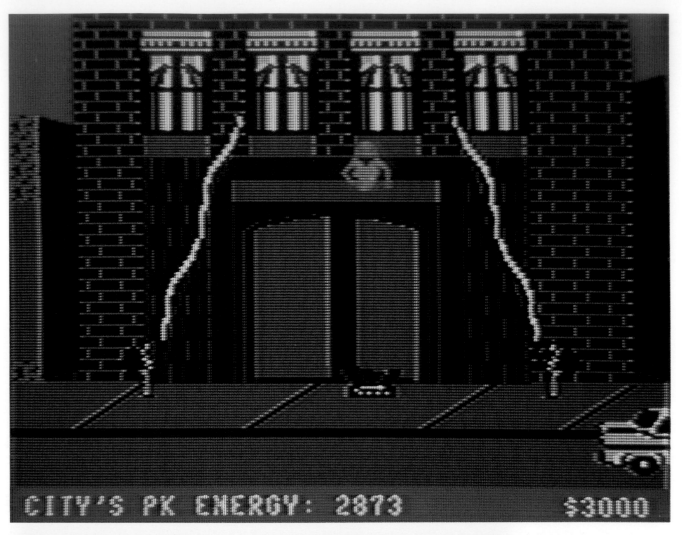

CITY'S PK ENERGY: 2873 $3000

>SURROUNDINGS
YOU'RE IN THE PARLOR OF THE ADMIRAL
BENBOW INN. THE FRONT DOOR IS TO THE
WEST, AND TO THE SOUTH IS A CURTAINED
PASSAGE TO THE BAR. SEATED AT ONE OF
THE TABLES IS A ROUGH LOOKING SEAMAN
NAMED BILLY BONES. HE HAS A SCAR ACROSS
HIS CHEEK.

TIME ELAPSED: 2 MINUTES

9-24. Action video game.
(Courtesy of Activision.
Graphics by Hillary Mills.)

9-25. Strategy game. (Courtesy of Byron Preiss Visual
Productions.)

9-26. Star Rider, a laser disk video game created by Computer Creations for Williams Electronics, presents a computer-generated race through a futuristic city. The images are retrieved from a videodisc and displayed on a video monitor while the view through a rearview mirror is calculated by the computer. (Courtesy of Computer Creations. Game design by Python Anghelo; animation by Eric Brown; software by Tom Klimek and Herman Towles.)

9-27. A system for teaching layout to design students. (Courtesy of the College of Fine and Applied Arts, Rochester Institute of Technology.)

are "plugged into" the support structure of computerized classroom rosters, scheduling, testing, grading, and financial exchange.

Imaginative graphics can be implemented on eight- and sixteen-bit home computers using sprites, look-up tables, and pull-down windows (fig. 9-27). The graphics can reinforce basic concepts even in nonvisual and abstract disciplines, such as typing, spelling, composition, science, history, or music.

Education and training systems often use ***instrumentation displays,*** which are similar to those in process control and many video games (fig. 9-28) and teach topics as diverse as golf, weight reduction methods, astrology, poker, chemistry, and instrument flight—a real time task. ***Virtual environments*** instruct by displaying synthetic physical environments, for example, a full-scale cockpit mock-up with working controls and a view out the window of land, clouds, airports, and other aircraft (fig. 9-29). Obviously, if you bank the plane, the point of view out the window changes. In fact, the cockpit can even be mounted on a hydraulically controlled platform, so the plane can pitch, bank,

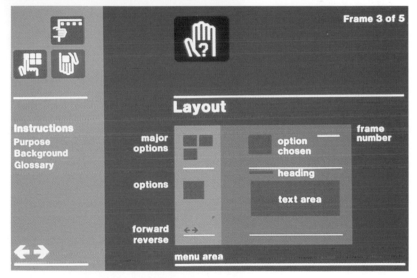

RELATED READING AND VIEWING

Herr, Laurin, and Judson Rosebush. *HDTV & The Quest for Virtual Reality,* ACM SIGGRAPH Video Review (Special Issue 60). New York: Association of Computing Machinery, 1990.

Herr, Laurin, and Judson Rosebush. *Visualization Software,* ACM SIGGRAPH Video Review (Special Issue 70). New York: Association of Computing Machinery, 1992.

Krueger, Myron W. *Artificial Reality II.* Reading, MA: Addison-Wesley, 1991.

9-28. An instrumentation display of a small aircraft is combined here with a moderately realistic view on the screen. Instrumentation includes an altimeter, artificial horizon, throttle, and rates of climb and descent. (Portrayed here is *Flight Simulator* by Microsoft, Inc.)

9-29. The virtual environment of an airplane cockpit includes full-scale seats and working controls. The views out the window are synthetically generated while the plane is "in flight." (Courtesy of Evans & Sutherland Corp.)

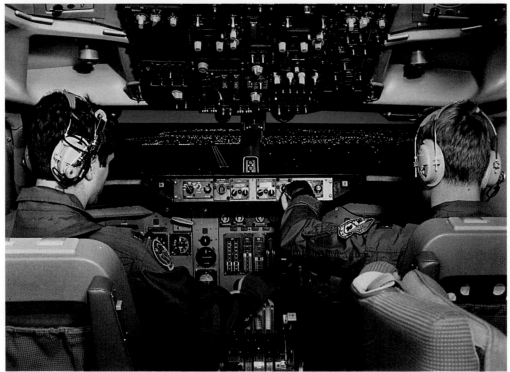

9-30. A rocker platform is used to support virtual environments, such as the one in figure 9-29, and adds an element of realism to the learning experience. The platform is mounted on hydraulic arms that can make it pitch or roll. (Courtesy of The Singer Co., Link Flight Simulation Division.)

and bounce from turbulence (fig. 9-30).

Image generation in virtual environments incorporates three-dimensional shaded computer graphics, using hardware and software to animate the screens in response to controls. Videodiscs can also be used by selecting from prerecorded images made from different points of view. One novel application by researchers at MIT's Architecture Machine Group recorded views down the streets of Aspen, Colorado, as well as all the corner turns. These fragments were stored on a disk, allowing a user to drive around the city without leaving the room.

A virtual environment can take many forms (fig. 9-31) and includes synthetic environments as well as synthetic instrumentation displays. The former includes visualizations of reality, the latter does not. As virtual environments become more tactile they can be used as substitutions for real world experience: training machines can already be connected, so two fighter pilots can practice dogfights. This is high-tech video, requiring motor skills to perform a precision task, and a closed environment is thus large enough to seem real.

VIRTUAL REALITY

The grand vision of multimedia is to build not only virtual media on the desktop but also virtual worlds that we can actually enter into and participate in. The characteristics of these virtual environments include head-mounted displays with stereoscopic vision and position tracking (fig. 9-31). The environment that is seen is created in real time and is interactive with current events and with extended body peripherals, like a data glove (fig. 3-49) or a full body suit (fig. 3-50). By tracking the location of the data glove the computer knows the position of your hand in the virtual world, and can detect when you touch things (9-32). Inside the virtual environment you can move around in 3D, hear sounds properly located in space, and see your own virtual hand (fig. 9-33). The term **virtunaut** may be used to indicate a person journeying into virtual space, and the term **virtuoid** to describe his or her virtual representation.

Virtual reality (VR) is a computer-mediated illusion of a real world that looks, sounds, smells, tastes, feels, and behaves real. Virtual reality is an infant art, and the way to get there from here involves perfecting and integrating several kinds of realism: visual realism demands smoothly rendered three-dimensional graphics (chapter 7). Sound may be delivered biaurally, but it must be environmentally positioned. Smell and taste are media that have not been mastered yet. Kinematic realism ensures that moving parts maintain permitted relationships (for example, a can can't pass through a wall). Behav-

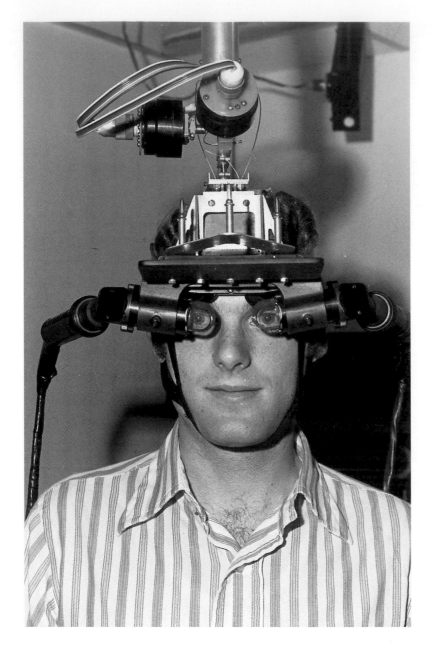

9-31. A head-mounted display tracks the user's head movements and simulates a three-dimensional environment that changes accordingly. (Courtesy of the University of Utah.)

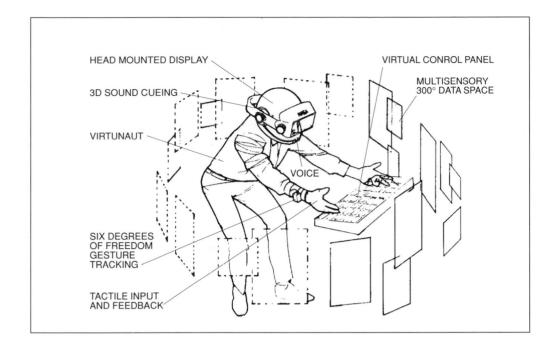

HEAD MOUNTED DISPLAY

3D SOUND CUEING

VIRTUNAUT

VOICE

SIX DEGREES
OF FREEDOM
GESTURE
TRACKING

TACTILE INPUT
AND FEEDBACK

VIRTUAL CONROL PANEL

MULTISENSORY
300° DATA SPACE

9-32. A virtual interface environment for management of large-scale integrated information systems shows an operator and virtual controls. Sensors measure the position of the hands, head, torso, and limbs. Feedback to the virtunaut includes two channels of vision, two channels of sound, and tactile sensing. Very smart interaction software recognizes gestures (pointing, waving hands) and voice commands. (Drawing adapted from Scott Fisher, et al., NASA Ames Research Center, 1986.)

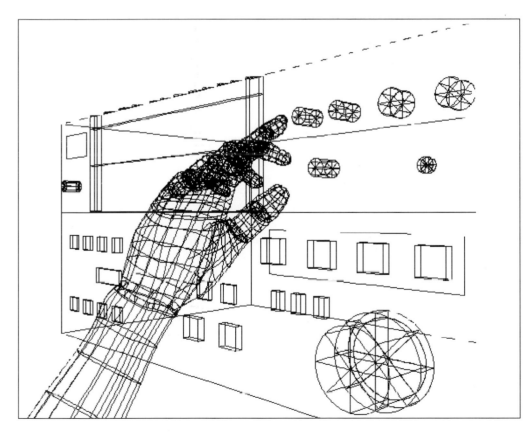

9-33. Inside the virtual world you can see you own virtual hand. (Courtesy of Yung Lim Jung, Prattt Institute.)

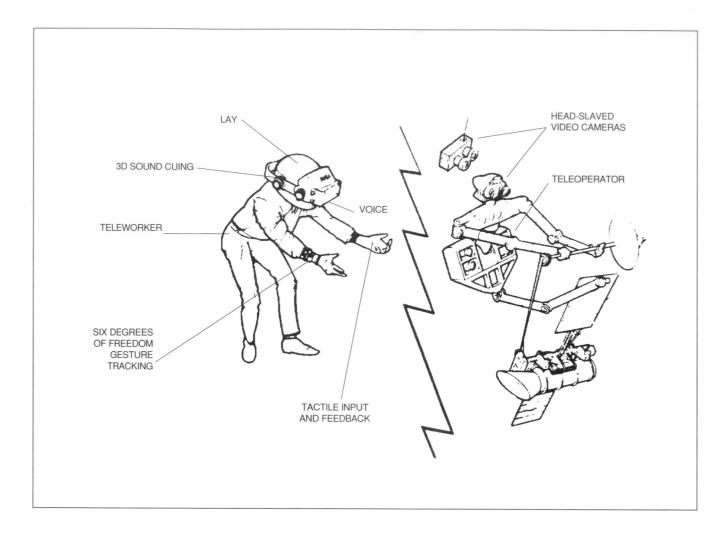

Labels on figure:
LAY

3D SOUND CUING

TELEWORKER

SIX DEGREES
OF FREEDOM
GESTURE
TRACKING

VOICE

TACTILE INPUT
AND FEEDBACK

HEAD-SLAVED
VIDEO CAMERAS

TELEOPERATOR

9-34. Teleworker and the remote-controlled teleoperator are connected together by a communications channel—perhaps the teleworker is at home or the office and the teleoperator is in space, underwater, or inside a nuclear reactor. As the teleoperator turns his real head, a position sensor measures the movement and turns the robot's head accordingly. The teleoperator sees through the TV camera eyes, and force feedback to the teleoperator lets him feel the shape of the part or the resistance of unscrewing a nut. (Drawing adapted from Scott Fisher, et al., NASA Ames Research Center, 1986.)

ioral realism is accomplished by incorporating dynamics into the virtual world, so it is embodied with forces of gravity, weight, momentum. In the near future the virtual world, and in particular the interaction paradigm, will be augmented with a dynamic new medium: force. Force feedback will enable virtual media and the virtual world to not only look real and behave real, but to *feel* real as well. You might be able to rub charcoal on a paper, squeeze a ball, touch a wall, or lift a weight. Finally, the processing must be real time, so fast that there is no perceptible lag between the actions of a virtunaut and the virtual world, or between one virtunaut and another.

Virtual reality is a science with its own variables. The **immersion level** determines

how surrounded you are in the environment. It is aided by wider field of view, stereoscopic vision, and motion platforms. A *vehicle paradigm* implies one can view a virtual world through a screen (for example, a driving simulator moves the virtual world past a stationary participant). An *immersive portal* implies a hand held TV screen that can be moved around inside the virtual environment so a participant can look through it into the virtual world. In an *immersive inclusive* experience virtunauts don goggles and gloves, and actually move themselves within the virtual world.

The **interaction level** determines how freely a virtunaut may move around in an environment. A *branching* system constrains one to predefined pathways, like tracks, roads, or sidewalks. A *free-roaming* system permits a virtunaut to move anywhere. The **participation level** specifies if the experience is *solitary* or *shared* and measures the number of virtunauts. The **reality level** is concerned with what virtual representations a virtunaut may encounter. These include not only the virtual environment, but also you own *virtual self* (parts of your own virtuoid—like your hand—seen from your normal perspective, or your own virtuoid seen from out-of-body views), *virtual representation of other real people* (virtuoids whom you encounter in the virtual world and interact with; they see your virtuoid from their perspective), and *simulacra* (also called *knobots,* these are virtual representations of characters synthesized by the computer with whom you and your associates interact). It is quite probable that you and your fellow virtual travelers will not be able to distinguish the look or behavior of simulacra from the look and behavior of a virtuoid (a virtual real person).

Besides the simple thrill of going virtual, it is expected that VR will profoundly change the workplace as well. A key reason lies in the mediation of force. Work, after all, is the product of force times distance, and a flavor of VR called **telework** provides a way to feel and exert force remotely, using a telephone line or a radio transmitter (fig. 9-34). One of the advantages of virtual reality is that force can be scaled—stronger and weaker.

The virtunaut of the future is expected to enjoy a range of fashions akin to those of the skier, surfer, or scuba diver. Datasuits may well resemble spandex exercise wear and be equipped with sensors for heartbeat, brainwaves, facial expressions, and eye position; and conversely, they will include tactile stimulators for all major parts of the body.

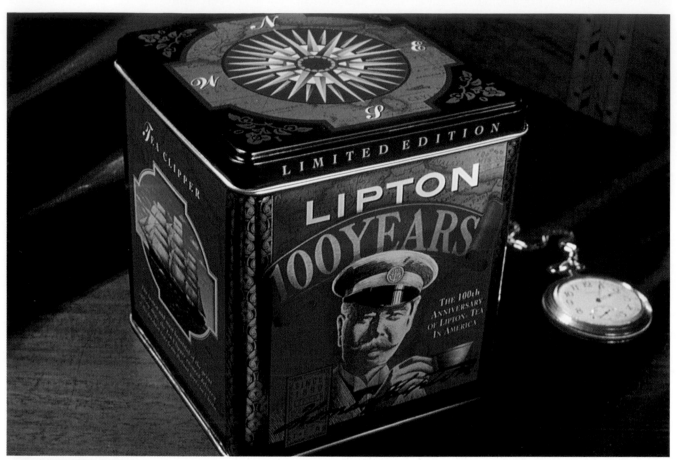

10-0. This could be a picture of a virtual tea tin but in fact it is a photograph of a real tea tin with artwork created on a computer. (*Lipton 100th Anniversary Tea Tin* courtesy of Primo Angeli Inc. Art Director: Carlo Pagoda, Designer: Primo Angeli, Computer Illustrators: Mark Jones and Mark Crumpacker, Illustrator: Anton Dayal.)

10

THREE-DIMENSIONAL MEDIA: THE PRODUCTION OF MATERIAL GOODS

INDUSTRIAL DESIGN
ARCHITECTURE AND INTERIOR DESIGN
PACKAGE DESIGN
CLOTHING AND TEXTILE DESIGN
SCULPTURE

Computer-aided design and manufacturing (CADAM) consolidates the design and production of three-dimensional material goods—packages, products, clothing, vehicles, and architecture.

The computer-aided design (CAD) component conceptualizes, models, previsualizes, tests, and documents the progress of a project. The computer-aided manufacturing (CAM) component automatically produces drafts, process plans, assembles—using numerically controlled robots and assembly tools—performs quality control, and accounts.

CADAM allows designs to be easily refined, increases design variety and accuracy, and shortens the cycle from design to production. Designers using CADAM

10-1. An overall view of an electronic circuit design (A), and a close-up of the area inside the rectangle (B). (Courtesy of NEC Information Systems.)

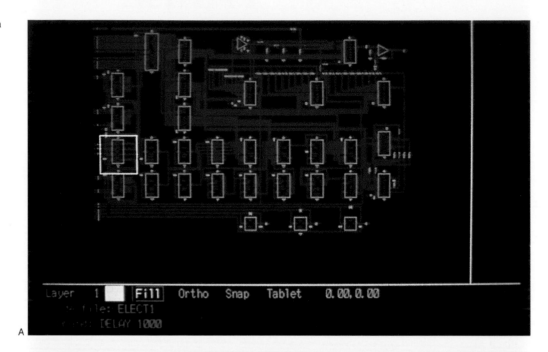

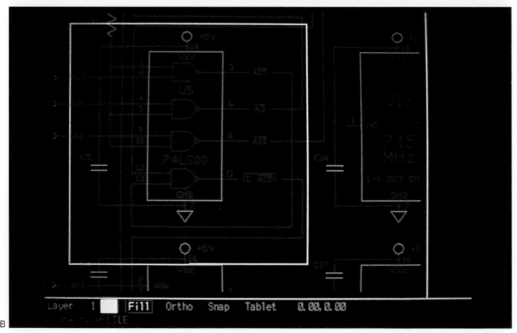

systems work in the positive, designing actual objects, rather than in the negative, where a mold is required. Since the data is digital, it can be archived when it becomes obsolete, yet restored and easily adapted should there be a need to redesign.

CADAM systems provide an alternative to the mass production of goods and can efficiently produce *prototypes* and *one-offs*, products manufactured in unit quantities, using mass production techniques.

INDUSTRIAL DESIGN

Applications in Industrial Design

Industrial design includes three-dimensional products used both by consumers and in manufacturing, such as hand tools, appliances, power and machine tools, furniture, electronic circuit components and products, farm equipment, automobiles, airplanes, musical instruments, drugs, and factories (fig. 10-1).

The products of industrial design can be solid objects made from a single material, such as a fork or baseball bat; static objects made from a combination of materials, such as a pencil; nonpowered objects built of moving parts, such as a stapler; or powered objects with many moving parts, such as a gasoline engine. The products may be manufactured by machine, cast from molds, stamped from dies, extruded, laminated, and grown, to name a few methods.

In all of these applications, whether objects are as small as atoms or as large as planets, computer graphics provides a way to model and preview the virtual product before it is actually manufactured, to test it in its domain, at a scale comfortable to the designer, and to convert the virtual model into a real product.

The CADAM Cycle of Production

The cycle of production of material goods begins with a design and concludes with a three-dimensional solid object. The steps of this production include needs

☛ **RELATED READING**

Earle, James H. *Engineering Design Graphics.* Reading, MA: Addison-Wesley, 1987.

Groover, Mikell P., and Emory W. Zimmers, Jr. *CAD/CAM Computer Aided Design and Manufacturing.* Englewood Cliffs, NJ: Prentice-Hall, 1984.

Hearn, Donald, and M. Pauline Baker. *Computer Graphics.* Englewood Cliffs, NJ: Prentice-Hall, 1986.

N-Nagy, Francis, and Andras Siegler. *Engineering Foundations of Robotics.* Englewood Cliffs, NJ: Prentice-Hall, 1987.

Schilling, Robert J. *Fundamentals of Robotics, Analysis and Control.* Englewood Cliffs, NJ: Prentice-Hall, 1990.

Tao, D. C. *Applied Linkage Synthesis.* Reading, MA: Addison-Wesley, 1964.

Tao, D. C. *Fundamentals of Applied Kinematics.* Reading, MA: Addison-Wesley, 1967.

Teicholz, Eric. *CAD/CAM Handbook.* New York: McGraw-Hill, 1987.

analysis, three-dimensional solid modeling, visualization, simulation, drafting, process planning, production, quality control, and accounting (fig. 10-2).

The *design concept,* a marketing-related term that refers to the design of the physical container or appliance as well as to the design of the idea, is the first concern when employing a CADAM system. The product design of frosted flakes, for example, refers not only to the design of the box and the graphics, but to the concept of frosting cornflakes and selling them as a breakfast cereal.

The development of a product in this context is shaped as much by the market research analyzed with a computer as by its interactive creation and the display of the product. Products today are often designed to fill sociological, psychological, and physical voids; a design that attracts buyers, therefore, is often not a physically innovative design, but one that has been shaped by a marketing plan based on demographics, research, and economics.

Once conceived, a product is modeled three dimensionally on an interactive vector graphic, or raster, work station that can rotate, size, and position the model.

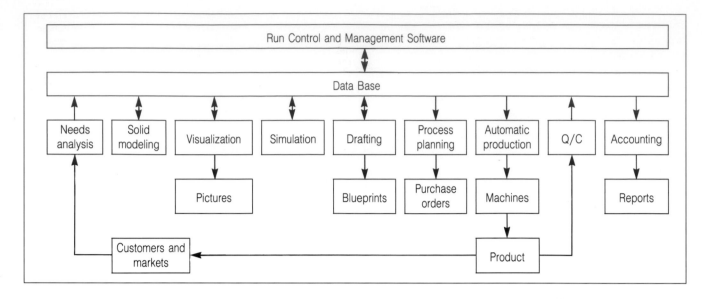

10-2. The CADAM cycle of production.

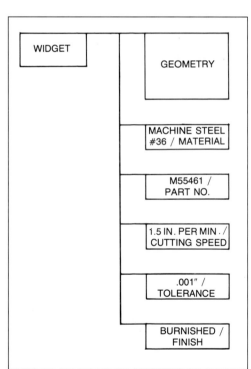

10-3. CADAM data bases combine geometric and nongeometric information.

Modeling for a CADAM system is not functionally different from the methods of three-dimensional modeling described in chapter 7. Models are constructed by digitizing and procedural techniques and are stored in graphics data bases. Standardized parts such as screws, nuts, brackets, and washers are modeled once and stored in on-line libraries.

A reliable and flexible data base is required at each stage, storing all relevant information about the product and how it is manufactured. *Geometric* data, about the shape of the object, as well as ***associated data,*** nongraphic information such as the materials used to make an object, manufacturing tolerances, and a part number are data-base components (fig. 10-3). Most CADAM data bases are relational and show how subassemblies together form a whole, and how parts are connected and move, their order of assembly, and functional relationships.

Previsualization provides a way to see the computer models before they are manufactured. The virtual models can be displayed either as wire frames, solid objects, or even cutaway views (fig. 10-4). Solid, shaded renderings are useful for thoroughly evaluating the look of a design, and realistic visualization routines include all of the aspects of surface and light interactions already discussed. Even animated movies and holograms can be made.

Simulation is the analysis of product design—testing the product while it is still a numerical model. The exact simulations performed depend on the product that is being designed; for example, a refrigerator design might be simulated to determine its heat loss under a variety of room temperatures. In all cases the results of the experiment are used to validate and modify designs.

Designs can be physically tested as well as market tested. Physical simulations include analyzing structures, calculating areas, testing electrical requirements and fracturing conditions, aerodynamics, and confirming tolerances between moving part. Air-conditioning, cooling, and power requirements can be simulated, as can human factors (fig. 10-5).

Market testing uses computerized previsualizations in research to test human responses to designs, determining which styles have appeal and which do not. The ability to generate variations in color, shape, and detail permits a researcher to quantify variations and hone in on successful design concepts within tight deadlines.

Drafting produces engineering drawings—geometric visualizations that represent data so that machinists, die makers, or assembly workers can follow it. Engineering drawings augment the basic geometry of a part with center lines, tolerances, surface finish, and measurements. Drafting is a characteristic of CADAM systems that distinguishes them from three-dimensional solid-modeling software.

When machines are computer controlled, engineering drawings are obsolete as communicative devices between designer and machinist. Applications that involve large constructions, such as ship building, architecture, or factory design, require drafting as a fundamental communication tool. In all cases drafting provides basic documentation, often in multiple colors, that depicts relationships between different systems (fig. 10-6).

Process planning techniques include assembly plans (fig. 10-7), schedules, pert

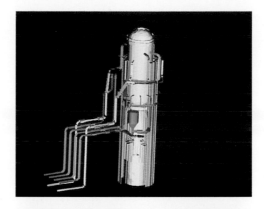

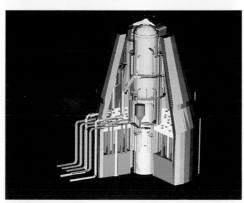

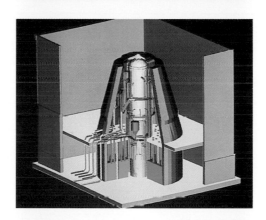

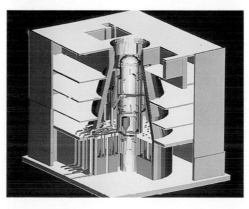

10-4. Previsualized cutaway views of nuclear reactor containment facility in varying degrees of complexity. (Courtesy of Everett I. Brown Company.)

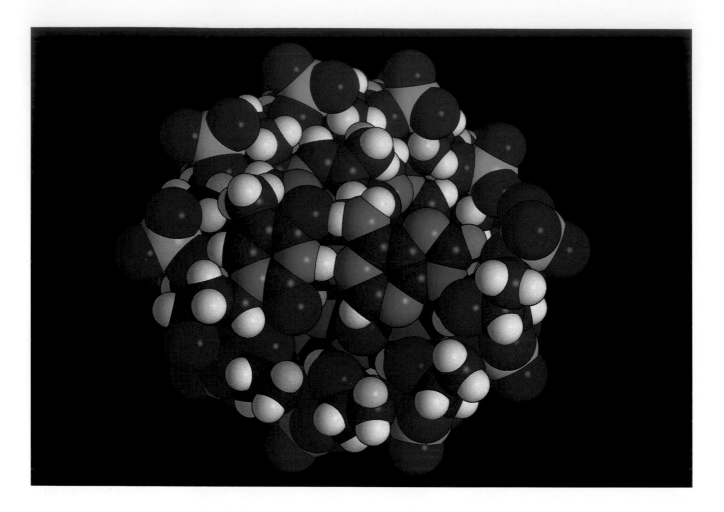

10-5. Simulation allows a product to be tested before it is created. For example, a new drug might be tested for side effects by simulating how it reacts chemically with other molecules in the body. The simulation uses calculations based on the rules of chemistry and molecular reactions. (Top view of DNA molecule courtesy of Nelson Max and Lawrence Livermore National Laboratory.)

and gant charts, which graphically depict critical paths of production, time allotments, raw materials and components lists used to generate purchase and work orders, and interfaces to sales, management, accounting, and production departments.

CADAM systems were developed to connect the three-dimensional digital data base directly with the manufacturing process for automated parts production and assembly. *Run control procedures* manage the entire design and manufacturing processes. Run control software interrelates the various components of a CADAM system and is akin in many respects to monitor and control processes, tracking production from order entry through delivery. The exact strategies involved vary according to the produc-

tion methods, but include numerically controlled machine tools and assembly robots. *Numerically controlled tools* are computer driven lathes, milling machines, and specialized machine tools of all types used to either make molds or to cut the material directly (fig. 3-46). *Assembly robots* (fig. 10-8) include machines that weld, integrate, and assemble products. Some are programmed to perform exact moves; others have computer vision and tactile sensors that allow them to pick up pieces in a random bin, or to orient themselves in situations that are not completely predictable.

After a product has been manufactured, each part can be tested to ensure *quality control*. These controls are computerized and are therefore clearly defined; solutions to past mistakes can be integrated

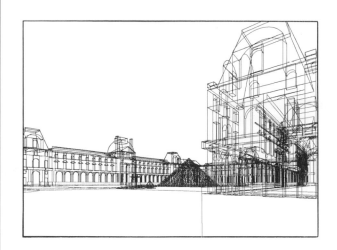

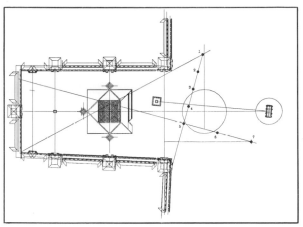

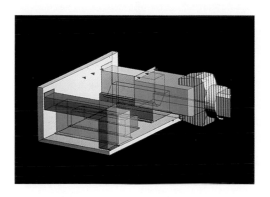

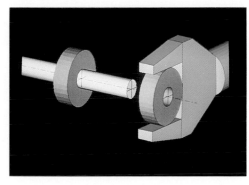

10-6. Drafting is a specialized visualization method used to show the relationships between different components of a project. Drafting includes plan and elevation drawings; structures can be also drawn in perspective. Depicted here is a remodeling of the Louvre Museum by I. M. Pei. (Courtesy of Computervision Corp.)

into the present system. The monitoring hardware can include digital scales that check weight, cameras and pattern recognition software that verify the shape of the part (fig. 10-9), and testing jigs, which operate the product (fig. 10-10).

Finally, *accounting software* produces reports either in a tabular or graphic format that detail profits, costs associated with specific jobs, and statistics about the production unit, such as what percent of its capacity is being used.

ARCHITECTURE AND INTERIOR DESIGN

Computers used in architecture and in interior design locate elements in three-

10-7. A Tokyo University research group led by Professor Kunii solves a product assembly problem. The product here is a copying machine that has been designed on a CAD system. The assembly solution begins by disassembling the product with a virtual disassembler, which tests pieces to see which can be removed, then removes them one by one— by sliding a bearing off a shaft, for example. After the disassembly sequence is stored, it is easily reversed, so either a virtual assembler, or a real machine performs the assembly. Kunii envisions a future with a standardization that enables real disassemblers to take apart real objects, service them, and put them together again. (Courtesy of Tosiyasu L. Kunii. © Tsukasu Noma, Tosiyasu L. Kunii, and Ricoh Co., Ltd.)

10-8. The robot (A) is first programmed using an interactive computer graphics display that simulates the robot's movements and checks for interferences (B). A variety of grippers can be affixed to the end of the robot arm. (Courtesy of Calma Company.)

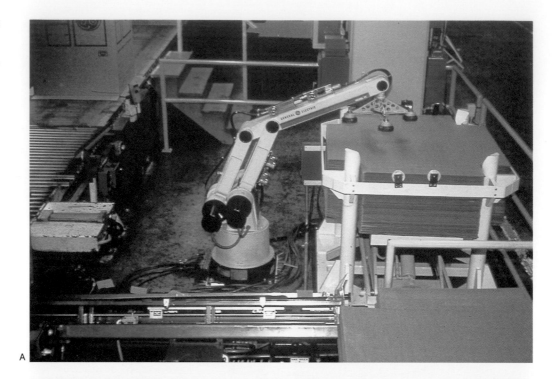

A

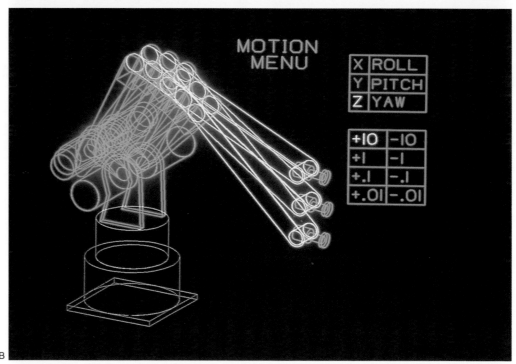

B

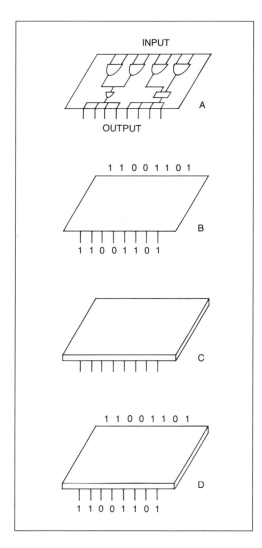

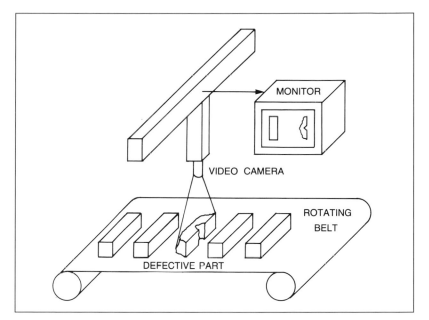

10-10. Testing may be closely allied to simulation. For example, a designer might make a computer model of a product such as a microprocessor chip (A). Next, a simulated electrical signal, essentially a machine language program, is applied to the virtual computer model to see if the results are predictable (B). If errors result, the original design is changed and retested. Once the virtual chip is perceived to be working, a real one is fabricated, using an automated production facility (C). The finished chip is mounted on pins and plugged into a testing machine, which applies the same software simulator, only this time to the real device (D). Once in production, the chips can be similarly tested on an individual basis.

dimensional space and simulate their appearance and performance. Computers assist in space design and planning, landscape studies, and the detailing and specifications of individual parts (fig. 10-11).

The design process for architecture generally follows the CADAM pattern and has much in common with the design of large structural objects like ships and airplanes. Models are input from coplanar blueprints, cross sections, and procedural techniques, and relational data bases and sophisticated software correlate designs for the various subsystems of a structure, such as the flow of water, electricity, communications, air conditioning, heat, and sewage.

Visualizations of an architectural project may be enhanced by color and realistic rendering techniques (fig. 10-12). Ground and air views of the structure in its proposed environment can incorporate the structure into existing urban data bases (fig. 10-13). The designer can animate the design and thus move through it, evaluating physical and social aesthetics.

Tests for structural properties, wind loading, and earthquakes, are performed on the digital architectural model (fig. 10-14). Energy studies analyze lighting, heating, and air-conditioning requirements.

10-9. A vision system checks gear tooth deviations using a video camera.

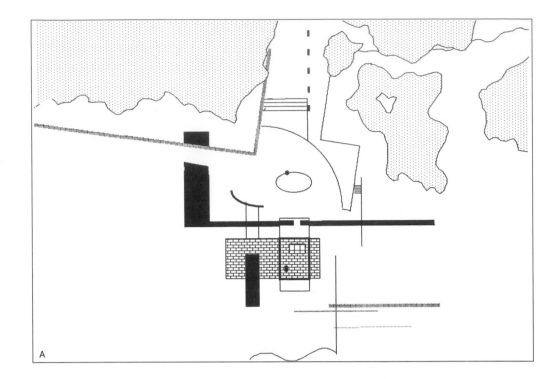

10-11. A site plan (A) as well as north (B) and east (C) elevations of a proposed residence created on a Macintosh personal computer. (Courtesy of UKZ: S. Unger, L. Kist, T. Zwigard, and M. Whitmore.)

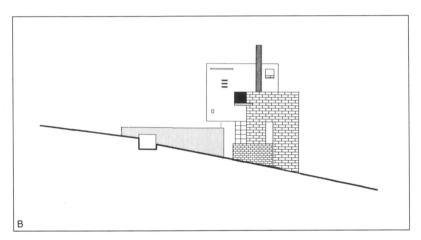

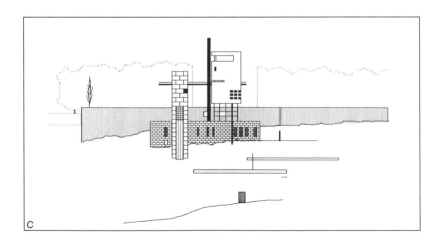

10-12. Realistic renderings can be produced with specialized software and assist in evaluating design decisions. (Courtesy of Cranston-Csuri Productions. Animation by Michael Collery.)

10-13. Medium-resolution color displays incorporate structures of the future into today's environments. (Courtesy of David M. McKeown Jr., Carnegie-Mellon University. Computer-generated scenes of Washington, D.C., using MAPS System, a three-dimensional map generation system.)

Color, light, and shadow studies (fig. 10-15) preview the structure as it might appear in the summer or winter. Zoning analysis plots allowable structures (fig. 10-16).

Finally, the graphic and nongraphic data in the relational data base are used to produce blueprints and engineering drawings that show any combination of sub-systems, testing them against each other to ensure they are properly structured and do not collide (fig. 10-17). The data bases can also feed numerically controlled machining of made-to-order parts, schedules of work orders, and material goods purchases.

The type of CAD system needed for an architectural application varies according to the size of the project. Initial sketching and massing studies, simple blueprints, line drawings, and even some structural analysis can be executed with a small computer (fig. 10-18). Only a larger system, however, can handle a complex project with extensive data bases that call for exhaustive analysis and realistic render-

☞ **RELATED READING**

Leighton, Natalie Langue. *Computers in the Architectural Office.* New York: Van Nostrand Reinhold, 1984.

Milne, M. *Computer Graphics in Architecture and Design.* New Haven, CT: Yale School of Art and Architecture, 1969.

Mitchell, William J. *Computer Aided Architectural Design.* New York: Van Nostrand Reinhold, 1977.

Mitchell, William J., and Malcolm McCullough. *Digital Design Media, A Handbook for Architects and Design Professionals.* New York: Van Nostrand Reinhold, 1991.

Negroponte, Nicholas, ed. *Computer Aids to Design and Architecture.* New York: Van Nostrand Reinhold, 1975.

10-14. Structural testing allows a structure to be stressed while still in the design stage. (Courtesy of Skidmore, Owings & Merrill.)

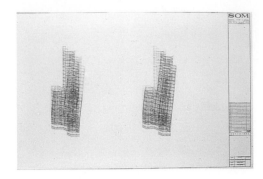

ing with solid volumes, transparencies, light reflections, shadows, and textures.

PACKAGE DESIGN

Package design considers the volume and shape of a container as well as its surface information (fig. 10-19). In other words, computer graphics in package design combines three-dimensional illustration, typography, and pagination. Graphic systems must therefore be highly flexible with two-dimensional makeup capabilities as well as the ability to map these designs on three-dimensional objects and view them in full color in perspective. An attractive alternative to building mockup packages, computer systems can test a variety of positions, proportions, and colors before creating the final package design (fig. 10-20).

Once the artwork is mapped onto a three-dimensional container, the finished model can be previewed as a full-color solid object, which permits many difficult container shapes to be explored and tested. The package, simulated in perspective

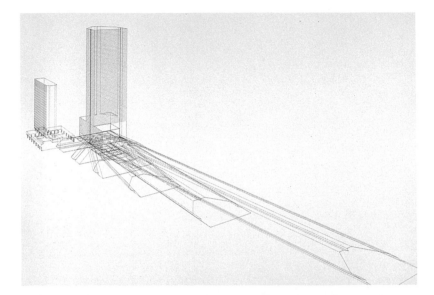

10-15. Shadow studies incorporate not only the location of shadows falling from a new structure, but how shadows from existing structures will affect heating and air-conditioning requirements. Shadow studies can be diagrammatic, as shown here, or incorporated into realistic renderings. (Courtesy of Skidmore, Owings, & Merrill.)

10-16. This illustration depicts a variety of allowable zoning setbacks (relationship between height and setbacks) in a New York City site study. (Courtesy of Skidmore, Owings, & Merrill.)

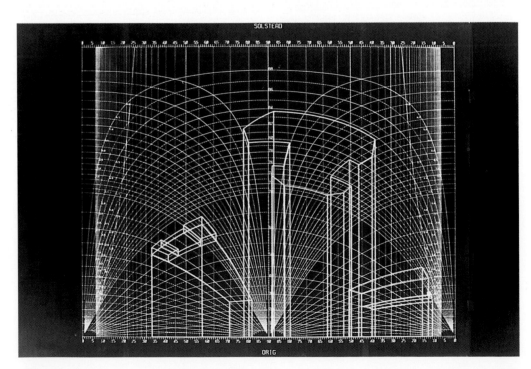

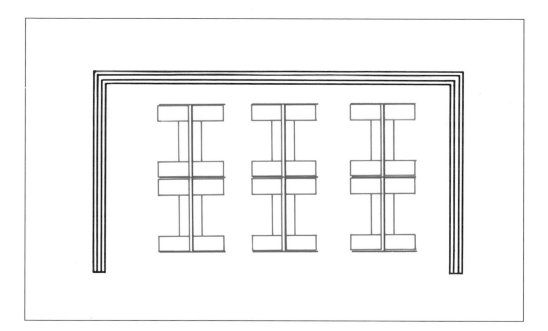

10-17. Overlays depict physical, electrical, and mechanical subsystems of the floor plan of a building. The furniture is drawn in black, the inner walls in green, the outer walls in red, and the lighting grid in blue.

10-19. Computer graphics can realistically simulate products and their packages. This Comet can is built by wrapping type and label information around a cylinder. The observant reader will notice that the effects of lighting do not appear in the label area, improving readability and creating a more effective graphic. (Courtesy of Digital Effects Inc.)

10-18. This small architectural system is built around a personal computer and can display color-shaded images of parts of structures. (Courtesy of Cubicomp. Corp.)

10-20. Computer graphic systems allow a variety of designs to be created for a single product. These two pictures show how a brand name, a bowl, and ears of corn form different design combinations. (Courtesy of Artronics.)

10-21. Computer-simulated products can be drawn in pattern repeats and in perspective as if they were actually on display. (Courtesy of Cranston-Csuri Productions, Inc. and Kornick Lindsay, Chicago.)

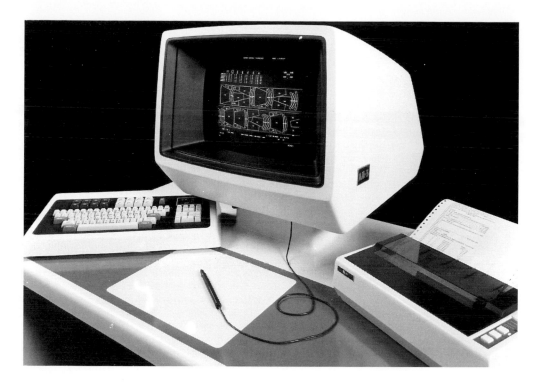

10-22. Pattern design systems are used to find the most effective way of cutting raw materials and arranging them in a limited shipping volume. (Courtesy of Gerber Camsco, Inc.)

on a supermarket shelf next to competing products, can be exposed to extensive market research in the early stages of design (fig. 10-21). Advertisements that incorporate the computer-generated package can also be tested.

A package design system must also be able to calculate the volume of the package and its gross weight; alternate materials can be compared for strength, weight, and cost. The distribution of a product, boxing and palletizing finished packages in a truck, also affect the final design (fig. 10-22).

Finally, prototypes can be produced quickly and cheaply using numerically controlled machine tools, thus allowing one to test physical objects. These same machines can then be used to fabricate production tools and dies. Computerized package design includes methods for identifying market appeal, optimizing resources, and reducing costs.

CLOTHING AND TEXTILE DESIGN

Computer graphics has a long tradition in the textile industry. Pixels are used in weaving and needlepoint, two-dimensional polygonal graphics are used for pattern design and textile printing, and two- and three-dimensional systems related patterns for cutting cloth with the three-dimensional structure of a finished garment. The Jacquard loom, created in the beginning of the nineteenth century, is an early example of a programmed machine. It used punch cards to weave complex patterns.

Weaving, like most textile applications, combines two-dimensional and three-dimensional technologies. In terms of pattern, weaving, like needlepoint and knitting, is a rectangular grid—an imaging technology that employs pixels. Cloth, however, is not just pattern, it is a material good, a matrix of yarn organized three dimensionally so it knots together.

Cloth is woven by stretching many parallel threads of yarn, called a *warp,* and then threading a horizontal thread, called a *weft,* back and forth through the warp (fig. 10-23) on a loom (fig. 10-24). Patterns are formed by varying which warp strings each weft string goes above and below. The control of this, along with the resulting

☞ **RELATED READING**

Creager, Clara. *Weaving.* Garden City, NY: Doubleday, 1974.

Davison, Marguerite. *A Handweavers' Pattern Book.* Swarthmore, PA: Davison Publishing, 1974.

Frey, Berta. *Designing and Drafting for Handweavers.* New York: Collier Books, 1958.

Lourie, Janice R. *Textile Graphics/Computer Aided.* New York: Fairchild Publications, 1973.

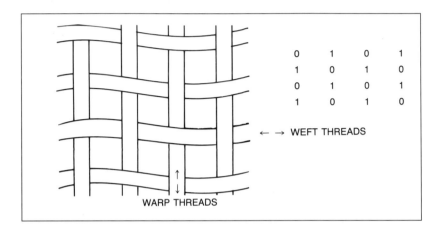

```
0   1   0   1
1   0   1   0
0   1   0   1
1   0   1   0
```

← → WEFT THREADS

↑ ↓ WARP THREADS

pattern, can be represented in ***draft notation***—a Boolean bitmap of the process and the result (fig. 10-25).

Draft notation can be executed on a computer, just as it can be executed on a real loom, allowing a designer to preview patterns. Furthermore, a computer, unlike a loom, can invert the operation—analyze a pattern and compose the draft notation.

Computer graphics are also employed in pattern design, textile printing, and are used to calculate pattern repeats (fig. 10-26), preview color combinations, alter designs, and calculate ***traps,*** which separate areas of different colors, so the textile inks have room to run without bleeding.

Computer systems to design and manufacture clothing combine two- and three-dimensional graphics and are similar to some metalworking processes, including the stamping of a steel sheet to form an automobile. Computers are used to preview patterns as they would appear three dimensionally (fig. 10-27) and also to deter-

10-23. Cloth is composed of weft threads, which alternatively stretch over and under warp threads. The over-and-under pattern of threads, a plain weave, can be represented as a Boolean bitmap.

10-24. On a loom the alternate warp threads pass through a heddle so they can be lifted up or depressed, allowing weft threads to be inserted between alternate warp threads. Two stages of the process are illustrated: lifting the heddle lifts the warp strings. The strings that are not connected to the heddle that is being lifted or depressed remain stationary.

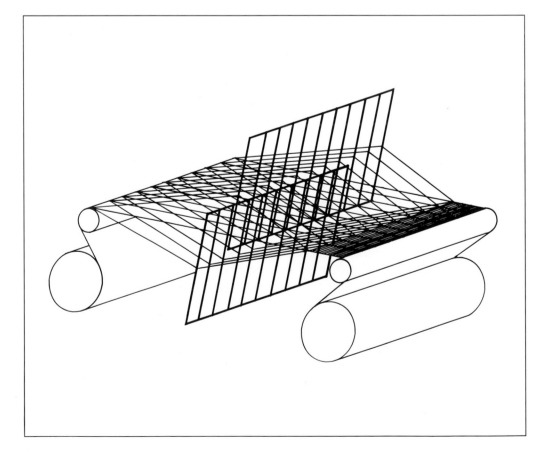

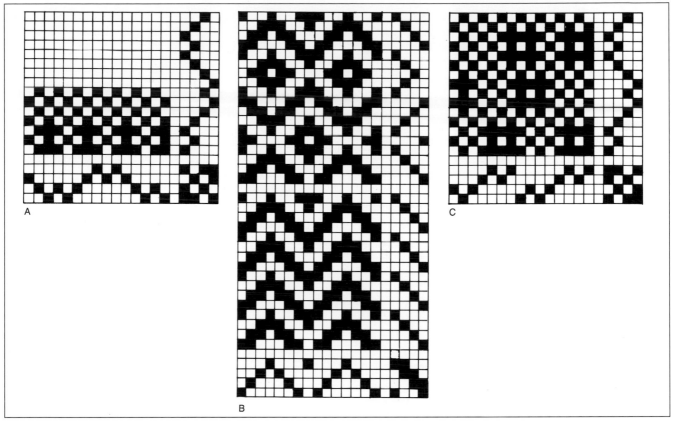

10-25. Draft notation consists of the threading draft, the tie-up, the treadling, and the web, or final pattern created by operating the loom. The threading draft, written across the bottom of each of these three diagrams, depicts four heddles. Black squares indicate that the heddle is connected to a string. The tie-up, in the lower right corner, indicates what foot pedals, or treadles, are connected to what heddles. For example, in diagram A treadle 1 is connected to heddles 1, 3, and 4; treadle 2 is connected to heddles 2 and 4, treadle 3 is connected it heddles 1 and 3, and treadle 4 is connected to heddles 1, 2, and 4. The treadles are the vertical column to the right of the drawing, and the black squares here indicate what treadle is pushed in what order. Finally, the web is the large area in the upper left of each drawing. The loom process works by depressing the treadles in the order indicated in the draft notation which in turn raises one or more heddles according to the tie-up; the heddles then lift up the corresponding warp threads so a new weft thread can pass underneath these strings horizontally. Thus the web grows away and up, with black web squares indicating where the warp threads will be visible in the final pattern, and white web squares indicating where the weft threads will be visible in the final pattern.

mine the position of the pattern on the raw material, minimizing the amount of material wasted.

SCULPTURE

Although artists are often not concerned with the analytical side benefits of CADAM (for instance, structural analysis, volume/surface area relationships, kinematic clearances), they often have a keen instinct for ways to employ the computer not only in the design and fabrication of pieces in a physical sense, but in their conceptual sense as well. Like other builders, sculptors may employ industrial design systems to previsualize concepts, draw plans, prepare parts lists, and even control cutting machines.

Other artists derive much of their cre-

10-26. The pattern printed on the fabric was created by duplicating the shape of a seashell that was scanned into the computer-aided design system. (*Cozumel* pattern design by Anna Ruohonen, Department of Clothing and Fashion Design, University of Industrial Arts, Helsinki, Finland. Photo by Kari Pyykönen.)

ative spirit from mathematics and geometry, and by structuring and juxtaposing the relationships of objects. Here too the computer can function as an ally, and enable what are basically proceduralist descriptions to be transformed into material objects (fig. 10-28). This ability to forge ideas into objects is very attractive to artists.

In the future we expect to see sculptors creating works by climbing into virtual worlds and shaping virtual clay, and at another extreme we might see sculptors directing their creations via intelligent agents. All the production tools in the middle (from drafting to holography) will continue to evolve.

10-27. After fabrics are designed on a computer, different choices may be previsualized as virtual clothes, drapery, or, as in this illustration, furniture coverings. (Courtesy of ModaCAD™ Computer-Aided Design, Los Angeles.)

10-28. This bronze sculpture is the result of a production process that started with two- and three-dimensional computer software. The artist then used tools and materials like bandsaws, gator-board, rubber, and wax for creating templates and molds. Patina was applied to the final bronze casts. (*Book of Ontology* courtesy of Robert G. Murray, F.T. Zone. Computer Art Lab, Indiana-Purdue University at Fort Wayne.)

11-0. The animation of characters represents the epitome of three-dimensional computer graphics. Not only must the creator fully understand the basic model-building and rendering techniques of three-dimensional computer graphics, but he or she must also master the subtleties of how to use motion to bring a character to life. (Courtesy of Allen Edwards and Thomson Digital Image.)

11

ANIMATION

FLIPPING FRAMES
SIMPLE 2D ANIMATION
CEL AND 3D ANIMATION
ACTIONS AND THE TIME AXIS
EASING, KINEMATICS, AND DYNAMICS

11-1. A rapid display of a sequence of individual, discrete frames with changes in movement is perceived as continuous motion. The simplest way to do this is to flip the whole frame for each increment. (*Thirteen Pyramids,* courtesy of Isaac V. Kerlow.)

FLIPPING FRAMES

Animation Defined

Animation is the representation and display of objects and motions across *time,* using a rapid sequence of individual pictures (fig. 11-1). The human perceptual system deploys special neural nets to analyze movement; these are in addition to networks to analyze color and space. Animation enables the artist, director, or communicator to introduce motion into otherwise static frames, and to communicate ideas and tell stories. Animation also enables a camera or a pair of virtual eyes to *move* through a virtual world; it allows scientists to make graphical visualizations of changing multivariable data.

Computer animation is produced using both interactive and batch tools. The difference between interactive animation and scripted animation is similar to the difference between a jazz musician and a composer; one improvises, the other creates a score that will be interpreted later. The production of animation is a process that takes place over hours, days, weeks, yet the experience—either just watching it or watching and interacting with it—is real time.

Computer animation is best designed and constructed with interactive real-time workstations that allow one to see the animation one is making in real time. ***Real-time animation*** is action that is updated in real time. It requires a fast CPU, especially when there are many objects or the objects are solid, in color, lit and shadowed, or otherwise enhanced. At some point there is a level of image complexity that cannot be computed and displayed in real time. In terms of a real-time preview, it is often possible to maintain the real-timeness of the display by ***reducing visual fidelity,*** that is, drawing some aspect of the object at reduced resolution (for example, representing a whole airplane with a rectangular box). The alternative to reducing visual fidelity is to compute ***non–real-time animation*** frames, single-frame record them one at a time, and then play them back at regular speed. An animation frame that takes 20 minutes to compute contains 36,000 times more computation than a real-time frame computed in 1/30th of a second (20 minutes × 60 seconds × 30 frames). This significant advantage can be used to enhance the detail of objects, lighting, and rendering ("representation"). So in this regard, animation is a compositional, batch process that uses interactive design tools.

Interactive real-time computer animation is action that plays in response to a user's control of a button or group of buttons. A simple case is a sprite (fig. 6-31) being animated on a screen in response to a button click. Note that the action does not involve flipping whole frames, only the sprite is flipping. A more sophisticated case of interactive real-time animation is merging the sprite and the button into a clickable animating object, for example, dragging a butterfly with flapping wings around the screen with a mouse. But here too, dragging the butterfly around is different than creating the animation.

Some computer processes enhance traditional animation, whereas others are techniques that simply never existed before. ***Computer-aided animation***

uses computers to control traditional (real-world) photographic hardware. It includes the control of animation stands (fig. 3-15), videotape and film recorders, and motion control. In ***computer-generated animation,*** all objects and actions are virtual and numerical (digital), either in a two-dimensional layered world (chapter 6) or a three-dimensional virtual world, lit with virtual lights, and viewed with a virtual camera (chapter 7). But all of these techniques involve the time axis.

General Production Process

The general description of producing and directing computer graphics provided in chapter 4 (including figs. 4-29 and 4-30) also pertains to animation. And although there are different animation production strategies they all share strategic processes. An animation begins with a clearly defined ***concept,*** the basic idea or design, of the project. A ***script*** is the text, including dialogue; it is often augmented with a ***storyboard,*** which illustrates the general characteristics of the objects or actors, the sets, the movement, and the mood, and shows the composition of each shot (fig 11-2). Camera movements and transition effects may also be plotted on storyboards. An ***animatic*** is used to derive a sense of action and pacing and is made by shooting the storyboard frames onto videotape (perhaps with pans and zooms to suggest action); it is edited in sync with a rough, but full-length, soundtrack. These steps constitute the ***preproduction*** phase.

The ***production*** phase covers the actual construction of virtual objects, their movement, and output to a recording medium. ***Modeling*** begins with designing two- or three-dimensional models of the backgrounds and characters and then digitizing them into the computer (chapters 6 and 7 are devoted to this topic). Movements are planned and blocked out on ***dope sheets,*** which show the position of each character (or

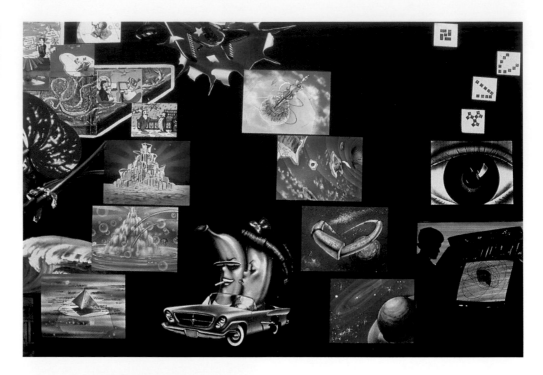

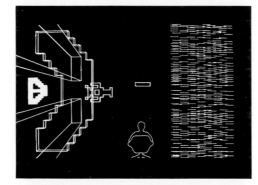

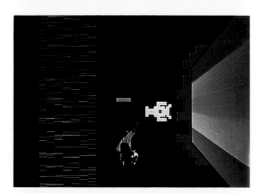

11-2. Storyboards combine script and visual compositions in a narrative sequence; this one is unusual in that the frames are not arranged in neat rows. (Drawn by Ikko Ono for Judson Rosebush Company.)

11-4. A set of high-resolution rendering tests from a news opening illustrates critical composition, coloring, and lighting. (Courtesy of Judson Rosebush and Digital Effects Inc.)

11-3. Motion tests often use diagrammatic representations of actions over time. In this example they are used to show size and position of live action as well as computer graphics. (Courtesy of Robert Abel Associates.)

object) at each frame. Action and lighting are previewed on sophisticated interactive displays (fig. 11-3). In productions that are too complex to preview interactively, a ***motion test,*** a wire-frame or low-resoulution test of the whole piece, is produced to describe the action, and selected frames are rendered in detail (fig. 11-4).

Once rendering and motion tests have been approved, the final, fully detailed animation is ***computed*** either in real time or frame by frame, and written to digital media, film, or videotape. Formats and resolutions vary widely, from animating icons on the desktop to video output of 480×640 pixels to $1,800 \times 2,400$ pixel 35mm film output and beyond.

After the scenes are completed they go into ***postproduction,*** where they are combined with sound and edited together. The ***editing*** process assembles the individual scenes into a complete work,

11-5. Postproduction involves many techniques to combine computer graphics and live action. The top photograph shows the shooting stage, with two bicycle riders, some real-world two-dimensional grass in front of them, and a black background. The shooting camera is just out of frame to the lower right, but a TV monitor (attached to the black pipe rigging in the foreground and visible in the right of the photograph) shows what the camera is seeing. The man in the lower center of the picture is operating a projector, which front-projects a computer-generated image onto the black screen behind the riders. The lower picture shows the final camera view.

perhaps using a nonlinear editor (see fig. 9-13). Postproduction also performs any optical or video **effects,** like matting (see figs. 6-19 through 6-25), fades (fig 6-25), dissolves (fig. 6-27), superimposition (fig. 6-28), glows (fig. 6-29), and titling. It is not unusual to combine computer animation and live action photography together in a single shot (fig. 11-5).

Given this strategic plan we will next inventory several strategies for fabricating animation, and then conclude the chapter with a study of action—the motion of things.

SIMPLE 2D ANIMATION

Cursor, Icon, and Sprite Animation

Creating animation by flipping whole frames (fig. 11-1) is conceptually simple, but usually involves redrawing or redisplaying much redundant picture information. A more efficient approach is to break an animation into a **foreground** and **background,** where the background is static, and a foreground has an object, called a **sprite.** Sprites

are groups of pixels able to (a) change shape, (b) move relative to the background, and (c) be in front of or behind other sprites (fig. 11-6). The foreground object is either a sprite or a cell, defined and discussed in detail in chapter 6. The difference between a sprite

11-6. A sprite is a rectangular matrix of pixels that is translated independently of the background and self-mattes over it. Conceptually the sprite is similar to a acetate cel riding on traveling peg-bar. A sprite is defined by a name, an X and Y position, a bitmap, and a flag indicating whether it is displayed or not. An animated sprite would have several bitmaps. The X and Y registration position may be a corner as shown, or an additional X and Y offset.

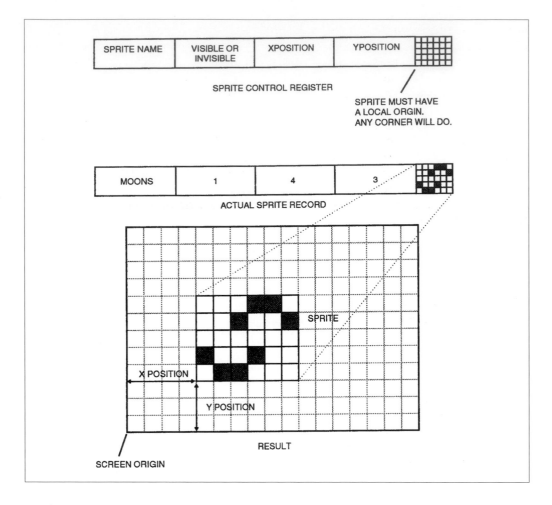

SPRITE NAME	VISIBLE OR INVISIBLE	XPOSITION	YPOSITION	

SPRITE CONTROL REGISTER

SPRITE MUST HAVE A LOCAL ORGIN. ANY CORNER WILL DO.

MOONS	1	4	3	

ACTUAL SPRITE RECORD

SPRITE

X POSITION

Y POSITION

RESULT

SCREEN ORIGIN

11-7. A puppet is an animated sprite that is interactive with the user. It may be dragged around, clicked on, or shot at. Semantically it is like a button in that it contains script that defines its behavior. The illustration shows a pivoting arm in an edit window registered at the shoulder and with the sprite before it drawn in onionskin mode. (Drawing made using ADDmotion software.)

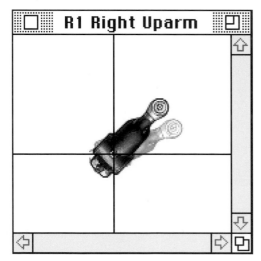

R1 Right Uparm

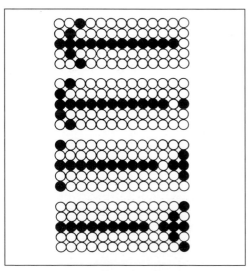

11-8. A marquee, like the light bulbs on a theater marquee, creates action simply by illuminating predefined areas in sequence, so limited animation is achieved without actually moving any shapes.

and a cell is that a *sprite* is a rectangle of pixels that can be translated and layered, and a *cell* is a polygon or group thereof that can be translated and layered (but be aware that these terms are not standardized nomenclature). Sprites often reserve one value for transparency so they will self-matte when laid anywhere over the background (fig. 6-30). An *animated sprite* consists of several different bitmaps that are alternated in sequence over a background (fig. 6-31). *Puppet sprites* may be dragged around the screen with the mouse or cursor while they are animating, or the mouse may be used to control their motion (fig. 11-7). An animated cursor can be a puppet sprite (fig. 4-12); a puppet sprite may also be thought of as a button with an animating icon that can be dragged around or clicked with the mouse.

Color Table Animation

Color table animation is a way of producing limited animation on a static display, without card flipping and without sprites. In its simplest form, action is created by sequentially illuminating fixed areas that are predefined, like an animating arrow made up of lightbulbs (fig. 11-8). The more common form of color table animation often involves an eight-bit color display and careful manipulation of the color lookup table (see chapter 5, and especially figs. 5-10 through 5-12). An object in the scene to be animated is created in several different positions, with each different position assigned a unique color number, which points to a row in the lookup table and thus a color value. The benefit of this setup is that it is computationally trivial to change the values in the lookup table, and when this is done the object appears to animate on the screen (fig. 11-9). Color table animation can be used many different ways; for example, two different lookup tables can be defined, and identical artwork can be used with either of them (fig. 11-10).

Motion Graphics

Motion control systems are computer-controlled hardware, such as an animation stand or live-action camera, which photograph real-world artwork and which repeat their movements precisely (fig. 3-15). An elaborate *motion control camera* might include three axes of translation and rotation (fig. 11-11); a similar translation and rotation strategy can be used to mechanically control a *platen,* a place where artwork is mounted (fig. 3-16).

Computer-aided applications include the recording of camera movements made by a human cameraman for sub-

11-9. Screen action (left) and an eight-row color look-up table (right) depict three successive animation frames. Between each frame, each row in the look-up table is translated one row down, in a loop. The design and format of the objects, and in particular their color-by-number assignments, set up the animation. Because the computation only involves the table and not the objects, it can be completed quickly. The effect on the screen is to blank certain pixels and to color others, so a single chevron appears to be descending.

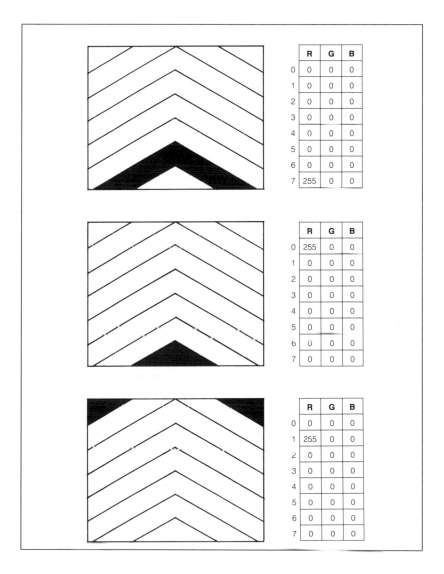

11-10. Look-up table animation showing sunny and stormy color palettes. The first twelve values in the look-up table dissolve from "sunny" to "stormy"; the values 13 and 14 are toggled on and off to simulate lightning.

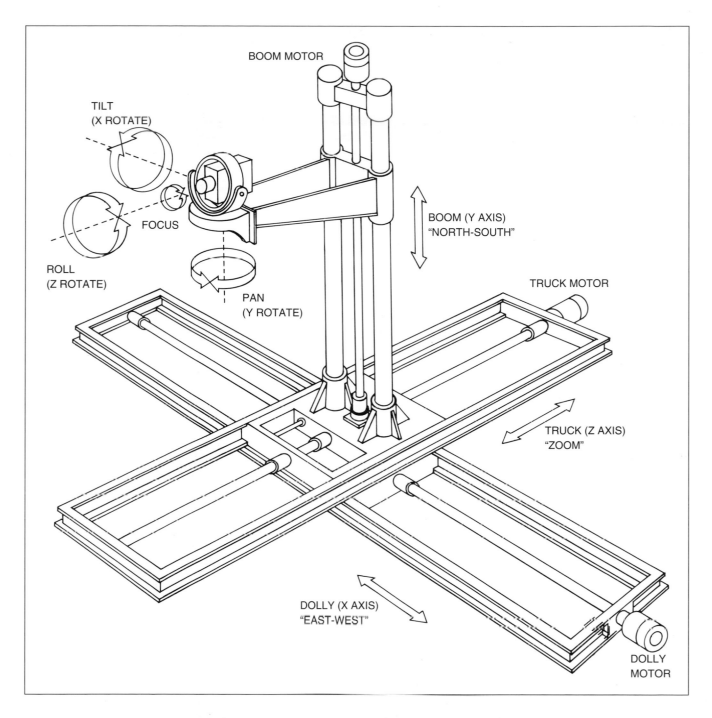

BOOM MOTOR

TILT
(X ROTATE)

FOCUS

ROLL
(Z ROTATE)

PAN
(Y ROTATE)

BOOM (Y AXIS)
"NORTH-SOUTH"

TRUCK MOTOR

TRUCK (Z AXIS)
"ZOOM"

DOLLY (X AXIS)
"EAST-WEST"

DOLLY
MOTOR

sequent playback, and the control of a real camera using actions created with a virtual camera (fig. 3-15). The computer control of cameras makes it possible to synchronize live action with computer-generated imagery (fig. 11-12), and to shoot multiple-pass cinematography where a camera photographs artwork

multiple times. This genre of motion control graphics includes images that often take advantage of the offset/repeat/multipass nature of motion control cameras. *Slit-scans* and *streaks* (fig. 11-13) are created by leaving the shutter open while simultaneously zooming the camera and panning the artwork. *Strobes*

11-11. Motion control camera with seven degrees of freedom, all of which may be operated with computer-controlled motors. The camera can translate position in X, Y, and Z axes, the camera head can rotate in all three axes, and focus can change.

11-12. Computer graphics and live action combined. In this image, the computer graphics are composited in front of live action, and a live action car is composited on the computer graphics. Photogrammetry techniques assist in synchronizing the graphics and live action. (Courtesy of Digital Effects Inc.)

11-13. Streaks are made by opening a camera shutter and then either moving the camera or the artwork to create a smear of light. (Courtesy of Shadow Light Productions, Inc., Director/Designer Marc Chelnik.)

are made by reshooting artwork multiple times but with subtle variations in color and cxposure (fig. 11-14).

CEL AND 3D ANIMATION

Cel Animation

Virtually all facets of hand-drawn (cartoon) animation can be computerized. A computer-simulated **cel animation** system enables a producer and director to construct shots of action that are generated primarily with layers of two-dimensional artwork. A **cel** is a physical piece of transparent acetate, often with a cartoon character inked and painted on it. A cel, or layers of cels, are laid over an opaque **background** and the visual result is recorded on film or tape. A full-blown cel animation production system consists of many computers networked together that share and exchange files pertaining to different facets of the process: scripting (word processing), storyboarding, drawing, inking and painting cels and backgrounds (draw and paint systems), in-betweening (interpolation of drawings), doping and composing cels over backgrounds (spreadsheets, animation systems, compositors), recording, editing, and—for the front office—scheduling and accounting software (fig. 11-15). We will detail most of these terms shortly.

In a virtual implementation of the cel paradigm the background is a bitmap or polygon graphic, and the front objects are cells or sprites (described above). The **cell** refers to a polygonal object that may be scaled, translated, rotated, and layered. A cell may be associated with a **layer** (**track, channel**), a priority list of who is closest to the background and who is the furthest in front. The layer may be represented as an integer, or it may be represented with a decimal number, in which case it resembles a Z-axis value. When the composited image is

☛ **RELATED READING**

Born, Robert, ed. *Designing for Television: The New Tools.* Tequesta, FL: Broadcast Designers' Association, 1983.

Felding, Raymond. *The Technique of Special Effects Cinematography.* New York: Hastings House, 1983.

Finch, Christopher. *Special Effects: Creating Movie Magic.* New York: Abbeville Press, 1984.

Imes, Jack. *Special Visual Effects.* New York: Van Nostrand Reinhold, 1984.

Levitan, Eli. *Electronic Imaging Techniques.* New York: Van Nostrand Reinhold, 1977.

Thomas, Frank, and Ollie Johnson. *Disney Animation: The Illusion of Life.* New York: Abbeville Press, 1981.

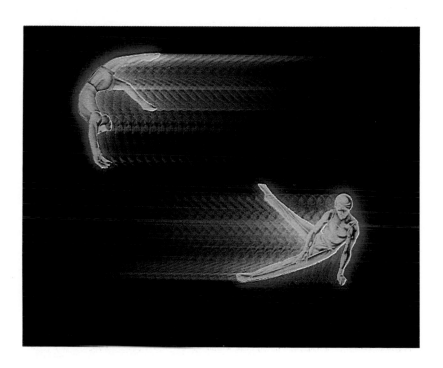

determined, the layer may be treated simply as rank order, in which case the picture is resolved back to front with each layer overlaying those beneath it, or the layer values may be used numerically to simulate a multiplane effect in which there is distance between the layers. **Animated cells** are a sequence of registered cells depicting action (fig. 11-16D). An **animated puppet cell** has button properties and animates; like a puppet

11-14. A strobe is a multiple exposure made by moving the camera or platen from position to position while the camera shutter is closed. (Courtesy of Animotion.)

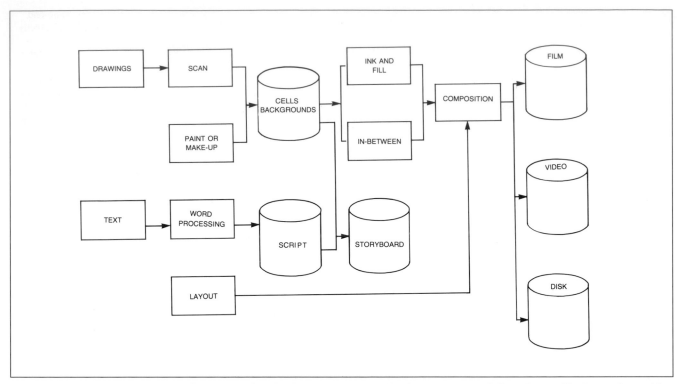

11-15. The steps of production in a computer-assisted cartoon system. Cell overlays and backgrounds are either hand drawn and scanned into the system, or made on a digital paint or display list system. Text is keyed in via a word processor. Illustrations and text are merged to form electronic storyboards. The cells are stored as polygon outlines, scan converted to make them opaque, and interpolated to calculate intermediary positions or in-betweens. Compositing or layout commands specify what cells and backgrounds are to be combined in what order, and the results are output to film, video, or digital disk.

sprite it can be translated interactively while it is animating.

The advantage of cells over sprites is that, in general, polygons are more flexible than sprites; the disadvantage is that a system needs a display list capability in hardware (or software) and must be more powerful. Like sprites, cells can translate around and over the background, but they can also scale and rotate continuously. Futhermore, since they are polygon outlines, their outline shape can be changed programmatically. Linear interpolation can be used to turn a keyhole into a circle, for example.

Key Frame Animation

The idea behind **key frame animation** is that action may be described as a series of key poses (or **key positions,** **key frames, keys, extremes**) that represent the extent of motion of a certain action (for instance, the top of a jump, the bottom of a jump where the shock is fully absorbed). A key pose is often typified by a moment of maximum position, zero velocity, and maximum acceleration, or as a moment of rest and no acceleration. The frames in between the keys are called **in-betweens,** and their images are formed by a breakdown of the information contained in the keys plus additional information about the nature of the object in motion (fig. 11-16).

Three-dimensional Computer Animation

The core ideas of the cel animation model can be extended into three dimensions. **Three-dimensional computer animation** uses computer pro-

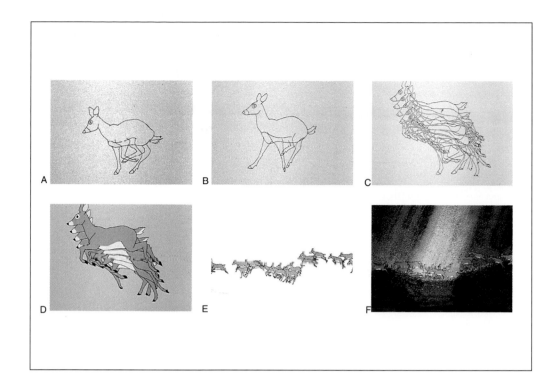

11-16. Beginning and end line drawings (A, B) specify two extreme, or key, positions that are used to determine the in-between drawings shown here both in line (C) and color (D). Apparent movement is achieved by repositioning successive inbetweens in a scene (E). The final animation is overlaid on a color background (F). (Courtesy of New York Institute of Technology.)

cedures to define, move, and display three-dimensional objects and procedures in an imaginary environment. The models are illuminated with imaginary lights, and viewed with a virtual camera. These modeling techniques include point digitizing, sectioning, coplanar blueprints, photogrammetry, and procedural methods. These are discussed in detail in chapter 7, as are parameters of lighting and rendering. The difference between 2D cel and 3D model animation is that in 2D animation the objects are flat and laid in layers atop a background, whereas in 3D animation the objects have volume and may be anywhere in space. The virtual camera sees them in correct perspective, and only the objects (or parts thereof) that are visible end up on the image (see, for example, fig. 7-43).

Like cel animation, three-dimensional animation requires scripts and storyboards. But instead of designing the action in a series of flat sliding planes using cells or sprites, the action must be thought through in the context of a three-dimensional environment. Objects are often designed with detailed blueprints, and instead of a background one thinks of *sets,* three-dimensional environments with lights, cameras, and objects. Sets in computer animation are very similar to sets in the theater or the movies.

A *motion pathway* is the line or curve an object or camera describes as it moves through the set over a sequence of frames (fig. 11-17). Just as objects and lighting require design, so too must a motion pathway be sculpted in space. A motion pathway is often defined by a series of transformations (figs. 7-23 through 7-33) that specify the successive positions of an object. Motion pathways are usually independent of whatever data describe the traveling object; in other words, many different objects can travel on the same motion pathway. This segregation of motion from object is a feature of most computer animation systems. Motion pathways can also be used in two-dimensional cell and sprite systems, and indicate the two-dimensional path of an object.

Everything in a computer animation set is parameterized. The computer animator's art lies in the manipulation of these parameters on a frame-to-frame basis. A *morph* is a change of the shape of an object on a frame-to-frame basis; it is often accomplished by interpolating points in one object into points in another. A morph may be done with polygon outlines, bitmap images (fig. 11-18), and three-dimensional volumetric objects (fig. 11-19). Other parameters that can animate include: positions of lights, cameras, and objects; colors of lights and objects; textures and reflections of objects; transparencies of camera filters;

even the atmospheric haze that fills up the set.

With three-dimensional model animation, there are at least two major approaches to calculating the parameterized values that are changing from frame to frame. A *parametric key frame* approach requires defining the beginning and end arguments of all the parameters, and then computes the intermediate parameter values for each frame, moves the objects accordingly, and displays or records the result. The computation of the in-between frames is not unlike the cel model except that the key positions are defined in terms of the parameters defining each object and not just their shapes. For example, a virtual articulated robot does not turn and salute by metamorphosing in two dimensions on the image plane, rather its body, shoulder, or elbow rotates. The key frame approach implies that the elbow (and all the other joints that are rotating) has an initial bend angle at the first frame and a terminal bend angle at the last frame, and that the computer calculates the rotations of the intermediate frames, and draws the robot as the virtual camera sees it (fig. 11-20).

The other major approach to calculating the positional locations of objects in space is *dynamics,* in which the virtual stage set is embued with simulated forces that model the laws of physics in the real world. These forces can then act on

11-17. A motion pathway (the red line) and an object (the number two) that is following the motion pathway. Given the two end positions and some rules, any number of intermediate in-between frames can be determined, making the action slow or fast.

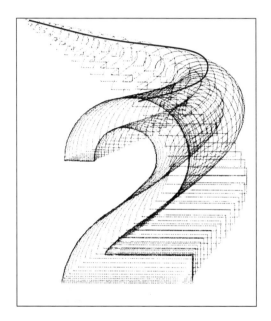

11-18. A two-dimensional morph works by selecting pixels paired between two different images and then interpolating the first image into the next. (*Funerary Stele* is courtesy of Mary Lowenbach, Pratt Institute.)

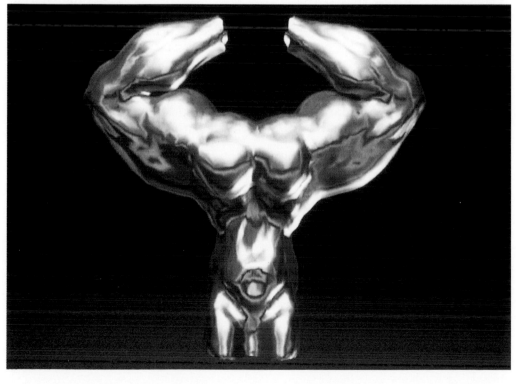

11-19. A three-dimensional morph changes the actual physical geometry of a volumetric object across a sequence of frames. (In *Search of Muscular Axis*, directed by Toshifumi Kawahara. © 1990 Polygon Pictures.)

11-20. The key frame approach to 3D animation implies, for the object, a rigid kinematic structure built out of joints and links, not unlike our human armature with rotating joints and fixed-length limbs. The XYZ positions of all the objects and all the angles in the scene are defined for a series of key positions. Individual frames are determined by in-betweening each of the parameters independently. The illustration shows four windows used by Life Forms, a program to make figureative animation. At the top left there is the stage—what the camera sees. The figure editor at the top right lets the animator define the key positions, and the timeline at the lower left allows the keys to be organized temporally. At the lower right is the controller to start and stop the action.

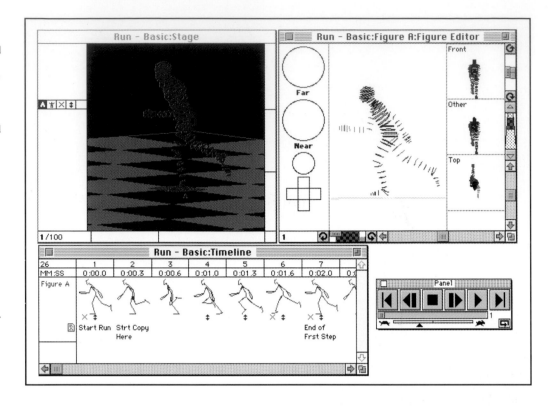

objects, causing specific actions to occur. For example, if a glass vase is released ten feet above the stage the gravity force would begin moving it through space; the distance the object travels in successive frames is a function of the law of gravity. Unlike key-framing, the object is not being moved between two key positions. Gravity has no idea where it is pulling the object to, it simply pulls it a certain distance each frame, a distance determined by the object's past. Key-framing has the advantage of the a priori from/to specificity, whereas dynamics has the advantage of letting forces act on objects to move them. Both are useful and sometimes only one or the other will do the job.

Animation is a temporal sequence of pictures in which at least one parameter is changed each frame. It is the variable of time that is unique to animation; *time* is a linear axis that passes from the past through the present into the future. This section focuses on the time management aspects of animation and how positions are determined in time.

ACTIONS AND THE TIME AXIS

Action refers to all kinds of motion—the position of objects in space, changes in object shape, changes in the position of camera, changes in the position of lights. Action is also created by changes in an object's geometry, by the brightness of lights, by rotations of objects and cameras, by surface patterns that are changing, by changes in the focus or focal length of the lens, and by special effects like fades and wipes. One creative aspect of computer animation is the search for new parameters to manipulate.

A *computer animation language* is one that permits images and events to be specified temporally; newer languages enable temporal events to be represented graphically on the desktop (figs. 4-4, 9-2, and 9-3). Animation languages aid in specifying when actions begin and end, and *how* objects move. The temporal layout of animation is

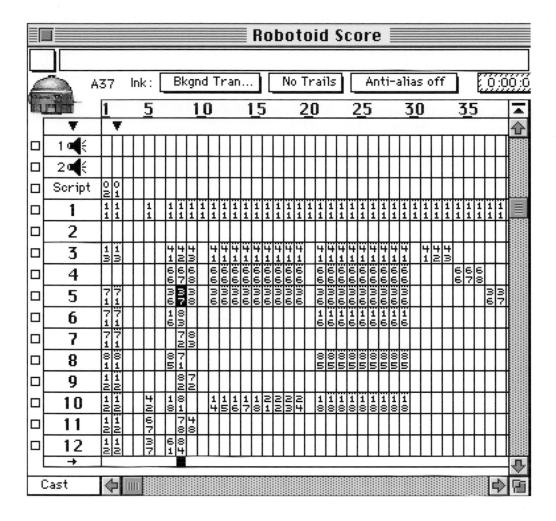

11-21. This virtual dopesheet has one column for each frame and one row for each cel layer (channel, track); it is also common to encounter the transposition of this, with one row for each frame and one column for each track. A cell or sprite stored in the matrix at a specific track-frame will appear on that frame. In this particular example, as the track numbers increment (and go toward the bottom of the page) the cells lie closer to the viewer. Clicking on a single square selects the sprite for that frame-layer, in this case, the robot head in the upper left. (Example from Macromind Director.)

done on what is called a **dopesheet** (**exposure sheet, score**), which is a spreadsheetlike matrix that allows an animator to place a cell or a sprite in a track at a frame (fig. 11-21). In a parameterized key frame model the tracks simply hold the individual parameter values, and there are as many tracks as there are parameters.

EASING, KINEMATICS, AND DYNAMICS

Eases and Rates of Change

Key frame animation implies a start position, an end position, a start time, an end time, and a motion rule, called an **ease,** which specifies how the in-between positions are calculated. Eases are used in all animation, be it hand-drawn, motion graphics, or computer-generated. They provide a way to depict **acceleration** and **deceleration,** the rate at which objects speed up and slow down. Eases are used to control the movement of objects, cameras, zooms, colors and lights, and special effects like fades and dissolves. Eases are designed using different mathematical formulas, including linear acceleration and deceleration (the simplest), sine waves, and logarithmic progressions. The parameters of an ease often include the length of time the ease should accelerate and decelerate.

11-22. Given two extremes, a keyhole and a circle, linear interpolation is used to create three in-betweens. The two extremes are designed to contain the same number of points; each point in the keyhole is interpolated into its corresponding point in the circle.

11-23. Positions, scalings, rotations, color values, and even normals can be interpolated. One merely supplies initial and terminal values and a frame count. The intermediary values, which the computer calculates, are equally spaced between the initial and terminal positions; the number of values plus the beginning and end points equals the number of iterations. The illustration shows a five-step interpolation between an initial position of (3, 4) and a final position of (7, 6). The interpolated positions can be described with a table:

3, 4
4, 4.5
5, 5
6, 5.5
7, 6

The interpolation is calculated by subtracting the initial position from the final position, thus creating a value that is equal to the total displacement. In this case, it would be [7,6] – [3,4] = [4,2]. Each increment of the displacement is equal to the displacement divided by one less than the count, here 4 (5 – 1). Thus the incremental displacement per frame is equal to [4, 2] ÷ 4 = [1, .5]. This incremental value is then successively added into the original position value to create the sequence of interpolated positions in the table above.

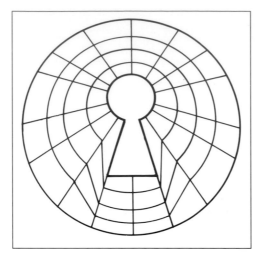

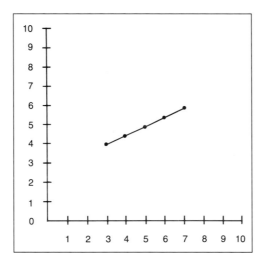

Linear Interpolation

The most rudimentary ease is *linear interpolation,* in which the in-betweens are equally spaced between two key positions and acceleration and deceleration are ignored (fig. 11-22). So in this regard a linear interpolation really does not "ease" at all. *Interpolation* is a method of calculating any number of new values between two existing values (fig. 11-23). The disadvantage of the linear interpolation is that objects in the real world do not accelerate and reach a constant velocity instantly; nature doesn't work this way and the visual result is jarring.

Eases that look real require knowledge about *kinematics,* the study of motion in terms of positions, velocity, and acceleration, but without regard to actual forces. A *position* is a two- or three-dimensional location in space expressed as XY or XYZ. A *velocity* is a rate of motion (for instance, 55 miles per hour) in a particular direction (for instance, northeast). *Acceleration* is the rate of change of velocity over time. A drag racer accelerates quickly; a blimp accelerates slowly. These differences in acceleration reveal differences in their character—and differences that are central to animation. Objects in nature begin to move in small increments that become larger until the object approaches a constant velocity; the increments then become smaller as the object slows down to a stop (fig. 11-24). An example of this is an ordinary automobile accelerating to a speed, cruising, and then braking to a stop. Easing, which is calculated using the acceleration formula, makes objects move in a natural manner. Another easing strategy specifies that an object be at certain places at certain times, and the computer is used to calculate a motion pathway with realistic acceleration (fig. 11-25).

Global and Local Actions

A *global action* is an action that is applied to an entire object or group of objects. A *local action* applies only to a component of the object. Global and local actions are applied by concatenating a series of individual transformations (described in chapter 7). Complex figures (for example, a robot character) are organized as a *hierarchical tree* of action transformations that propagate from the trunk of the body out through its joints (fig. 11-26). A complex character often requires many simultaneous arguments, or parameters, to specify actions, and there is at least one parameter for every joint in the actor. A hierarchical object may be animated using a **parameter table,** a matrix that contains one column for each joint angle parameter in the body and one row for each key frame (fig. 11-27). A parameter table is not unlike a dopesheet used in traditional animation (fig. 11-21), except it is transposed and contains parameters, not cells. The parameter values for in-between frames are determined by easing each parameter individually. A **gesture** is a collection of parameters that animate in synchronization and that may be temporally scaled.

A **cycle** is a series of transformations that repeat periodically and are controlled using a single parameter. Consider animating an automobile engine, a complicated but predictable collection of pistons and rods connected to a crankshaft (fig. 11-28). The cyclic action is controlled by specifying an angle for the crankshaft and letting the computer determine the position for all the engine parts that belong to the hierarchical tree. The engine is not defined for a finite number of positions; it is procedurally defined for any **phase,** that is, any angle of rotation specified by an argument. Animating the engine is therefore a process of specifying beginning and end phase angles, calculating the phase angles for all the in-between frames, and then calling the engine function for each frame and passing it the appropriate angle. This is a kinematic approach: the engine is rotating as if it were being turned by an electric starter motor. By changing the sequence of arguments the animation can make the engine run faster, slower, or even backward. Accelerations and decelerations are accomplished by applying an ease to the rotary angle.

All of these easing methods involve **forward kinematics** in which, for example, the position of each angle is specified in advance of each frame. **Inverse kinematics** is a method whereby the animator specifies only a final position or rotation, and the computer determines

☞ **RELATED READING**

Halas, John, ed. *Computer Animation.* New York: Hastings House, 1974.

Halas, John. *Graphics in Motion.* New York: Van Nostrand Reinhold, 1984.

Halas, John, and Roger Manvell. *The Technique of Film Animation.* 3d ed. New York: Hastings House, 1971.

Magnenat-Thalmann, Nadia, and Daniel Thalmann. *Computer Animation, Theory and Practice,* 2d ed. New York: Springer-Verlag, 1990.

Magnenat-Thalmann, Nadia, and Daniel Thalmann. *Synthetic Actors in Computer-Generated 3D Films.* New York: Springer-Verlag, 1990.

Roncarelli, Robi. *The Computer Animation Dictionary.* New York: Springer-Verlag, 1989.

Rosebush, Judson. *Computer Animation.* New York: Van Nostrand Reinhold, 1993.

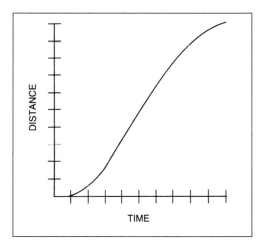

11-24. This ease illustrates linear acceleration or deceleration. A command such as "17 EASE .3 .2" produced the ease in this drawing. It is 17 frames long, accelerates for 30 percent of the time, and decelerates for 20 percent of the time. The drawing shows an object moving from bottom to top, with time plotted on the horizontal axis. The initial increments of distance are small, but increase from frame to frame until the motion consists of a constant velocity; the increments are equal here. Finally, as the object slows to a stop, each increment of distance gets progressively smaller.

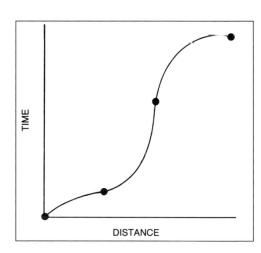

11-25. A compound ease is defined first by selecting points at specific space/time intervals (X, Y coordinates in the graph) and then fitting a curve through the points.

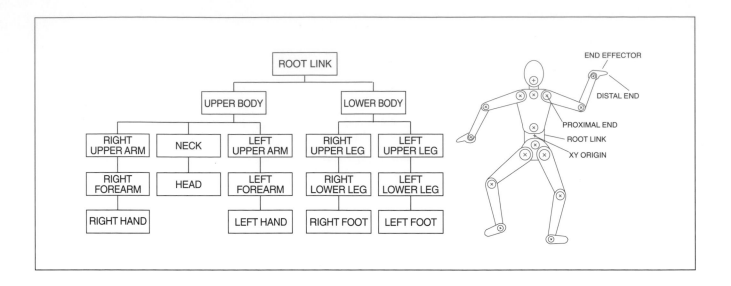

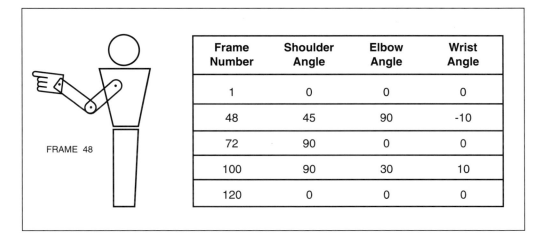

11-26. This simplified two-dimensional human skeleton represents major body joints as single axis rotations. A global transformation moves the entire skeleton as a unit. A local transformation, for example, a rotation of the shoulder, orients the upper arm as well as the forearm and hand below it; the elbow is more local than the shoulder and only orients the forearm and hand. The most local transformation is the wrist rotation, which only affects the orientation of the hand.

FRAME 48

Frame Number	Shoulder Angle	Elbow Angle	Wrist Angle
1	0	0	0
48	45	90	-10
72	90	0	0
100	90	30	10
120	0	0	0

11-27. The two-dimensional robot has an origin in its chest and an arm with an articulated shoulder, elbow, and wrist. Each of these joints is rotated to move the arm. Whereas a global transformation might apply to the entire body, increasing local actions applied to the shoulder would affect the movement of the elbow, which in turn would concatenate to the wrist. (After all, a shoulder pivots everything below it.) Also shown is the parameter table used to describe the robot, which shows frame numbers and the corresponding angles for key positions of each of the three joints. A computer program will evaluate the table, construct the appropriate transformations, and calculate inter-mediate frames.

the position or rotation of all the intermediate pieces. Inverse kinematics is used to solve problems like a robot reaching for an object (fig. 11-29).

Dynamic Modeling

Dynamics (also known as *physical modeling* or *simulation*) is a way to produce animation by modeling the physical forces that actually affect objects, instead of manually positioning objects where they are supposed to be. A *force* is a push or a pull that produces or prevents motion; forces include mass, gravity, inertia, friction, momentum, and elasticity. Dynamic animation techniques enable one to

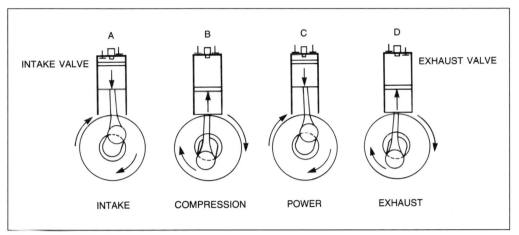

11-28. A single parameter often controls the action of many connected parts—here, a simple engine is controlled by the rotary angle of its crankshaft. The rate of change of this parameter controls the speed at which the engine turns. For example, if the engine were running at 10 rpm (3,600 degrees per minute) and the animation consisted of 24 frames per second (1,440 frames per minute), then the engine would advance 2.5 degrees per frame (3,600 ÷ 1,440). The animation would be performed by calling the function once for each frame, with a sequence of arguments: 0, 2.5, 5, 7.5, 10, 12.5 . . . degrees. The program might look like this, with function ENGINE taking a single argument ANGLE. ANGLE is initially zero, and increases in increments of 2.5 per frame:

```
ANGLE = 0
BEGIN 1440
    DRAW ENGINE ANGLE
    ANGLE = ANGLE + 2.5
    FRAMEADVANCE
END
```

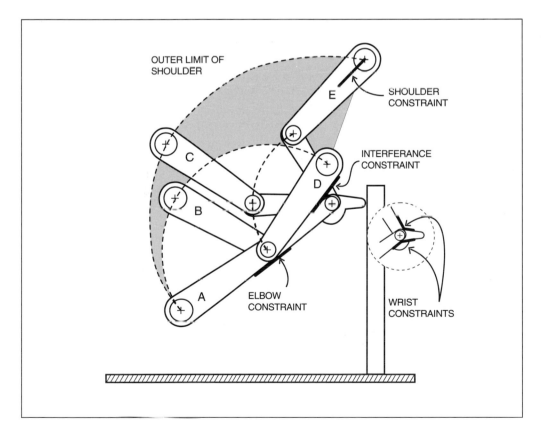

11-29. Inverse kinematic problems can often have multiple solutions, as you can see in this solution diagram. Here, the animator specifies that the finger of the hand must touch the wall. The position of the wrist is thus constrained, but the elbow is now free to move in an arc and the shoulder can be placed anywhere in the shaded area. Instead of concatenating transformations from global to local to placing the last link, inverse kinematics positions the most local link first, and then solves more global transformations.

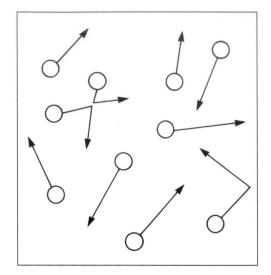

11-30. Simulation of gas molecules. In a closed room, each molecule in a simulation has a location, a direction in which it is moving, and a speed. For each frame of the simulation, the computer advances the molecule the distance in space along the direction of its motion. It then tests to see if any molecule has collided with any other molecule or if any molecule has collided with the exterior. When two molecules collide, they ricochet away from each other like two Ping-Pong balls hitting in space, and the simulation program calculates a new direction vector and speed for each. Should a molecule hit the wall, it will bounce off in a new direction. The gas pressure in the room is the number of molecules that hit the wall each second, and this simulation determines how the pressure changes when the temperature is increased and the molecules move faster.

make animation that moves according to the laws of physical nature.

For example, the cycling automobile engine described above is a kinematic description—the procedure does model the motion of the engine, but it does so by declaring where it is to be positioned. A dynamic engine simulation would consider the physics of engine operation; it would calculate the rate of exploding gas in the top of the cylinder, the resistance of the piston and the connecting rod, and determine how far the piston gets pushed, then draw it. The position of the piston is calculated this way for each successive discrete frame in time, creating animation.

Kinematic actions, like cranking the automobile engine, require no history: the sequence of frames can be calculated in any order, and successive frames are not dependent on previous frames. On the other hand, dynamics equations are solved incrementally. A dynamic simulation of an automobile engine must solve the position for "frame one" before it can begin to solve the position for "frame two." Indeed, to get to an advanced state like "frame one hundred," it may be necessary to calculate all ninety-nine prior frames. Dynamic simulations provide us with a way to answer "what-if" questions by making scientific visualizations of our experiments (fig. 11-30). Dynamics can be applied to the position or the shape of an object, and thus provides a practical way to animate natural phenomena like walking, cloud formations, or a leaf falling in the wind (fig. 11-31).

One of the goals of computer graphics during the past forty years has been to make *images* that *look* more and more realistic. In a parallel way, one of the goals of computer animation is to make *actions* that *behave* more and more realistically, and dynamics is a tool to accomplish this. Dynamics is also essential to virtual reality, because virtual worlds must not only look but also behave realistically.

11-31. The motion of the leaves is generated by simulating wind and then blowing the leaves about. The wind is represented as a 3D velocity vector, and the leaves are represented as flexible triangulated polygons modeled as networks of masses and springs. The forces the wind exerts on each triangle of the leaf are calculated, affecting how the leaf bends and twists as it is blown and carried along by the wind. (From *Leaf Magic* courtesy of IBM Research. Image by K. Argu, R. Bacon, D. Haumann, A. Khornsanl, A. Norton, P. Sweeney, and J. Wejchert.)

CONCLUSION

Many people ask us, your authors, about jobs and the art of the future. If you have read this book it should be obvious that we are advocates of using computers in design and art projects, not only because they make some aspects of graphics easier, but also because they empower us—as artists, as communicators, as agents of evolution—to engage in new horizons.

Computers can be easy to use, but their successful use is not without craft, diligence, or knowledge. One sure step toward success is understanding the tool. In general, the broader and deeper your knowledge is, the more valuable a role you can play and the easier it is to get ahead. Although you may become conceited about your knowhow, remember that a little humility goes a long way. There is really no limit to what one can learn about computer graphics, and it is impossible to learn everything in a lifetime. There are also other factors (like personality, promptness, reliability) that contribute to goodwill and how the universe responds to you. The professional world has small tolerance for missed deadlines, sloppy work, or conceit.

Another fact of life you must face up to is that the all-digital world is very flexible and can be expected to continue to evolve rapidly. Software ingenuity is a main driving force of our culture, and you must learn to live by your wits. So accustom yourself to a lifetime of perpetual education. This learning must be sensitive to at least two levels. First, there is **tactical knowledge**—the latest workstation, the hottest rendering software, the newest paint system feature. Second, there is **strategic knowledge**—this is the "big picture" and deals with trends and a deeper vision of the future. Strategic issues today include portability, cellularity, wirelessness, smart interfaces, agents, and telecommunications. Be forewarned that it is possible to acquire a great deal of tactical information without really knowing anything. Training is not education.

This is a world where you may find yourself thrust into the role of expert or leader with very few, if any, senior advisors to turn to. If you are unsure where you are going, take small steps and verify what you think to be true by testing it. Buy one of something before you buy fifty. Things that are true today will not be necessarily true in the future (or were not in the past).

Take notes, write down directions, write down changes that are supposed to be made in work-in-progress. You may be quite able to remember the three things you agreed to fix in an animation, but the client, your boss, or your employee may remember things differently. Write it down. When you need to solve a problem be methodical, keep notes, and only change one thing at a time. This may try your patience, but it is the only way to avoid flailing around. If you change two things (a cable and a switch) and something works that didn't before, you have the satisfaction of it working, but you don't know if it was the switch, the cable, or both that fixed the problem. Precision counts, and in many organizations the only difference between the hotshots and the sheep is that the hotshots know how to open up a manual and read it.

Remember that chance is one of nature's many ways. Some unlucky events, like having a meteorite fall on your computer, are truly unpredictable. Others, like having your disk crash, are inevitable (although the "when" is unpredictable). Getting hit by a meteorite is bad luck, but losing a job because the disk didn't get backed up is incompetence.

This said, your authors would like to wish you all the good luck in the world.

BOOKS AND PERIODICALS

Adobe Systems. *PostScript Language, Tutorial and Cookbook.* 2d ed. Reading, MA: Addison-Wesley, 1990.

Agfa Compugraphic: *An Introduction to Digital Color Prepress.* Rev. ed. Wilmington, MA: Agfa Corporation, 1990.

Ahuja, Narendra, and Bruce J. Schachter. *Pattern Models.* New York: John Wiley & Sons, 1983.

Ambron, Sueann, and Kristina Hooper. *Interactive Multimedia.* Redmond, WA: Microsoft Press, 1988.

Anderson, Allan Ross, ed. *Minds and Machines.* Englewood Cliffs, NJ: Prentice-Hall, 1964.

Arijon, Daniel. *Grammar of the Film Language.* Los Angeles: Silman-James Press, 1992.

Artwick, Bruce. *Applied Concepts in Microcomputer Graphics.* Englewood Cliffs, NJ: Prentice-Hall, 1983.

Ashley, Ruth, and Nancy B. Stern. *Background Math for a Computer World.* 2d ed. New York: John Wiley & Sons, 1980.

Auble, J. Woodward. *Arithmetic for Printers.* 2d ed. Peoria, IL: Bonnett, 1954.

Backer, David, and Andrew Lippman. *Future Interactive Graphics: Personal Video.* Cambridge, MA: MIT, Architecture Machine Group, 1980.

Badler, Norman, ed. *Motion Representation and Perception,* New York: Association for Computing Machinery, 1983.

Baeker, Ron. *Readings in Human Computer Interaction, A Multidisciplinary Approach.* Des Moines, IA: Morgan Kaufmann, 1987.

Ballard, Dana H., and Christopher M. Brown. *Computer Vision.* Englewood Cliffs, NJ: Prentice-Hall, 1982.

Barnett, M. P. *Computer Typesetting.* Cambridge, MA: The MIT Press, 1985.

Barnhill, Robert E., and Richard F. Reisenfeld. *Computer Aided Geometric Design.* New York: Academic Press, 1984.

Beatty, John C., and Kellogg Booth. *Tutorial: Computer Graphics.* 2d ed. Long Beach, CA: IEEE Computer Society, 1982.

Bernstein, Saul, and Leo McGarry. *Making Art on Your Computer.* New York: Watson-Guptill, 1986.

Bertin, Jacques. *Semiology of Graphics.* Madison: University of Wisconsin Press, 1983.

Birren, F., ed. *The Elements of Color.* New York: Van Nostrand Reinhold, 1970.

Black, Roger. *Roger Black's Desktop Design Power.* New York: Bantam Books, 1991.

Bolt, Richard. *Spatial Data-Management.* Cambridge, MA: The MIT Press, 1979.

Bolt, Richard. *The Human Interface, Where People and Computers Meet.* New York: Van Nostrand Reinhold, 1984.

Bonifer, Michael. *The Art of Tron.* New York: Simon & Schuster, 1982.

Booth, Kellogg S. *Tutorial: Computer Graphics.* Long Beach, CA: IEEE Computer Society, 1979.

Boraiko, Allen A. "The Chip." *National Geographic* (October 1982): 421–57.

Born, Robert, ed. *Designing for Television: The New Tools.* Tequesta, FL: Broadcast Designers' Association, 1983.

Bourgoin. J. *Arabic Geometric Patterns and Design.* New York: Dover Press, 1973.

Bove, Tony, Cheryl Rhodes, and Wes Thomas. *The Art of Desktop Publishing, Using Personal Computers to Publish It Yourself.* New York: Bantam Books, 1986.

Bradbeer, Robin, Peter DeBono, and Peter Laurie. *The Beginner's Guide to Computers.* Reading, MA: Addison-Wesley, 1982.

Brand, Stewart. *The Media Lab, Inventing the Future at MIT.* New York: Viking, 1987.

Bruno, Michael H., ed. *Pocket Pal, A Graphic Arts Production Handbook.* 14th ed. Memphis, TN: International Paper Company, 1989.

Burke, Harry. *Handbook of Barcoding Systems*. New York: Van Nostrand Reinhold, 1987.

Burson, Nancy, Richard Carling, and David Kramlich. *Composites, Computer Generated Portraits*. New York: Beech Tree Books, 1986.

Burtnyk, Nestor, and Marcelli Wein. "Computer Animation." In *Encyclopedia of Computer Science and Technology*. New York: Marcel Dekker, 1976.

Cage, John. *Notations*. New York: Something Else Press, 1969.

Cakir, A. D., D. J. Hart, and T. F. M. Stewart. *Visual Display Terminal*. New York: John Wiley & Sons, 1980.

Campbell, Russell. *Photographic Theory for the Motion Picture Cameraman*. San Diego: A. S. Barnes & Co., 1970.

Card, Stuart. *The Psychology of Human-Computer Interaction*. Hillsdale, NJ: Lawrence Erlbaum Associates, 1983.

Cardamone, T. *Chart and Graph Preparation Skills*. New York: Van Nostrand Reinhold, 1981.

Carey, Tom. "User Differences in Interface Design." *Computer* (November 1982): 14–20.

Cavuoto, James, and Stephen Beale. *Linotronic Imaging Handbook*. Torrance, CA: Micro Publishing Press, 1990.

Chambers, John M., William S. Cleveland, Bert Kleiner, and Paul A. Turkey. *Graphical Methods for Data Analysis*. Belmont, CA: Wadsworth, 1983.

Chasen, Sylvan H. *Geometric Principles and Procedures for Computer Graphic Applications*. Englewood Cliffs, NJ: Prentice-Hall, 1978.

Ching, Francis D. K. *Space, Form and Order*. New York: Van Nostrand Reinhold, 1979.

Clark, David R., ed. *Computer for Imagemaking*. Oxford, England: Pergamon Press, 1981.

Cohen, Luanne Seymour, Russell Brown, Lisa Jeans, and Tanya Wendling. *Professional Studio Techniques: Design Essentials*. Mountain View, CA: Adobe Press, 1992.

Conrac Corp. *Raster Graphics Handbook*. Covina, CA: Conrac, 1980.

Crawford, Chris. *The Art of Computer Game Design*. Berkeley, CA: Osborne/McGraw-Hill, 1984.

Creager, Clara. *Weaving*. Garden City, NY: Doubleday, 1974.

Cundy, H. Martyn, and A. P. Rollett. *Mathematical Models*. 2d ed. London: Oxford University Press, 1961.

Cunningham, Steve. "Computer Graphics Education Directory." *Computer Graphics* (October 1987): 253.

David, Douglas. *Art in the Future, History/Prophecy of the Collaboration Between Science, Technology and Art*. New York: Praeger, 1973.

Davis, William S. *Computing Fundamentals, Concepts*. 2d ed. Reading, MA: Addison-Wesley, 1989.

Davison, Marguerite. *A Handweaver's Pattern Book*. Swarthmore, PA: Davison Publishing, 1974.

Deken, Joseph. *Computer Images*. New York: Stewart, Tabori & Chang, 1983.

Deken, Joseph. *The Electronic Cottage*. New York: William Morrow, 1982.

Dennis, Ervin A., and John D. Jenkins. *Comprehensive Graphic Arts*. 2d ed. Indianapolis: Bobbs-Merrill, 1983.

Descargues, Pierre. *Perspective*. New York: Van Nostrand Reinhold, 1982.

Dictionary of Computing. 3d ed. New York: Oxford University Press, 1990.

Diffrient, Niels, Alvin R. Tilley, Joan C. Bardagjy, and David Hartman. *Humanscale*. Cambridge, MA: The MIT Press, 1981.

Drexler, K. Eric, and Peterson. *Unbounding the Future: The Nanotechnology Revolution*. New York: William Morrow, 1991.

Dubery, Fred, and John W. Illatz. *Perspective and Other Drawing Systems*. London: Herbert Press, 1983.

Dunn, Linwood G., and George E. Turner. *The ASC Treasury of Visual Effects*. Hollywood, CA: American Society of Cinematographers, 1983.

Earle, James H. *Engineering Design Graphcs*. Reading, MA: Addison Wesley, 1987.

Eastman Kodak Company. *Ergonomic Design for People at Work*. Rochester,

NY: Eastman Kodak Company, Human Factors Section, 1983.

Encarnacao, J., and E. G. Schlechtendahl. *Computer Aided Design.* New York: Springer-Verlag, 1983.

Faux, I. D., and M. J. Pratt. *Computational Geometry for Design and Manufacture.* New York: John Wiley & Sons, 1979.

Favre, Jean-Paul. *Color and Communication.* Zürich: ABC Verlag, 1979.

Feigenbaum, Edward A., and Pamela McCorduck. *The Fifth Generation.* Reading, MA: Addison-Wesley, 1983.

Felding, Raymond. *The Technique of Special Effects Cinematography.* New York: Hastings House, 1983.

Fenton, Erfert. *The Macintosh Font Book, Typographic Tips, Techniques and Resources.* Berkeley, CA: Peachpit Press, 1989.

Finch, Christopher. *Special Effects: Creating Movie Magic.* New York: Abbeville Press, 1984.

Foley, James, Andries Van Dam, Steve Feiner, and John Hughes. *Computer Graphics, Principles and Practice.* 2d ed. Reading, MA: Addison-Wesley, 1990.

Fox, David, and Mitchell Waite. *Computer Animation Primer.* New York: McGraw-Hill, 1983.

Frank, Mark. *Discovering Computers.* Washington, DC: Stonehenge Press, 1981.

Franke, Herbert. *Computer Graphics—Computer Art.* 2d ed. Berlin: Springer-Verlag, 1985.

Frates, Jeffrey, and William Moldrup. *Computers and Life.* Englewood Cliffs, NJ: Prentice-Hall, 1982.

Freeman, H., ed. *Tutorial and Selected Readings in Interactive Computer Graphics.* Long Beach, CA: IEEE Computer Society, 1980.

Frey, Berta. *Designing and Drafting for Handweavers.* New York: Collier Books, 1958.

Friedhoff, Richard Mark, and William Benzon. *Visualization, The Second Computer Revolution.* New York: Harry N. Abrams, 1989.

Frutiger, Adrian. *Type Sign Symbol.* Zurich: ABC Editions, 1980.

Fu, K. S., and T. L. Kunii, eds. *Picture Engineering.* New York: Springer-Verlag, 1982.

Gassée, Jean-Louis. *The Third Apple: Personal Computers and the Cultural Revolution.* New York: Harcourt Brace Jovanovich, 1987.

Gasson, Peter C. *Geometry of Spatial Forms.* New York: John Wiley & Sons, 1983.

Gayeski, Diane, and David Williams. *Interactive Media.* Englewood Cliffs, NJ: Prentice-Hall, 1985.

Gerken, J. Ellen, ed., *Click 1, The Brightest in Computer-Generated Design and Illustration.* Cincinnati, OH: North Light Books, 1990.

Gerritsen, Frans. *Theory and Practice of Color.* New York: Van Nostrand Reinhold, 1975.

Gerstner, Karl. *Compendium for Literates: A System of Writing.* Cambridge, MA: MIT Press, 1974.

Giloth, Copper, and Lynn Pocock-Williams. "A Selected Chronology of Computer Art: Exhibitions, Publications, and Technology." *Art Journal* (Fall 1990): 283–97.

Gips, Terry, ed. "Computers and Art: Issues of Content." *Art Journal.* (Fall 1990).

Glassner, Andrew S. *3D Computer Graphics, A User's Guide for Artists and Designers.* 2d ed. New York: Design Press, 1989.

Gonzalez, Rafael C., and Paul Wintz. *Digital Image Processing.* Reading, MA: Addison-Wesley, 1977.

Goodman, Cynthia. *Digital Visions, Computers and Art.* New York: Harry N. Abrams, 1987.

Gottschall, Edward M. *Typographic Communications Today.* Cambridge, MA: The MIT Press, 1989.

Gottschall, Edward M., ed. *Graphic Communication/Visions 80.* Englewood Cliffs, NJ: Prentice-Hall, 1981.

Graham, Frank. *Mathematics and Calculations for Mechanics.* New York: Audel & Co., 1948.

Green, William B. *Digital Image Processing.* New York: Van Nostrand Reinhold, 1983.

Greenberg, Donald, Aaron Marcus, Allan H. Schmidt, and Vernon Gorter. *The Computer: Image Applications of Computer Graphics.* Reading, MA: Addison-Wesley, 1982.

Gregory, Richard L. *Eye and Brain, The Psychology of Seeing*. 3d ed. New York: McGraw-Hill, 1978.

Greiman, April. *Hybrid Imagery, The Fusion of Technology and Graphic Design*. New York: Watson-Guptill, 1990.

Grimson, Eric. *From Images to Surfaces: A Computational Study of the Human Early Visual System*. Cambridge, MA: The MIT Press, 1981.

Groover, Mikell P., and Emory W. Zimmers, Jr. *CAD/CAM Computer-Aided Design and Manufacturing*. Englewood Cliffs, NJ: Prentice-Hall, 1984.

Hafner, Katie. *Cyberpunk, Outlaws and Hackers on the Computer Frontier*. New York: Simon & Schuster, 1991.

Halas, John. *Graphics in Motion, From the Special Effects Film to Holography*. New York: Van Nostrand Reinhold, 1984.

Halas, John, ed. *Computer Animation*. New York: Hastings House, 1974.

Halas, John, and Roger Manvell. *The Technique of Film Animation*. 3d ed. New York: Hastings House, 1971.

Hall, Roy. *Illumination and Color in Computer Generated Imagery*. New York: Springer-Verlag, 1989.

Handbook of Pricing and Ethical Guidelines. 7th ed. New York: Graphic Artists' Guild, 1992.

Hanson, Dirk. *The New Alchemists*. Boston: Little, Brown, 1982.

Harrington, Steven. *Computer Graphics: A Programming Approach*. New York: McGraw-Hill, 1983.

Hearn, Donald, and M. Pauline Baker. *Computer Graphics*. Englewood Cliffs, NJ: Prentice-Hall, 1986.

Heckel, Paul. *The Elements of Freindly Software Design*. New York: Warner Books, 1984.

Heidegger, Martin. *The Questions Concerning Technology and Other Essays*. New York: Harper & Row, 1977.

Hiebert, Kenneth. *Graphic Design Processes,. . . Universal to Unique*. New York: Van Nostrand Reinhold, 1992.

Hildebrandt, Stefan, and Anthony Tromba. *Mathematics and Optimal Form*. New York: W. H. Freeman, 1984.

Hoffman, E. Kenneth, and Jon Teeple. *Computer Graphics Applications*. Belmont, CA: Wadsworth, 1990.

Holden, Alan. *Shapes, Space, and Symmetry*. New York: Columbia University Press, 1971.

Hubbard, Stuart W. *Computer Graphics Glossary*. New York: Van Nostrand Reinhold, 1984.

Hubel, David H. *Eye, Brain and Vision*. New York: W. H. Freeman, 1988.

Hurvich, L. M. *Color Vision*. Sunderland, MA: Sinauer Assoc., 1981.

IBM. *Informatique #13*. Paris: IBM, 1975.

Imes, Jack. *Special Visual Effects*. New York: Van Nostrand Reinhold, 1984.

Jankel, Annabel, and Rocky Morton. *Creative Computer Graphics*. Cambridge, England: Cambridge University Press, 1984.

Jarett, Irwin M. *Computer Graphics and Reporting Financial Data*. New York: John Wiley & Sons, 1983.

Judd, D. B., and G. Wyszecki. *Color in Business, Science, and Industry*. 3d ed. New York: John Wiley & Sons, 1975.

Katsui, Mitsuo, and Toshifumi Kawahara, eds. *World Graphic Design Now 6, Computer Graphics*. Tokyo: Kodansha, 1989.

Kawaguchi, Yoichiro. *Digital Image*. Tokyo: Ascii Publishing, 1981.

Kawaguchi, Yoichiro. *Morphogenesis*. Tokyo: JICC Publishing, 1985.

Kawaguchi, Yoichiro. *The Computer Graphics*. Tokyo: Graphic-sha Publishing, 1982.

Kerlow, Isaac. *Illusion and Technology*. Master's Thesis, Pratt Institute. New York, 1983.

Kerlow, Isaac Victor, ed. *Computers in Art and Design, SIGGRAPH '91 Art and Design Show*. New York: Association for Computing Machinery, 1991.

Kim, Scott. *Inversions*. New York: W. H. Freeman, 1989.

Knowlton, Ken. *EXPLOR*. Murray Hill, NJ: Bell Laboratories, 1974.

Knuth, Donald E. *TEX and Metafont: New Directions in Typesetting*. Bedford, MA: American Mathematical Society, Digital Press, 1979.

Kobler, Helmut. *The Little Mac Word Book*. Berkeley, CA: Peachpit Press, 1992.

Kranz, Stewart. *Science and Technology in the Arts*. New York: Van Nostrand Reinhold, 1974.

Krueger, Myron W. *Artificial Reality II*. Reading, MA: Addison-Wesley, 1991.

Lalvani, Haresh. *Transpolyhedra*. New York: Red Ink Productions, 1977.

Lange, Jerome C., and Dennis P. Shanahan. *Interactive Computer Graphics Applied to Mechanical Drafting and Design*. New York: John Wiley & Sons, 1984.

Larish, John. *Electronic Photography*. Blue Ridge Summit, PA: TAB Books, 1990.

Laurie, Peter. *The Joy of Computers*. Boston: Little, Brown, 1983.

Leavitt, Ruth, ed. *Artist and Computer*. New York: Harmony Books, 1976.

Leighton, Natalie Langue. *Computers in the Architectural Office*. New York: Van Nostrand Reinhold, 1984.

Leopoldseder, Hannes. *Meisterwerke Der Computerkunst, Prix Ars Electronica*. Bremen, Germany: TMS-Verlag, 1988.

Levitan, Eli. *Electronic Imaging Techniques*. New York: Van Nostrand Reinhold, 1977.

Levy, Steven. *Artificial Life, The Quest for a New Creation*. New York: Random House, 1992.

Lewell, J. *Computer Graphics*. New York: Van Nostrand Reinhold, 1985.

Lindsay, Peter H. *Human Information Processing, An Introduction to Psychology*. New York: Academic Press, 1977.

Linehan, Thomas E., ed. "SIGGRAPH 1990, Digital Image, Digital Cinema." *Leonardo* (Supplemental Issue, 1990).

Lipton, Lenny. *Foundations of the Stereoscopic Cinema*. New York: Van Nostrand Reinhold, 1982.

Lombardo, Josef V., Lewis S. Johnson, W. Irwin Short, and Albert J. Lombardo. *Engineering Drawing*. New York: Harper & Row, 1956.

Lourie, Janice R. *Textile Graphics/Computer Aided*. New York: Fairchild Publications, 1973.

Lovejoy, Margot. *Postmodern Currents: Art and Artists in the Age of Electronic Media*. Amherst, MA.: UMI Research Press, 1989.

Lu, Cary. *The Apple Macintosh Book*. 4th ed. Redmond, WA: Microsoft Press, 1992.

Lyotard, Jean-Francois. *The Postmodern Condition, A Report on Knowledge*. Minneapolis: University of Minnesota Press, 1988.

Machover, Carl. *Display Systems: Computer Graphics*. Pittsfield, MA: Optical Publishing, 1979.

Machover, Carl. *Understanding Computer Graphics*. New York: Van Nostrand Reinhold, 1980.

Madsen, Roy. *Animated Film*. New York: Interland Press, 1970.

Magnenat-Thalmann, Nadia, and Daniel Thalmann. *Computer Animation, Theory and Practice*. 2d ed. New York: Springer-Verlag, 1990.

Magnenat-Thalmann, Nadia, and Daniel Thalmann. *Image Synthesis: Theory and Practice*. New York: Springer-Verlag, 1987.

Magnenat-Thalmann, Nadia, and Daniel Thalmann. *Synthetic Actors in Computer-Generated 3D Films*. New York: Springer-Verlag, 1990.

Malina, Frank J., ed. *Kinetic Art Theory and Practice*. New York: Dover, 1974.

Mandelbrot, Benoit B. *The Fractal Geometry of Nature*. New York: W. H. Freeman, 1983.

Marks, Robert W. *The New Mathematics Dictionary and Handbook*. New York: Bantam, 1981.

Martin, J. *Design of Man-Computer Dialogues*. Englewood Cliffs, NJ: Prentice-Hall, 1973.

Marx, Ellen. *Optical Color and Simultaneity*. New York: Van Nostrand Reinhold, 1983.

McCorduck, Pamela. *Machines Who Think*. San Francisco: W. H. Freeman, 1979.

Meadows, A. J., ed. *Dictionary of New Information Technology*. New York: Random House, 1983.

Milne, M. *Computer Graphics in Architecture and Design*. New Haven, CT: Yale School of Art and Architecture, 1969.

Minsky, Marvin. *The Sociey of Mind*. New York: Simon & Schuster, 1987.

Mitchell, William J. *Computer Aided Architectural Design.* New York: Van Nostrand Reinhold, 1977.

Mitchell, William J., and Malcolm McCullough. *Digital Design Media, A Handbook for Architects and Design Professionals.* New York: Van Nostrand Reinhold, 1991.

Mitchell, William J., Robin S. Liggett, and Thomas Kvan. *The Art of Computer Graphics Programming, A Structured Introduction for Architects and Designers.* New York: Van Nostrand Reinhold, 1987.

Moles, Abraham. *Art et Ordinateur.* Paris: Casterman, 1971.

Monmonier, M. S. *Computer Assisted Cartography.* Englewood Cliffs, NJ: Prentice-Hall, 1982.

Moore, Patricia, ed. *Harvard Library of Computer Graphics.* Cambridge, MA: Harvard University Laboratory for Computer Graphics, 1980.

Mortenson, Michael E. *Geometric Modeling.* New York: John Wiley & Sons, 1985.

Muller, W., ed. *Dictionary of the Graphic Arts Industry.* Amsterdam: Elsevier Scientific Publishing, 1984.

N-Nagy, Francis, and Andras Siegler. *Engineering Foundations of Robotics.* Englewood Cliffs, NJ: Prentice-Hall, 1987.

Negroponte, Nicholas. *The Architecture Machine.* Cambridge, MA: The MIT Press, 1970.

Negroponte, Nicholas, ed. *Computer Aids to Design and Architecture.* New York: Van Nostrand Reinhold, 1975.

Nelson, Kay Yarborough. *The Little DOS 5 Book.* Berkeley, CA: Peachpit Press, 1992.

Nelson, Kay Yarborough. *The Little Windows Book.* 2d ed. Berkeley, CA: Peachpit Press, 1992.

Nelson, Thedore H. *Dream Machines/Computer Lib.* Chicago: Hugo's Book Service, 1977.

Nelson, Thedore H. *Literary Machines.* Strathmore, PA: Nelson Publishing, 1987.

Nevatia, R. *Machine Perception.* Englewood Cliffs, NJ: Prentice-Hall, 1982.

Newman, William M., and Robert F. Sproull. *Principles of Computer Graphics.* 2d ed. New York: McGraw-Hill, 1979.

Norman, Donald. *Memory and Attention, An Introduction to Human Information Processing.* New York: John Wiley & Sons, 1976.

Norman, Donald A. *The Psychology of Everyday Things,* New York: Basic Books, 1988.

Olson, Gary. *Getting Started in Computer Graphics.* Cincinnatti, OH: North Light Books, 1989.

Pavlidis, T. *Algorithms for Graphics and Image Processing.* New York: Springer-Verlag, 1982.

Pearce, Peter. *Structure in Nature as a Strategy for Design.* Cambridge, MA: The MIT Press, 1978.

Penley, Constance. *Technoculture.* Minneapolis: University of Minnesota Press, 1991.

Pfeiffer, Katherine Shelly. *Silicon Mirage.* Berkeley, CA: Peachpit Press, 1992.

Porter, Tom, Bob Greenstreet, and Sue Goodman. *Manual of Graphic Techniques.* 4 vols. New York: Charles Scribner's Sons, 1980, 1985.

Poster, Mark. *The Mode of Information, Poststructuralism and Social Context.* Chicago: University of Chicago Press, 1990.

Pratt, William K. *Digital Image Processing.* New York: John Wiley & Sons, 1978.

Prueitt, Melvin. *Art and the Computer.* New York: McGraw-Hill, 1984.

Prueitt, Melvin. *Computer Graphics.* New York: Dover, 1975.

Prusinkiewicz, Przemyslaw, and Aristid Lindenmayer. *The Algorithmic Beauty of Plants,* New York: Springer-Verlag, 1990.

Pulgram, William L., and Richard E. Stonis. *Designing the Automated Office.* New York: Whitney Library of Design, 1984.

Raymond, Eric, ed. *The New Hacker's Dictionary.* Cambridge, MA: The MIT Press, 1991.

Reichardt, Jasia. *Cybernetic Serendipity.* New York: Praeger, 1969.

Reichardt, Jasia. *The Computer and Art.* New York: Van Nostrand Reinhold, 1971.

Resch, Mark, ed. "SIGGRAPH 1989, Computer Art in Context." *Leonardo* (Supplemental Issue 1989).

Rivlin, Robert. *The Algorithmic Image, Graphic Visions of the Computer Age.* Redmond, WA: Microsoft Press, 1986.

Rock, Irvin. *Perception.* New York: W. H. Freeman, 1984.

Rogers, David F. *Procedural Elements for Computer Graphics.* New York: McGraw-Hill, 1985.

Rogers, David F., and J. Alan Adams. *Mathematical Elements for Computer Graphics.* New York: McGraw-Hill, 1976.

Roncarelli, Robi. *The Computer Animation Dictionary.* New York: Springer-Verlag, 1989.

Ronell, Avital. *The Telephone Book, Technology-Schizophrenia-Electric Speech.* Lincoln: University of Nebraska Press, 1989.

Rosebush, Judson. *Computer Animation.* New York: Van Nostrand Reinhold, 1993.

Rosenfeld, Azriel, and Avinash C. Kak. *Digital Picture Processing.* 2d ed. Orlando, FL: Academic Press, 1982.

Ross, Andrew. *Strange Weather, Culture, Science, and Technology in the Age of Limits.* New York: Verso, 1991.

Ross, David A., and David Em. *The Art of David Em.* New York: Harry N. Abrams, 1988.

Russett, Robert, and Cecile Starr. *Experimental Animation: An Illustrated Anthology.* New York: Van Nostrand Reinhold, 1976.

Roth, Stephen, ed. *Real World Postscript.* Reading, MA: Addison-Wesley, 1988.

Schachter, Bruce J., ed. *Computer Image Generation.* New York: John Wiley & Sons, 1983.

Schilling, Robert J. *Fundamentals of Robotics, Analysis and Control.* Englewood Cliffs, NJ: Prentice-Hall, 1990.

Schillinger, Joseph. *The Mathematical Basis of the Arts.* New York: Philosophical Library, 1966.

Schneider, Derrick. *Zen and the Art of Resource Editing.* Berkeley, CA: Peachpit Press, 1992.

Schneider, Steve. *That's All Folks.* New York: Henry Holt, 1988.

Schneiderman, Ben. *Designing the User Interface, Strategies for Effective Human-Computer Interaction.* Reading, MA: Addison-Wesley, 1987.

Scott, J. E. *Introduction to Interactive Computer Graphics.* New York: John Wiley & Sons, 1982.

Scott, Joan. *Computergraphia.* Houston: Gulf Publishing, 1984.

Sherman, Chris. *The CD ROM Handbook.* New York: McGraw-Hill, 1988.

Siegel, Efrem. *Videotex: The Coming Revolution in Home/Office Information Retrieval.* White Plains, NY: Knowledge Industry Publications, 1980.

Skidmore, Owings and Merrill. *Computer Capacity.* Chicago: Skidmore, Owings and Merrill Co., 1980.

Smith, David. *Computer Literacy: Coping with Terminal Anxiety.* New York: McGraw-Hill, 1983.

Smith, H. T. *Human Interaction with Computers.* New York: Academic Press, 1980.

Smith, Ross. *Learning PostScript, A Visual Approach.* Berkeley, CA: Peachpit Press, 1992.

Snelson, Kenneth. *The Nature of Structure.* New York: New York Academy of Sciences, 1989.

Soppli, Charles. *Microcomputer Dictionary.* Ft. Worth: Radio Shack, 1981.

Spear, Mary Eleanor. *Practical Charting Techniques.* New York: McGraw-Hill, 1969.

Sterling, Bruce. *Mirrorshades: The Cyberpunk Anthology.* New York: Arbor House, 1986.

Stone, Sumner. *On Stone, The Art and Use of Typography on the Personal Computer.* San Francisco: Bedford Arts, 1991.

Tao, D. C. *Applied Linkage Synthesis.* Reading, MA: Addison-Wesley, 1964.

Tao, D. C. *Fundamentals of Applied Kinematics.* Reading, MA: Addison-Wesley, 1967.

Talbot, Michael. *The Holographics Universe.* New York: HarperCollins, 1991.

Teicholz, Eric. *CAD/CAM Handbook.* New York: McGraw-Hill, 1984.

Thomas, Frank, and Ollie Johnson. *Disney Animation: The Illusion of Life.* New York: Abbeville Press, 1981.

Thomas, Frank, and Ollie Johnson. *Too Funny For Words, Disney's Greatest Sight Gags.* New York: Abbeville Press, 1987.

Thompson, D'Arcy. *On Growth and Form.* London: Cambridge University Press, 1971.

Truckenbrod, Joan. *Creative Computer Imaging.* Englewood Cliffs, NJ: Prentice-Hall, 1988.

Tufte, Edward R. *Envisioning Information.* Cheshire, CT: Graphics Press, 1990.

Tufte, Edward R. *The Visual Display of Quantitative Information.* Cheshire, CT: Graphics Press, 1983.

Tukey, John W. *Exploratory Data Analysis.* Reading, MA: Addison-Wesley, 1977.

Ulichney, Robert. *Digital Halftoning.* Cambridge, MA: MIT Press, 1997.

Understanding Computers, Computer Images. Alexandria, VA: Time-Life Books, 1986.

Upstill, Steve. *The RenderMan Companion, A Programmer's Guide to Realistic Computer Graphics.* Reading, MA: Addison-Wesley, 1990.

Von Arx, Peter. *Film Design.* New York: Van Nostrand Reinhold, 1984.

Ward, Fred. "Computer Images: The New Creation." *National Geographic* (June 1989): 719–51.

Weinstock, Neal. *Computer Animation.* Reading, MA: Addison-Wesley, 1986.

Weizenbaum, Joseph. *Computer Power and Human Reason: From Judgment to Calculation.* New York: W. H. Freeman, 1976.

Wenninger, Magnus J. *Polyhedron Models.* Cambridge, England: Cambridge University Press, 1971.

Wenninger, Magnus J. *Principles of 3-Dimensional Design.* New York: Van Nostrand Reinhold, 1977.

Wexelblat, Richard L. *History of Programming Languages.* New York: Academic Press, 1981.

Whitney, John. *Digital Harmony: On the Complimentarity of Music and Visual Art.* Peterborough, NH: McGraw-Hill, 1980.

Whitney, Patrick. *Design in the Information Environment.* New York: Knopf, 1985.

Williams, Robin. *The Little Mac Book.* 2d ed. Berkeley, CA: Peachpit Press, 1992.

Williams, Robin. *The Mac Is Not a Typewriter.* Berkeley, CA: Peachpit Press, 1992.

Wilson, Mark. *Drawing with Computers.* New York: Putnam, 1985.

Wilson, Stephen. *Multimedia Design with Hypercard.* Englewood Cliffs, NJ: Prentice-Hall, 1991.

Wong, Wucius. *Principles of Three-Dimensional Design.* New York: Van Nostrand Reinhold, 1977.

Wong, Wucius. *Principles of Two-Dimensional Design.* New York: Van Nostrand Reinhold, 1972.

Woodson, W. E. *Human Factors Design Handbook.* New York: McGraw-Hill, 1981.

Youngblood, Gene. *Expanded Cinema.* New York: E. P. Dutton, 1968.

VIDEOGRAPHY

The following is a list of videotapes and programs on computer animation. Of the published material available on videotape the largest selection is found on the *Siggraph Video Review.* The material produced by other sources includes anthologies, which are basically "Best Of" collections, instructional programs, and montage.

Amayakan Japan Ink. *Computer Graphics Anthology.* Tokyo: Polydor K.K, 1988, videodisc. This 10-volume videodisc collection includes technical animation as well as art and demo reels.

Churchill, Steve, and Odyssey Visual Design, producer. *State of the Art of Computer Animation.* Beverly Hills, CA: Pacific Arts Video, 1988, videotape. Also distributed on laserdisc by Image Entertainment, Los Angeles.

DeFanti, Tom, editor. *Siggraph Video Review.* New York: Association of Computing Machinery, 1980–present, videotape. Dozens of hours of computer animation embracing many topics and personalities in multivolumes.

de Valois, Geoffrey, producer. *Computer Animation Magic.* Los Angeles: Digital Vision Entertainment, 1987, videotape.

de Valois, Geoffrey, producer. *Computer Dreams.* Los Angeles: Digital Vision Entertainment, 1988, videotape.

Dupont, Colyer, producer. *The World of Computer Imagery.* San Francisco: Cinemagic Productions, 1986, videotape.

Eaker, Dean, producer. *Computer Pictures Showcase Reel.* Clifton, NJ: Computer Pictures Magazine, 1981, videotape.

Eaker, Dean, producer. *Creative Computer Graphics.* Clifton, NJ: Computer Pictures Magazine, 1982, videotape.

Herr, Laurin, and Judson Rosebush. *HDTV & The Quest for Virtual Reality,* ACM SIGGRAPH Video Review (Special Issue 60). New York: Association of Computing Machinery, 1990, videotape.

Herr, Laurin, and Judson Rosebush. *Visualization Software,* ACM SIGGRAPH Video Review (Special Issue 70). New York: Association of Computing Machinery, 1992, videotape.

Herr, Laurin, and Judson Rosebush. *Visualization: State of the Art—Update,* ACM SIGGRAPH Video Review (Special Issue 35). New York: Association of Computing Machinery, 1989, videotape (also available on laserdisc with HyperCard stack).

Herr, Laurin, and Judson Rosebush. *Volume Visualization: State of the Art,* ACM SIGGRAPH Video Review (Special Issue 44). New York: Association of Computing Machinery, 1989, videotape.

Kawahara, Toshifumi, producer. *The Art of Bob Abel.* Japan: Pioneer Electronics Corporation, 1985, laserdisc.

National Computer Graphics Association. *International Computer Animation Competition Finalists (1987–91).* Fairfax, VA: National Computer Graphics Association, 1987–91, videotape.

Nickman, Jan, and Steven Churchill. *The Mind's Eye.* Seattle: Miramar, 1991, videotape. Orchestrated montage composition of clips into a working visual piece.

Palfreman, Jon, and Robert Hone. *The Machine that Changed the World.* Boston: WGBH Foundation, 1992, 5-volume videotape.

Rosebush, Judson. *Principles of Computer Animation.* New York: Association of Computing Machinery, 1991, videotape.

Rosebush, Judson, and Gwen Sylvan. *History of Computer Animation,* ACM SIG- GRAPH Video Review (Special Issue 90). New York: Association of Computing Machinery, 1991, videotape.

Silas, Steve, producer. *Fresh Video Portfolio: Computer Graphics Animation (1989–92).* Los Angeles: Fresh Electronic Publishing, 1989–92, videotapes. Five volumes of work from commercial computer animation companies.

Thorens, Terry, producer. *Anthology of Computer Animation.* Los Angeles: Expanded Entertainment, 1987, 35mm and 16mm distribution only.

Thorens, Terry, producer. *International Tournee of Animation Collection,* Los Angeles: Expanded Entertainment, 1986–present, videotape. These contain conventional as well as computer animation.

PUBLICATIONS

AIGA Journal of Graphic Design. American Institute of Graphic Arts, 1059 Third Avenue, New York, NY 10021, (212) 752-0813, Quarterly.

Aldus Magazine. Aldus Corporation, 411 First Avenue South, Seattle, WA 98104-2871, Bimonthly.

Amiga World. TechMedia Publishing, 80 Elm Street, Peterborough, NH 03458, (603) 924-0100, Monthly.

Business Publishing. Hitchcock Publishing Company, 191 South Gary Avenue, Carol Stream, IL 60188, (708) 665-1000, FAX (708) 462-2225, Monthly.

Byte. One Phoenix Mill Lane, Peterborough, NH 03458, (603) 924-9281, FAX (603) 924-2550, Monthly.

Computer Graphics & Applications. IEEE Computer Society, 10662 Los Vaqueros Circle, P.O. Box 3014, Los Alamitos, CA 90720-1264, (714) 821-8380, Monthly.

Computer Graphics World. One Technology Park Drive, P.O. Box 987, Westford, MA 01886, (508) 692-0700, FAX (508) 692-0525, Monthly.

Computer Pictures. 25 Bischoff Avenue, Chappaqua, NY 10514, (914) 238-0752, FAX: (914) 328-9093, Bimonthly.

Desktop Communications. 530 Fifth Avenue, New York, NY 10036, (212) 768-7666, Bimonthly.

Education by Design. Autodesk, Inc., 2320 Marinship Way, Sausalito, CA 94965, FAX (415) 491-8305.

Educom Review. 1112 16th Street NW, Suite 600, Washington, DC 20036, (202) 872-4200, FAX (202) 872-4318, Bimonthly.

Emigre. 4475 D Street, Sacramento, CA 95819, (916) 451-4344.

Human Factors. Human Factors Society, 1124 Montana Avenue, Santa Monica, CA (310) 394-1811.

ID Systems. 174 Concord Street, P.O. Box 874, Peterborough, NH 03458-0874, (603) 924-9631, Monthly.

Infoworld. 155 Bovet Road, San Mateo, CA 94402, (415) 572-7341.

Iris Universe. 2011 North Shoreline Boulevard, Mail Stop 415, Mountain View, CA 94039-7311, (415) 335-1278, Quarterly.

Mac Artist. 901 East Santa Ana Boulevard, Suite 103, Santa Ana, CA 92701, (714) 973-1529, Monthly.

Mac Publishing and Presentations. 530 Fifth Avenue, New York, NY 10036, (212) 768-7666, Monthly.

MacWeek. One Park Avenue, New York NY 10016.

MacWorld. MacWorld Communications., 501 Second Street, 5th Floor, San Francisco, CA 94107, (415) 243-0505, Monthly.

MicroStation Manager. Austin Office: (512) 250-1991.

New Media. Hypermedia Communications Inc., 901 Mariners Island Boulevard, Suite 365, San Mateo, CA 94404, (415) 573-5170, FAX (415) 573-5131, Monthly.

PC Magazine. One Park Avenue, New York, NY 10016, (212) 503-5100.

PC Publishing & Presentations. 530 Fifth Avenue, New York, NY 10036, (212) 768-7666, Bimonthly.

Personal Publishing. Hitchcock Publishing Company, 191 South Gary Avenue, Carol Stream, IL 60188, (708) 665-1000, FAX (708) 462-2225, Monthly.

Pixel Vision. P.O. Box 1138, Madison Square Station, New York, NY 10159.

Pre-. South Wind Publishing Co., 8340 Mission Road, Suite 106, Prairie Village, KS 66206, (913) 642-6611, FAX (913) 642-6676, Bimonthly.

Publish. Integrated Media Inc., 501 Second Street, San Francisco, CA 94107, (415) 243-0600, Monthly.

Silicon Graphics World. 12416 Hymeadow Drive, Austin, TX 78750-1896, (512) 250-9023, FAX (512) 331-3900, Monthly.

Syllabus. P.O. Box 2716, Sunnyvale, CA 94087-0716, (408) 773-0670, FAX (408) 746-2711, Bimonthly.

The Journal. Desktop Publishing Institute, 1260 Boylston Street, Boston, MA 02215, (800) 874-4113, Monthly.

The Journal. Technological Horizons in Education, 150 El Camino Real, Suite 112, Tustin, CA 92680-3670, (714) 730-4011, FAX (714) 730-3739, Monthly.

The Mac Street Journal. The New York MacUsers' Group, Inc., 688 Sixth Avenue, 3rd Floor, New York, NY 10010, (212) 691-0496, Monthly.

The Seybold Reports. P.O. Box 644, Media, PA 19063, (215) 565-2480.

Type World. One Stiles Road, Suite 106, P.O. Box 170, Salem, NH 03079, FAX (603) 898-3393, published 18 times annually.

Verbum. Verbum, Inc., P.O. Box 12564, San Diego, CA 92112, (619) 233-9977, FAX (619) 233-9976, Quarterly.

Windows. 600 Community Drive, Manhasset, NY 11030, (516) 562-5370, FAX (516) 562-5482, Monthly.

Luster, in three-dimensional modeling, 181

McCarthy, John, 41
Machine languages, 38
Main memory, 28
Management systems, 97
Man-machine interface, 102–103
Mapping
  image, 133
  in three-dimensional modeling, 180–181
Matching, image analysis and, 154
Matrix, 6
Mattes, 110–111
  continuous contrast, 138–140
  key, 137–138
  static, 140
  traveling, 142
Megabyte, 3
Memory, 28–31
  main, 28
  peripheral, 29
  virtual, 29–30
Menubar, 85
Menus, pulldown, 85
Mflops, 27
Microcomputer, 27
Microphones, 56
Mips, 27
Modeling. *See also* Three-dimensional modeling
  in animation, 269
Moiré pattern, 22
Monadic image processes, 1 28–133
Monitors
  calibration of, 125
  ergonomic considerations, 101
Morphs, 280
Mosaic, 147
Motion control systems, 273–277
Motion pathway, 279
Motion test, 270
Mouse, 61
MPEG compression, 229
Multiaxial point peripherals, 79
Multimedia, digital unified, 224
Multimedia applications, 230–233
Multimedia systems, 227–229
Multiplex holograms, 74
Multispectral imaging, 111
Multiuser systems, 37

NAPLPS (North American Presentation Level Protocol Standard), 233
Negative look-up tables, 116
Networks, 45–49
Noise, 150
Noise reduction, 150
Normal determination, 154
Novell, 46–47
Number of degrees of freedom of a peripheral, 52
Numbers, 3–5
Numerical code (NC), 78
Numerically controlled tools, 252

Objects. *See also* Three-dimensional modeling
  definition of, 160
Objects of revolution, 161
Oblique projections, 194
Occultation, 186–187
Offsetting, 171
Omnidirectional light, 183
One-byte-per-pixel-per-primary resolution, 123
Opaque surface rendering, 187
Opcode, 38
Operand, 38
Operating system, 36–37
Operators, 104
Optical character recognition (OCR), 56
Origin, 9
Orthogonal projection, 194
Overlays, 140

Package design, 258–261
Page, 91
Pagination, 214–216
Paint programs, 213
Palettes. *See also* Look-up tables
  button, 85
Pan, 177
Pantographs, raster, 74, 77
Paperless office, 231
Papert, Seymour, 43
Parallel ports, 31
Parameter table, 285
Parametric key frame, 280
Particle systems, 164, 168
PASCAL, 43
Pattern repeats, 128
Perception, 152
Peripheral memory, 29
Peripherals, 31, 52–81
  ergonomic considerations, 101–102

force, 80–81
one-dimensional (speech and text), 56–61
  alphanumeric text entry, 56
  alphanumeric text output, 57
  potentiometers and dials, 59, 61
  shaft encoders and stepping motors, 57, 59
three-dimensional, 72–80
  clothing and multiaxial peripherals, 79–80
  point input peripherals, 72–73
  point output peripherals, 73–74
  voxel input peripherals, 78
  voxel output peripherals, 78–79
  zel input peripherals, 72, 74–78
topologies of, 52–55
two-dimensional (graphics), 61–71
  pixel input peripherals, 66
  pixel output peripherals, 66, 69
  point input peripherals, 61–63
  point output peripherals, 63–66
zero-dimensional (switches), 55–56
Perlis, Alan J., 41
Personnel, 103
Perspective, 11, 174–177
Phigs, 43
Photogrammetric techniques, 73
Photogrammetry, 154, 157, 163–164
Picas, 208
Picture Descripton Instructions (PDIs), 233
Pitch, 11
Pixelation, 147
Pixel input devices, 61
Pixels, 12–13, 52
Plane, 9
Platen, 59
Plotters, 63–64
  electrostatic, 70
  ink jet, 69
  rotary drum, 69–70
Point, 9
Point and normal digitizers, 79
Point digitizing, 161
Pointing, 87–88
Point input peripherals, 61–63
Point list table, coplanar method and, 163
Point of delivery, in contracts, 100
Point of view (POV), 176
Point output peripherals, 61
Point radars, 72–73